AIRPORT
ENGINEERING

AIRPORT ENGINEERING

Second Edition

NORMAN ASHFORD
University of Technology, Loughborough

PAUL H. WRIGHT
Georgia Institute of Technology, Atlanta

A Wiley-Interscience Publication
JOHN WILEY & SONS
New York / Chichester / Brisbane / Toronto / Singapore

Library of Congress Cataloging in Publication Data:

Ashford, Norman.
  Airport engineering.

  "A Wiley-Interscience publication."
  Includes index.
  1. Airports—Planning.   I. Wright, Paul H.   II. Title.

TL725.3.P5A83   1984   629.136   83-23494
ISBN 0-471-86568-0

Printed in the United States of America

10 9 8 7 6 5 4 3 2

PREFACE

In the five years since the appearance of the first edition of this book, there have been numerous changes in the world of air transport. In this most rapidly changing mode, significant developments in practice have necessitated major updating in some chapters. The major changes to Annex 14 introduced in 1983 have been included in Chapter 7, Geometric Design of the Airside, and changes in the approach to airside capacity analysis are reflected in Chapter 6, Airport Capacity and Configuration. Other major updating has been applied to the areas of the book relating to demand analysis, the design of passenger and freight terminals, pavement design, and environmental impact. We ourselves have used the first edition as an instructional text in North and South America, Europe, Africa, and the Far East. Based on our experiences, we have included in this edition a great number of illustrative examples that have been developed as teaching examples yet serve to show the principles of design of the various elements making up the airport.

In this edition too, we wish to express our sincerest thanks to all those organizations in the air transport industry that have given generous advice on the preparation of this text.

NORMAN ASHFORD
PAUL H. WRIGHT

Loughborough, Leicestershire
Atlanta, Georgia
April 1984

PREFACE
TO THE FIRST
EDITION

This book is a basic text for airport planning and design courses in civil engineering. It should also be valuable as a professional reference for architectural, engineering, and planning consultants who deal with airport planning and design.

The book begins with a concise description of the various international, national, and local organizations and agencies that affect air transportation, as well as the means by which airports are financed. It includes helpful background material on aircraft characteristics and the air traffic control systems that facilitate safe aerial navigation.

Principles of airport master planning and system planning are presented, and chapters are devoted to airport capacity and configuration and the planning and layout of passenger terminals. Fundamental principles of airport layout and design are covered, including geometric design, airport drainage, and pavement design.

We have attempted to emphasize areas of emerging concern and significance. Thus chapters are included on forecasting air transport demand, air cargo facilities, airport access, requirements of V/STOL systems, and the environmental impact of airports.

In preparing this book we have drawn freely from publications of the Federal Aviation Administration and the International Civil Aviation Organization. Materials published by the Air Transport Association and the International Air Transport Association were also useful sources of reference, as were publications of various aircraft manufacturers, airline companies, and other government agencies and industry organizations. We appreciate the use of these materials. Finally, we gratefully acknowledge the assistance of Mr. Robert

Caves, Research Fellow, University of Technology, Loughborough, who prepared the material on aircraft characteristics.

NORMAN ASHFORD
PAUL H. WRIGHT

Loughborough, Leicestershire
Atlanta, Georgia
February 1979

CONTENTS

AIRPORT
ENGINEERING

THE STRUCTURE AND ORGANIZATION OF AIR TRANSPORT

1.1 THE NEED FOR NATIONAL AND INTERNATIONAL ORGANIZATIONS (1)

For those who have matured in an age marked by the noise, bustle, and efficiency of jet aircraft travel, it is difficult to realize that it is barely three-quarters of a century since the first brief flight of the Wright brothers at Kitty Hawk, N.C., and Bleriot's later historic crossing of the English Channel. Before the early years of this century, except for the infrequent use of nonpowered balloons, man had been restricted to the earth's surface. Now civil aviation is a major international industry that carries three quarters of a billion passengers each year in aircraft that fly for an aggregate of over 10,000 million km. Since aviation is largely international, problems are created that individual nations cannot solve unilaterally; consequently, from the earliest days of civil aviation, there has been an attempt to find international solutions through the creation of international bodies. Typically, civil aviation requires the building of airports to accepted international standards, the establishment of standard navigational aids, the setting up of a worldwide weather reporting system, and the standardization of operational practices to minimize the possibility of error or misunderstanding.

National institutions can assist in the general aims of providing safe and reliable civil air transport. Their role is to furnish procedures for the inspection and licensing of aircraft and the training and licensing of pilots, and to provide the necessary infrastructure—that is, navigation aids and airports. Although the establishment of an infrastructure for a country's civil air transport is a national concern that cannot realistically be assumed by an international body, it is clear that there is need for the standardization of procedures, regulations, and equipment, as well as infrastructure, on a worldwide basis.

1.2   THE INTERNATIONAL CIVIL AVIATION ORGANIZATION (1)

The first attempt to reach an international consensus was unsuccessful; in 1910, representatives of 19 European nations met to develop an international agreement. Another attempt was made to internationalize civil aviation standards after World War I, when the Versailles Peace Conference set up the International Conference for Air Navigation (ICAN). Although this organization lasted from 1919 until World War II, its effectiveness was extremely limited because of the regionality of air transport even up to the early 1940s.

World War II provided a huge impetus to civil aviation. New types of fast monoplane aircraft had been developed, and the jet engine was in its infancy; navigational aids that had been developed for military purposes were easily adapted to civilian use, and many countries had built numerous military airports that would be converted to civilian use in peacetime. A generation of peacetime development had been crammed into the period of the European war from 1939 to 1945. In early 1944, the United States sought out its allies and a number of neutral nations, 55 in all, to discuss postwar civil aviation. The result of these exploratory discussions was the Chicago Convention on Civil Aviation in November 1944, attended by 52 countries. Its purposes are best described by the preamble to the convention:

> WHEREAS the future development of international civil aviation can greatly help to create and preserve friendship and understanding among the nations and peoples of the world, yet its abuse can become a threat to the general security; and
>
> WHEREAS it is desirable to avoid friction and to promote that cooperation between nations and peoples upon which the peace of the world depends;
>
> THEREFORE the undersigned governments, having agreed on certain principles and arrangements in order that international civil aviation may be developed in a safe and orderly manner and that international air transport services may be established on the basis of equality of opportunity and operated soundly and economically;
>
> HAVE accordingly concluded this Convention to that end.

The Chicago Convention established 96 articles, which outlined the privileges of contracting states, provided for the establishment of international recommended practices, and recommended that air transport be facilitated by the reduction of formalities of customs and immigration. After ratification by the legislatures of 26 national states, the International Civil Aviation Organization (ICAO) came into existence on April 4, 1947. By 1983, the original 26 ratifying states had grown to 150 member states. The modus operandi of ICAO is stated in Article 44 of the Convention:

> ICAO has a sovereign body, the Assembly, and a governing body, the Council. The Assembly meets at least once in three years and is convened by the Council.

Each Contracting State is entitled to one vote and decisions of the Assembly are taken by a majority of the votes cast except when otherwise provided in the Convention. At this session the complete work of the Organization in the technical, economic, legal and technical assistance fields is reviewed in detail and guidance given to the other bodies of ICAO for their future work.

Although the sovereign body of ICAO is the Assembly, in which each contracting state has one vote, the governing body of the organization is the 30 member Council, which emphasizes in its makeup the states of chief importance to air transport, with a provision for geographical balance. One of the principal functions and duties of the Council is to adopt international standards and recommended practices. Once adopted, these are incorporated as Annexes (Table 1.1) to the Convention on International Civil Aviation.

1.3 NONGOVERNMENTAL ORGANIZATIONS

There are a number of industrial organizations active in the area of air transportation, both at the international and national levels. The most important of the international organizations are as follows:

1. *International Air Transport Association (IATA).*   An organization with more than 100 scheduled international carrier members. Its role is to foster the interests of civil aviation, to provide a forum for industry views, and to establish industry practices.
2. *International Civil Airports Association (ICAA).*   An association of civil airport authorities established to serve as a forum and focus for the views and interests of civil airport operators.
3. *Institute of Air Transport (ITA).*   An association of individuals and organizations with interest in civil aviation.

In the United States, the more important domestic organizations with views and policies affecting the civil aviation industry are the Air Line Pilots Association, the Aircraft Owners and Pilots Association, the Air Transport Association of America, the National Association of State Aviation Officials, the Airport Operators Council International, and the American Association of Airport Executives.

1.4 U.S. GOVERNMENTAL ORGANIZATIONS (2)

The administration, promotion, and regulation of aviation in the United States is carried out at the federal level by three administrative bodies:

TABLE 1.1 Annexes to the ICAO Convention on International Civil Aviation

Annex[a]	Covers
1. Personnel Licensing	Licensing of flight crews, air traffic control officers and aircraft maintenance personnel
2. Rules of the Air	Rules relating to the conduct of visual and instrument flights
3. Meteorological Service for International Air Navigation	Provision of meteorological services for international air navigation and reporting of meteorological observations from aircraft
4. Aeronautical Charts	Specifications for aeronautical charts for use in international aviation
5. Units of Measurement to be used in Air and Ground Operations	Dimensional systems to be used in air and ground operations

6. Operation of Aircraft
    Part I—International Commercial Air Transport
    Part II—International General Aviation
	Specifications that will ensure in similar operations throughout the world a level of safety above a prescribed minimum

7. Aircraft Nationality and Registration Marks	Requirements for registration and identification of aircraft
8. Airworthiness of Aircraft	Certification and inspection of aircraft according to uniform procedures
9. Facilitation	Removal of obstacles and impediments to movement of passengers, freight and mail across international boundaries
10. Aeronautical Telecommunications	Standardization of communications equipment and systems (Vol. 1) and of communications procedures (Vol. 2)
11. Air Traffic Services	Establishment and operation of air traffic control, flight information, and alerting services
12. Search and Rescue	Organization and operation of facilities and services necessary for search and rescue
13. Aircraft Accident Investigation	Uniformity in the notification, investigation of, and reporting on aircraft accidents
14. Aerodromes	Specifications for the design and equipment of aerodromes
15. Aeronautical Information Services	Methods for the collection and dissemination of aeronautical information required for flight operations
16. Environmental Protection	Specifications for aircraft noise certification, noise monitoring, and noise exposure units for land use planning
17. Security	Specifications for safeguarding international civil aviation against acts of unlawful interference
18. Safe Carriage of Dangerous Goods by Air	The storage, handling and carriage of dangerous and hazardous cargo

Source: Memorandum on ICAO, Montreal: International Civil Aviation Organization, July 1975.

[a] All Annexes, except 9, are the responsibility of the Air Navigation Commission. Annex 9 is the responsibility of the Air Transport Committee.

1. The Federal Aviation Administration (FAA).
2. The Civil Aeronautics Board (CAB).
3. The National Transportation Safety Board (NTSB).

The Federal Aviation Administration

The FAA has prime responsibility for civil aviation. Formerly called the Federal Aviation Agency, it was absorbed into the Department of Transportation under the terms of the reorganization contained in the Department of Transportation Act of 1967 (80 Stat. 932). It is charged with the regulation of air commerce to "foster aviation safety; promoting civil aviation and a national system of airports; achieving efficient use of navigable airspace; and developing and operating a common system of air traffic control and air navigation for both civilian and military aircraft." It discharges these responsibilities with programs in eight principal areas:

1. *Safety Regulation.* Issuance and enforcement of regulations relating to the manufacture, operation, and maintenance of aircraft; rating and certification of airmen, certification of airports serving air carriers; flight inspection of air navigation facilities in the United States and, as required, abroad.

2. *Research and Development.* Research and development activities aimed to provide a safe and efficient system of air navigation and air traffic control for civil aviation and the air defense system; this now also includes the development and testing of improved aircraft, engines, and other aircraft technology.

3. *Air Navigation Facilities.* The location, construction, maintenance, and operation of federally owned visual and electronic aids to air navigation.

4. *Airspace and Air Traffic Management.* The operation of a network of air traffic control towers, air route traffic control centers, and flight service stations; the promulgation of air traffic rules and regulations, and the allocation of the use of airspace.

5. *Airport Planning and Development Programs.* Identification of the type and cost of development of public airports necessary for a national airport system; the provision and administration of grants of funds to assist public agencies in airport system planning, airport master planning, and public airport development.

6. *Registration and Recordation.* Provision of a system for the registration of an aircraft's nationality, engines, propellers, and appliances as well as a system for recording aircraft ownership.

7. *Civil Aviation Abroad.* Promotion of civil aviation abroad by means of technical assistance, information exchange, and training of foreign nationals.

8. *Other Programs.*   A variety of programs including the publication of airways and airport service information and other technical materials and the administration of aircraft loan guarantee programs.

The Civil Aeronautics Board

Under the original terms of the Civil Aeronautics Act of 1938 (52 Stat. 973) and the Federal Aviation Act of 1958 (72 Stat. 731), the Civil Aeronautics Board (CAB) was established and continued as an independent commission for the promotion and regulation of the interstate civil air transport industry in the United States, and between the United States and foreign countries. The five-member board granted licenses to provide air transportation services and approved or disapproved proposed rates, fares, agreements, and corporate relationships involving air carriers by issuing general rules or by considering individual applications. Board functions were significantly affected by the Airline Deregulation Act of 1978. The goals of the Act were promoted by the board, which relaxed barriers to the entry of new airlines into markets by the policy of "multiple-permissive entry." Competition in both fares and quality of service were the aim of the Act, which engendered a policy of fare flexibility, allowing broad upward and downward discretion in setting fare levels. After December 31, 1981, the board no longer made findings of public convenience and necessity and did not name points of service on domestic certificates of operation. Certificates after this date were issued on grounds of carrier fitness only. All board authority over domestic fares was abolished on January 1, 1983. The functions that still accrued to the board after this date were:

1. Authorization to U.S. air carriers to engage in interstate and foreign air transportation and to foreign carriers to operate between the United States and foreign countries.
2. The setting and adjusting of foreign fare levels and the suspension of rates and fares it finds unlawful.
3. Operation of Subsidy and Small Community Service, which identifies and, if necessary, subsidizes the essential level of air service to 500 small communities.
4. The approval and disapproval of various relationships and agreements involving air carriers only, or others, to ensure that no unfair competitive practices occur.
5. The negotiation and implementation of bilateral agreements for international air transportation.
6. The administration of a uniform carrier accounting and reporting system.
7. The analysis and publication of industry statistics.
8. Enforcement of compliance with the Federal Aviation Act and the board's rules and regulations.

The Deregulation Act of 1978 provided for the abolition of the board in 1985, unless it could demonstrate the need for its continued existence.

The National Transportation Safety Board

The NTSB was established as an independent agency of the federal government in April 1975, under the terms of the Independent Safety Board Act of 1974 (88 Stat. 2156; 49 U.S.C. 1901). Its five members are appointed by the President. Its function is to ensure that all types of transportation in the United States are conducted safely. The board assumed responsibility for the investigation of aviation accidents, which previously had been carried out by the CAB. Within NTSB the Bureau of Aviation Safety is under the management direction of the Office of the General Manager, as is the Bureau of Surface Transportation Safety, but it reports directly to the five-member board on aviation accidents.

1.5 AVIATION PLANNING AND REGULATION AT STATE LEVEL

In the early days of civil aviation, the federal government saw no role for itself in the provision of airports. This was stated to be a local responsibility that should be financed principally by the municipalities or by private sources (3). The Air Commerce Act of 1926 gave the Secretary of Commerce authority "to designate and establish civil airways and, within the limits of available appropriations hereafter made by Congress, to establish, operate and maintain along such airways all necessary air navigation facilities except airports."

In that municipalities draw all their powers from the authority delegated by the sovereign states, government at the state level necessarily became involved in aviation. Consequently, state aviation departments and bureaus and, in some cases, state aeronautical commissions were established. Most states have some form of user taxation on aviation, which is channeled back into airport development in the form of matching fund grants.

The planning and financing of airports varies from state to state, and the practice of a particular state depends greatly on the organizational structure of the overall administration of transportation within the state. More than half the states have reorganized their administration of transportation to form state Departments of Transportation (DOTs), which frequently act as intermediaries in federal-local negotiations. A number of different organizational forms of state DOTs have evolved in the last 10 years. In extremes they vary from *functional* structures, where individual departments are multimodal, to *modal* structures, which reflect more closely the structures of the individual agencies prior to reorganization into the DOT format. Frequently the structure is a hybrid form of organization somewhere between these two extremes. Figure 1.1 illustrates three types of state DOT structure.

Where no state DOT exists, aviation at the state level is usually administered by a specialized agency. This is frequently a bureau or division, in many cases

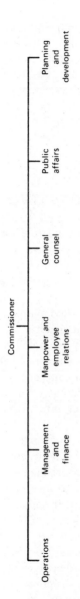

Functional organization

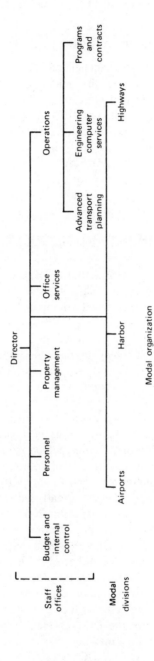

Modal organization

Hybrid organization

FIGURE 1.1 The aviation function within State Departments of Transportation. (*Source*: Reference 4.)

8

within the state Department of Commerce, reflecting the federal structure before the Civil Aeronautics Act of 1938. (In some states civil aviation was administered by a Civil Aeronautics Commission.)

In the regulation of air transportation at the state level, public service commissions still play an important role. Whereas interstate services, fares, and tariffs are set by the CAB, for intrastate traffic control over the provision of services and the power to set and control fares and tariffs fall entirely within the jurisdiction of Public Service Commissions.

1.6 PATTERNS OF AIRPORT OWNERSHIP (5)

In the early days of civil aviation in the United States, airports typically were owned by local authorities or private organizations. Massive increases in passenger volumes, however, required extensive building infrastructure in the passenger terminal area; at the same time the increasing weight and sophistication in aircraft necessitated greater investment in extensive pavements for runways, taxiways, and aprons; equally necessary were navigational and landing aid systems. These requirements were generally beyond the capability of private finance, and the private airport operator has tended to disappear, except at the smallest airports. The trend toward public ownership is generally international, but the form of public ownership varies from country to country. The principal forms of ownership include the following:

1. Ownership by a governmental agency or department, whereby airports are centrally owned and operated either by a division of the overall Ministry of Transport or by the more specialized Ministry of Civil Aviation.
2. Quasi-governmental organizations—public corporations set up by government for the specific purpose of airport ownership and operation; the governmental unit may be national or regional (including state or provincial governments).
3. Authorities for individual airports or for groups of airports authorized by a consortium of state, provincial, or local governmental units.
4. Individual authorities that run one airport on the behalf of one local authority.
5. Departments of a local authority.
6. Private organizations.

An examination of international patterns of ownership indicates no special trends. France, Italy, West Germany, Holland, and the United States have the majority of their airports run by individual airport authorities. The same is true of the United Kingdom, except that 80% of British air traffic operates through airports that are owned by a public corporation, the British Airports

Authority. Most developing countries, as well as South Africa, Australia, Canada, Sweden, Spain, Japan, Mexico, and Belgium, own and operate their airports through centralized organizations that are part of the national government. In Brazil, where commercial aviation exhibits considerable growth potential, airport policy matters are decided by the Ministry of Aeronautics; administration of the airports is carried out by a national holding company INFRAERO (Empresa Brasiliera de Infraestrutura Aeroportuaria). This responsibility is further devolved to smaller regional organizations: for example, ARSA (Aeroportos de Rio de Janeiro, S.A.) manages the three airports of Rio de Janeiro in much the same way as the Port Authority of New York and New Jersey manage the three airports of Kennedy, La Guardia, and Newark.

1.7   REVENUES AND EXPENDITURES AT U.S. AIRPORTS

Since the feasibility of developing and building an airport rests heavily on the anticipated revenue and expenditure, the financial aspects of airport planning must take into consideration both *revenues* and *expenses*; these two principal divisions may be further grouped into the operating and nonoperating areas.

Revenues

Operating Revenues.   The operating revenues at airports may be categorized into five major groupings (6).

1. *Landing Area.*   Revenues are produced directly from the operation of aircraft in the form of landing fees and parking ramp fees.
2. *Terminal Area Concessions.*   Nonairline uses in the terminal areas produce income from a varied range of activities including *specialty areas* (e.g., duty-free stores, souvenir vendors, bookshops, newsstands, banks), *food and drink areas* (e.g., restaurants, cafeterias, bars), *leisure areas* (e.g., television, movie, and observation areas), *travel services* (e.g., lockers, washrooms, nurseries, insurance desks, car rentals, rest areas, telephones), *personal service areas* (e.g., barber shops, beauty salons, valet service), and *off-terminal facilities* (e.g., office rentals, advertising).
3. *Airline Leased Areas.*   Within the terminal itself or in the general airport site, substantial revenues can be generated by leasing facilities to the airlines. Airlines normally rent offices, hangars, ticket and check-in counters, operations and maintenance areas, and cargo terminals. Ground rents are paid when the facility is provided by the airline.
4. *Other Leased Areas.*   Many larger airports function as industrial and transport complexes incorporating a number of nonairline operations.

These operations, which constitute another source of revenue, typically include industrial areas, fuel and servicing facilities, fixed base operators, freight forwarders, and warehousing.

5. *Other Operating Revenue.* The sources that can contribute to this category include equipment rental, resale of utilities, and at some airports, services such as baggage handling.

Nonoperating Revenues. All income that accrues from sources that are not directly connected to airport functions is nonoperating revenue. Such income may derive, for example, from the rental of nonairport land or from interest on accumulated surpluses.

Expenditures

Operating Expenses. Numerous operating expenses are associated with the provision of airport services. These can be categorized into maintenance costs and operations costs.

1. *Maintenance Costs.* Expenditures are required for the upkeep of facilities; these are largely independent of traffic volumes. Maintenance must be provided to the landing area (runways, taxiways, aprons, lighting equipment, etc.), the terminal area (buildings, utilities, baggage handling, access routes, grounds, etc.), and to hangars, cargo terminals, and other airport facilities.

2. *Operations Costs.* This category, which includes administration and staffing, utilities, and to some extent security, reflects to a greater degree the amount of traffic. To some degree these costs are escapable when demand is low.

Nonoperating Expenses. The inescapable costs that would have to be met even if the airport ceased operation are said to be nonoperating expenses. Typically, they include the interest payments on outstanding capital debt and amortization charges on fixed assets such as runways, aprons, buildings, and other infrastructure.

Table 1.2 shows the effect of the magnitude of passenger operations on the sources of income and expenditure for 43 airports in the United States. The data reveal a moderate tendency for nonoperating income and expenses to increase as airports become larger. The overwhelming source of both revenue and expenditure remains in the operating category. The low level of nonoperating expense at U.S. airports reflects high levels of FAA funding for infrastructure. In fundamentally differently financed systems, nonoperating costs could rise substantially higher.

TABLE 1.2   Income and Expense Breakdown for Airports Having Different Levels of Operational Activity

	Annual Enplanements		
Income or Expense	<500,000 (17 airports)	500,000- 2,000,000 (15 airports)	>2,000,000 (11 airports)
Income			
Operating income (%)	95.7	98.5	92.2
Nonoperating income (%)	4.3	1.5	7.8
Expenses			
Operating expenses (%)	91.4	86.4	87.0
Nonoperating expenses (%)	8.6	13.6	13.0

Sources: Airport Operators Council International Uniform Airport Financial Report and S. Bauml, "Airport Revenues and Expenses" (based on a sample of 43 airports) in *Airport Economic Planning*, G. P. Howard (Ed.), Cambridge, Mass.: MIT Press, 1974.

The Structure of Revenues

Operating revenues vary considerably from airport to airport, in structure and in size. Their structure depends greatly on operating volume. (Since nonoperating revenues are, by their nature, not dependent on the operating characteristics of the airport, they tend to be unpredictable.) As the number of airport operations increases across the range of airport size, the busier airports attract a higher proportion of commercial air carrier operations. The large passenger capacity of commercial carrier aircraft ensures a disproportionate increase in passenger traffic in comparison with the increase in aircraft movements. Consequently air terminal income increases rapidly in importance in the overall revenue structure with growing operational activity.

Operational growth that accompanies increasing air carrier traffic requires substantial investment in terminal infrastructure to provide for the rapid increase in passenger movements. Table 1.3 indicates, for airports across a range of operational volumes, the declining relative importance of the landing area as a source of revenue and the increasing dominance of terminal income. The financial stability of the operation of large airports is strongly related to the income generated by the terminal area. More than half this income relates to surface access in the form of parking charges and leases to car rental firms (Table 1.4); but more than a quarter of terminal income is almost discretionary, coming from restaurants, bars, shopping concessions, and similar sources. Careful design can optimize this income relative to expenditure.

1.8   SOURCES OF CAPITAL FINANCING FOR U.S. AIRPORTS

All airports are to some degree self-financing, and some large airports give a healthy return on invested capital. The initial capital requirements for the construction and development of airports is very large, and frequently the owning authority is unable to supply the necessary amount from its own resources. In the United States, ownership of airports rests almost entirely in the hands of local governmental units with slender capital resources. Airport development therefore proceeds on the basis of money aggregated from a variety of sources such as general obligation bonds, self-liquidating general obligation bonds, revenue bonds, local taxes, and state and federal grants.

General Obligation Bonds

General obligation bonds are issued by a governmental unit. They are secured by the full faith, credit, and taxing power of the issuing governmental agency.

TABLE 1.3   Operating Revenue Source Distributions by Annual Enplaning Passenger Numbers at Air Carrier Airports

	Enplaned Passengers (%)				
Category	Over 2 Million	500,000– 2 Million	250,000– 500,000	125,000– 250,000	Under 125,000
Airfield area					
Air carrier landing fees	25.1	22.5	19.0	16.5	8.9
Other landing fees	0.4	0.6	1.0	1.2	2.3
Fuel and oil sales	0.9	4.6	10.0	10.6	8.4
Airline catering fees	1.1	3.3	—	—	—
Aircraft parking	0.1	1.1	1.9	1.9	2.6
Total airfield	27.6	32.1	31.9	30.2	22.2
Hangar and building area	11.4	11.6	13.6	20.2	43.9
Terminal area	12.8	13.3	18.7	14.8	10.5
Systems and services	4.3	3.1	4.0	4.0	4.0
Concessions					
Airport parking	19.7	15.5	11.5	11.0	2.1
Car rental	8.2	10.3	10.2	8.0	6.8
Restaurant and lounge	4.8	5.5	5.9	3.5	2.5
Advertising	0.6	1.2	0.9	1.5	1.2
Ground transportation	1.9	1.9	0.7	1.9	0.2
Flight insurance	2.3	2.4	0.7	0.7	0.5
Hotel/motel	1.8	1.6	0.1	1.5	0.1
Miscellaneous	4.6	1.5	1.8	2.7	6.0
Total concessions	43.9	39.9	31.8	30.8	19.4

Source: Neiss, J. A., *Economics of Airport Operation* (7).

TABLE 1.4   Average Annual Terminal Concession Revenues by Categories

Category	Small Hubs	Medium Hubs	Large Hubs
Number of operations	172,311	146,841	338,554
Number of enplanements	215,375	649,118	3,891,175
Revenues	$743,153	$2,066,931	$7,270,592
Landing Area[a]	$255,153	$ 830,754	$1,928,648
Terminal Area			
Car rentals	$ 61,562	$ 182,610	$ 575,267
Parking	80,170	317,648	1,231,019
Restaurant, bars, etc.	36,585	103,331	450,293
Hotel	—	1,554	3,150
Advertising	5,444	12,018	63,635
Limousines and taxis	4,405	14,402	28,202
Flight insurance	7,408	38,372	136,021
Coin-operated devices	3,538	15,732	116,069
Specialty shops, stores, and facilities	—	13,537	395,061
Parking meters	—	38,003	90,547
Personal services	—	—	5,629
Buses	—	—	112,739
Miscellaneous	1,670	7,342	3,037
	$200,782	$ 744,079	$3,210,669
Aviation leased areas[b]	$188,195	$ 340,379	$1,199,953
Other leased areas[c]	$ 22,399	$ 54,262	$ 483,935
Other areas[d]	$ 76,624	$ 97,457	$ 447,387

Source: Airport World, December 1970.

[a] Includes leasing fees, fuel, fixed base operations (FBO), hangar rentals, ramp tiedowns, etc.

[b] Includes terminal and building.

[c] Includes buildings, grounds, farms, residences, parking leases, warehouses, FBOs, and facilities.

[d] Includes services, utilities, equipment rental, government reimbursements, gross business over-rides, military.

Although the level of anticipated revenues is considered in the initial deter-mination of the level of investment, the bonds themselves are guaranteed from the general resources of the issuing body, not from the revenues themselves. With this degree of investment security, general obligation bonds can be sold at a relatively low interest rate, requiring a lower level of expenditure on debt servicing. Since local authorities are constitutionally limited in the total debt that can be secured by general obligation, the use of this type of bond reduces the available debt level. Because of the high demand on local authorities for capital investment, usually for facilities that produce no revenue, most gov-ernment agencies consider it unwise to use general obligation bonds for income-generating projects such as airports.

Self-Liquidating General Obligation Bonds

Self-liquidating general obligation bonds have been recognized by the courts of some states. These instruments are secured in exactly the same way as ordinary general obligation bonds; however, since it is recognized that the bonds are financing a revenue-producing project, the issue is not considered to contribute toward the overall debt limitation set by the state. This type of financing is particularly desirable in that it bears low interest rates without limiting other general obligation debt.

Revenue Bonds

Revenue bonds can be issued where the entire debt service is paid from project revenues. Although subject to the general debt limitation, these bonds bear substantially higher interest rates than general obligation bonds, the interest rate often being dependent on the anticipated level of coverage of revenues to debt service. Before issuing revenue bonds, it is normal practice to prepare a traffic and earnings report that includes the forecasting of revenues and expenses during the life of the bond issue. Revenue bonds are sold on the open market, but they suffer from the disadvantage that banks are forbidden to deal in revenue bond issues. Banks, on the other hand, are responsible for a large share of the underwriting of general obligation issues.

Some authorities have negotiated airport-airline agreements to provide a greater degree of security to revenue bond issues in order to assure a lower interest rate. Under these agreements, the airline guarantees to meet all airport obligations with respect to the issue. Usually, however, this sort of agreement requires that capital decisions be made by the airline, a restriction that few airports are prepared to accept.

In the past, almost all airports were financed by general obligation bonds, but the rapidly increasing sophistication of the required facilities has necessitated an increasing trend toward the use of revenue bonds, with an increasing level of commitment by the airlines in guaranteeing the revenues for debt service.

Local Government Taxes

In the early days of aviation, most airports were supported by general local government taxes. As facilities grew, the fiscal requirements rapidly outpaced the local governments' abilities to provide capital from their own annual revenues. As a source of capital, this form of finance is now unimportant.

State Finance

The individual states contribute substantially to the financing of airports. About half these states require federal funding to be channeled to local government through state agencies. It is normal in these circumstances for the state to share equally in the nonfederal contribution of matching finance for federal funds. Where no federal funds are involved, state funds may be matched to local funds. Much of state funding comes from taxes on aviation fuel, which are largely reused for airport development. In 1982, combined state and local government expenditures for airports amounted to $2.9 billion.

Federal Grants

The federal government has provided substantial support for the development of inputs through a series of peacetime programs in the 1930s; the Federal Airport Act of 1946 as amended in 1955, 1959, 1961, 1964, and 1966; and, currently, by the Airport and Airways Development Act of 1970, as amended in 1976, as the Airport Development Acceleration Act of 1973 and the Airport and Airway Improvement Act of 1982. Federal financing is discussed more extensively in the following section.

1.9 FEDERAL FINANCING

Up to 1933, the financing of airports in the United States was carried out almost entirely by local government and by private investors. The first significant infusion of federal monies into the development of airports came in 1933, at the height of the Depression. In that year, through the work relief program of the Civil Works Administration, approximately $15.2 million was spent on airports. After a short period of support by the succeeding work relief program of the Federal Emergency Relief Administration in 1934, the Works Progress Administration (WPA) assumed responsibility for the administration of federal aid to airports and spent approximately $320 million between 1935 and 1941 (7). The WPA programs required a degree of matching local support, and it was at this time that the practice of sharing airport development costs among federal, state, and local governments became established.

In 1938, the Civil Aeronautics Administration (CAA) was created to formulate policies to promote the overall development of the aviation industry; this body, several reorganizations and retitlings later, is now the Federal Aviation Administration (FAA). During the war years the Civil Aeronautics Administration, in the interests of national defense, spent approximately $353 million for the development and construction of military airports; approximately $9.5 million went for civilian airports in the same period.

Toward the end of the war, Congress was aware that postwar civil aviation was likely to achieve a remarkable growth rate. The CAA was authorized by House Resolution 598 (78th Congress) to carry out a survey of airport needs in the postwar period. This survey, and the clear need for federal funds, led to the Federal Airport Act of 1946. This legislation authorized the spending of approximately $500 million in federal aid to airports over seven years, with a further $20 million for the Virgin Islands, Puerto Rico, Alaska, and Hawaii. In 1950, the original seven-year period was extended to 12 years, reflecting the realization that federal appropriations were falling significantly below the levels of authorization.

Further major amendments were made in 1955, 1959, 1961, 1964, and 1968. During that period, the authorizations grew from $40 million in 1956, with a further $2 million for Alaska, Hawaii, Puerto Rico, and the Virgin Islands, to $75 million for the period 1968–1970. By the late 1960s, however, it was clear that the scale of capital investment required to provide airports and airways to meet the sustained growth in aviation that could be expected in the 1970s and 1980s called for a restructuring of airport financing beyond what could reasonably be achieved by further amendment of the Federal Airport Act.

The Airport and Airways Development Act of 1970 established the Airport and Airways Trust Fund, amounting to $2.5 billion for airports over a period of 10 years, and a further $2.5 billion for airways and air traffic control systems. Financing was by a series of user taxes: 8% tax on airplane tickets, flat rate airport head taxes of $3 for passengers going abroad or to Hawaii and Alaska, a domestic cargo tax of 5% on tariffs, a 7¢/gal tax on noncommercial aviation fuel, and an airplane registration tax of $25 plus a levy based on the engine weight type. The act substantially increased the amount of federal funds available for airport development. Each year, $250 million was to be made available for air carrier and reliever airports; one-third of this fund was earmarked for air carrier airports based on the number of enplaning passengers, one-third was for air carrier and general aviation reliever airports on the basis of state population and state area, and one-third was to be disbursed at the discretion of the Secretary of Transportation. Grant agreements were to extend over three years, rather than the one-year basis of funding authorized by the Federal Airport Act.

For a project to be eligible to receive funds under the Airport Development Aid Program (ADAP), the airport had to be publicly owned and in the National Airport System Plan. The 1970 act retained the federal share of eligible project costs at 50%, a holdover from the Federal Airport Act; this federal share was subsequently modified by amendments in 1973 and 1976.

Under the terms of the development act, airport facilities associated with safety and necessary operation were eligible for federal grants. Included were the purchase of land for physical facilities and the purchase of long term easements to protect navigable airspace in the clear zones; construction and reconstruction of runways, taxiways, and aprons; resurfacing of runways, taxiways, and aprons for structural but not maintenance purposes; runway and taxiway lights; touchdown lights for category II and III runways (see Section 5.7), high intensity runway lights, obstruction lights, beacons, taxiway guidance lights, runway centerline lights; buildings associated with safety, such as the airport fire and emergency buildings; and roads, streets, and rapid transit facilities. In the original version (1970) of the act, terminals, car parking hangars, and administration buildings were absent from the list of facilities for which federal funds could be used.

Over the 10-year period of the act, planning funds were made available to a limit of $15 million for airport system planning on a regional basis and the master planning of individual airports. Federal planning funds were available on a 75% cost sharing basis, with a limit of $1.5 million to any one state.

The Airport Development Acceleration Act of 1973 made some substantial changes to the operation of the trust fund. Federal funds for airport development were increased from $280 million to $310 million annually, with the federal proportion going from 50 to 75% for airports with passenger enplanements less than 1% of total national passenger enplanements; the federal share of airport certification and security requirements costs was set at 82%. This act also specifically prohibited the collection of state airport "head taxes."

Further significant amendments to the 1970 act were made in 1976 (Public Law 94-353). These amendments increased the level of annual authorization for airport development to $500 million in 1976, climbing to $610 million in 1980. For airports enplaning less than 1% of national enplaning passengers, the federal share of allowable project costs was increased to 90% in 1976–1978 and 80% in 1979–1980; for the busier airports, the federal share was increased to 75%. This act also permitted the use of federal funds for non-revenue-producing areas in the passenger terminal and for passenger transfer vehicles on both the airside and the landside.

Significant changes to airport financing were made by the Airport and Airway Improvement Act of 1982. Major funding over a six-year period was authorized for airport improvement, ranging from $450 million in 1982 to $1017 million in 1987. The same act authorized sums over the same period, ranging from $261 million to $1164 for facilities and equipment associated with air traffic control and navigation, and a further $800 million to $1362 million for airspace system operation and maintenance. Fifty percent of the total authorization was designated for primary airports (see Section 1.10), with the apportionment formula remaining the same as that for air carrier airports under the ADAP, with increases between 10% in 1984 to 30% in 1987. State apportionments amount to 12% of total apportionment. In the contiguous United States, 99% of the state's apportionments are for nonprimary airports. Other fund limitations legislated were that at least 10% of total apportionment was for reliever airports, at least 8% for noise compatibility, and at least 5.5% for commercial service airports that are not primary airports and for public noncommercial service airports that had scheduled service in 1981. At least 1% of total funds were designated for planning, with ι3.5% remaining to be used at the discretion of the Secretary.

1.10   THE U.S. NATIONAL INTEGRATED AIRPORT SYSTEM

Under the terms of the Airport and Airway Improvement Act of 1982, airports in the United States are functionally classified as shown in Figure 1.2 for purposes of federal administration (8):

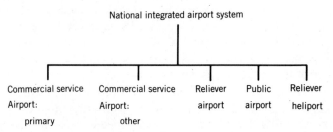

FIGURE 1.2   Functional classification of the U.S. National Integrated Airport System.

Commercial Service Primary Airport: A public airport that receives scheduled service and enplanes 0.01% or more of total annual enplanements of all commercial service airports. In 1982, this lower limit of 0.01% approximated to 31,000 enplanements.

Other Commercial Service Airport: A public airport receiving scheduled service and enplaning 2500 or more annual passenger enplanements, but less than the 0.01% required for the primary category.

Reliever Airport: An airport designated by the Secretary as having the function of relieving congestion at a commercial service airport and providing more general aviation access to the overall community.

Public Airport: Any other public airport. (This classification equals basically the old General Aviation class.)

Reliever Heliport: A heliport designated by the Secretary as having the function of relieving congestion at a commercial airport by diverting potential fixed-wing enplaned passengers to helicopter carriers.

Additionally, there is an operational classification that is used to categorize airports according to the size and performance characteristics of aircraft using the facility (9, 10). Airports are operationally classified into *utility* and *transport* airports

Utility Airports

These airports serve general aviation aircraft and are generally suitable for lightweight airplanes with approach speeds of 120 knots or less. Reference 9 defines four categories of utility airports:

1. *Basic Utility Stage I.*   This type of facility accommodates approximately 75% of single-engine and small twin-engine airplanes under 12,500 pounds. It is primarily intended for low activity locations that serve personal and business flights.

2. *Basic Utility Stage II.*   This type of airport accommodates the same fleet of aircraft suited to Basic Utility Stage I airports plus a broader array of small business and air-taxi type twin-engine airplanes. It is

primarily intended to serve medium-sized communities, with a diversity of usage and a potential for increased aviation activities.

Basic utility airports are designed to serve airplanes with wingspans of less than 49 ft. Precision approach operations are not anticipated for either of the Basic Utility airport classes.

3. *General Utility Stage I.*   General utility airports are primarily intended to serve the fringe of metropolitan areas or large, remote communities. General Utility Stage I airports are designed to accommodate all aircraft of less than 12,500 pounds. These airports are usually designed for aircraft with wingspans of less than 49 ft and are not intended to accommodate precision approach operations.

4. *General Utility Stage II.*   This class of airports accommodates airplanes with approach speeds up to 120 knots. These airports are designed to serve airplanes with wingspans of up to 79 ft. They usually have the capabilities for precision approach operations.

Transport Airports

Transport airports accommodate, or are expected to accommodate, airplanes with approach speeds of more than 120 knots. Such airports are usually capable of accommodating turbojet-powered aircraft. Many of these airports are served by air carriers, while others accommodate only general aviation aircraft.

REFERENCES

1. *Memorandum on ICAO*, Montreal: International Civil Aviation Organization, July 1975.
2. *U.S. Government Manual, 1982–83*, Office of the Federal Register, General Services Administration, Washington, D.C.: Government Printing Office, 1982.
3. *The Federal Turnaround on Aid to Airports, 1926–1938*, Washington, D.C.: Federal Aviation Administration, 1973.
4. Rubino, Richard G. *A Quest for Integrated and Balanced Transportation Systems in State Government*, Transportation Center Report 5, Tallahassee: Florida State University, September 1972.
5. *Airports International Directory 1981*, London: IPC Transport Press Ltd., 1981.
6. Bauml, S., "Airport Revenues and Expenses," in *Airport Economic Planning*, G. P. Howard (Ed.), Cambridge, Mass.: MIT Press, 1974.
7. Neiss, J. A., *Economics of Airport Operation*, AD/4-005 892, Washington, D.C.: Report for Federal Aviation Administration, 1974.
8. *Airport and Airway Improvement Act, 1982*, Washington, D.C.: U.S. Congress, 1982.
9. *Utility Airports—Air Access to National Transportation* AC 150/5300–4B, including Changes 1–6, Washington D.C.: Federal Aviation Administration, February 24, 1983.
10. *Airport Design Standards—Transport Airports*, AC 150/5300-12, Washington, D.C.: Federal Aviation Administration, February 28, 1983.

2

FORECASTING
AIR TRANSPORT
DEMAND

Air transport in the 1980s will be characterized by traffic volumes many times greater than those of today. In meeting this demand, the resolution of the economic and political aspects of the general problem will present greater difficulties than resolving the technical aspects. World airline passenger traffic should double by 1980 and increase sixfold by 1990. Scheduled air freight by 1980 will be 3.5 times, and by 1990 ten times, present volumes. Industrial countries will continue to predominate air passenger and freight traffic. Today's turbojet fleet of 4000 will expand to about 6000 by the early 1980s and some aircraft may have over 1000 seats. Cargo capacity will increase proportionately. Congestion of airport runways, passenger and cargo terminals, inspection and ground transport facilities is expected to increase, as will demand for additional and improved airport systems. Continued traffic growth creates a need for effective longer range advance planning and requires a coordinated approach to design, development and operation of future airports. Rapid technological change, traffic expansion and environmental considerations underline the need for cooperation and coordination between aviation system planners, builders, operators and users in successfully meeting the challenges of the 1980s (1).

However unrealistic when viewed in retrospect in the light of increases in oil prices and recessions, forecasts such as this by the then Director of IATA were not simply the dreams of futurists, but were the best estimates of future levels of demand made by planners in the air transport industry. By 1980, passenger traffic had in fact increased by a factor of 1.76, and the aircraft manufacturers estimated that the rate of growth of passenger traffic should slow to between 6.4 and 6.1% over the decade of the 1980s (2, 3). Even so it is estimated that by 1990, passenger traffic will be over three times that of 1973.

The forecasting of future demand is difficult, and when forecasts are incorrect, an entire mode of transportation's ability to react to changing traffic is affected.

Until the early 1970s, the growth rate of air transport had been almost consistently underestimated. Expansion of air transport traffic had been associated with rapid population growth, increasing industrialization in developing countries, changes in the form of industrial structure in developed countries, worldwide urbanization and, not least, rapid and marked technological changes. Forecasters of the early 1970s attempted to correct for the underestimations of previous years, and for projected passenger and freight growths which were serious overestimates in the climate of increased real oil prices, inflation, and a worldwide economic recession of unprecedented depth.

In spite of the difficulties associated with making forecasts of air transport demand, such estimates are necessary, however, for the following reasons:

1. To assist manufacturers in industry to anticipate levels of aircraft orders and to develop new aircraft.
2. To aid airlines in their long term planning for both equipment and personnel.
3. To assist central governments to facilitate the orderly development of the national and international airways system, and to aid all levels of government in the planning of infrastructure (including, e.g., terminal facilities, access routes, runways, taxiways, aprons, and terminal air traffic control).

2.1 POSTWAR TRENDS IN AIR TRANSPORT

Accurate forecasts of air passenger and freight demand proved to be extraordinarily difficult in the past, when over an extended period, rapid advances in technology continued to lower the real costs of air transport to the consumer. For example, a 1963 forecast by the FAA predicted that 100 million passengers would be transported by U.S. carriers in 1975 (4). By the year 1971, however, the number of persons carried was already 174 million, and, by 1979, this figure was 321 million. This pattern of very buoyant expansion of demand at an exponential growth rate is typical of a demand curve of an infant industry, in which supply costs fall as demand rises. As the industry matures, real air transport costs will tend to stabilize at the higher level of demand, given that input costs such as labor, fuel, and vehicle costs remain constant in real terms. High early growth will give way to lower, steadier rates of increase that reflect population growth, modified by the factors of socioeconomic change.

Figure 2.1 shows the historic trends and long term projections of world passenger movements (5). The exponential nature of air transportation demand between 1950 and 1970 is clear. Most forecasters expect air transport to increase its share of total passenger kilometers over the next 20 years because of technological improvements of the mode, even given substantial real increases in fuel costs.

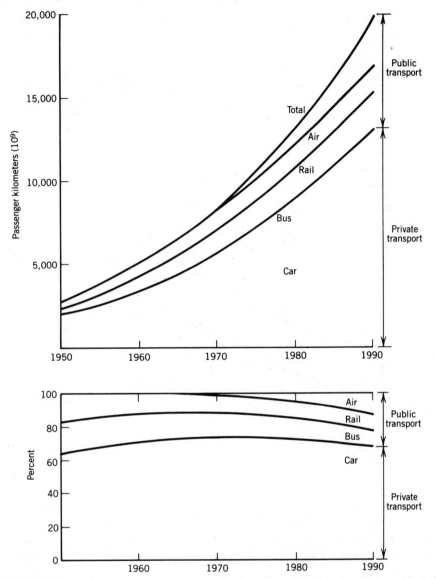

FIGURE 2.1 World total passenger movements distributed by principal modes. (*Source:* Adapted from Reference 5.)

Between the period 1972 and 1981, the overall world growth rate of scheduled passenger kilometers grew at an average rate of 7.9%, freight tonne kilometers at 8.1% and total tonne kilometers at 7.8% (6). However, growth rates have varied considerably by region from these average rates. Figure 2.2 expresses this variation graphically for total passenger and freight tonne kilometers where North America with a flatter graph line is seen to lag behind the more buoyant

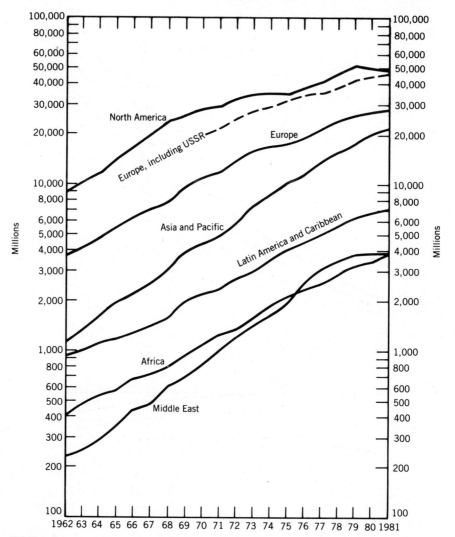

FIGURE 2.2 Long term regional trends: total tonne-kilometres in all operations performed by scheduled services of airlines registered in ICAO states in each region, 1962–1981. (*Source: Reference 6.*)

growth curves of Asia, Africa, and the Middle East. These developing regions have growth rates significantly above the world average; this is also shown in the statistics of Table 2.1.

When considered in terms of overall freight movement, air freight represents a minuscule portion of total freight ton mileage; in the United States, less than 0.2%. However, if the cost of transport is measured this share becomes 1.6%, since modal choice is affected by commodity value, length of haul, and commodity vulnerability.

TABLE 2.1 ICAO World Air Passenger Traffic 1970–1990. (Excludes domestic traffic of the USSR; includes Taiwan; excludes E. Germany. Traffic defined by on-flight origin/destination.)

| | Revenue Passenger (billions of kilometers) | | | | Average Annual Growth Rate | | |
| | Actual | | Forecast | | Actual | Forecast | |
	1970	1980	1985	1990	1970–1980	1980–1985	1985–1990
U.S. Domestic[a]	177.3	331.7	425.3	534.1	6.5%	5.1%	4.6%
Non-U.S. Domestic	50.6	146.3	211.5	304.6	11.2	7.6	7.6
Total Domestic	227.9	478.0	636.8	838.7	7.7	5.9	5.7
North Atlantic[b]	48.2	110.6	139.5	172.8	8.7	4.8	4.4
Trans-Pacific[c]	16.1	46.4	70.1	98.3	11.2	8.6	7.0
Western Hemisphere	20.4	50.7	75.4	108.6	9.5	8.3	7.5
European intercontinental flows[d]	29.8	123.7	185.3	264.4	15.3	8.4	7.4
Intra Asia/Oceania	9.9	44.6	71.5	109.5	16.2	9.9	8.9
Intra Europe[e]	34.6	88.6	120.0	162.4	9.9	6.2	6.2
Total international[f]	159.4	466.2	664.1	919.2	11.3	7.3	6.7
Total scheduled	387.3	944.2	1300.9	1757.9	9.3	6.6	6.2
Total nonscheduled	84.3	106.0	128.7	148.5	2.5	3.6	2.9
Total world	471.6	1052.2	1429.6	1906.4	8.4	6.3	5.9

Source: World Air Traffic Forecast 1970–1990, Lockheed, California (3).

[a] Includes 50 states plus Puerto Rico and U.S. Virgin Islands. Includes all certificated carriers.
[b] Includes IATA & Non-IATA carriers, includes Miami-Europe.
[c] North America-Far East/Oceania
[d] Europe, including North Africa and Middle East, to Asia, Oceania/Latin America/Sub Sahara Africa
[e] Includes North Africa and Middle East.
[f] Includes a small amount of miscellaneous (mainly African flows) traffic.

TABLE 2.2 U.S. Domestic Shares of Passenger and Goods Movement

Mode	Year			
	1945	1960	1970	1980
A. Intercity Travel: Billions of Passenger Miles (Percentages shown in parentheses)				
Private auto	220.3 (63.8)	706.1 (90.4)	1026.0 (86.9)	1312.1 (83.6)
Private air	Negligible	2.3 (0.3)	9.1 (0.8)	15.0 (1.0)
Public air	4.3 (1.2)	31.7 (4.1)	109.5 (9.3)	203.2 (12.9)
Bus	27.4 (7.9)	19.3 (2.5)	25.3 (2.1)	27.7 (1.8)
Rail	93.5 (27.1)	21.6 (2.8)	10.9 (0.9)	11.5 (0.7)
Total	345.5 (100.0)	781.0 (100.0)	1180.8 (100.0)	1569.5 (100.0)
B. Intercity Freight: Billions of Ton Miles (Percentages shown in parentheses)				
Rail	691 (67.2)	579 (44.1)	771 (39.7)	932 (37.5)
Truck	67 (6.5)	285 (21.8)	412 (21.3)	560 (22.5)
Oil pipeline	127 (12.4)	229 (17.4)	431 (22.3)	579 (23.3)
Great Lakes	113 (11.0)	99 (7.5)	114 (5.9)	93 (3.7)
Rivers and canals	30 (2.9)	121 (9.2)	205 (10.6)	318 (12.8)
Air	0.09 (0.01)	0.89 (0.07)	3.3 (0.17)	4.27 (0.17)
Total	1028 (100.0)	1314 (100.0)	1936 (100.0)	2486 (100.0)

Source: Transportation Facts and Trends, 17th Ed. (7).

In the United States, the domestic air transport industry has matured since World War II, and now represents a strong and significant mode, catering to intercity movement of freight and passengers. U.S. air passenger mileage grew from 4.3 billion passenger miles in 1945 to 203 billion passenger miles in 1980, representing approximately 13% of all intercity passenger mileage (7) (see Table 2.2). During the same period, domestic air freight has increased from 0.09 to 4.27 billion ton miles, an average increase of 11.6%. However, during the 1970s, the growth rate in domestic cargo declined significantly. During the period of severe recession, air cargo traffic declined by 7% between 1978 and 1980. It is clear that air cargo demand is closely related to domestic economic conditions, and tends to fluctuate more than passenger traffic. It is a general rule, however, that while the air mode accounts for only a tiny fraction of the total ton mileage of freight carried, it represents a significantly large proportion of traffic on a value basis.

2.2 CONVENTIONAL METHODS OF FORECASTING

Conventionally, forecasting of future air traffic demand has been carried out at the macroscopic scale, viewing demand as a response to the overall levels of change of a number of variables, without examining in detail the individual effect of the particular variables. These very simple methods have been applied with reasonable success at the local, national, and international levels, where rates of growth of traffic have been remarkably constant over time. Methods that have been used include judgment, surveys of expectation, trend forecasting, and base forecasting, which we now consider in turn.

Judgment

Under conditions of very limited growth, a crude but effective method of forecasting is the judgment estimate by a forecaster who is close to the problem and able to integrate and balance the factors involved in the specific situation. The chances of success diminish as the complexity of the situation increases and the need for long term forecasts predominates. Use of judgment can easily result in forecasting by hunches, a procedure that is abhorrent to analytical planners.

Surveys of Expectation

A technique not very widely used is the survey of expectation, directed to individuals in the air transport industry who might be said to be in a position to judge future trends. By selection of a broad range of interests in the selection of those surveyed, the forecaster hopes for a balanced view.

A refined procedure, which is becoming more widely used in general transportation planning, is *delphi analysis*—approaching the estimate of the future by applying an iterative procedure to a survey of expectation. In this procedure, experts make forecasts and then receive a feedback of results from the entire group of forecasters. After each iteration, the range of responses tends to narrow, and consensus is ultimately reached. In general, however, surveys of expectation are more suitable to aggregate forecasts at the regional or national levels than to disaggregate estimates at the airport level.

Trend Forecasting

Extensive use has been made of trend forecasting, where the planner simply extrapolates, basing judgment on past growth figures. In the short term this technique is reasonably reliable, especially when the extrapolation procedure is carried out with modified growth rates to account for short term disturbances in secular trends. In the long term this type of extrapolation is likely to be most unreliable and is theoretically difficult to substantiate. Past experience with long term trend forecasting has been less than satisfactory. Early trend forecasts were straight-line extrapolations that were almost always too low in the rapid growth years of the 1950s and the early 1960s. Forecasts made in the later 1960s were exponential. Opinion now is more conservative, reflecting a sense that the curve of growth is more likely to be logistic (Figure 2.3).

Base Forecasts on Ratios of National Forecasts

In the United States, a widely used technique for air traffic forecasting is the *base forecast* method, which assumes that a city's percentage of the annual national passenger volumes remains relatively constant over time. Airport forecasts are obtained by step-down percentages of national forecasts. The method suffers from two serious limitations:

1. A percentage of national figures does *not* necessarily remain constant; rapidly growing areas attract more traffic, whereas the traffic demand

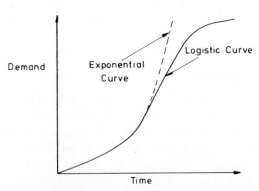

FIGURE 2.3   The logistic curve.

in more static areas with primary sector economic bases may not change significantly.

2. National forecasts have been historically incorrect, as noted earlier.

Certainly the method presents severe limitations in its application to Western Europe, where charter traffic is an important segment of total air passenger traffic; this traffic is particularly vulnerable to changes in fares.

Typically, two techniques have been used in the United States:

Method A

1. Determine the percentage of national enplaned passengers that the airport has attracted in the past.

2. Adjust this percentage to reflect anticipated abnormal growth trends.

3. Obtain data for national passenger volumes for the design year.

4. Calculate step-down design figures as the product of the percentage of step 2 and the national figure from step 3.

Method B

1. Obtain the number of passengers per 1000 population that the airport has experienced in the past.

2. Compare the figure computed in step 1 with the number of passengers nationally per 1000 population.

3. Compute the following ratio:

$$\frac{\text{passengers}/1000 \text{ population for airport}}{\text{passengers}/1000 \text{ population for nation}}$$

4. Obtain the national forecast of air passenger volumes per 1000 population for the design year.

5. From the ratio computed in step 3 and the national forecast of step 4, calculate the local passenger volumes per 1000 population.

The step-down method is useful when the catchment area of an airport can be reasonably well defined (e.g., the United States and Canada). In smaller countries such as those of Western Europe, where catchment areas are less well defined, the method is less useful (8). Typical of this method is the model used in a Washington State study (9) where:

$$E_i = M_{i/j} \cdot M_{j/s} \cdot M_{s/us} \cdot E_{us} \tag{2.1}$$

where

E_i = domestic enplanement at i
$M_{i/j}$ = percent market share for airport i of scheduled domestic total enplanement in region j

$M_{j/s}$ = percent market share for region j of total state market s
$M_{s/us}$ = percent market share of state s of total U.S. market
E_{us} = total scheduled domestic enplanements in the United States.

2.3 ANALYTICAL METHODS OF AIR TRAVEL DEMAND FORECASTING

Trend forecasting is simplistic in that the technique looks at experience over time and attempts to continue the curve of historical demand in the light of general prognostications of overall conditions. Upturns or downturns in the general state of the economy are applied to past trends and are used to modify this macroscopic model.

In the past, in most nations, air transport has appeared to exhibit an exponential growth, with air passenger traffic figures compounding at a growth rate of approximately 10% per year during the 1950s and 1960s. Clearly exponential growth can continue for a limited period, but in the long term it is more reasonable to expect that growth in the industry will adhere more to the logistic curve, which is the conventional historical curve of demand for a new technology.

The exponential curve leads fairly rapidly to unattainable levels of demand, but the logistic curve more realistically reflects the very rapid growth rates of demand at the point of introduction of the technology, where marginal production costs fall rapidly to an eventual saturation of the market at fairly constant marginal production costs. Thus when trend forecasting is applied to the early part of the curve, it tends to give absurdly high long term forecasts for demand functions that in fact follow the logistic form.

Analytical methods endeavor to overcome the grosser errors of trend analysis in trip generation by attempting to relate the level of traffic to changes in the level of a variety of causal or closely associated factors (10, 11). In the case of air traffic demand, it has been found that the number of trips made by the individual traveler depends not only on a number of socioeconomic variables outside the air transport system, such as income, employment type, and family structure, but also on system-based variables including frequency and level of service (including speed). As changes occur in these variables across the area being investigated, changes in demand levels can be predicted; these predictive procedures are capable of reflecting realistic changes over time in a manner that cannot be hoped for in trend forecasting.

Conventional analysis of traffic demand divides the modeling procedure into four distinct consecutive steps: generation, distribution, modal split, and assignment as shown below:

Generation → Distribution → Modal choice → Assignment

Generation models indicate how many trips originate or terminate in a specific area; these models are often based on the socioeconomic characteristics of the area and the nature of the transport system. In the *distribution* phase the trips are modeled as trip interchanges between specific pairs of origins and destinations, usually using some form of equilibrium model, with time or distance as the parametric impedance to travel.

Modal choice models split the interchanges into those specific to individual modes; choice normally is a function of the structure and nature of the transport system and the socioeconomic status of the trip maker. *Assignment* models indicate which route is taken by the individual traveler from a choice of all available routes. The assignment model is of little use in much air transport work, where as a rule a number of alternate routes are not available. The reader is referred to standard references on transport modeling for a more complete description of the model chain (12).

In the case of air transport, the model chain has frequently been simplified to a mode-specific chain of the following form:

$$\text{Air trip generation} \rightarrow \text{Air trip distribution}$$

This simplified chain is inadequate insofar as it assumes that air traffic generations are peculiar to the model itself and are not subject to modal choice dependent on the nature of the competing modes. Sections 2.5 to 2.8 give a more complete description of the various analytical models.

2.4 THE VARIABLES FOR PASSENGER DEMAND MODELING

Travel can be recognized as the product of four basic factors that must be accounted for in any realistic analysis attempting to predict demand over time. These basic factors are as follows:

A supply of people.
A motivation to travel.
Resources available for expenditure on travel in terms of time and money.
A transport infrastructure capable of supporting travel demand.

Over the long term it is necessary to consider the nature of the factors underlying demand when attempting to make forecasts. Where a complete demand analysis is to be carried out, the procedure should consist of the following steps:

1. Observation of past trends.
2. Identification of exogenous variables that act as surrogates for the basic factors causing changes in level of air transport demand.
3. A base survey collecting the socioeconomic data that describe the status of the population, the nature of the area, and the technological status of the system.

4. Establishment of relationships between the predictive variables and both levels and changes in levels of air transport demand.

5. Prediction of the anticipated level of the exogenous variables in the design year.

6. Prediction from the design year levels of the exogenous variables and predictive relationships of future demand levels.

Simplistic methods of prediction such as trend forecasting take explicit account of the first step only, and steps 2 to 6 are mixed with subjective judgment, with varying degrees of success.

In attempting to make predictions the analyst must enumerate and quantify the variables that are likely to affect the level of demand. In the past variables in the following areas have been used:

1. Demographic variables, including city size and population density.

2. Proximity to other large cities.

3. Economic character of the city.

4. Governmental activity, including promotional and regulatory policies, subsidy of competing modes, and energy conservation and balance-of-payments policies.

5. Fare levels.

6. Developments in competing transport modes.

7. Technological developments in the aircraft industry.

8. Adequacy of infrastructure provision of the air mode and competing modes.

9. Urban and regional development character.

10. Various other imponderables, such as sociocultural changes in leisure and work patterns, changes in communication technology, and secular changes in life patterns.

2.5 AIR TRIP GENERATION MODELS

In the process of generation, the analyst models directly the number of trip ends (or trip origins and destinations). The scale of the generation model can vary. At one end of the range it is possible to produce macromodels to describe and forecast aggregate levels of trip making at the national level, or disaggregated models related to individual airports and different trip purposes. Two principal techniques of analysis have been used: market analysis and multiple regression.

Market Analysis

The market analysis approach normally assumes that an area's share of the total air transport market remains constant over time. National demand totals are estimated for the design date, usually by using straightforward trend forecasting or cross-classification (category analysis). In the short term the assumption of constant total market share is likely to be reasonably valid, but clearly under changing economic and demographic conditions, the analyst can be less sanguine with respect to the accuracy of the premise.

Trend analysis for national demand totals can be carried out in a manner similar to that described in Section 2.2. Alternatively, the cross-classification analysis technique can be used: here it is assumed that individuals with different social, economic, and demographic characteristics demonstrate different and predictable air travel behavior that is constant over time. Based on a surveyed information base, travel demand is categorized for the different elements that comprise the total population; the variables used include income, age, employment type, family structure, and education. Demand rates are computed at each level of the predictive variables from base year survey data. Next, these trip rates are applied to the forecast national population disaggregated into its component parts by level of predictive variable. The aggregation of the component demand levels then gives total projected demand for the future population.

A somewhat modified form of cross-classification market analysis was used in conjunction with forecasting traffic in the inquiry into the siting of the third London airport (13). In that case, the categorization related to strata of trip purpose, income, and family structure. For each category the demand level was computed as a *propensity to fly*, which was further modified by the relative accessibility to the site in question.

Regression Analysis

It is also possible to forecast air passenger transport demand with regression techniques. Statistical models for demand analysis have been widely used for many years in the prediction of urban passenger transport (12). When applied to air transport a statistical relationship is established between rate of air trip generation (the dependent variable) and a number of predictive variables (the independent variables). The analysis is usually carried out by observing air trip generations from survey data and recording associated levels and changes of levels of socio–economic data of the area and the physical characteristics of the overall origin-to-destination air-ground transport system. By the use of correlation analysis, factor analysis, or other multivariate statistical methods, suitable predictive variables are chosen that seem to be best capable of modeling air trip generation. Then regression models can be constructed to describe existing relationships, and these are used to forecast future air trip generations.

Typically, the air trip generation regression model would be of the following form:

$$T = a_0 + a_1 x_1 + a_2 x_2 + \cdots + a_n x_n \qquad (2.2)$$

where

$$T = \text{the number of air trips generated}$$
$$x_1, \ldots x_n = \text{the independent or predictive variables}$$
$$a_0, \ldots a_n = \text{regression constants}$$

Models of this form are suitable for both national and local demand analysis. Variables most commonly used for the projection of travel generated in an area are population, income, type of employment, and accessibility of catchment population to the airport. For national aggregate levels of demand, gross domestic product has been found to be a most useful variable.

It is essential that in the relationships modeled there be not only statistical correlation, but also a logical or implied causal relationship between the predicted and predictive variables. It is also most important that the predictive variables be largely independent of each other (12).

A example of a regression model used to predict the total air trip generation at an airport is that developed in Virginia (9):

$$\ln \frac{E_i}{P_i} = 10.8 - 0.172F + 1.41 \ln (Y_i) \qquad (2.3)$$

where

$$E_i = \text{predicted emplanements}$$
$$P_i = \text{population of hinterland}$$
$$F = \text{U.S. average airfare/mile}$$
$$Y_i = \text{per capita income of hinterland}$$

2.6 AIR TRIP DISTRIBUTION MODELS

The trip distribution model predicts the level of trip interchange between designated airport pairs, once the level of generation of air trip ends at the individual airports has been computed. The most widely used distribution model applied to the transport situation has been the gravity model. This model, analogous to Newton's law of gravity, has grown from the knowledge developed in the social sciences that interactions between human settlements appear to be in accord with principles that are in many ways similar to the physical law of gravity. The gravity model in transport practice distributes trips between city pairs according to measures of the attractiveness of the cities, allowing for the impedance effects of cost, time, and other factors.

As early as 1943, the use of the gravity model was advocated for predicting the air trip interchange between cities. The model took the following form:

$$T_{ij} = \frac{kP_iP_j}{d_{ij}^x} \qquad (2.4)$$

where

T_{ij} = travel by air passengers between cities i and j
P_i = population of the origin city
P_j = population of the destination city
d_{ij} = distance between i and j
k = a constant of proportionality
x = a calibrated constant

Using distance as the measure of impedance, it was found that the value of x appeared to vary from 1.3 to 1.8. Other forms of this model have been developed that attempt to define the measure of impedance in terms other than distance alone. Using travel cost, the following model was calibrated:

$$T_{ij} = \frac{kT_iT_j}{C_{ij}^x} \qquad (2.5)$$

where

T_i = total air trips generated in city i
T_j = total air trips generated in city j
C_{ij} = cost of travel between i and j
K = a constant of proportionality
x = a calibrated constant

In a study of the U.S. airline interstation traffic, it was found that this model could be used only for city pairs less than 800 miles apart (14). For larger distances, traffic appears to be independent of both travel cost and distance and dependent only on the level of trip generation at either node. Thus, for greater air trip distances, the form of the model can be simplified to

$$T_{ij} = k(T_iT_j)^p \qquad (2.6)$$

where p is a calibrated parameter.

A modified form of gravity model was used in Canada (15):

$$T_{ij} = K \cdot \frac{P_i^{0.62} \; P_j^{0.35}}{D_{ij}^{0.56}} \cdot R_i^{4.88} \cdot A_j^{0.83} \cdot S_{ij}^{1.25} \; F_{ij}^{0.38} \; C_{h_i}^{-0.38} C_{h_j}^{-1.4} \qquad (2.7)$$

where

P_i = population at i
D_{ij} = distance between i and j
R_i = indicator of road condition around city i

A_j = indicator of attraction to city j
S_{ij} = seats available between i and j
F_{ij} = service reliability indicator
C_{h_i} = percent of manufacturing and retail employment of total employment at i

A predictive equation of a similar form was developed by the British Airports Authority for the Western European Airports Association (16):

$$Y_{it} = a_i(F_{it})^{\alpha_i} (I_{it})^{\beta_i} (1 + \gamma_i)^{t-1} \qquad (2.8)$$

where

Y_{it} = number of air trips in year t in trip category i
i = trip category—cross classified for business/leisure, European resident/nonresident, long haul/short haul
F = real cost of fares in year t
I = real income in year t
γ = an autonomous trend
α = elasticity of demand (fares)
β = elasticity of demand (income)
a = a regression constant

2.7 MODAL CHOICE MODELS

As previously stated, the analytical forecasting method has frequently been applied to mode-specific air trip generations that have been separately distributed. A more rational approach is to generate non-mode specific intercity movements, distribute these according to travel limitations and finally to determine modal selection by the application of modal choice models (12, 17). A generalized cost model is given here for illustrative purposes; it should be borne in mind, however, that many other model types are available which, in the right context, have shown equal or better validity.

Many factors affect modal choice, such as convenience, comfort, and safety. Though such factors are often difficult to quantify, a simple method of allowing for them and for individual variability among travelers is to construct the model from parameters that reflect the degree of randomness of the traveler's choice. In general, the traveler will usually choose the mode with the lowest generalized cost, but there is a finite probability that some other mode will be selected. One model that incorporates this factor is of the form:

$$\frac{T_{ijk}}{T_{ij}} = \frac{\exp(-\alpha C_{ijk})}{\sum_{r=1}^{n} \exp(-\alpha C_{ijk})} \qquad (2.9)$$

where

T_{ij} = total trips by all modes from i to j
T_{ijk} = trips by mode k from i to j
α = some calibration constant
C_{ijk} = generalized costs of travel from i to j by mode k
n = number of available modes

The generalized cost of any mode is the total direct and indirect costs incurred in traveling. Theoretically the generalized cost is capable of reflecting in monetary terms *all* factors affecting travel. In the absence of complete knowledge of social and attitudinal cost tradeoffs, the generalized cost concept has its limitations. In practice, generalized cost is frequently expressed in terms of direct monetary costs and cost of travel time. Where this is so, and where two alternate modes p and q are being considered, equation 2.9 reduces to

$$\log \left[\frac{T_{ijp}}{T_{ijq}} \right] = -\alpha \left[(M_{ijp} - M_{ijq}) + \lambda (t_{ijp} - t_{ijq}) \right] \qquad (2.10)$$

where

α, λ = calibration constants
$(M_{ijp} - M_{ijq})$ = difference in money costs for modes p and q for the journey from i to j
$(t_{ijp} - t_{ijq})$ = difference in travel times by modes p and q for the journey from i to j

This form of model has been successfully used to analyze air transport's share of a short haul market in competition with high speed conventional rail travel and a high speed tracked hovercraft mode (18).

2.8 GENERATION-DISTRIBUTION MODELS

Some analysts do not agree that the decision to make an air trip is separated from the decision of where to go, which is the implied in accepting the independent generation and distribution models. In an attempt to reflect the integrated decision process, combined generation–distribution models have been produced. Typically two types are available, *mode-specific* and *multimode* models. Both are generally of the multiple regression type.

Mode-Specific Models

Air travel volumes can be generated and distributed directly between city pairs by means of mode-specific models. In this analysis technique, the generation of air travel is considered entirely separately from the demand levels of other intercity and interregional movements. These models are usually of the regression type, with predictive variables related to the socioeconomic characteristics of the population and the economic characteristics of the cities themselves.

One form of this type of model can be written as follows:

$$T_{ij} = r \, P_i^s \, P_j^t \, d_{ij}^u \, l_i^v \, l_j^w \tag{2.11}$$

where

$$
\begin{aligned}
T_{ij} &= \text{the volume of air passenger traffic between city } i \text{ and city } j \\
P_i, P_j &= \text{the populations of cities } i \text{ and } j \\
d_{ij} &= \text{the distance between } i \text{ and } j \\
l_i, l_j &= \text{the respective portions of the cities' populations with income} \\
&\quad \text{in excess of \$10,000 annually} \\
r, s, t, u, v, w &= \text{regression-calibrated parameters}
\end{aligned}
$$

(In logarithmic form the structure of the equation is of standard linear type.)

The structure of equation 2.11 can be extended to include other applicable variables including the economic characteristics of the cities. An examination of the model indicates that it is "backward-looking," specific to the mode concerned—the calibrated value of the regression constants reflecting the relative levels of air and other technologies at the time of calibration. New technological options or radical changes in existing systems cannot be accommodated within this form of model, making it of questionable utility in the long term.

The Canadian Transport Commission produced a mode-specific time trend analysis of the form (15):

$$\frac{F_{ij}}{P_i P_j} = \alpha + \beta t + Q_{ij} \tag{2.12}$$

where

$$
\begin{aligned}
F_{ij} &= \text{air trips between } i \text{ and } j \\
P_i &= \text{population at } i \\
t &= \text{time in years} \\
Q_{ij} &= \text{factor to adjust for quantum effects such as new surface links}
\end{aligned}
$$

A mode-specific econometric model has been produced of the form (19):

$$T_{ij} = a(\alpha_i \text{GNP}_i)^b \, (\alpha_j \text{GNP}_j)^c \, \beta_{ij}^d \left(F_{ij} + A + \frac{B}{F_{ij} - C} \right) \tag{2.13}$$

where

$$
\begin{aligned}
T_{ij} &= \text{air traffic between stations } i \text{ and } j \\
\alpha &= \text{station share of gross national product (GNP)}
\end{aligned}
$$

$$\beta = \text{country pair relation index}$$
$$F = \text{economy fare}$$
$$A, B, C = \text{currency scale constants}$$
$$a, b, c, d = \text{regression constants}$$

A two-category model has been developed for both the business and leisure categories of air trips (20). These models are:

Business

$$\left(\frac{\Pi}{P}\right)_B = A + Mf_{y_B}\left[R_1(Z_0, Z_D)^P_{y-1} + \frac{R_2}{1 + [K(\bar{F}/I)]^q}\right] \quad (2.14)$$

Leisure

$$\left(\frac{\Pi}{P}\right)_L = A + Mf_{y_L}\left[\frac{1}{1 + [K(\bar{F}/I)]^q}\right] \quad (2.15)$$

where

$$\Pi = \text{trips in year } y$$
$$P = \text{population at origin}$$
$$A, M = \text{constants}$$
$$f_{y_B} = f(\text{income, station affinity, propensity to invest and trade}) \text{ in year}$$
$$y \text{ for business}$$
$$R_1, R_2 = \text{constants}$$
$$Z_0, Z_D = \text{ratios in real terms of origin and destination countries economies}$$
relative to base date.
$$\bar{F} = \text{mean total effective fare (fare, supplements, and travel time)}.$$
$$I = \text{mean income of households of potential travelers in origin country}$$
$$K = \text{constant reflection surface route saturation}$$
$$p, q = \text{constants}$$

A number of distribution models have been developed using *growth factors*. However these are simplistic models, and it is difficult to justify their use in long term forecasting. The reader is referred to Paquette et al. (12) for a reasonably complete discussion of these models.

Multimodal Models

In an attempt to overcome the shortcomings of mode-specific models, multimodal models that can simultaneously predict the generation rates, distribution patterns, and modal choice of travelers have been introduced. Perhaps the best known multimodal model is the abstract mode model, which emphasizes modal characteristics and is inherently capable of representing any existing or hypothetical mode by a set of variables that completely describe the pertinent attributes of a transport mode for the type of travel being considered (21). For passenger transport, therefore, variables such as travel time, frequency of service, and indices of comfort and safety may be used. For each mode under consideration, the abstract mode model represents the characteristics in a ratio relative to the best mode available. These ratios are then used as predictive variables in the calibrated equation. In one of its forms, the model can be written in the following way:

$$T_{kij} = \alpha_0 P_i^{\alpha_1} P_j^{\alpha_2} Y_i^{\alpha_3} Y_j^{\alpha_4} M_i^{\alpha_5} M_j^{\alpha_6} N_{ij}^{\alpha_7}$$
$$\times f_1(H_{ij}, H_{kij}), f_2(C_{ij}, C_{kij}), f_3(D_{ij}, D_{kij}), \ldots \qquad (2.16)$$

where

$$
\begin{aligned}
\alpha_0, \alpha_1, \ldots, \alpha_7 &= \text{regression constants} \\
P_i, P_i &= \text{the populations of the two nodes} \\
Y_i, Y_j &= \text{the median incomes at the two nodes} \\
M_i, M_j &= \text{the institutional (industrial) indices of the two nodes} \\
H_{ij} &= \text{the least required travel time} \\
H_{kij} &= \text{the travel time by the } k\text{th mode} \\
N_{ij} &= \text{the number of modes between } i \text{ and } j \\
C_{ij} &= \text{the least cost of travel between } i \text{ and } j \\
C_{kij} &= \text{the travel cost by the } k\text{th mode} \\
D_{ij} &= \text{the best departure frequency from } i \text{ to } j \\
D_{kij} &= \text{the departure frequency by the } k\text{th mode}
\end{aligned}
$$

The advantage of abstract mode models is that they can be used to predict demand for some novel transport system that does not now exist but for which a set of characteristics can be specified. Such applications include predicting demand for short haul. V/STOL transportation, or for interurban third level carrier transportation, and in the projection of the impact of new technologies for which only the performance standards can be specified at the time of analysis.

The abstract mode model was used to assign trips by mode in the California Corridor Study (22). This model was applied to absolute levels of demand derived from the following regression models:

Business

$$\ln(T_{ij}) = -7.32 + 0.29 \ln(P_i) + 0.37 \ln(P_j) + 0.89 \ln(Y_{ij})$$
$$- 0.33 \ln(t_{ij}) \qquad (2.17)$$

Leisure

$$\ln(T_{ij}) = -15.65 + 0.31 \ln(P_i) + 0.42 \ln(P_j) + 1.40 \ln(Y_{ij}) \qquad (2.18)$$

where

i = origin
j = destination
P = zonal population
Y_{ij} = average zonal mean income of zones i and j
t_{ij} = shortest travel time between i and j

2.9 LOAD FACTORS AND AIRCRAFT MIX

Any analysis of air transport demand must take account of the relationships between air passenger movements and aircraft movements. This relationship hinges on two factors: the load factor and aircraft mix.

The *load factor* is the ratio of passenger miles carried to seat miles operated. Operators naturally wish to maintain high load factors which make operation of the aircraft equipment profitable. Since average load factors cover both peak and off-peak operation, high load factors may indicate that some traffic is being turned away in peak times. This condition may be less profitable than accepting a lower overall load factor. Figure 2.4 shows international trends in load factors since 1962. Since the oil crisis of 1973, airlines have attempted to increase their efficiency by increasing load factors. This has frequently been achieved by lowering the net yield per passenger kilometer by the introduction of low fares with restrictions on availability and by accepting standby passengers at very low fares. Because of the requirements of positioning aircraft and scheduling to avoid airport operational restrictions, load factors of over 80% are impossible on a system-wide basis.

In computing the number of aircraft operations that a facility can anticipate handling, a planner must keep abreast of expected changes in aircraft fleet mix which will affect the operations under consideration. Figure 2.5 shows projected aircraft fleet mix changes across the industry. Clearly it is essential in designing an individual facility for the airport planner to confer with airlines to ensure that assumed fleet mix changes are in conformity with airline plans and that these plans correspond to the long term expectations of the industry. Trends observable from Figure 2.5 appear to indicate the long term phasing out of most propeller and turboprop aircraft and the increased use of wide-bodied jets. Judging what aircraft will be available and the timing of their introduction is extremely important and is perhaps the most difficult element of demand forecasting.

2.10 ESTIMATES OF AIR CARRIER MOVEMENTS

Estimates of aircraft movements can be obtained by simple trend analysis, projecting growth rates of movements from past experience. This approach is

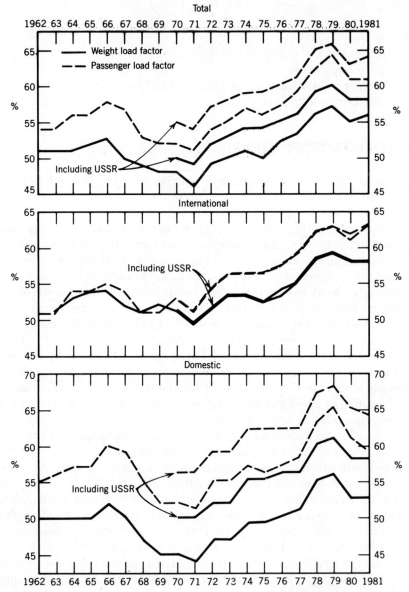

FIGURE 2.4 Trends in load factors on scheduled services—world averages (ICAO States), 1962–1981. (*Source:* Reference 6.)

likely to be satisfactory only for short term forecasting, since it takes no account of changes in technology and equipment, nor does it allow for possible market saturation—all factors that can have significant effects in the long run. Whereas simple extrapolation methods can give reasonable estimates of general aviation activity, air carrier movements are better predicted using refined analysis of estimates of air passenger volumes gained from the modeling procedures discussed previously.

To convert annual estimates of air passenger movements to peak air carrier movements, it is necessary to understand the temporal variations of demand as they relate to the design facilities. Figure 2.6 shows that pattern of variation of passenger and aircraft movements throughout the year depends greatly on the function of the airport. Heathrow, the principal airport for London, shows typical variations of demand, with a peak during the summer and lowest flows during February. The peak/average ratio for this airport, which serves large volumes of business traffic with a limited number of charter flights, is the

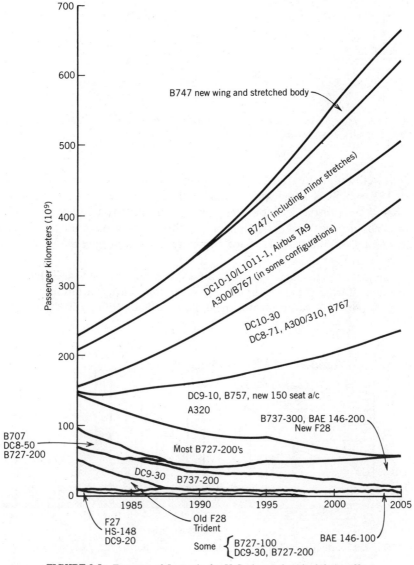

FIGURE 2.5 Forecast of fleet mix for U.S. domestic scheduled traffic.

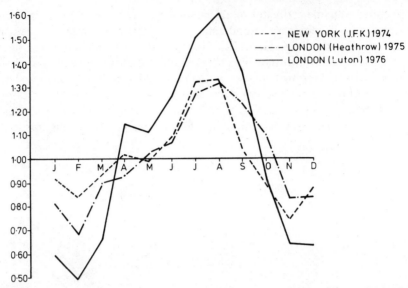

FIGURE 2.6 Monthly variations in passenger traffic in three airports. (*Source:* FAA Airport Activity Statistics, CAA Monthly Statistics.)

relatively low figure of 1.31. This is a similar ratio to that observed at New York JFK which is somewhat similar in function. By comparison, Luton, another airport in the London area, serving principally holiday and charter traffic, has a very large variation in monthly flow throughout the year, as indicated by the ratios of 1.54 for commercial air transport movements and 1.61 for passenger flow.

As important as the large variation of traffic throughout the year is fluctuation of volumes during the day. Figure 2.7 gives the hourly variation of flow at Logan Airport in Boston. Airport peak hours (0800–1000, 1500–1800) tend

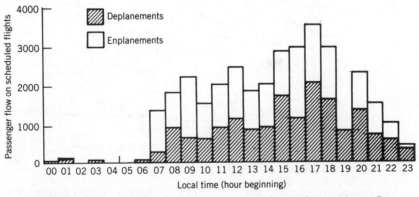

FIGURE 2.7 Hourly variation of scheduled passenger flows at Logan Airport, Boston.

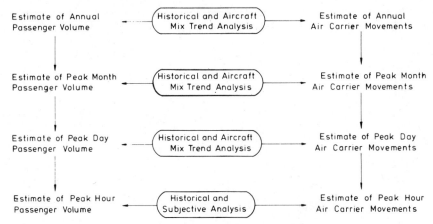

FIGURE 2.8 Procedure for computing monthly, daily, and hourly peak volumes.

to coincide closely with the peak condition of urban transport; this unfortunately complicates the surface access problem, since major reliance is often on road-based modes (see Chapter 11).

Figure 2.8 outlines a procedure to compute the peak hour passenger and aircraft movement figures necessary for facility design. Using factors gained from past experience at the airport in question, annual passenger volumes can be factored to provide peak month, peak day, and peak hour passenger volumes. These are converted at each stage to aircraft movements from an estimate to aircraft mix, using historical data and trend analysis of fleet replacement. The

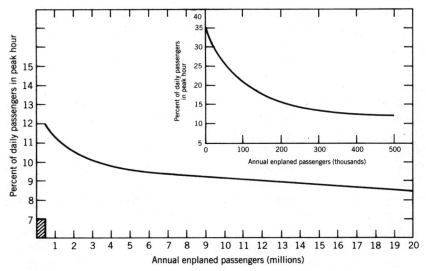

FIGURE 2.9 Percent of daily passengers in peak hour versus annual enplaned passengers. (*Source:* Reference 25.)

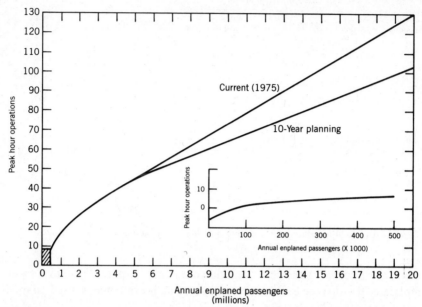

FIGURE 2.10   Estimated peak hour operations versus annual enplaned passengers. (*Source:* Reference 25.)

following alternative approach to the peak hour design figure has been used by the Port Authority of New York (24).

$$
\begin{aligned}
\text{Average monthly passengers} &= 0.08417 \times \text{annual passenger flow}\\
\text{Average daily passengers} &= 0.03226 \times \text{average monthly flow}\\
\text{Peak day flow} &= 1.26 \times \text{average daily flow}\\
\text{Peak hour flow} &= 0.0917 \times \text{peak daily flow}
\end{aligned}
$$

Peak hour passenger flows were converted into peak aircraft flows using estimates of average passenger load per aircraft computed from projected load factors and projected seatings per aircraft movement.

In Section 8.2, the FAA relationship between peak hour flows and annual volumes is given in conjunction with other estimates used for peak planning (25). Figures 2.9 and 2.10 show graphs recommended for planning purposes which relate peak hour passenger flows and peak hour aircraft operations to annual passenger throughput in terms of enplanements.

Throughout the rest of the world, the concept of the 30th highest hour or *Standard Busy Rate* is often used. This is the passenger traffic flow which is exceeded by only 29 other hours of operation. Figure 2.11 shows the log–log relationship between the SBR and total annual passenger flows that has been observed over an eight-year period for a range of British airports (26). For comparative purposes the Typical Peak Passenger Flow (FAA) relationship has been plotted on the same graph.

2.11   AIR FREIGHT DEMAND

National Projections

Theoretically, the movement of freight by any mode is likely to be more amenable to analysis and prediction than passenger travel because the element of subjective choice or personal taste is lessened where freight movements are concerned. Additionally, social variables, which have been found to be so important in passenger demand models, are absent in the analysis of freight movements, greatly simplifying the procedure. However, the forecasting of freight movements by all modes, including air, is currently in its infancy, reflecting the great scarcity of historical data at a necessary level of detail. Consequently, aggregated projections at the national level are more easily made than disaggregated forecasts of freight movements between specific lo-

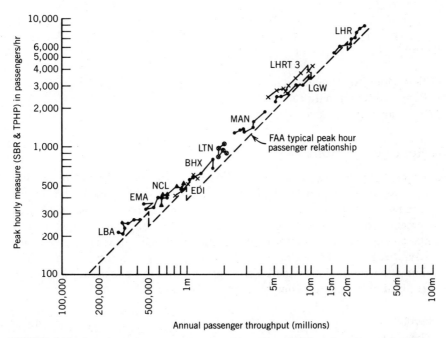

FIGURE 2.11   Relationship between Standard Busy Rate (SBR) and total annual passenger throughput. (*Source:* Reference 26.)

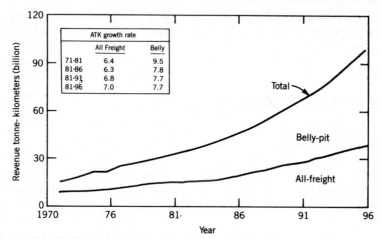

FIGURE 2.12   World air cargo forecast. (*Source:* McDonnell Douglas.)

cations. Figure 2.12 presents a forecast for world air cargo traffic made by one major aircraft manufacturer.

Using regression techniques, excellent correlations can be achieved from equations of the form:

$$F = f(\text{GNP}, P_A) \tag{2.19}$$

where

F = domestic scheduled air freight traffic (revenue ton-miles)
GNP = gross national product
P_A = air freight rates

Regional Projections

At the level of predicting actual regional freight movements, the lack of specific data on city pairs has prevented the calibration of satisfactory models. Whereas large sums have been expended on the collection and analysis of urban passenger movement data, and to a lesser degree intercity passenger movement data, a similar amount of detailed information relating to freight traffic is not available. Ideally, freight traffic can be considered to move according to some cost-minimization rationale. In fact, air freight appears to be responsive to some generalized cost function composed of the following elements:

Freight tariff.
Time in transit.
Frequency of service.
Time of scheduling.

Security of product.

Reliability of service.

Quality of service.

Value of freight per unit weight.

2.12   AIR FREIGHT GENERATION MODELS

The two principal approaches to freight forecasting are regression analysis and input–output analysis.

Regression Analysis

Regression analysis has been applied in the hope that the method would be as successful for freight as it has been with respect to passenger movements (see Section 2.5). Successful calibration has not been possible, however, because of the lack of adequate data on movements between specific city pairs. It has been proposed that freight movement is likely to be strongly correlated to a surplus of specific commodities at the origin ends of the trips and a demand for the same commodities at the destination ends. In the absence of detailed knowledge of commodity supply and demand, surrogate variables describing the industrial makeup of the city pairs are used, in conjunction with variables descriptive of the level of air service. Experience with these models has been less than satisfactory.

Input–Output Analysis

In the United States, some effort has been made to use the interindustry model, a macroeconomic model sometimes designated as input–output analysis. This model can be used to determine supply and demand of commodities of different types for individual sectors of industry. This information, in turn, can be applied to the industrial structure of specific city pairs to determine the generation of freight flows. The model is still at an embryonic stage.

2.13   AIR CARGO DISTRIBUTION AND MODAL SPLIT MODELING

Distribution of freight movements has been carried out using gravity models to distribute the demand between origins and destinations. These standard procedures are described in readily accessible reference works.

In the sequence of models, the generation and distribution stages are followed by commodity modal choice. The most successful *modal choice* model appears to be a cost-minimization approach that includes freight rates, damage costs, security, travel times, inventory and warehousing costs, commodity deterioration, and en route handling costs.

2.14 GENERAL AVIATION FORECASTS

A considerable amount of subjective judgment goes into making general aviation forecasts, which rely heavily on national trends and forecasts and, to the extent such are available, local historical records. Three basic types of forecast are normally made: (1) number of based aircraft, (2) number of aircraft operations, and (3) passenger forecasts.

The number of based aircraft forecast calls for an inventory of presently based aircraft, historical growth trends, and employment of FAA National Forecast Growth Ratios for General Aviation Based Aircraft (given for various areas of the United States).

The number of aircraft operations (local and itinerant) can be forecast from actual counts of present activities, from FAA surveys (Towered Airports), and by obtaining a relationship between the number of operations per based aircraft. If local data are not available, the following FAA data could be used:

	Annual Operations per Based Aircraft		
Type	Typical Low	Median	Typical High
Local operations	170	375	690
Itinerant operations (nontower airport)	125	210	450
Itinerant operations (tower airport)	225	425	745

Passenger forecasts are made by multiplying the average number of passengers per plane by half the total number of general aviation itinerant operations. The FAA has given data on the average number of passengers per plane.

	Average Number of Passengers per Plane	
Airports	1975	1980
Air carrier	3.26	3.36
Other	2.20	2.50

A brief treatment of modelling general aviation activity is contained in *Manual on Air Traffic Forecasting* (11).

REFERENCES

1. Hammarskjold, K., "Demands for Air Transport: 1980–1990," in *Airports for the Eighties, Proceedings of the Fourth World Airports Conference*, London: Institution of Civil Engineers, April 1973.

2. *Outlook for Commercial Aircraft 1982–1996*, Long Beach, California: Douglas Aircraft Company, 1982.

3. *World Air Traffic Forecast 1970–1990*, Burbank, California: Lockheed, September 1981.

4. Pulling, R., *Journal of Aerospace Transportation*, Proceedings of the American Society of Civil Engineers, April 1965.

5. Silverleaf, A., "Overall Trends in the Development of Transport: 1980–1990," Proceedings of the Fourth World Airports Conference. London: Institution of Civil Engineers, 1973.

6. *ICAO Bulletin*, Montreal: International Civil Aviation Organization, July/August 1982.

7. *Transportation Facts and Trends*, 17th ed., Washington, D.C.: Transportation Association of America, 1981.

8. Ashford, N., and McGinity, P., "Access to Airports Using High Speed Ground Modes," *High Speed Ground Transportation*, Vol. 9, No. 1, Spring 1975.

9. Jacobsen, I. D., "Demand Modelling of Passenger Air Travel," NASA Report CR-157469.

10. Kanafani, A., *Transportation Demand Analysis*, New York: McGraw-Hill, 1981.

11. *Manual on Air Traffic Forecasting*, Montreal: International Civil Aviation Organization, 1972.

12. Paquette, R. J., N. Ashford, and P. H. Wright, *Transportation Engineering: Planning and Design*, 2nd ed., New York: John Wiley and Sons, Inc., 1982.

13. *Report of the Commission on the Third London Airport*, London: Her Majesty's Stationery Office, 1971.

14. Belmont, Daniel, *A Study of Airline Interstation Traffic*, Berkeley: University of California, Institute of Transportation and Traffic Engineering, 1958.

15. *Canadian Domestic and Transborder Traffic, 1971–1981*. Research Publication 29, Ottawa: Canadian Transport Commission, June 1972.

16. *Forecasts of Traffic at Western European Airports to 1990*, British Airports Authority.

17. Lowry, Ira S., "A Short Course in Model Design," Santa Monica, California: Rand Corporation, 1965.

18. "Comparative Assessment of New Forms of Intercity Transport," Report SR 3, Crowthorne, England: Transport and Road Research Laboratory, December 1971.

19. Bjorkman, B., *Methodology in Air Traffic Forecasting*, Paris: Civil Aviation Forecasting Workshop, International Civil Aviation Organization, 1974.

20. Wimhurst, J., O. W. N. Cock, and D. H. Jagger, *Travel Demand Forecasting Study, Part 1—North Atlantic Travel*, Hatfield, Herts: Hawker Siddeley Aviation, Ltd., 1976.

21. Quandt, R. E. and W. J. Baumol, *Regional Science*, Vol. 6, No. 2, 1964.

22. Fan Shing Leung, R. Horonjeff, and A. Mogharabi, *Forecasting the Demand Potential for STOL Air Transportation*, NASA Report CR-114572, February 1973.

23. *Federal Aviation Forecasts: Boston*, Washington, D.C.: Federal Aviation Administration, July 1982.

24. Johnson, N. L., "Forecasting Airport Traffic," in *Airport Economic Planning*, George P. Howard (Ed.), Cambridge, Mass.: M.I.T. Press, 1974.

25. *Planning and Design Considerations for Airport Terminal Building Development*, AC 150/5360-7, Washington, D.C.: Federal Aviation Administration, October 1976.

26. Ashford, N., H. P. M. Stanton, and C. Moore, *Airport Operations*, New York: Wiley-Interscience, 1984.

3

CHARACTERISTICS OF AIRCRAFT AS THEY AFFECT AIRPORTS

ROBERT CAVES
Department of Transport Technology
Loughborough University

3.1 RELATIONSHIPS BETWEEN AIRCRAFT AND AIRPORTS

In a conventional air transport system, aircraft and airports are dependent on each other in providing a service for the passenger. In the past the system evolved largely with separate planning of the airport, the route structuring, and the aircraft technology. Advances in technology, the major factor in the growth of the mode, have been quickly utilized by the airlines in expanding their route structures. Those responsible for the provision of airports have sought to acquire the necessary facilities to ensure that they were not left behind and that they could participate to the full in this high growth industry.

Advances in engine and airframe technology have allowed significant reduction in the real cost of air travel and at the same time have led to improvements in system performance. These improvements in speed, range, ticket price, comfort, and reliability have been responsible for the high growth rates. In addition, the operating costs of the aircraft have constituted 85% of the operating costs of the entire air transport system; the airports have contributed 10%, and the remaining 5% have been spent on navigation charges and overheads of governmental control. This has resulted in a natural tendency for the airports to accommodate any changes in aircraft design and performance that could maintain the trend to lower aircraft direct operating cost (DOC). The result is illustrated in Figure 3.1, which shows how the runway length of a major

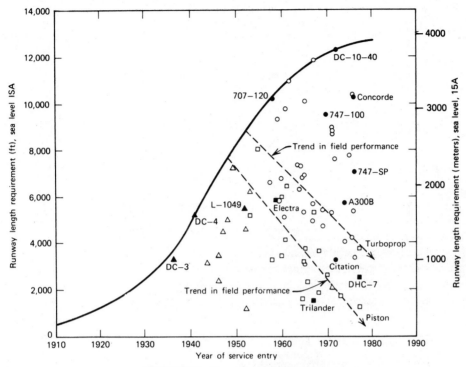

FIGURE 3.1 Trends in runway length.

intercontinental airport has had to be progressively increased to keep ahead of aircraft field length requirements.

The trend of allowing aircraft DOC to dominate in the design of the air transport system was broken in the late 1960s by several factors. Environmental considerations, primarily in the neighborhood of the airport, are causing compromises between aircraft design and airport location. Rising land values and construction costs are increasing the airport contribution to the total system capital costs, which is already considerably greater than its contribution to operating costs. The increasing cost and scarcity of capital add importance to the correct definition of the role of the airport to the total system. A new trend is to bring into the air route system more and more airports with relatively low frequency operation and relatively short stage lengths. The low utilization of such facilities implies a greater contribution of the airports to the total system cost and makes it unreasonable for aircraft designers to call for increases of runway length on a massive scale. Figure 3.2 charts the variation in the ratio of airport costs to total system operating costs with route throughput and stage length in an assumed air transport system.

The short range aircraft needs less runway than the long range type, since there is a smaller fuel requirement. In addition, advances in the technology of producing high lift for takeoff and landing allow a further reduction in the

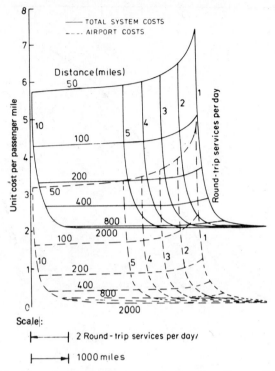

FIGURE 3.2   Airport and total air system operating costs. (*Source:* Reference 1.)

runway requirement without too much penalty in DOC. Therefore, the pressures from the airport to reduce runway length requirements can be met by the aircraft operator. New runways are often shorter, where the main market is for short range operations.

At the same time, the growth in runway length for long range operations has leveled off as new demands for increased range no longer appear,* and because the operating costs for this type of flight are acceptably low. This double trend of both increasing and decreasing runway length is depicted in Figure 3.1.

Runway length is only one of many areas where the requirements of aircraft performance and cost affect the airport layout. Other important areas are the number of runways required, cargo handling facilities, and the design of taxiways, aprons and terminals. These control the airport layout and capacity requirements. All these areas are discussed in detail in this chapter, together with the issue of noise control. The layout effect is emphasized, however,

---

* Between short and long haul designs the proportion of empty to maximum weight varies from 63 to 49%, while the proportion of fuel to maximum weight varies from 20 to 42%—though some of this difference is due to the smaller size of the shorter range aircraft.

since the problems of capacity are more amenable to treatment with a flexible approach to design.

3.2 THE INFLUENCE OF AIRCRAFT DESIGN ON RUNWAY LENGTH

All commercial aircraft design has its roots in the development of propulsion systems and the application of aerodynamic theory. In parallel with advances in type and efficiency of aircraft power plants (Figure 3.3) have come increases in absolute power. Aerodynamic advances have been made allowing the full use of propulsive improvements. In particular, speed capability has increased (Figure 3.4). The combination of improvements in speed and absolute size has resulted in the upward trend in seat mile per hour productivity shown in Figure 3.5. With the exception of the early pure jets, a similar upward trend also occurred in seat miles per gallon because of advances in engine fuel efficiency. All these effects, combined with economies of scale, generated the reduction in real costs per tonne kilometer plotted in Figure 3.6.

In the days of the DC-3, a wing design that gave economical cruising flight also allowed a reasonably short field length because the aircraft could sustain flight at quite a low speed.

For level flight,

$$\text{lift}(=\text{weight}) \propto \rho V^2 S C_L \tag{3.1}$$

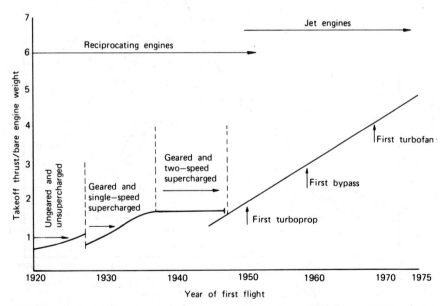

FIGURE 3.3 Trends in ratios of takeoff thrust to bare engine weight. (*Source:* Reference 2.)

where

ρ = air density
V = forward speed of the aircraft
S = area of the wing
C_L = coefficient of lift (nondimensional): approximately proportional to the angle of attack of the wing

or

$$\frac{W}{S} \propto \rho V^2 C_L$$

where W = aircraft weight and W/S = wing loading.

Thus, at a given value of C_L, higher speeds allow a smaller wing, hence a lower weight and drag. Unfortunately, high speed wings tend to have a lower maximum value of C_L (at which the wing stalls and loses lift abruptly), so the ratio of cruise speed to stall speed is naturally lower, and this leads to much

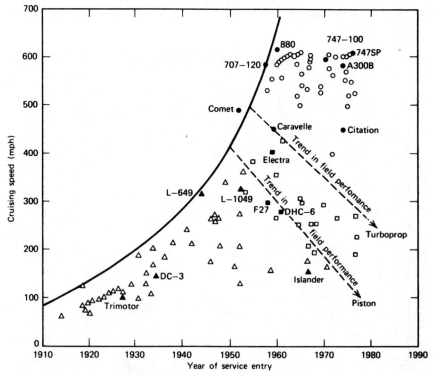

FIGURE 3.4 Trends in cruising speeds.

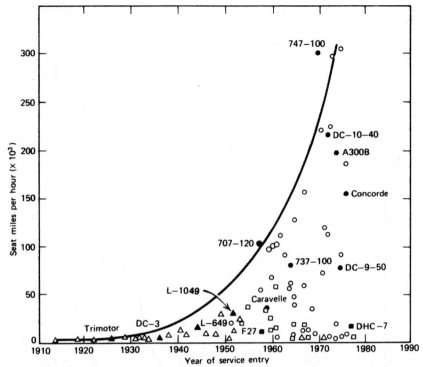

FIGURE 3.5 Trends in productivity in terms of passenger seat miles per hour.

higher takeoff and approach speeds. Even if it were possible to have infinitely long runways, high approach speeds would be unacceptable because of problems associated with landing gear design, pilot judgment, airspace requirements, and air traffic control. Hence high lift devices are employed to reduce the stalling speed by increasing the effective wing area and increasing the maximum value of C_L.

Wimpenny (4) suggests that a twin turbofan aircraft designed for 1000 nautical mi range from a 6000 ft runway is penalized in productivity by 23% compared with an aircraft of similar specification designed to unlimited field length.* The penalty arises from a combination of increased wing area, the high lift devices, extra thrust for takeoff, and extra fuel. The high lift devices have more influence on the landing field length and the extra thrust is of more value on takeoff. The increase in wing area provides a lower minimum flying speed regardless of the amount of flap or slat being used, thus reducing both the takeoff and landing field length requirements. The takeoff usually leads to the greater field requirement, except with aircraft designed exclusively for

---

* In this case "productivity" is defined as seat miles per hour per pound all-up-weight (AUW).

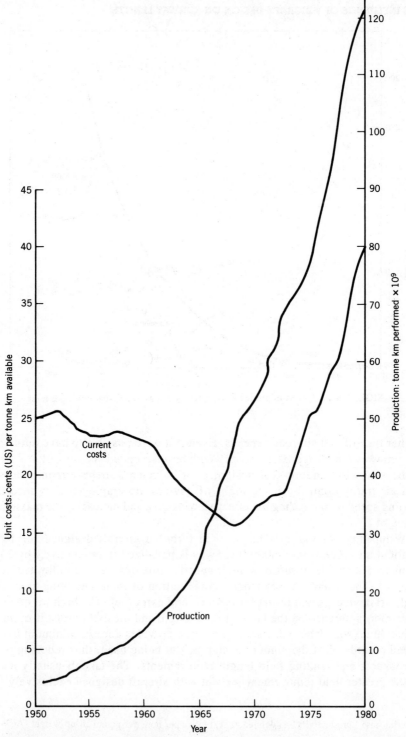

FIGURE 3.6 Air transport passenger traffic in relation to air transport costs. (*Source:* Reference 3.)

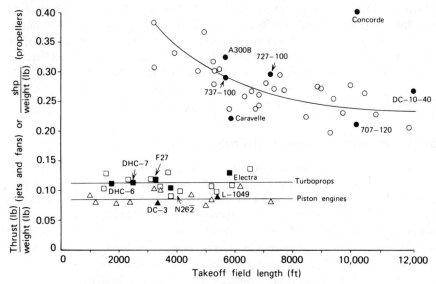

FIGURE 3.7 Effect of power-to-weight ratio on field length.

short stage lengths; in the latter case, the maximum landing weight is usually very similar to the maximum takeoff weight.

Figures 3.7 and 3.8 illustrate the tendencies for aircraft designed to different field lengths to use different thrust-to-weight ratios and wing loadings. From the range of types of powerplant and categories of operation selected, it can be seen that propeller-driven aircraft achieve adequate field performance without

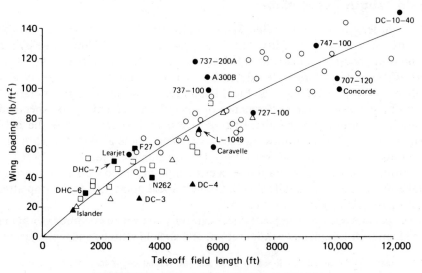

FIGURE 3.8 Effect of wing loading on field length.

increased thrust-to-weight ratio because of their use of relatively low wing loadings and the high static efficiency of their low disc loading.* Similarly, the helicopter achieves vertical takeoff with the same installed power as a light conventional aircraft of the same weight. On the other hand, pure jet aircraft require much higher installed thrust if their takeoff field length is to be reduced substantially, with commensurate reductions in wing loading, or more powerful flaps if the landing field length is to be similarly reduced.

Requirements of Present Aircraft Types

The discussion above has attempted to indicate the interactions that take place in aircraft design between the field length and other factors. There are fundamentally three different types of interaction. With long range aircraft, a long takeoff is dictated by the large fuel requirements. Medium and short range aircraft for trunk and local airline operation have to compromise their cruise performance with the need to use a large number of medium length fields. Aircraft for feeder and general aviation roles normally operate over short ranges where cruise speed is not essential; thus a low wing loading is permissible and they can operate with short field lengths without a significant design penalty.

Tables 3.1a, b, and c present the characteristics of a wide range of present-day aircraft. The variation in runway length illustrates the preceding discussion. It is important to realize that the speeds, field lengths, weights, and maximum stage lengths given are all for quite specific conditions of operation, which are held constant over the range of aircraft types for ease of comparison. Cases of variation from these specific conditions having an important effect on the field length requirements are discussed in detail below.

Field Length Regulations

The field lengths listed in Table 3.1 are determined not only on the basis of the aircraft's design capability, but also by the safety regulations made by the responsible bodies. In the United States, the regulating authority is the FAA. The ICAO issues worldwide advisories that are similar in philosophy and content to the FAA regulations. Field length requirements for a given class of aircraft are based on the performance of several critical and rigidly specified operations. In essence, an aircraft type is required to demonstrate the field length required for the following cases: (a) to complete a takeoff to 35 ft (11 m) altitude with all engines operating, (b) to complete a takeoff to 35 ft (11 m) altitude with an engine failure at a critical point, (c) to stop after aborting a takeoff with an engine failure at the same critical point, and (d) to stop after landing from a height of 50 ft (15 m).

The demonstrations take place under carefully controlled conditions of flying speed, aircraft weight and configuration, and airfield altitude and temperature.

---

* Disc loading is the thrust developed by a fan per unit frontal swept area. Static efficiency is inversely proportional to disc loading.

TABLE 3.1a Aircraft Characteristics of Air Carriers: Powerplant, Dimensions, and Number of Passengers

Aircraft Type	Powerplant	Dimensions (ft)						Number of Passengers (max)
		Span	Length	Height	Turning Radius	Wheel Base	Track	
Intercontinental								
747-200B	4 × 46,950 lb	195.7	231.3	63.4	146.0	84.0	36.0	500
DC-10	3 × 50,000 lb	165.3	182.2	58.1	123.9	72.3	35.0	380
Concorde	4 × 30,850 lb	83.8	203.8	37.9	127.0	59.7	25.3	128
707-320B	4 × 19,000 lb	145.8	152.8	42.5	—	59.0	22.1	219
Transcontinental								
L-1011 Tristar	3 × 42,000 lb	155.3	178.6	55.3	141.3	70.0	36.0	400
A300 B4	2 × 51,000 lb	147.1	175.8	54.3	111.5	61.1	31.5	345
727-200[a]	3 × 16,000 lb	108.0	133.2	34.0	82.0	63.3	18.8	189
A 310-200	2 × 48,000 lb	144.0	153.1	51.9	103.3	40.9	31.5	265
767-200	2 × 48,000 lb	156.3	159.2	52.0	110.5	64.6	30.5	255
Short haul								
757-200	2 × 37,400 lb	124.5	155.3	44.5	92.0	60.0	24.0	233
1 11-475	2 × 12,550 lb	93.5	93.5	24.5	51.5	33.1	14.3	119
737-200[a]	2 × 15,500 lb	93.0	100.0	37.0	56.4	37.4	17.3	130
Trident 3B	3 × 11,960 lb[b]	98.0	131.2	28.3	80.0	52.4	19.1	180
DC-9-50	2 × 16,000 lb	93:3	125.6	28.0	68.0	56.1	16.4	139
F28-2000	2 × 9,850 lb	77.3	97.2	27.8	58.0	33.9	16.5	79
146-200	4 × 6,700 lb	86.4	93.7	28.3	41.2	36.8	15.5	106
Commuters								
Brasilia	2 × 1,500 eshp	64.9	64.7	20.7	58.4	22.3	19.9	30
HS-748-2A	2 × 2,280 eshp	98.5	67.0	24.8	74.0	20.7	24.8	60
F27-500	2 × 2,140 eshp	95.2	82.3	28.6	65.9	31.6	23.7	56
DHC-7	4 × 1,174 eshp	93.0	80.3	26.2	62.0	27.5	23.5	54
Nord 262C	2 × 1,145 eshp	74.1	63.3	20.3	57.0	23.8	10.3	29
SD 3-30	2 × 1,120 eshp	74.7	58.1	15.7	53.8	20.2	13.9	30

[a] Advanced version.

[a] One RB 162 booster.

Source: References 5, 6, Manufacturers' brochures.

61

TABLE 3.1b Aircraft Characteristics of Air Carriers: Weight, Field Length, Cruise Speed, and Payload

Aircraft Type	Weight (lb × 1000)			FAR Field Length (ft)		Cruise Speed (knots)	Payload Range: ISA, Still Air, No Reserves			
							Range at Max Payload		Max Range Payload	
	Takeoff (max)	Landing (max)	Empty, Operating	Takeoff	Landing		(nautical mi)	lb × 1000	(nautical mi)	lb × 1000
Intercontinental										
747-200B	770	564	367.4	10,500	6,150	506	4,330	159.1	7,140	62.6
DC-10-30	555	403	267.3	10,490	5,960	499	4,390	104.5	6,660	47.8
Concorde	400	245	174.8	10,280	8,000	1,176	4,430	28	4,480	23.5
707-320B	333.6	247	147.8	10,000	6,250	478	5,175	53.9	6,500	33.3
Transcontinental										
L-1011 Tristar	430	358	239.4	7,750	5,700	495	2,885	85.6	4,845	32.0
A300 B4	330.7	293.2	191.3	8,740	5,950	481	1,820	77.6	3,400	39.8
727-200[a]	207.5	160	103	10,080	4,800	495	2,615	41	3,190	33.9
A310-200	291	261	169.5	6,050	5,460	488	2,210	69.7	4,430	27.1
767-200	300	270	178.3	5,650	4,700	506	2,220	67.7	4,900	15.9
Short haul										
757-200	220	198	129.8	6,180	4,820	494	1,200	64.0	4,660	11.8
1 11-475	99.7	87	54.8	7,470	4,770	457	1,303	26.2	2,026	20.2
737-200[a]	115.5	103	60	6,550	4,290	460	1,280	35	2,740	21.4
Trident 3B	158	130	82.4	8,595	5,680	480	1,990	35.4	2,375	28.3
DC-9-50	120	110	65	7,880	4,680	465	1,275	33	2,420	21.4
F28-200	65	59.6	37	5,490	3,540	457	920	17.5	2,620	5.1
146-200	88.3	77	47.2	5,100	3,480	419	1,535	22.1	1,646	20.9
Commuters										
Brasilia	21.7	21.7	12.3	3,540	4,000	287	575	6.0	1,570	3.2
HS-748-2A	46.5	43	26	5,380	3,370	242	1,160	12.5	1,740	9.0
F27-500	45	42	26.3	5,470	3,290	248	825	13.2	2,180	5.66
DHC-D7	41	39	24.4	1,800	1,900	238	637	11.1	1,740	6.44
Nord 262C	23.8	23	15.9	3,510	1,720	211	270	6.78	1,280	4.53
SD3-30	22	21.7	14.2	3,900	3,400	197	395	5.85	910	4.00

[a] Advanced version

Source: References 5, 6, manufacturers' brochures.

TABLE 3.1c Characteristics of General Aviation Aircraft

Aircraft	Powerplant	Dimensions (ft)			Number of Passengers (max)	Weight (lb × 1000)			FAR Field Length (ft)[a]		Cruise Speed (knots)[b]
		Span	Length	Height		Takeoff (max)	Landing (max)	Empty, Operating	Takeoff	Landing	
Gulfstream 2	2 × 11,400 lb	68.9	79.9	24.5	19[c]	62.0	58.5	35.6	5000	3190	480
BAe 125-700	2 × 3,750 lb	47.0	50.7	17.6	14[c]	25.5	22.0	14.0	5800	2550	441
Learjet 36	2 × 3,500 lb	38.1	48.7	12.3	8[c]	17.0	13.3	8.76	3500	3690	460
Citation	2 × 2,200 lb	43.8	43.5	14.4	6[c]	11.7	11.0	6.35	3275	2300	351
Beech 99	2 × 715 eshp	45.8	44.6	14.4	15[c]	10.9	10.9	6.00	3100	2220	248
Twin Otter	2 × 715 eshp	65.0	51.7	18.6	20[c]	12.5	12.5	6.70	1200[d]	1050[d]	165
Merlin 3	2 × 904 eshp	46.3	42.2	16.8	7[c]	12.5	11.5	6.99	3080	2860	275
MU 2K	2 × 724 eshp	39.2	33.3	12.9	6[c]	9.92	9.44	5.92	1700	1490	318
BNZA-21	2 × 300 hp	53.0	39.5	13.9	8[c]	6.60	6.60	3.74	1090	960	157
Cessna 421	2 × 375 hp	41.9	36.1	11.6	8[e]	7.45	7.45	4.43	2507	2178	235[e]
Piper PA-31P	2 × 425 hp	40.8	34.6	13.1	8[e]	7.80	7.80	4.90	2200	2700	244[e]
Cessna 337	2 × 225 hp	38.0	29.9	9.1	6[e]	4.63	4.63	2.71	1675	1650	170[e]
Aztec E	2 × 250 hp	37.2	31.2	10.3	6[e]	5.20	5.20	3.04	1250	1620	183[e]
Cessna 210	1 × 285 hp	36.9	28.3	9.7	6[e]	3.80	3.80	2.12	1900	1500	164[e]
Cherokee 180	1 × 180 hp	32.0	23.3	7.3	4[e]	2.15	2.15	1.27	1700	1075	115[e]
Cessna 150	1 × 100 hp	32.7	23.8	8.10	2[e]	1.60	1.60	1.00	1385	1075	102[e]

Source: References 6, 7

[a] Figures refer to sea level, 59°F (international standard atmosphere), dry runway, and zero wind for the worst applicable FAR regulations.
[b] Cost-economic true air speed (TAS).
[c] Plus two crew, but may need only one.
[d] Short takeoff and landing (STOL) regulations.
[e] Includes crew, maximum speed.

Safety margins are then added to these demonstrated distances to allow for variation in pilot performance, aircraft performance, and environmental conditions in service. The margins are typically 15% in the all-engine-operating takeoff case and 67% in the landing case; the difference is due mostly to the extra difficulty of controlling and monitoring an approach compared with the relatively fixed and known conditions on takeoff.

Extra margins are implicit in the procedure just described insofar as most airports accepting commercial flights do not have obstructions at the ends of their fields and most airfields have either visual or electronic guidance on the approach path. However, experience has shown that margins of this order are necessary if a satisfactorily low rate of hazardous incidents associated with field length is to be maintained. In this way, a required field length is assigned to each certificated aircraft, for every practical combination of variations in weight, altitude, and temperature, and the information is published in the official flight manual as a series of charts. This information is collated by the FAA (8). Figure 3.9 is an example taken from the ICAO *Aerodrome Manual* (9). The dotted lines on the figure show the method of reading the chart, the runway length required at a given airfield altitude and temperature being determined either by the aircraft's takeoff weight (line 1,220,000 lb) or by its ability to maintain climb capability after takeoff (line 2, for airfield altitude of 3000 ft). Allowance is also made for wind strength and direction, runway

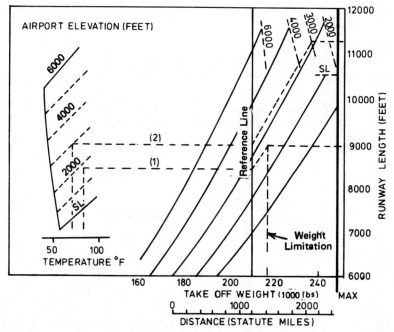

FIGURE 3.9 Aircraft performance on takeoff: example ICAO requirements for large aircraft. (*Source:* Reference 9.)

slope, runway surface conditions, and the need to retain some minimum climb capability on the takeoff flight path with one engine inoperative.*

Published field length requirements can be used for the following purposes:

Checking the ability of an aircraft to take a specified payload from, or land at, a specified airfield in specified environmental conditions.

Calculating the allowable maximum payload that may be moved under those specific conditions when the payload is limited by available field length.

Planning the field lengths that must be provided at an airport to allow operation of a specific aircraft type from that airport to specific destinations on a specified percentage of occasions annually (determined by local environmental history), with a specified percentage of its maximum payload.

This chapter is mostly concerned with the last of these uses. In this case, the altitude and temperature are fixed and the runway slope and obstacles below the flight path are largely predetermined. It is unwise to rely on any advantage from wind effects, and equipment is provided to ensure that aircraft performance is not compromised by runway surface conditions. Then the main variables are runway length, aircraft type, and aircraft weight, the weight being adjustable between useful payload and fuel as described below.

There are, however, two further variables to be considered in defining the field length requirement. The takeoff distances that must be demonstrated for transport category aircraft are presented in Figure 3.10; the speeds to be controlled during the demonstration are symbolized as follows:

V_1 = takeoff decision speed chosen by the aircraft manufacturers: > 1.10 V_{mc}, $<$ speed at which brakes overload, $< V_R$, $< 1.10 V_s$.

V_{mc} = minimum control speed: minimum speed at which engine failure can occur and still allow straight flight at this speed in a fully controlled manner.

V_{LOF} = liftoff speed: $\geqslant 1.1 V_{mu}$ ($\geqslant 1.05 V_{mu}$ with one engine out)

V_{mu} = minimum unstick speed: $>$ minimum speed that allows safe continuation of the takeoff.

V_2 = takeoff safety speed at 35 ft (11 m) $\geqslant 1.2 V_s$, $\geqslant 1.1 V_{mc}$

V_s = stall speed in takeoff configuration

V_R = speed at which nosewheel can be lifted from runway and $\geqslant V_1$, $\geqslant 1.05 V_{mc}$

The first variable is V_1, which can be chosen by the manufacturer within the limits of controllability, rotation speed, and brake failure. If the engine fails before this speed is reached, the pilot must abort the takeoff; if failure

---

* All major manufacturers include runway design information in the airport design manuals for each of their aircraft types, but the actual approved field lengths are to be found in the individual operator's flight manual.

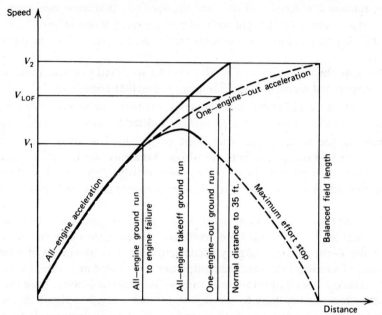

FIGURE 3.10 Takeoff field length demonstration requirements for transport category aircraft. (*Source:* References 9 and 10.)

occurs at or above this speed, the pilot must continue the takeoff despite the loss of power. When only a normal hard runway is available, the minimum engine-out runway requirement is obtained if V_1 is chosen so that the distance needed to stop is equal to the distance to reach 35 ft (11 m). This is called the *balanced field length*. The field length in this case is determined as the larger of the balanced field length and 115% of the all-engine distance to a height of 35 ft (11 m). This was the only definition applicable to piston-engine aircraft.

Turbojet engines have proved to be so reliable that engine failure on takeoff has become very uncommon. This has allowed the introduction of a second variable, namely, the ability to substitute stopways and clearways for some portions of the hard runway. Stopways and clearways are defined in Code of Federal Regulations (CFR), Title 14, Part 1 (11, 12) as "an area beyond the runway, not less in width than the width of the runway, centrally located about the extended centerline of the runway, and designated by the airport authorities for use in decelerating the aircraft during an aborted takeoff. To be considered as such, the stopway must be capable of supporting the aircraft without inducing structural damage to it." A clearway is defined as follows:

An area beyond the runway not less than 500 feet (150 m) wide, centrally located about the extended centerline of the runway, and under the control of the airport authorities. The clearway is expressed in terms of a clearway plane, extending from the end of the runway with an upward slope not exceeding 1.25% above which no object nor any portion of the terrain protrudes, except that threshold lights may protrude above the plane if their height above the end of the runway is not greater than 26 inches (66 cm) and if they are located to each side of the runway.

A clearway may not be longer than half the difference between 115% of the distance between the liftoff point and the point at which 35 ft (11 m) altitude is reached for a normal all-engine takeoff nor longer than half the difference between the liftoff point and the point at which 35 ft (11 m) altitude is reached for an engine-out takeoff. A stopway may be used as a substitute only for the part of the accelerate-stop distance that is greater than the full-strength runway requirement determined from clearway allowances; that is, the hard runway must extend for the full length of the take-off run, defined as the point equidistant between the point at which V_{LOF} is reached and the point at which a height of 35 ft (11 m) is attained. The use of stopways and clearways in the declaration of available field lengths is shown in Figure 3.11. Also shown is the way in which the demonstrated performance is converted to the factored performance as scheduled in the aircraft's flight manual.

The takeoff field lengths scheduled in the flight manual and listed in Table 3.1 must be the greater of the demonstrated engine-out accelerate-stop distance, the demonstrated engine-out distance to 35 ft (11 m) altitude, or 115% of the demonstrated all-engine distance to 35 ft (11 m) altitude. The take-off decision speed (V_1) may be chosen by the manufacturer, within the limits noted in Figure 3.10, but the same speed must be used for both the aborted and the continued takeoff.

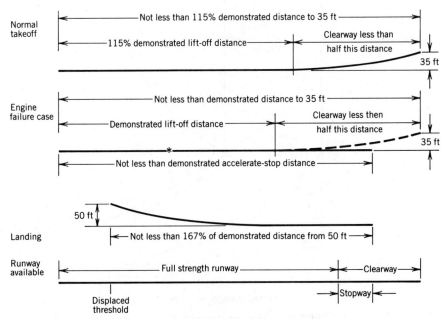

FIGURE 3.11 Field length definitions. (Asterisk indicates engine failure at speed V_1.)

This flexibility of choice is extended to the pilot faced with a particular runway situation, so that the greater the takeoff distance available, relative to the emergency stop distance available, the lower he will choose his V_1 speed. Similarly, the airport planner can take advantage of these alternatives. It is frequently advantageous to use a clearway because it saves on full-strength runway without penalizing the operation. Then a low decision speed can be chosen, to keep stopway requirements to a minimum. Conversely, a high V_1 will give an even shorter full-strength runway requirement at the expense on a long stopway in the engine failure case, but the normal takeoff or landing cases may then become critical from the point of view of the length of full-strength runway. These choices are depicted in Figure 3.12. Specific recommendations are impossible because the decision depends on the geography of the airport, the possible critical speeds of the aircraft, and the fuel requirements for the critical flight plan.

General Aviation Aircraft

Many general aviation aircraft used for executive business, air taxi, and commuter operation are now certificated under Federal Aviation Regulations, Part 25, and so must meet the same field length requirements as those applicable to aircraft greater than 12,500 lb all-up-weight (AUW) and/or 30 seats as

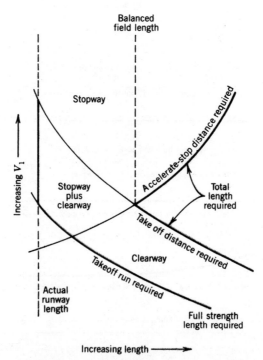

FIGURE 3.12   Use of unbalanced field performance.

described earlier. Other aircraft are certificated under Federal Aviation Regulations, Part 23 (13), which requires only demonstration of all-engine takeoff distance to 50 ft altitude and landing from 50 ft altitude for aircraft weighing between 6000 and 12,500 lb. No specific demonstration is required for aircraft below 6000 lb, but Table 3.1c gives some data relating to normal takeoff and landing distances to 50 ft to assist in runway design.

Reference 12 provides guidance on the recommended runway lengths for turbojet-powered airplanes of 60,000 lb or less maximum certificated takeoff weight. In that circular, the FAA presents temperature and altitude-dependent curves to cover 75% and 100% of the basic turbojet fleet at 60% and 90% load factors. That fleet includes Learjets, Sabreliners, Cessna Citations, and Fan Jet Falcons. Load factors greater than 90% are not considered because the likelihood of that load occurring on a day when this category of aircraft is not climb limited is very small. For those airports expected to accommodate general aviation aircraft over 60,000 lb, the runway length requirement is calculated on the critical aircraft as it is at a commercial airfield.

Reference 14 gives the runway lengths recommended as a basis for planning the various classes of utility airports, as well as the effects of altitude and temperature.

Restrictions on Payload-Range Performance

It is important to realize that the field lengths given in Table 3.1 refer to maximum takeoff weight at sea level and 59°F (15°C) (ISA). Equation 3.1 (Section 3.2) indicates that lift is proportional to air density. Since air density falls with increase of either altitude or temperature, either the takeoff and landing speeds must rise, which requires a greater field length, or the lift, hence the weight, must fall. This is demonstrated by Figure 3.9 and Table 3.2. The illustrations refer to transport category operation, but the effects on general aviation are equally substantial. The situation is complicated by the effect on engine performance, which tends to produce a greater deterioration in the takeoff case unless the engine is flat rated (i.e., its output at high air densities is deliberately limited to avoid overloading its components). It frequently happens that different criteria become critical in defining the field length because of the need to choose a V_1 speed, discussed above. Therefore, under hot and high conditions, it becomes necessary to use longer field lengths or to reduce weight. In addition, the hot and high cases frequently make it difficult to meet the requirements for engine-out climb gradients at a given weight, even if the runway is long enough to meet the field length regulations at that weight.

The previous discussion has shown how the payload range can be compromised by runway length and by altitude and temperature. The allowable operating weights, hence the payload-range capability, can also be affected by runway strength limitations. This is illustrated by Figure 3.13, which indicates the relative effects of strength and length limitations for a given set of operating

TABLE 3.2 Increases in Field Length (ft × 1000) Due to Changes in Altitude and Temperature

Aircraft	Takeoff				Landing			
	Sea Level		5000 ft		Sea Level		5000 ft	
	ISA	ISA + 20°C	ISA	ISA + 20°C	ISA	ISA + 20°C	ISA	ISA + 20°C
Concorde	10.28	12.35	12.50	13.08	8.00	8.00	9.28	9.28
707-320B	10.00	11.40	12.65[a]	12.84[a]	6.25	6.25	6.94	6.94
L-1011	7.75	9.25	12.95[a]	13.30[a]	5.70	5.70	6.40	6.40
767-200	5.65	6.10	7.70	8.60	4.75	4.75	5.35	5.35
727-200	10.08	13.19	13.81[a]	14.12[a]	4.80	4.80	5.31	5.31
737-200	6.55	7.73	8.80[a]	10.20[a]	4.29	4.29	5.14	5.14
DC-9-50	7.88	9.80	10.85[a]	12.15[a]	4.68	4.68	5.30[b]	5.10[b]
HS-748-2A	5.38	5.70[a]	5.50[a]	5.90[a]	3.37[b]	3.36[b]	4.76[b]	4.67[b]
Nord 262C	3.51	3.68[a]	3.84[a]	3.94[a]	1.72[b]	1.72[b]	1.94[b]	1.88[b]

[a] Weight limited by climb gradient requirement on takeoff.
[b] Weight limited by climb gradient requirement on overshoot.

Source: References 5, 6.

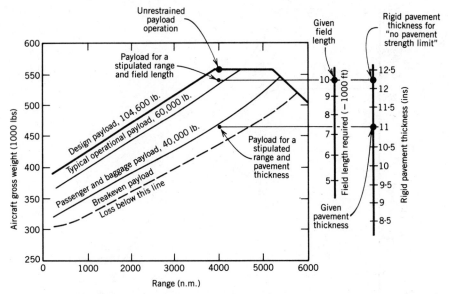

FIGURE 3.13 Aircraft gross weight versus range. (*Source:* Reference 15.)

conditions, as well as the reduction in potential profit margin. However, these limitations only apply for frequent use above the pavement's structural limits.

Weight Components

It is not always difficult to reduce weight to meet runway requirements because aircraft usually are flexible in the makeup of their maximum weight, as indicated by the following definitions:

1. Empty operating weight is a constant weight for a type, made up of all items except payload and fuel.
2. Zero fuel weight is the sum of empty operating weight and the maximum payload, the latter normally being volume limited.
3. Maximum takeoff weight is determined by structural limits and performance requirements and is made up of the empty operating weight and a flexible combination of payload and fuel.
4. Maximum ramp weight is usually slightly higher than the maximum takeoff weight so that the fuel required for queueing and taxiing does not prejudice the load that can be lifted for the flight.
5. Maximum landing weight is less than the maximum takeoff weight by an amount dependent on a reasonable mean expectancy of the weight of fuel burned during a flight. Thus the landing gear can be designed for lower landing loads without prejudice to the aircraft's lifting ability,

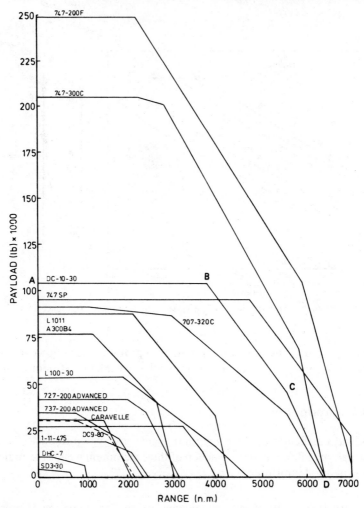

FIGURE 3.14 Payload ranges of various commercial aircraft. (*Source:* Adapted from Reference 5.)

on condition that sufficient fuel will always be burned or jettisoned before a landing is attempted.

Tables 3.1b and 3.1c list the maximum takeoff, maximum landing, and empty operating weights.

It can be seen that there is flexibility in both the size and the makeup of the difference between the takeoff weight and the empty operating weight. This is usually expressed in terms of a payload-range diagram (Figure 3.14). The payload is the useful load that may be carried—passengers, cargo, or mail. It is normally volume limited, but may on occasion be limited by structural, weight, or balance factors. The fuel is limited by volume or by the maximum ramp weight. Some fuel is always needed even for a zero range flight for ground taxiing and reserves, the latter depending on whether the flight is to be under visual or instrument flight rules (VFR or IFR).* A further reserve is required as a function of range, to allow for winds and loss of engine efficiency.

For short ranges and low payloads, the aircraft may take off with a weight below the maximum takeoff weight. Indeed, even if maximum payload is to be carried, the aircraft may still take off below the maximum takeoff weight for the short ranges over which the payload remains constant (A–B in Figure 3.14). Above this range, the aircraft must use its maximum takeoff weight, and the more fuel it needs to carry, the less payload it can accept (B–C). Finally, it is operating with full tanks, and the only extra range capability comes from the slight reduction of drag if even less payload is carried (C–D). Thus the lack of runway for maximum weight takeoff will not necessarily penalize the operator if he has a smaller payload or range for a particular stage than is average for the aircraft type under consideration. It would not, however, be wise to rely too much on this in airport planning, since traffic normally is expected to grow and the operator may prefer to carry extra fuel rather than buy it elsewhere.

The foregoing discussion of field length applies in principle to all types of aircraft, though the detail is mainly concerned with conventional transport category aircraft. Reduced and short takeoff and landing (R/STOL) designs generally find that the landing case can be as limiting as the takeoff case. This is normally true of general aviation designs, which naturally have these R/STOL characteristics. Such aircraft have less rigorous requirements to meet but are more sensitive to environmental effects and generally have less flexibility with regard to payload and fuel. As a first approximation, it may be assumed that a 10% increase in takeoff run can be caused by a 5% increase in weight, a 1000 ft (305 m) increase in altitude, a 5°C increase in temperature, a 2% increase in runway slope, or a tail wind of 5% of the unstick speed. Also, long grass, soft ground, or snow can lengthen the takeoff run by 25% (16).

3.3 OTHER AIRPORT LAYOUT FACTORS

Aircraft characteristics significantly affect other airport layout factors, including the number of runways, the type and strength of pavement, and the dimensions of parking areas and taxiway systems.

Number of Runways; Crosswinds

The number of runways required is influenced both by the number of each type of aircraft to be accepted and by their capability to operate in crosswinds.

---

* These terms are defined in Section 5.2.

TABLE 3.3   Maximum Crosswinds Permissible for Different Runway
Lengths and Aircraft Types

Reference field length[a] (m)	1500 and over	1200–1500	1200 and less
Maximum permissible crosswind component (kts)	20	13	10

[a] Balanced field length at maximum takeoff weight with standard atmospheric conditions at sea level (see this chapter: Field length regulations).

Source: Annex 14, Amendment 36, ICAO.

The former is largely a capacity problem, whereas the latter is an aircraft design problem. The more slowly an aircraft is designed to fly, the more difficult it is to compensate for a given crosswind without too severe a penalty in other areas of design. This is because there is an increase in the angular difference between the resultant direction of airflow and the required track on the ground. Transport category aircraft must demonstrate their ability to operate in crosswinds of 25 knots* (CFR, Title 14, Part 25), but other categories of aircraft with lower flying speeds and shorter field lengths have less crosswind capability. This is reflected in ICAO airport requirements (17), which call for runways to be usable for 95% of the time in the maximum crosswinds listed in Table 3.3.

These crosswind limits on runways are for design purposes. They are quite conservative in comparison with the 25 knot speed used in transport aircraft design to allow for variation in runway surface conditions. In general aviation, where combinations of sideslip, crab, and the use of crosswind landing gear can allow operation in 20 knot crosswinds, the airport design criteria are more conservative: it is frequently more difficult to taxi in crosswind than to land (18).

The validity of the criterion of 95% usability is debatable. Not only does it appear low, but the criterion remains constant over all categories of airport, whereas one might have expected that the investment in other areas to improve operational reliability at major airports would have called for commensurate improvement in the area of crosswinds.

Runway and Taxiway Strength and Surface

The strength requirement is a function of absolute weight, weight per wheel, pressure per wheel, and the frequency of operation. In addition, the type of surface that is acceptable depends on the jet exhaust or slipstream effects, and the vulnerability of intakes and flying surfaces to damage from debris thrown up by tires. In aircraft intended for shorter fields at low frequencies, the

---

* 1 knot = 1 nautical mi/hr = 1.15 statute mi/hr = 1.85 km/hr.

designers generally attempt to minimize aircraft sensitivity to rough surfaces*
and to minimize the weight and pressure per wheel. In this way, the least
expensive surface can be used. However, this approach leads to increased
empty weight and drag from the landing gear housing, and is thus less appropriate
to high speed, long range designs. The only economic solution to increasing
size for these aircraft is to increase the number of wheels per bogie and the
number of bogies, particularly for the main wheels, which, between them,
take approximately 95% of the aircraft weight.

Limitations Due to Aircraft Dimensions

The principal dimensions of the more common aircraft are given in Table 3.1.
The spacing of taxiways and nose-in bays is determined largely by the wing
span. The length is important in determining queueing distances, spacing of
pretakeoff waiting areas, and the length of loading bays. The height to the top
of the tail fin is of interest in sizing maintenance hangars and also, together
with the other dimensions, in the location of electronic aids to minimize any
interference due to reflection. The primary use of the minimum radius swept
by the extremity of the aircraft is in determining the size of apron and parking
space. The pivot point can be derived by projecting through the axes of the
main wheels and the axis of the nose wheel at its maximum angle, which gives
a reference point from which the minimum radius swept by the landing gear
can be found. The minimum radius on taxiways and turning points is based
on this, though in practice the more important criterion is the minimum radius
that can be negotiated at a given taxi speed. The width of the taxiways is
influenced by the track width between the wheels, and the size of full strength
apron and waiting area surfaces is related to the wheelbase (i.e., the distance
between the nose and main wheels).

Cargo Implications

The layout of the facilities for handling cargo is influenced by all the parameters
that determine the airside design to the passenger handling terminal. However,
the increasing average size of aircraft is influencing the degree to which cargo
can be considered separately from passenger handling.

The air cargo industry has always looked forward to the day when it would
be able to commission its own dedicated freighter aircraft design. Such aircraft
do not yet exist in quantity because it is so much cheaper to utilize surplus
carrying capacity in the holds of scheduled passenger services—normally
available because the average passenger load factor seldom exceeds 65%,
hence the aircraft is seldom operated at its maximum takeoff weight unless
cargo is carried. As aircraft have increased in size, the volumetric capacity

---

* Example, the VFW-614 has its engines placed over the wing primarily to avoid ground ingestion
problems.

available for underfloor cargo has increased in greater proportion. Hence, although air cargo is growing at a faster annual rate than passenger traffic, it is likely that the majority of cargo will continue to be handled in belly holds of scheduled passenger service aircraft. The siting of cargo terminals and the associated taxiways and service roads should reflect careful consideration of this trend.

3.4 FACTORS AFFECTING AIRPORT CAPACITY

The characteristics of aircraft using an airport have an important effect on the capacity of runway systems, as well as that of the passenger processing terminal facilities.

Runway Capacity

The capacity of a given runway under given meteorological conditions and control procedures depends on the average aircraft size and the mix of types of aircraft using the runway. The variation in capacity with fleet mix is due to differences in the approach and climbout speeds of the various aircraft, and to the vorticity generated in the wake of large aircraft. The vorticity gives rise to control problems for smaller aircraft attempting to fly through.

Lift is produced by the achievement of a pressure on the upper surface of a wing that is lower than the pressure on the lower surface. This produces a tendency for air to flow up around the wing tips. At the same time, the lift generated by the pressure differential must be balanced by a downward component of momentum in the airstream behind the wing. The combined effect of these forces is for a pair of vortices to roll up behind and below each wing tip, the radii of the cones increasing with distance downstream. The effect of these vortices is severe enough to have caused a DC-9 to bank through 90° while attempting to follow a DC-10 in to land (19).

Much research is being done to contain the effect of the vortices. The most promising approach—namely, to prevent the vortices from developing—requires modifying the wing producing the vortices, without destroying the lift or increasing the drag.

The progress being made in this direction is illustrated by changes in the level of rolling moment required by a Learjet to overcome the vorticity generated by a Boeing 747 in the landing configuration in the three cases appearing in Figure 3.15. The spoiler reduces the rolling moment required below that available when the separation between the aircraft exceeds 0.5 nautical mi. This is achieved with no loss of maximum lift and only a 4% increase in drag. There is little inducement for operators of large aircraft to go to the expense of fitting devices, though there is some hope that wing-tip "sails" might offer a reduction in vortex strength while actively improving the aerodynamic performance of the wing. Thus, in the short term, either the separation between large aircraft

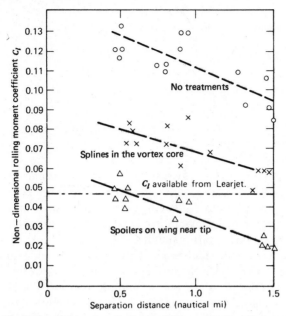

FIGURE 3.15 Effect of the wake of a Boeing 747 on a Learjet. (*Source:* Reference 19.)

and following small aircraft must be increased, with consequent loss of runway capacity, or the smaller aircraft must be segregated to other airfields.

The loss of capacity caused by differences in approach speed can be avoided by the same extreme measure, which is very inconvenient if connecting flights are involved. Alternatively, since the small aircraft usually only require short runways, a parallel runway can be utilized, at least in VFR conditions. This solution is not readily available to overcome the vorticity problem, because the vortices tend to drift across in crosswind situations.

The runway capacity in terms of operations per hour is a function of aircraft size. The smaller aircraft can be accommodated at a higher rate, particularly in VFR conditions. This is because of their lower runway occupancy time and their ability to perform tighter maneuvers in the air. Both these advantages stem from their lower takeoff and approach speeds. Thus an increase in average aircraft size does not necessarily result in an increase in passenger throughput.

Terminal Capacity

Despite the qualification above, the advent of large aircraft has tended to transfer the capacity problem from the runway to the passenger processing terminal. Problems arise particularly in the areas of:

1. Apron requirements.
2. Location of airbridges, etc.

3. Access to upper decks of 747s.
4. Baggage handling.
5. Handling large batches inside the terminal.

3.5 NOISE

The noise generated by aircraft creates problems in making decisions on layout and capacity. The correct assessment of future noise patterns, to minimize the effect on surrounding communities, is essential to the optimal layout of the runways. Failure in this regard may result in capacity problems due to curfews and maximum allowable noise and number index (NNI) limits.

The FAA noise regulations (FAR Part 36: 20) came into force in 1969 for jet-powered aircraft with bypass ratios greater than 2. In 1973, they were modified to apply to all aircraft manufactured after that date. The regulation with respect to noise on the sideline and below the approach path is indicated by the solid line in Fig. 3.16; the broken line shows regulations for takeoff. The Stage 2 regulations are shown because they do not vary with the number of engines. The Stage 3 regulations, applicable to aircraft certificated after 1975, are approximately 4 dB lower than Stage 2 levels. Both in timing and in their variation with weight, the regulations are carefully tailored to demand only what current technology can provide, without undue economic penalty. It can be seen that the first- and some of the second-generation jets would not meet the regulations on approach noise, though they would have less trouble with the sideline limits (the aircraft can be identified with respect to sideline noise, since they are plotted at the same gross weight as the approach measurements). Although this tendency is not shown, the aircraft generally meet the takeoff requirement more easily than the approach case, but less easily than the sideline case. Some small allowance is given for one or more of the criteria to be exceeded, provided any such excess is completely offset in the remaining cases. The third-generation jets have little difficulty meeting the current requirements. However, future legislation will ensure continuous reduction down to the level at which aerodynamic slipstream noise over the aircraft structure becomes the limiting factor,* at a rate commensurate with technological capability. Meanwhile, many countries have made the noise regulations retroactive—in which case the current fleet of first- and second-generation jets would have to be replaced rather earlier than anticipated (typically 1986) or be reengined or fitted with hush kits.

Similar remarks about the status and the realistic levels of the regulations apply to general aviation noise, except that current legislation applies only to flyover noise at maximum cruise power at 1000 ft.

---

* This so-called self-noise is likely to create approximately 80 EPNdB. (EPNdB = effective perceived noise decibels; units of noise are defined in Chapter 13).

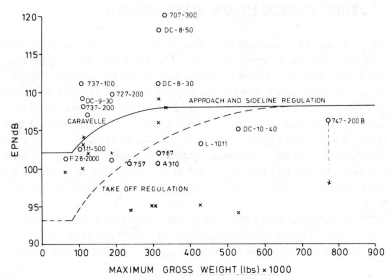

FIGURE 3.16 Aircraft noise (EPN&B) measured with reference to CFR, 14, Part 36. (*Source: Reference 5.*)

One of the most effective ways of minimizing the impact of aircraft noise on communities near airports is to reduce field length. Although subject to the crosswind difficulties mentioned earlier and to a penalty in terms of DOC per seat mile, aircraft that can utilize the shorter runways do tend to increase runway occupancy rate, reduce expenditure on new runways, and improve aircraft utilization at the trip ends—an important factor in short-haul operations that tends to offset the inherent DOC disadvantage. The combined effect of the shorter field length with the steeper approach and takeoff paths is potentially quite dramatic (Table 3.4) when taken with other improvements.

TABLE 3.4   Effect of Field Length on Noise Footprint

| | Noise Footprint (km²) | |
Technology	90 PNdB	80 PNdB
1960 Long haul CTOL	180	450
1970 Short haul STOL	60	250
1970 Short haul STOL (FAR, Part 36)	20	55
1970 Short haul STOL + engines silenced to 10 PNdB[a]	5	20
Future RTOL with engines silenced to 10 PNdB[a]	3	10
Future STOL	1	3

Source: Reference 21.

[a] PNdB = perceived noise decibels (see Chapter 13).

3.6 FUTURE TRENDS IN AIRCRAFT DESIGN

This chapter has indicated that aircraft design has, in the past, improved productivity by increasing speed and size. The air transport product has now become much more diverse, with particular emphasis on aircraft-mile costs as well as seat-mile costs. Several established trends have now been broken. The introduction of the turbo fan has helped to allow a more efficient match between cruise performance and field performance, so relieving the pressure on runway length (see Figure 3.1). The fuel efficiency of the turbofan makes it relatively more expensive to consider supersonic flight. While it is undoubtedly feasible technologically, it is therefore unlikely that the logarithmic growth of speed with time (Figure 3.17) will continue as a major stimulant to air travel.

Many advances in aerodynamics, structures, propulsion, systems, and control technology (22, 23) are moving from the development stage to production. These advances should allow a continuous improvement in fuel efficiency of

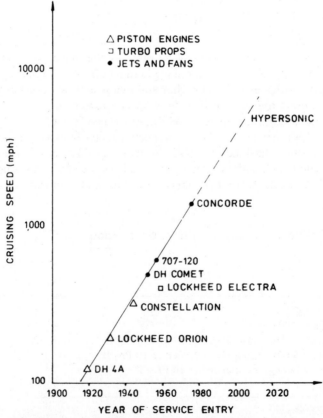

FIGURE 3.17 Historical and projected growth in air transport speed.

at least 25% by the year 2000, allowing real unit costs to remain approximately constant. Technological development is now becoming so expensive that only a strong demand for fuel, causing a return to the fuel crises of the 1970s, is likely to warrant the development of advances like boundary layer control or a hydrogen technology.

The search for fuel efficiency is causing more attention to be focused on turboprops, particularly for the short-haul market. They provide an easy way of obtaining the short field lengths that these markets need, in order to:

1. Serve the very many smaller airports that could not justify runway expenditure for low density operations.
2. Reduce noise footprint areas at airports close to built-up areas.
3. Increase runway capacity with the use of early turnoffs, parallel STOL runways, and stub runways, so supplementing the trend toward more frequent services with smaller aircraft in this time-sensitive sector of the market.

The potential demand for ever larger aircraft exists on the routes that have adequate frequency already. Whether these designs are accepted into service will depend increasingly on their ability to match their runway strength and terminal design requirements to the airports' capabilities. The additional capacity is likely to be offered in the form of standard seating in extended upper decks of the Boeing 747, with all the subsequent problems for the airport of servicing this higher deck level. The other main problem for all sizes of airport is likely to be the increased span of new aircraft at a given seating capacity, as the aircraft manufacturers aim for greater aerodynamic efficiency.

REFERENCES

1. Caves, R. E., "Air System Costs," Cranfield, Bedford, England: Cranfield Centre for Transport Studies, CTS Memo 12, November 1975.
2. Stamper, J. T., "Airports for the Eighties," Paper No. 6, in VSTOL *Fourth World Airports Conference*, Institution of Civil Engineers, April 1973.
3. *Annual Financial Data Reports*, International Civil Aviation Organization.
4. Wimpenny, J. C., "The Design and Application of High Lift Devices," *Annals of New York Academy of Sciences*, Vol. 15A, Art. 2, November 22, 1968.
5. Hofton, A., "Commercial Aircraft of the World," *Flight International*, October 23, 1982.
6. "Business Jets and Turboprops," *Flight International*, November 14, 1981.
7. "International Private Aircraft Survey," *Flight International*, March 14, 1981.
8. *Runway Length Requirements for Airport Design*, U.S. Federal Aviation Administration, Advisory Circular AC 150/5325-4, including Changes 1 through 11.
9. *Aerodrome Design Manual, Part 1: Runways*, Montreal: International Civil Aviation Organization, 1st Ed., 1980.
10. *Airworthiness Standards—Transport Category Airplanes*, Federal Aviation Regulations, Part 25, Revised January 1, 1982.
11. *Definitions*, U.S. Code of Federal Regulations, Title 14, Part 1, January 1982.

12. *Airport Design Standards—Transport Airports*, U.S. Federal Aviation Administration, AC 150/5300-12.

13. *Airworthiness Standards—Normal, Utility and Acrobatic Category Airplanes*, Federal Aviation Regulations, Part 23.

14. *Utility Airports—Air Access to National Transportation*, U.S. Federal Aviation Administration, AC 150/5300-4B, June 24, 1975.

15. O'Massey, R. C., "Industry Needs—Airport Pavement Strength Evaluation System," in *American Society of Civil Engineers Conference on Airports: Key to the Air Transportation System*, April 1971.

16. Information Circular No. 73/1982, London: U.K. Civil Aviation Authority, 1973.

17. *Airport Planning Manual: Part 1; Master Planning*, 1st Ed., Montreal: International Civil Aviation Organization, 1977.

18. Fisher, B. D. et al., "A Flight Investigation of Piloting Techniques and Crosswind Limitation During Visual STOL-type Landing Operations," National Aeronautics and Space Administration TN-D-8284, October 1976.

19. Lee, G. H. "Trailing Vortex Wakes" *Aeronautical Journal*, September 1975.

20. *Noise Standards—Aircraft Type and Airworthiness Certification*, U.S. Code of Federal Regulations, Title 14, Part 36.

21. *The Future of Short-Haul Air Transport Within Western Europe*, The Hague: Netherlands V/STOL Working Group, June, 1973.

22. Stewart, D. J. and B. S. Campion, "New Technology in Commercial Aircraft Design for Minimum Operating Cost," *Aeronautical Journal*, February 1980.

23. Klineberg, John M., "NASA's Aircraft Energy Efficiency Program," Washington, D.C.: Transportation Research Board, January 1978.

4

AIRPORT MASTER PLANNING

4.1 THE AIRPORT MASTER PLAN: DEFINITION AND OBJECTIVES

The planner's idealized concept of the form and structure of the ultimate development of the airport is contained in the airport master plan. This plan is not simply the physical form of ultimate development but a description of the staging and both the financial implications and the fiscal strategies involved. Master planning can apply to the construction of new airports as well as to significant expansion of existing facilities. The FAA describes the objectives of the master plan as follows (1):

To provide an effective graphical presentation of the ultimate development of the airport and of the anticipated land uses adjacent to the airport.

To establish a schedule of priorities and phasing for the various improvements proposed in the plan.

To present the pertinent back-up information and data which were essential to the development of the master plan.

To describe the various concepts and alternatives which were considered in the establishment of the proposed plan.

To provide a concise and descriptive report so that the impact and logic of its recommendations can be clearly understood by the community the airport serves and by those authorities and public agencies which are charged with the approval, promotion, and funding of the improvements proposed in the master plan.

4.2 FAA RECOMMENDATIONS FOR THE STRUCTURE OF THE AIRPORT MASTER PLAN

The planning procedure recommended by the FAA consists of four separate phases.

Phase I: Airport Requirements

Essentially, the first phase is an examination of the scale and timing of new facilities with respect to the anticipated demand; the status of existing facilities is described in the context of anticipated environmental implications.

Phase II: Site Selection

Once a prima facie case for the construction of a new airport or the major expansion of existing facilities has been established, the second phase begins. Evaluation of the available sites should include study of airspace requirements, environmental impact, development, access, availability of utilities, land costs and availability, site development costs, and political implications.

Phase III: Airport Plans

After the site for the location of a new airport or the area of expansion of an existing facility has been selected, the proposed facility is represented precisely with respect to the following points:

1. *The Airport Layout Plan.*   Indicates the configuration, location, and size of all physical facilities.
2. *The Land Use Plan.*   Details land use within the proposed airport boundary and shows the land use of areas outside the boundary that are affected by the siting of the airport.
3. *Terminal Area Plans.*   Show the size and location of the various buildings and activity areas within the terminal area complex.
4. *Airport Access Plans.*   Show proposed routings for the various access modes to the transportation infrastucture for the region.

Phase IV: The Financial Plan

The final phase involves collecting data in the four principal areas of financial importance:

1. *Schedules of Proposed Development.*   Indicate the short, intermediate, and long term stagings of development, timed to coincide with demand estimates.

2. *Estimates of Development Costs.* Staged to conform to the scheduled development strategy.

3. *Economic Feasibility Analysis.* Examines whether the expected revenue generation will cover the anticipated costs.

4. *Financial Feasibility Analysis.* Undertaken to determine whether the scale of facility under consideration can be financed within the fiscal capability of the authority involved.

Although many of the items of airport master planning that are considered in the FAA procedure are also covered in the more generally applicable procedure detailed by the ICAO (9), there are significant differences. Comparison of ICAO master planning procedures, detailed in Section 4.7, with the FAA structure indicates a much stronger emphasis by the United States on capital programming and economic and financial feasibility analysis. This is understandable in that the FAA is the agency responsible not only for safeguarding aviation and airport standards, but also for administering grant aid for airports through federal aid (see Section 1.9).

4.3 AIRPORT REQUIREMENTS (PHASE I)

The determination of airport facility requirements necessitates a detailed examination of the following aspects:

Inventory.
Forecasting.
Demand-capacity analysis.
Facility requirement analysis.
Environmental impact.

Inventory

The inventory is a large data collection exercise that allows the airport planner to gain complete understanding of the nature and scale of existing facilities. For all potential sites, the planner needs data relating to the following: the physical and environmental characteristics of the site; the presence nearby of any existing airport; the structure of airspace in the area and the availability and location of navigational aids; existing and projected land uses at and in the general affected area of the site; the location of utilities, schools, hospitals, and other public infrastructure; and the legislative constraints related to ordinances, by-laws, zoning, building codes, and so on, which could affect the nature and scope of any projected airport development.

Forecasts

There is a need to develop short, medium, and long term forecasts of aeronautical demand to permit well-conceived planning leading to the ultimate development of the airport site. The discussion of forecasting procedures appearing in Chapter 2 is not repeated here. The planner has need of forecasts of passenger volumes, as well as movements of aircraft and cargo both at the annual and peak levels. Knowledge of annual movements is necessary for estimating the magnitude of revenues that will accrue to the facility; peak movement levels determine the scale of facility required to assure a balance of capacity to demand. For forecasting purposes, the FAA recommends employing base data in the areas of demography, personal income, economic activity and industrial status, geography, alternative technology, sociological and political factors, and historical air traffic data.

Demand-Capacity Analysis

With a knowledge of forecast demand for a proposed airport site, and with different estimates of staged development beyond existing infrastructure levels, the analyst is able to test a variety of options of development in a demand-capacity analysis. The analysis should be broad and should cover the following areas of operation in sufficient detail to permit preliminary facility sizing:

1. Forecast of aircraft operations vis-à-vis airspace capacity (2, 3).
2. Forecast of aircraft operations vis-à-vis air traffic control facilities (4).
3. Forecast of aircraft operations vis-à-vis airfield capacity (5).
4. Forecast of passenger movements vis-à-vis passenger terminal capacity (see Chapter 8).
5. Forecast of cargo volumes vis-à-vis air cargo terminal capacity (see Chapter 9).
6. Forecast of access traffic vis-à-vis surface access route capacity (6).

Facility Requirements

The type of new facilities required, their scale, and the staging of their construction are determined as a result of the demand-capacity analysis. These elements are developed according to FAA standards in the United States, and according to ICAO or applicable national standards elsewhere. The facilities required and the elements requiring consideration are as follows (1):

1. *Runways.* Length, width, clearances, clear zones, approach slopes, orientation, crosswind runway provision, grades, capacity, staged construction, cost implications of delay to aircraft, and cost effectiveness.

2. *Taxiways.* Width, location, clearances, design and location of exits, grades, effect on runway capacity, staged construction, and cost effectiveness.

3. *Terminal Area.* Clearances, grades, gate positions, aircraft parking clearances, space requirements, and terminal design concept.

4. *Service and Hangar Areas.* Service equipment buildings, cargo facilities, and fire and rescue equipment buildings.

5. *Heliports.* Planning and design, rooftop and elevated pads.

6. *Obstructions.* Required standards for approach, horizontal, and other control surfaces, and clear zones.

7. *Drainage.* Structures, layout, and grades.

8. *Paving.* Fillets, jet blast protection, pavement types, and construction details.

9. *Lighting and Marking.* Approach lighting, runway lighting, taxiway lighting, runway and taxiway marking, helicopter landing area, and obstructions.

10. *Wind Data.* Source of data.

11. *Aids to Navigation.* Location and grading requirements.

Environmental Study

One of the requirements of the Airport and Airway Development Act of 1970 is that environmental factors be considered both in the site selection process and in the design of the airport. Furthermore the National Environmental Policy Act of 1969 established the Council of Environmental Quality to develop guidelines for federal agencies affected by the policy law. Any federal actions regarding proposals with respect to airport development that significantly affect environmental quality must be accompanied by a statement of the following (1):

1. The environmental impact of the proposed action.

2. Any adverse environmental effects that could not be avoided if the proposal were implemented.

3. Alternatives to the proposed action.

4. The relationship between local short term users of the environment and the enhancement of long term productivity.

5. Any irreversible and irretrievable commitments of resources in the proposal.

It is therefore suggested that any airport master plan be evaluated factually in terms of the following potential effects:

Changes in ambient noise level.

Displacement of significant numbers of people.

Aesthetic or visual intrusion.

Severance of communities.

Effect on areas of unique interest or scenic beauty.

Deterioration of important recreational areas.

Impact on the behavioral pattern of a species.

Other interference with wildlife.

Significant increase in air or water pollution.

Major adverse effects on watertable.

4.4 SITE SELECTION (PHASE II)

Before World War II, when air travel was still a relative rarity, aircraft were
small and lightly powered, and even metropolitan airports had a low number
of daily flights. Airports then were not considered by the community to be
undesirable neighbors. Indeed aviation was still new enough to exert a novelty
attraction among its close neighbors. Site selection under these conditions was
relatively simple and depended principally on aviation and civil engineering
requirements. Because of the dramatic increase in air travel, accompanied and
engendered by larger and more powerful aircraft over the last 15 years, airports
have come to be identified as land users that cause severe environmental deterioration to their neighbors, generate high volumes of surface traffic, and
bring economic and community development that may not accord with the
desires of surrounding land users. Thus, site selection has become more difficult.

In the late 1960s and early 1970s, prolonged planning battles have been
fought over the location of the proposed fourth New York airport, the third
London airport, the second Atlanta airport, and the proposed Everglades (Miami)
airport, to name only a few. Accordingly, site selection is now as complex as
the problem it seeks to solve. In the master planning procedure, the FAA
recommends a minimum site selection analysis that includes the following
factors:

Airspace analysis.

Obstructions.

Environmental impact and nature of surrounding development.

Proximity to areas of aviation trip generation.

Ground access.

Physical site characteristics, including atmospheric conditions.

Utilities.

Land cost and availability.

Comparative analysis of alternative sites.

Analysis of Available Airspace

Very large amounts of airspace are necessary for the unimpeded functioning of airports. Airspace is required for arriving and departing aircraft on the airways, for inbound aircraft in holding stacks, and for arriving and departing aircraft in the approach and climb outpaths, respectively. It is not unusual for large metropolitan areas to have more than one airport, so that airspace is effectively partitioned or shared. If two or more airports are not far enough apart, there can be a loss of individual and overall capacity under IFR conditions, due to interference of traffic, which must maintain proper separation standards.

Many factors such as the size of airport, runway configuration, type of aircraft, volume of air traffic, and environmental conditions affect airport spacing and traffic patterns in the vicinity of an airport. It is therefore not possible to apply hard-and-fast rules to determine minimum spacing between airports. However, the FAA has published guidelines for airport spacing in order to promote standardization in the performance of airport airspace analyses (2, 3). The guidelines recommend rectangular airspace areas for planning new airports or establishing IFR radar control procedures at existing airports. The approximate size of these areas range from about 1.5 by 3.0 nautical miles for the smallest category of aircraft in VFR conditions to 10 by 25 nautical miles for the largest category in IFR conditions. Where there is a possibility of airspace interaction, a detailed study using such techniques as simulation are frequently necessary. Since the FAA has the responsibility for the planning and design of airspace, where interaction is possible it is necessary to consult the federal agency.

Obstructions to Airspace

The airspace in which aircraft approach, turn, and climb out from airports is "protected airspace." Obstructions are not permitted to penetrate certain protected surfaces, which are called "controlled surfaces." In the United States, the geometry of controlled surfaces is set by regulations contained in FAR Part 77 (4); the international standards, which are generally similar with some significant differences, are set out by the ICAO in Annex 14 (5). The United Kingdom has a similar code, the Civil Air Publication (CAP) 168. During site selection, it is necessary to check that the sites under consideration have no man-made or natural obstructions that significantly violate the controlled surfaces. In the later stages of master planning, the zoning ordinances adopted must incorporate height restrictions that will prevent future violation of protected airspace throughout the life of the airport.

Environmental Impact and Nature of Surrounding Development

The anticipated environmental impact on the various sites is established in the work carried out in the preparation of the statement of environmental impact in Phase I (airport requirements). Without doubt, this factor is one of the most important of the criteria to be considered in the choice of siting of a modern, high volume airport. The environmental impact of an airport is closely related to the nature of the surrounding land use, from the viewpoint of both existing and proposed uses. Proximity to an airport is not particularly detrimental to some land uses, but for other types of development, the presence of an airport nearby is likely to have serious impact on the suitability of the area for that type of land use. Consequently, different types of land use can be ranked in descending order of suitability to the near-airport location.

Rural, agriculture.
Industrial.
Office and commercial.
Public buildings (schools, hospitals, universities, etc.).
Residential.

Experience with Heathrow Airport, which is surrounded by urban development, has caused the British Department of the Environment to promulgate standards, based on noise levels, which restrict the development of a number of types of land use, with different degrees of limitation, depending on type of use (6). Similar and more up-to-date standards have been developed in the United States (7).

Examination of the compatibility of the airport to surrounding development must extend to an estimation of the degree of protection that can be given to the airport, with respect to encroachment from new development likely to be spawned by the building of the airport itself. This involves study of the zoning ordinance, building codes, and development procedures for all the local authorities and jurisdictions in affected areas.

Location with Respect to Aeronautical Demand

In selecting the location of an airport, the planner should endeavor not to complicate unnecessarily patterns of surface movement in the area served by the airport. Because air trips are not complete trips from air terminal to air terminal, but are normally the line haul portion of a mixed mode trip, site selection should take into account the prime origins and destinations of these trips. Since airports should be sited to minimize surface access time, they should be as close as possible to the major generators of air travel demand.

Two locational problems arise when a supplementary airport is to be located close to a metropolitan area. To avoid problems of overlapping airspace and to spread the environmental impact, it might appear desirable to locate the new airport on the opposite side of the metropolitan area. This, however, can mean that some passengers on transfer flights are obliged to make a connecting ground journey, which is normally unacceptable; such a situation faced planners attempting to locate a new proposed Atlanta airport. Another type of problem presented overwhelming difficulties in the choice of Maplin for the site of the third London airport. Most air passengers with access trips in the London area were destined or originating in the West End of London, the center of tourist shopping and the hotel portion of the metropolis. Consequently, their access trips required crossing the very congested central core of the City of London itself.

Availability of Suitable Ground Access

Ensuring adequate ground access by providing freeway or rail surface routes can be a very expensive proposition, yet it is critical to the ability of the airport to function at balanced levels of capacity throughout the system chain from access to airspace. Location decisions should favor sites with good proximity to freeways, which can give immediate regional access. When it is feasible to connect the airport to available conventional rail systems, the possibility of connecting to the rail systems by means of a short spur line or an extension to a rapid transit system is another favorable condition. The economics of dedicated, high speed rail systems is discussed with some detail in Chapter 11.

Physical Site Characteristics, Including Atmospheric Conditions

Airports are ideally situated in large open areas of flat land, since the grades and grade changes of runway areas are limited, and the use of runway gradients increases the requirements for runway length. Given the large physical scale of airports, even gently rolling ground can involve heavy construction expense in regrading. Where possible, therefore, a flat site should be used. Flat areas are frequently low lying, however, and if the site chosen is too low, there may be heavy construction costs in fill. Clearly a balance must be struck.

Low-lying land presents another difficulty in the area of drainage. Both waste and storm drainage requirements from a major airport development can be very large. Usually, the inverts of both sewerage systems will fall well below the level of their outfalls into surface rivers and watercourses. In the case of the storm water runoff, this may necessitate the installation of large and expensive pumping facilities, adding to the overall construction cost.

For maximum utilization of the airport, it is essential that the site be as free as possible from poor atmospheric conditions such as fog, haze, industrial smog, and smoke. Fog incidence tends to be predictable and is a function of the degree to which the site is naturally sheltered from atmospheric clearing winds and breezes. Sites close to the ocean and on estuaries are likely to be fog free, whereas sites in natural basins offer less clear conditions.

Availability of Utilities

All airports have the normal commercial utilities requirements: electricity, water, sewers, and telephone; in some cases, natural gas is used for heating.

Some large airports have a substantial worker population in addition to the many transients—for example, more than 50,000 people work at London's Heathrow. In such cases, the demand for utilities may be on the scale of a new town rather than on the scale of more usual commercial developments such as shopping centers. The ideal remoteness of the site to overcome environmental problems may present problems in securing utility services.

Although not strictly a utility, the aviation fuel supply may be considered at this time. The daily usage of aviation fuel at major airports is so great that frequently the fuel is piped in to avoid congestion problems on the access roads and to reduce handling costs.

Land Cost and Availability

The size of the airport site is determined by a number of factors, including the type of aircraft using the site, the altitude of the runways, and the number of runways required, considering both air traffic volume and the requirement of a crosswind runway. Choice of location depends on the developer's ability to assemble sufficient parcels of land at an acceptable cost. In most countries, including the United States, sale of land for public purposes such as airports can be compelled under the laws of eminent domain. However, the planner should look at the pattern of land ownership and should determine which persons and organizations hold title to key pieces of land. Delays in land assembly can be most time-consuming, hence very expensive in terms of overall development costs. Ease of purchase is a positive locational variable, both for immediate land needs and for land required for expansion at an undetermined date.

Overall Evaluation Procedure

Alternate sites must be evaluated with respect to the range of factors discussed earlier. There is a wide divergence of views among planners and decision makers on the best form of evaluation procedure. Most sites are subjected to a traditional cost comparison; that is, costs are computed for land acquisition and easements, site developments, major utilities, foundations, access facilities, and ground travel. More complex cost analyses have been adopted, which additionally attempt to take into account monetary values of environmental costs on surrounding areas in terms of noise, air and water pollution, safety, and difficulty of access to the airport user (8).

The lack of agreement on the social costs of the development of major transport facilities has hindered acceptance of cost-benefit analysis. In general, the inability to associate any cost with some of the quantitative and qualitative factors involved in facility development has meant that these factors have been omitted from the analysis, therefore effectively ignored. Even when some monetary values have been imputed (e.g., in the value of saved travel time), these values have become the subject of impassioned debate.

To overcome the simplistic assumptions necessary to apply cost-benefit analysis (i.e., that all factors can be expressed in monetary terms and that there are definable tradeoffs between decision variables), a range of more complex evaluation procedures has been suggested (9). These procedures include rational systems analysis, cost effectiveness techniques, factor profiles, and planning balance sheets. The last technique named, in which decisions are arrived at on the basis of a mix of quantitative and qualitative factors, appears to be one of the most successful procedures to date.

4.5 AIRPORT LAYOUT PLAN (PHASE III)

The airport layout is likely to consist of a number of drawings that show both existing and proposed facilities in the development of the selected airport site. The proposed facilities may be depicted at the various levels of staged development. Drawings give the scale of development anticipated at each stage but detail the anticipated location in the overall development, including necessary dimensions and clearances. Layout drawings show the configurations of runways, taxiways, and aprons, the position and size of terminal facilities, and the location of runway approach zones. Figure 4.1 illustrates the airport layout plan for a small international airport, indicating current facilities and the ultimate development. Figure 4.2 shows the ultimate layout plan for Kansas City International Airport.

Land Use Plan

The land use plan can be a clear statement of the way in which the airport has been sited and designed, not simply in accordance with local land use plans, but as an integral part of that planning. There should be coordination not only of current and future land uses, but also of planning policies and programs at the local and regional levels. Generally, the airport master plan will include a land use plan for the airport area.

Two levels of land use are generally designated. Within the airport boundary, there is a detailed plan of land use; outside the boundary, land use is depicted at the general level only. Since noise is the major negative effect on the environment, a plan should be made showing noise exposure of the surrounding areas throughout the design period, to clarify the areas of significant environmental impact. The FAA further recommends setting out a plan designating areas where height and hazard zoning ordinances are necessary and suggesting land use zoning in areas where some environmental impact is predicted.

Terminal Area Plans

The FAA recommends that terminal area plans form part of the airport master plan. Under the terms of U.S. legislation, the terminal area includes:

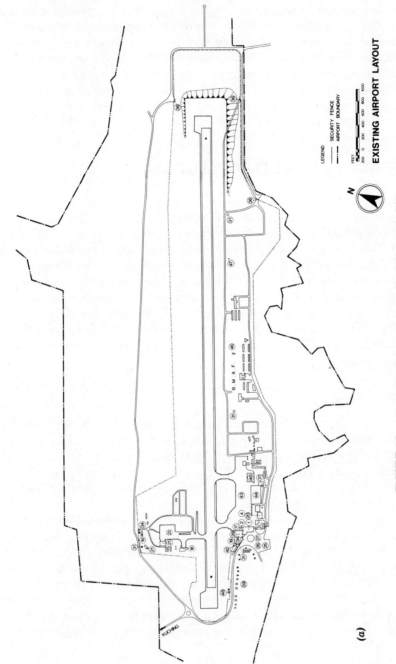

FIGURE 4.1a Example of airport layout plan—Current facilities.

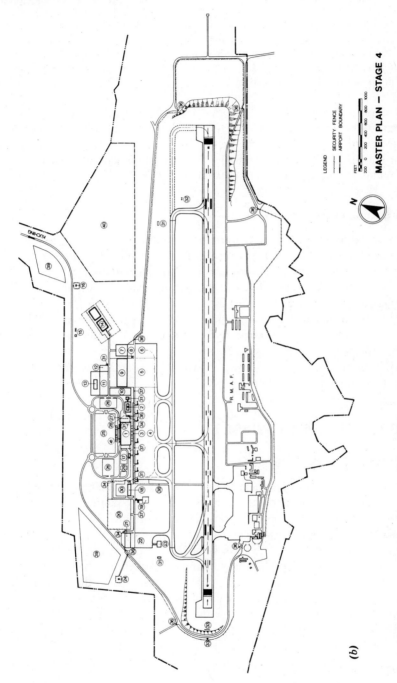

(b)

FIGURE 4.1b Example of airport layout plan—Ultimate development. (*Sources*: Malaysian Associate Architects and Sir Frederick Snow and Partners by permission of Department of Public Works, East Malaysia.)

that area used or intended to be used for such facilities as terminal and cargo buildings, gates, hangars, shops, and other service buildings; automobile parking, airport motels and restaurants, and garages and vehicle service-facilities used in connection with the airport; and entrance and service roads used by the public within the boundaries of the airport.

The location and layout of the terminal facilities should be indicated with conceptual rather than detail drawings to show the accommodation of passenger, baggage, cargo, and vehicle flows. In the context of master planning, it should be clear how the design concept handles the multiple functions of the terminal and provides for the activities anticipated in that area.

Airport Access Plans

The plan must show explicitly the proposed routing of airport access to the central business districts of the areas served and to other major air trip generators; points of connection to regional and metropolitan transportation systems should also be indicated. All available and anticipated modes should appear in the plan, and trip data should be estimated in terms of the volumes of anticipated trips along the principal facilities. Since it is unlikely that ground access will be totally independent of non-airport urban travel, data should be supplied on the non-airport-bound traffic using the same corridors of movement, to place the surface access problem in its proper context as part of the general urban and regional transportation problem.

4.6   FINANCIAL PLAN (PHASE IV)

Development and Costs

Schedules of proposed development and estimates of costs can now be developed on the basis of short, intermediate, and long range aeronautical demand. Normally these are the 5-, 10-, and 20-year planning horizons. Quantity estimates are made from the staged airport layout plans drawn up in Phase III, and from these preliminary cost estimates can be made for the staged developments. Table 4.1 gives a typical preliminary estimate, broken into broad categories of construction and other costs that could be presented in the master plan. Such costs would be based on more refined estimates, but for master planning purposes, it is necessary to present only the broad-based costs, which are needed for economic and financial planning.

Economic Feasibility

Economic feasibility is considered at every stage of the master planning process: in the determination of whether to expand an existing airport or to develop a new site, in the selection of the site itself, and in the choice of design concept

TABLE 4.1   Example of Master Plan Cost Estimates for a Typical
Project with Three-Stage Expansion of Existing Facility

Type of Expenditure	Stage 1 1985–1989	Stage 2 1990–1994	Stage 3 1995–2004
Paving			
Airfield (includes lights)			
Runway	$ 629,370	$ 144,126	$ 1,706,022
Taxiways	1,130,176	631,706	1,610,490
Aprons	274,444	246,677	1,385,100
Roads			
Terminal and service	265,680	243,000	1,127.520
Parking lot	72,900	—	234,900
Buildings			
Expansion of existing terminal	1,814,400	615,600	—
New terminal	—	—	10,206,000
Fire and crash equipment	—	—	162,000
Airport maintenance	—	—	267,300
Relocation			
Fixed base operator	324,000	—	—
Military	64,800	162,000	—
Airport maintenance	56,700	—	—
Miscellaneous			
Electrical	218,700	35,640	136,080
Utilities	72,900	—	324,000
Drainage	48,600	24,300	283,500
Landscaping	—	—	243,000
Fencing	16,200	—	64,800
Site preparation	366,120	217,080	955,800
Total estimate for construction	5,354,990	2,320,129	18,706,512
Legal, administrative, engineering costs	1,147,703	509,715	4,115,433
Total project	6,502,693	2,829,844	22,821,945
Land acquisition	2,612,250	—	—
Total estimated cost	$9,114,943	$2,829,844	$22,821,945

in the access-terminal-airfield system. In each case, preliminary cost elements
must be used to assess capital investments and revenues. In the last phase of
master planning, a final economic evaluation must be made of the 5-, 10-, and
20-year stage plans, to predict whether at each stage the planned development
will be able to produce revenues to cover the annual capital and operating
costs, supplemented as they may be by federal, state, and local subsidies and
grants in aid. In general, revenue comes from user charges, lease rentals, and

concession revenues from the various airport operations. An examination of the estimated contributions enables the planner to determine whether the respective areas would be contributing a proportionate or proper share of costs, according to the policy that is to be adopted.

Investment is either *non-depreciable* or *depreciable*. Non-depreciable investment has an infinite economic life—in other words, it never wears out. Land acquisition is a good example. For items of permanent value, the annual capital costs are simply the interest on the investment. Normally, no interest costs are assumed in the economic analysis for investments using federal grant funds under the Federal Aviation Act of 1958 or the Airport and Airway Development Act of 1970. With investments of a finite economic life or capital that must be repaid in a shorter period, the annual capital costs are the interest plus a depreciation cost. Again, interest and depreciation costs are not computed when federal grant funds are computed. Airport revenues can be estimated to be available from the landing area, the terminal apron, airplane parking areas, the passenger terminal building, public car parking areas, aviation fuel sales, hangars, commercial facilities, concessions, and a variety of minor sources.

Examination of capital costs and revenues will indicate whether the staged development program is realistic; if not, it must be adjusted. In the early days of civil aviation growth there was a tendency to underestimate potential revenues; consequently, development plans were too modest. In the late 1960s, many aviation forecasts were too buoyant, producing development programs that have proved to be financially troublesome to some airports (10).

Financing

Once economic feasibility has been determined, a financial analysis must be made of the forms of capital available for carrying out the development. These include the following:

General obligation bonds.
Revenue bonds.
Private finance.
Financing from specially formed non-profit corporations.
Federal grants.
State and municipal grants.

4.7   MASTER PLANNING ACCORDING TO ICAO GUIDELINES

A planner operating outside the United States is likely to use ICAO Manual procedures or national procedures based on the ICAO manual (11). In general terms, the ICAO procedure is very similar to that recommended by the FAA.*

---

* It is interesting to note that the preface to the ICAO manual states that the material contained in the document does not necessarily reflect the views of the ICAO.

However, since member countries of the organization range from highly industrialized states to quite undeveloped nations, the procedures outlined are less specific with respect to the form of the master plan, the methods of analyzing problems of environmental impact, and the manner in which economic analysis is to be carried out.

The ICAO manual states that the airport master plan is a guide for:

- development of physical facilities on the airport
- development of land uses for areas surrounding the airport
- determination of environmental effects of aerodrome construction and operation
- establishment of airport access requirements.

In addition, the plan can be used to provide guidance on policy and decisions in both the long and short term, to identify potential problems and opportunities, to assist in securing financial aid, to serve as a basis for negotiations between the airport authority and its tenants, and to generate local interest and support. The manual identifies a number of areas that will be included in any master planning activity. These are policy and coordinative planning, economic planning, physical planning, environmental planning, and financial planning. The master planning process itself is made up of a number of defined steps:

1. Preparing a master planning work plan.
2. Inventory and document existing conditions.
3. Forecast future air traffic demand.
4. Determine scale and time phasing of facilities.
5. Evaluate existing and potential constraints.
6. Determine the relative importance of constraints and other considerations.
7. Develop a number of master plan options.
8. Evaluate and screen all plan options.
9. Select most acceptable and appropriate option, refining and modifying it in response to the evaluation process.
10. Prepare master plan documents in final form

The ICAO manual states that the master plan is no more than a guideline that must later be developed into a more detailed implementation program. Table 4.2 outlines the ICAO master planning process.

4.8   DATA REQUIREMENTS FOR MASTER PLANNING

Notwithstanding the method used, all master plans must be founded on assumptions and forecasts built from an extensive and valid data base. The collection and validation of data is therefore an important and time-consuming element of the master planning process. In a master planning exercise, the following data requirements could be expected:

TABLE 4.2 Outline of ICAO Master Planning Process

Planning Step	Description
Preplanning considerations	Coordination, planning procedure, planning organization, goals, and policy objectives.
Forecasting for planning purposes	Requirements, forecasts required, accuracy, methods and principles of forecasting, factors, presentation of forecasts.
Financial arrangements and controls	Capital costs: currency requirements, source of funds, domestic and foreign financing. Operational costs: sources of income. Financial control and accounting.
Site evaluation and selection	Land required, location of potential sites, factors affecting airport location, preliminary study of possible sites, site inspection; operational, social, and cost considerations, environmental study, review of potential sites, outline plans and estimates of costs and revenues, final evaluation.
Runways and taxiways	Dimensions, strength; aircraft characteristics, performance, and runway length; configuration. Airfield capacity.
Aprons	Layout of aprons, size of stands, parking, service, and hangar aprons, holding bays, security, apron accommodations.
Air and ground navigational and traffic control aids	Visual aids, radio navigation aids and their buildings, demarcation of critical areas, air traffic services, search and rescue services, apron control, communications.
Passenger building	Planning principles, airport traffic and service characteristics, factors affecting scale of services to be supplied, capacity and demand. Connection of passenger building to access system, passenger and baggage processing, waiting areas, governmental frontier controls, airside linkages, apron passenger vehicles, transit and transfer passengers, passenger amenities and other passenger building services.
Cargo facilities	Siting, building function and type, apron, facility requirements, access, parking, inspection, and control.
Ground transport and internal airport vehicle circulation and parking	Private and public transport modes, traffic data, internal roadway circulation, curbside, vehicle parking.
Airport operations and support facilities	Administration and maintenance, medical center, ground vehicle fuel stations, generating stations, water supply and sanitation, flight catering, kitchens; meteorological services, aircrew briefing and

TABLE 4.2 (continued)

Planning Step	Description
	reporting, aircraft maintenance, rescue and fire-fighting, general aviation facilities, aircraft fuel facilities.
Security	Airside security: roads, fencing, isolated parking position, security parking area, emergency explosive holding area.
	Landside security: passenger buildings, public storage lockers.

Demand and Traffic

Passengers:

Annual passenger movements over the last ten years;
monthly passenger movements over the last five years;
hourly passenger movements for ten peak days of last five years.

Aircraft:

Annual movements over the last ten years;
monthly movements over the last five years;
hourly movements for ten peak days of the last five years.

Airlines' and ICAO estimates of regional passenger growth both domestic and international.

Current and future aircraft fleet mix over next fifteen years.

Historic patterns of military movements and estimates of growth of these movements if airport is a shared facility.

Schedule patterns of operating airlines.

General socioeconomic data—economic base data on size and projected growth rates in locality and region of airport, including data on population, employment, income, tourism, building activity, retail sales, industrial output, and so on. Current income distribution within city, region, and nation, with projected changes in distribution pattern.

Cost and service levels of competing land (and if applicable, sea) transport modes.

Environmental Data

Local planning regulations.

Local development plans, both detailed and structural, indicating plans for metropolitan and regional development.

Existing land uses and status of development in the airport environs.

Local transportation plans.

Relationship between local transportation plans to national transportation plans and investment strategies at various governmental levels.

Local and national noise regulations, both current and planned.

Physical Data

Description and modal share of existing access modes.

Meteorological data—wind records, rainfall, snow, periods of low visibility.

Topographical details to approximately 30 km (18 miles) around each airport with contours to 10 m at a scale of 1:50,000.

More detailed topography 3–5 km (2–3 miles) outside airport boundary to a contour of approximately 1 m, at a scale of 1:2000.

As built plans of existing facilities with details of ownership.

Detailed breakdown of square footage of existing building space allotted to various functions.

Architectural detail plans of any existing terminal designating usage to various facilities: for example, immigration, customs, departure lounge, check-in, baggage claim, administration, concessions, and so on. Structural details of construction of aprons, taxiways, runways, and major buildings. Evaluation of the strength and surface condition of these structural elements.

Appraisal of the structural soundness of existing buildings plus an indication of structure type (permanent, light construction, or temporary).

Condition and extent of existing drainage and sewerage.

Condition and extent of existing of lighting on runways, taxiways, aprons, and approaches.

Condition and extent of existing markings.

Condition, type, and capability of existing navigation and telecommunication aids.

Data on hazards to aircraft penetrating protected surfaces.

Details of existing services/firefighting/apron services, and so on.

Other necessary physical data including environmental data on flora and fauna.

General

Other transportation and major development plans in the environs of the airport site.

Commercial, tourist, industrial, governmental development plans.

Financial data on existing airport operations.

Aeronautical

Holding stacks, approaches, missed approaches, takeoff, and climbout procedures.

Airways.

Construction

Detail costs of unit prices of construction materials: for example, earth, steel, concrete, and masonry prices. Finish costs.

Equipment costs.

4.9 THE STRUCTURE OF THE MASTER PLAN REPORT

The presentation of the master plan is in the form of a report which describes:

Demand:

Passenger traffic forecasts.
Cargo traffic forecasts.
Air transport movement forecasts.
General aviation and military movement forecasts.
Ground access traffic movements by public and private modes.

Capacity:

The sequenced and staged provision of capacity in accordance with the development of demand. Capacity will be computed for:

    Airside: runways, taxiways, apron, holding areas.
    Terminals: passenger and cargo.
    Landside: access modes and parking.

This section of the report will explain the logic underlying the developments of the selected airside configuration and the reasons for siting the major facilities on the airport.

Cost estimates:

Runways, taxiways, aprons, and holding areas.
Cargo and passenger terminals.
Navaids, control tower.
Utilities and support facilities (meteorological, fire, etc.)
Roads, parking, and other access facilities.

Military areas.

General aviation facilities.

Maintenance areas.

It is usual to provide at least the following drawings:

Orientation plan.

Location plan.

Existing site plan.

Vicinity land use plan.

Regional land use plan.

Ultimate airport land use plan.

Ultimate layout plan.

Staged layout plans.

Location of navaids.

Location of aeronautical protected surfaces.

Access facilities—staged plans.

Drainage, earth-works and landscaping.

Noise contours—staged.

REFERENCES

1. *Airport Master Plans*, FAA Advisory Circular AC 150/5070-6, February 1971.
2. *Guidelines for Airport Spacing and Traffic Pattern Airspace Areas*, FAA Order 7480. 1A, August 1971.
3. *Capacity of Airport Systems in Metropolitan Areas: Methodology and Analysis*, Federal Aviation Administration, FAA/BRD 403.
4. *Objects Affecting Navigable Airspace*, FAR Part 77, 1965 (as amended).
5. *Aerodromes*, Annex 14 to the International Convention on Civil Aviation, 8th Ed., Montreal: International Civil Aviation Organization, 1983.
6. *Airport Planning Manual, Part 2, Land Use and Environmental Control*, Montreal: International Civil Aviation Organization, 1977.
7. *Airport Land Use Compatibility Planning* AC 150/5050-6, Washington D.C.: Department of Transportation, Federal Aviation Administration, 1977.
8. *Commission on the Third London Airport*, London: Her Majesty's Stationery Office, 1970.
9. Paquette, R. J., N. Ashford, and P. H. Wright, *Transportation Engineering*, 2nd Ed., New York: Wiley, 1982.
10. Doganis, R. S., and G. F. Thompson, *The Economics of British Airports*, London: Transport Studies Group, Department of Civil Engineering, Polytechnic of Central London, 1973.
11. *Airport Planning Manual, Part 1, Master Planning*, Montreal: International Civil Aviation Organization, 1977.

5

AIR TRAFFIC CONTROL, LIGHTING, AND SIGNING

5.1 PURPOSE OF AIR TRAFFIC CONTROL

The two factors underlying the need for air traffic control (ATC) are safety and efficiency. The individual user must have enough airspace to avoid the risk of near misses or collisions; but to maintain sufficient capacity of movement in heavily trafficked areas, efficiency demands that the individual use of airspace be minimal within the constraints of safety. Furthermore, any ATC system must consider and balance the needs of all users of airspace: the military, the commercial carriers, and general aviation.

Air traffic control measures were instituted only when it became apparent that there was a necessity for control under traffic conditions having a high probability of human failure. As air traffic activity grows, increasing traffic density and its concomitant problems will undoubtedly necessitate further air traffic regulations and the development of a more sophisticated and extensive system to provide for the safe and efficient movement of all aircraft. The increasing range of aircraft technology will certainly mean that more attention must be given to the allotment of airspace and the compatibility of equipment between air carrier and general aviation aircraft. As the number of general aviation aircraft continues to increase, the range of air carrier technology embraces a great variety of aircraft types, which includes CTOL, VTOL, SST, STOL, and giant conventional subsonic aircraft. The air traffic control system, which must accommodate the wide variety of airspace needs, is responsive in its development to the underlying factors of safety, technology, regulation, and financing.

Formal federal involvement in air traffic began with the Air Commerce Act of 1926, which provided for the establishment, maintenance, and operation of lighted civil airways. Federal rather than state authority governs air traffic control because the implications of air travel are interstate by nature and have no general relation to or respect for state boundaries. In the United States, the

Federal Aviation Administration is the governmental authority responsible for providing control and navigation assistance for the movement of air traffic. One of the major functions of the 1982 Airway and Airport Improvement Act was to provide the FAA with a financial structure that would permit an extensive modernization program for air traffic control in the United States.

5.2   VISUAL FLYING RULES (VFR) AND INSTRUMENT FLYING RULES (IFR)

Air traffic moves under visual flight rules (VFR) or instrument flight rules (IFR), depending on weather conditions as well as on the location and altitudes of flight paths. In general, VFR operations prevail when weather conditions are good enough for the aircraft to be operated by visual reference to the ground and to other aircraft, and when traffic densities are sufficiently low to permit the pilot to depend on vision rather than on instrument readings. IFR conditions exist when the visibility or the ceiling (height of clouds above ground level) falls below that prescribed for VFR flight or when air traffic densities require IFR controlled conditions.

In VFR conditions, there is essentially no en route air traffic control except where prescribed; aircraft fly according to "rules of the road," using designated altitudes for certain headings, and pilots are responsible for maintaining safe distances between their respective aircraft. Positive traffic control is always exercised in IFR conditions and in designated control areas. Responsibility for maintaining safe aircraft separation passes to the air traffic controller. Essentially, the controller follows the IFR procedures, which call for the controlled assignment of specific altitudes and routes, and minimum separation of aircraft flying in the same direction at common altitudes.

5.3   THE U.S. AIRWAYS SYSTEM

Flights from one part of the United States to another are normally channeled along navigational routes that are as well identified as the surface road system. Three separate route systems can be identified: (1) VOR airways,* (2) the Jet route system, and (3) the Area navigation (RNAV) system.

VOR Airway Systems

VOR airways are a low altitude system consisting of airways from 1200 ft above the surface up to, but not including, 18,000 ft above mean sea level (MSL). The extent of the system is indicated in the En Route Low Altitude Charts (1).

---

* VOR = very high frequency, omnidirectional range.

The VOR system, known as the Victor airways, uses an alphanumeric code with V followed by a number (e.g., V21). These airways use only VOR/VORTAC navigational aids (see below). VOR navigation is free from radio static and is easily picked up by the receiver on a line of sight basis; therefore, the range of the ground facility is dependent on aircraft altitude (see Section 5.5). Victor airways are a minimum of 8 nautical mi wide; where the distance between VOR stations is greater than 120 mi, the airway width increases to the envelope encompassed by planes at an angle of 4½° about the centerline joining the two ground stations.

The Jet Route System

Airways from 18,000 ft above mean sea level (MSL) to 45,000 ft (flight level* FL450) designed for aircraft that customarily operate at these altitudes, comprise the jet route system. These routes also operate using VOR ground navigation stations, but the system requires significantly fewer stations, since line of sight operation gives the VORs substantially greater range when dealing with aircraft at high altitudes. The width of the airways of the jet route system is similar to that of the Victor airways. Figure 5.1a shows a portion of a typical Victor airways chart; a jet route chart in the same area appears in Figure 5.1b.

The Area Navigation System (RNAV)

RNAV is a skeletal structure of more than 160 high altitude routes from 18,000 ft MSL to FL450 covering 48 states. Aircraft that are properly equipped and certificated with area navigation equipment may use these routes. Frequently used RNAV routes are published and designated. Below 18,000 ft MSL, RNAV routes are designated in the V700 series with an "R" added to indicate the use of area navigation (e.g., V725R). Above 18,000 ft MSL, the J800 and 900 series is reserved for area navigation routes, also with the R designation (e.g., J814R). Low altitude RNAV routes are planned for flights operating at altitudes below 18,000 ft MSL.

The distinguishing feature of area navigation is the ability to fly over a predetermined track without the need to overfly ground-based navigational facilities. A small airborne computer converts the azimuth and distance to ground VORs into cockpit data indicating whether and by how much the aircraft is deviating from a selected route that is not directly between VORs. The result is much more flexible use of airspace with much less needless congestion on highly trafficked routes. The load on air traffic controllers is substantially lowered in certain cases—for example, when aircraft must be moved off Victor airways to vector around bad weather conditions.

Operation above FL450 is carried out on an individual flight, point to point basis. Navigational guidance is provided on an area basis using the U.S. Series H En Route High Altitude Charts.

* Flight level = altitude above mean sea level ÷ 100 (in feet).

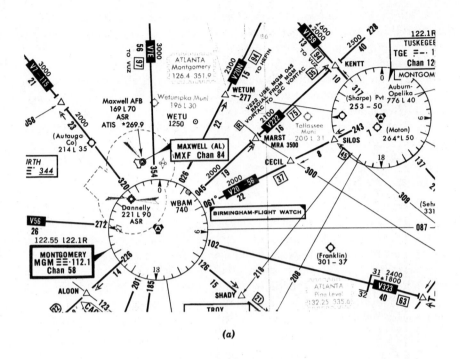

(a)

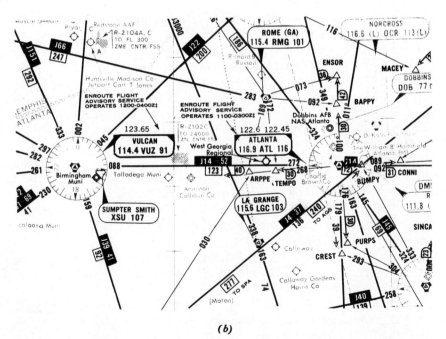

(b)

FIGURE 5.1 (a) Portion of a Victor airways chart. (*Source:* FAA.) (b) Portion of a jet route chart. (*Source:* FAA.)

5.4 CONTROLLED AND UNCONTROLLED AIRSPACE

Airspace is both controlled and uncontrolled: in controlled airspace, flight is conducted in accordance with promulgated altitude and heading combinations (Figure 5.2). Controlled airspace, extending upward from 700 ft above ground level (AGL), and, in a few areas from 1200 AGL, exists in almost all areas of the contiguous United States, where Control Areas and Transition Areas have been designated. In addition, controlled airspace extends upward from the ground in areas immediately surrounding an airport in Control Zones. The nature and variety of demand points up the need for shared airspace. Increased communications have aided and will become more important as they link computers and automatic air traffic control systems. To achieve greater airspace utilization and safety, an area above 14,500 ft MSL has been designated as a Continental Control Area. Aircraft flying above this altitude are higher performance aircraft, usually jet powered. In Positive Control Areas, above 18,000

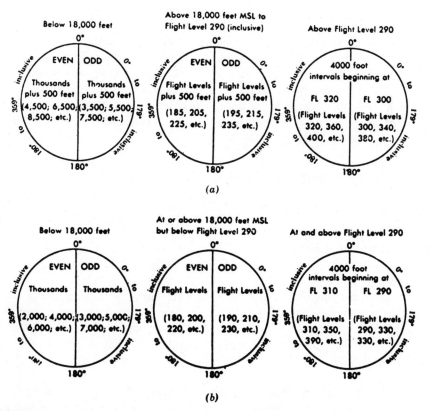

FIGURE 5.2   IFR and VFR altitudes and flight levels. (a) Under VFR at 3,000 ft or more above surface, controlled and uncontrolled airspace. (b) Under IFR, outside controlled airspace. (*Source:* Reference 2.)

ft MSL, all aircraft are controlled by continuous surveillance and are required to have certain equipment to permit the higher aircraft densities of the higher performance aircraft.

Terminal Control Areas, such as the one shown in Figure 5.6, are designated around major aviation hub areas to impose special operating requirements on all flights in this airspace. In addition, special purpose areas are delineated, either to prohibit or to caution flight operations. These are designated respectively as Restricted Areas, such as weapons ranges, and Warning Areas, such as areas of intense air traffic or student pilot training.

In the end it is public interest in safety and efficiency that causes regulation of the aeronautical use of space; in the United States, this results in the designation and use of positive air traffic control, in accordance with IFR flight rules in the Continental Control Area and in transition areas at airports, as well as at other designated areas.

5.5 NAVIGATIONAL AIDS

As air traffic activity continues to grow, there is an increasing need for navigational aids to narrow the limits of navigational error in horizontal or vertical separation. At low traffic densities the degree of navigational sophistication required is generally quite low, but as air traffic congestion grows, more navigational aids are needed to give all-weather operation that is highly reliable and safe. Navigational aids that are either ground based or airborne may be conveniently functionally classified as en route navigation aids and terminal area navigation and landing aids.

En Route Air Navigation Aids (2)

A number of locational aids, operating outside terminal areas, permit in-flight aircraft to achieve accurate navigation using instruments only.

Non-Directional Radio Beacon (NDB).   The NDB is a general purpose, low or medium frequency radio beacon on which an aircraft equipped with a loop antenna can home in or can determine his bearing relative to the sender. Operating in the frequency band 200–425 kHz, these facilities transmit with 1020 Hz modulation, which is keyed with a continuous three letter code to provide identification, except during voice transmission. NDBs are subject to atmospheric noise and communications interference, but can be useful for longer ranges (200 mi).

Very High Frequency Omnidirectional Range (VOR).   VOR navigation uses a very high frequency, day-night, all-weather, static-free radio transmitter, operating within the 108.0–117.95 MHz frequency band with a power output matched to the operational service area. Since the units are limited to line of sight reception, the range is dependent on aircraft altitude. Reception at an altitude of 1000 ft is limited to approximately 45 mi, but the range increases with altitude. High altitude aircraft can suffer mutual VOR interference (multiple reception of facilities with similar frequencies), because of the greatly increased horizon of the aircraft. VOR facilities form the basis of the Victor airways, with stations set along the airways and at intersections. The accuracy of the indicated course alignment is usually excellent—generally on the order of $\pm 1°$.

Distance Measuring Equipment (DME).   The slant range to the DME facility is measured by a device located at the VOR site. Its maximum range is 199 mi, using the very high frequency range (962–1213 MHz) with line of sight operation, and subject to the same performance criteria as VOR. The DME operates by sending out paired pulses at a specific spacing from the aircraft; these pulses are received by a transponder at the ground VOR station. The ground station transmits paired impulses back to the aircraft at the same pulse spacing, but at a different frequency. The time between signal transmission and signal reception is measured by the airborne DME unit, and the slant distance in nautical miles is computed and displayed. The equipment is accurate to 0.5 mi or 3% of the distance, whichever is greater.

Tactical Air Navigation (TACAN) and VHF Omnidirectional Range/Tactical Air Navigation (VORTAC).   These navigational aids represent the incorporation of VOR and DME functions into a single channelized system utilizing frequencies in the ultra-high frequency range. Although the technical principles of operation of TACAN are quite different from those of VOR-DME, from the pilot's viewpoint, the outputs or information received are similar. Operating in conjunction with fixed or mobile ground transmitting equipment, the airborne unit translates a UHF pulse into a visual presentation of both azimuth and distance information. TACAN is independent of conventional VOR facilities but is similarly constrained to line of sight operation.

VORTAC is a combined facility composed of two different components, VOR and TACAN. It has a triple output: VOR azimuth, TACAN azimuth, and range. Although it consists of more than one component, operating at more than one frequency, VORTAC is considered to be an integrated navigational unit providing three simultaneous information outputs. The jet route high altitude airways have been created for use with VORTAC stations separated by long distances.

In 1983, the FAA installed the first of 950 new solid state VORTACs to be located in the United States, replacing existing vacuum tube equipment.

Marker Beacons.   Marker beacons identify a specific location in airspace along an airway, by means of a 75 MHz directional signal, which transmits to aircraft flying overhead. They are used to determine the exact location on a given course. Markers are primarily used in instrument approaches or departure procedures, as holding fixes or position reporting points, in conjunction with en route navigational aids or instrument landing systems.

Communications (3).   Communications are accomplished by radio receivers and transmitters located both in the aircraft and on the ground. Civilian aircraft primarily use VHF radio ranges, whereas military aircraft use UHF radio ranges. Air-to-ground communications are necessary to enable pilots to receive flight instructions as they progress along the airways to their destinations if not on flight plans, to obtain reports of weather ahead, and to alter flight planning as required.

Air Route Surveillance Radar.   This is a system of long range radar designed to provide a display of aircraft operating over a large area, especially en route aircraft flying the airways. Scanning through a 360° azimuth, the equipment provides the ground-based air traffic controller with information on the azimuth and distance position of each aircraft in the airway. Used either in conjunction with other navigational equipment or separately, the radar can be employed to locate with precision an aircraft's position, without reliance on the accuracy of the pilot's reporting. Consequently there is a substantial reduction in the frequency of voice communication necessary between the controller and the pilot. These radars are being installed on a nationwide basis with a range of 200 mi; they will eventually produce an increase in airways' capacity by permitting a reduction in separations between aircraft flying at the same altitude.

Air Traffic Control Radar Beacon System (ATCRBS).   ATCRBS is a system having three main components: *interrogator*, *transponder*, and *radarscope*. This system is frequently termed *secondary* surveillance radar. Whereas primary radar, a passive system, relies on the bouncing back of the transmitted radar signal, the ATCRBS is an active system in which the interrogator transmits, in synchronism with primary radar, discrete radio signals requesting all transponders on that mode to reply. The airborne radar beacon (transponder) receives the signal from the interrogator and replies with a specific coded pulse group signal, which is much stronger than the primary radar return. The radarscope displays the targets, differentiating between coded aircraft and ordinary primary radar targets (Figure 5.3). Radarscopes are also equipped to indicate aircraft identification and altitude on an alphanumeric display. The advantage is obvious; the controller is able to differentiate between aircraft rapidly and with certainty, and to be assured of correct identification of equipped aircraft in the airspace under surveillance.

Terminal Area Navigation and Landing Aids

In the immediate area of the terminal, special aids are necessary to assist in the operations of landing and takeoff, and to provide safe navigation in the crowded air space.

AIR NAVIGATION RADIO AIDS

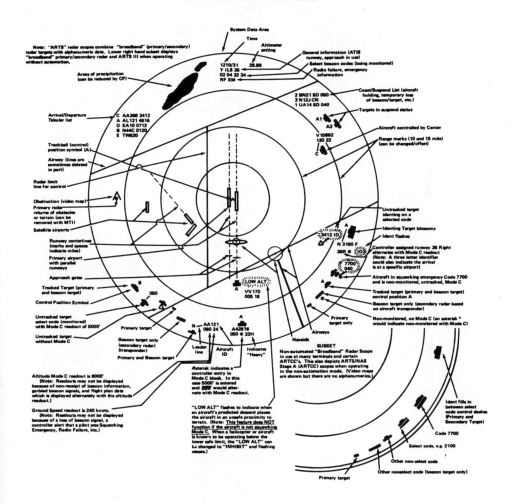

FIGURE 5.3 Controller's secondary surveillance radarscope display. (*Source:* Reference 2.)

Instrument Landing System (ILS). ILS is an approach and landing aid designed to identify an approach path for exact alignment and descent of an aircraft making a landing. It is the most commonly used system for instrument landings. Functionally, the system is composed of three parts:

1. *Guidance Information.* Localizer, glide slope.
2. *Range Information.* Marker beacons.
3. *Visual Information.* Approach lights, touchdown zone and centerline lights, runway lights.

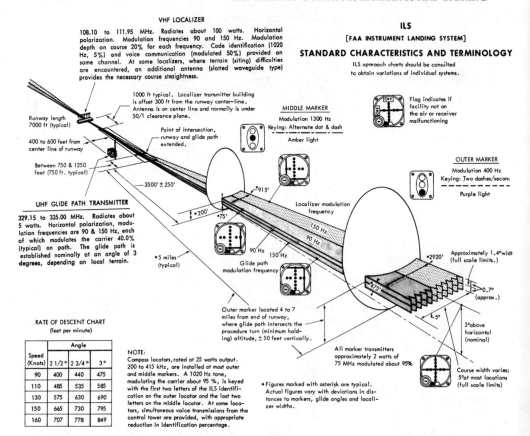

FIGURE 5.4 FAA instrument landing system. (*Source:* Reference 2.)

Figure 5.4 depicts the layout of the non-visual elements of the ILS system. The ground equipment consists of two highly directional transmitting systems and at least two marker beacons. Guidance information is provided in the cockpit by an adaptation of the VOR equipment.

The *localizer* transmitter is located typically 1000 ft beyond the end of the runway; it emits signals that give the pilot course guidance to the runway centerline. Deviation to the left or right of the extended centerline is indicated on the VOR receiver display, as shown in Figure 5.4. The UHF glide slope transmitter is normally set back 750 ft from the runway threshold, usually offset at least 400 ft from the runway centerline. The directional beam provides a radio signal indicating the glide slope; deviation above or below this slope can be displayed on the cockpit VOR receiver.

To help the pilot further on an ILS approach, two low power fan markers furnish range information, to indicate how far along the approach path the aircraft has progressed. The glide path is normally adjusted to 3° above horizontal so that it intersects the middle marker (MM) at 200 ft altitude, about 3500 ft from the threshold. The outer marker (OM) is approximately 5 mi from the threshold, at which point the glide path is 1400 ft above the threshold altitude. Thus a pilot using the ILS approach has continuous information on position, relative to the correct glide path and the extension of the runway centerline. The pilot is further alerted by visual signals when passing over first the outer marker and the middle marker. On some ILS systems (ICAO categories II and III: see below), there is an inner marker (IM) close to the threshold.

The ICAO promulgates a number of categories into which a designated ILS at an airport is assigned, according to the conditions of runway visual range (RVR) and decision height at which a landing may be made with that particular ILS system. It is not possible to categorize a facility until equipment has been installed and is operating. The level of categorization is dependent on three principal factors: the quality of signal produced by the navigation equipment, the monitoring and standby arrangements, and the environmental conditions imposed on the equipment in general by the terrain and other surroundings. Table 5.1 shows the ICAO and FAA categories in terms of RVR and decision heights.

Precision Approach Radar (PAR). Frequently called ground-controlled approach (GCA), PAR is independent of airborne navigation equipment. PAR equipment is located on the ground adjacent to the runway. These facilities may be used as a primary landing aid or, as frequently, in conjunction with ILS. Two antennas are used, one scanning the vertical plane, the other the horizontal. The PAR radarscope gives the controller a picture of the descending aircraft in azimuth, distance, and elevation, permitting an accurate determination of the aircraft's alignment relative to the runway centerline and the glide slope. Range is limited to 10 mi, azimuth to 20°, and elevation to 7°. Therefore, the PAR equipment can be used only on the final approach area, where corrections to the approach are given to the pilot by voice communication from the monitoring air traffic controller.

TABLE 5.1   Visibility Minima by ILS Categories

ILS Category (CAT)	Lowest Minima	
	RVR	Decision Height
Precision CAT I	FAA: 1800 ft (600 m)	200 ft (60 m)
	ICAO: 2500 ft (800 m)	
Precision CAT II	1200 ft (400 m)	100 ft (30 m)
Precision CAT IIIa	700 ft (200 m)	0 ft (0 m)
Precision CAT IIIb	150 ft (50 m)	0 ft (0 m)
Precision CAT IIIc	0 (0 m)	0 ft (0 m)

Source: ICAO and FAA.

Airport Surveillance Radar (ASR).   Airport tower operators receive their terminal area traffic control and aircraft location information from ASR. Within a range of 30 to 60 mi ASR provides information for aircraft transiting from the airways to holding areas through to the final approach. It is a two-dimensional aid and does not give information on aircraft altitude. Surveillance radars scan through a full 360° of azimuth, presenting target information on radar displays in the control tower or the air traffic control center. The equipment is used in conjunction with other navigational aids for instrument approaches.

Airport Surface Detection Equipment (ASDE).   ASDE is a specially designed radar system for use at large, high density airports to aid controllers in the safe maneuvering of taxiing aircraft that may be difficult to see and identify because of airport configuration, aircraft size, or poor visibility conditions. At the moment, ASDE is available only at a very few of the world's busier airports.

Instrument Approach Procedures and Standard Instrument Departures.   Though these are not navigational aids, they afford the means of using the en route as well as the terminal area navigational aids. They are not only indispensable to IFR landing approaches, but are also helpful to the VFR pilot landing at an unfamiliar airport. Instrument approach charts diagram every airport in the country that has some kind of instrument landing aid installation (NDB, VOR, DME, TACAN, VORTAC, PAR/ASR, ILS, etc.).

The charts indicate prescribed instrument approach procedures from a distance of about 25 mi from the airport, and present all related data such as airport elevation, obstructions, navigational aid locations, and procedural turns. Each recommended procedure—and even a simple airport has several—is designed for use with a specific type of navigational aid. The pilot's choice of procedure depends on instrumentation and prevailing weather conditions. To aid pilots on takeoff, standard instrument departures (SID) have been developed to facilitate the transition between takeoff and en route operation, alleviating the need for extensive oral communication between controllers and pilots.

Microwave Landing Systems (MLS).   The ILS system, developed mainly by the military, was adopted as a standard approach aid by the ICAO in 1947. It is not, however, without problems. Very large aerial arrays are required to radiate sufficiently narrow beams at the wavelengths employed. Also, the signals from both the glide slope and localizer antennas are affected by the movement of vehicles and taxiing aircraft in their vicinity. Sharp variations in terrain topography and the presence of buildings near the antennas also create difficulties with the signals, which are at their best when reflected from a smooth, featureless ground plane. Consequently, it cannot be guaranteed that a system will reach a required level of performance; exact categorization depends on *in situ* testing of installed equipment.

Possibly more serious than the readily apparent limitations imposed by terrain and buildings is the inherent limitation of the system itself, which can

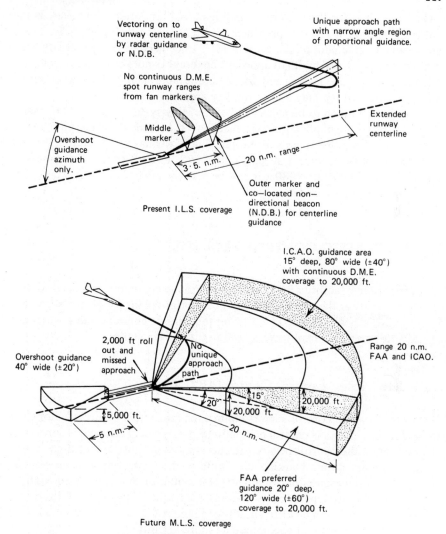

Vectoring on to
runway centerline
by radar guidance
or N.D.B.

Unique approach path
with narrow angle region
of proportional guidance.

No continuous D.M.E.
spot runway ranges
from fan markers.

Extended
runway
centerline

Middle
marker

Overshoot
guidance
azimuth
only.

3·5. n.m.   20 n.m. range

Outer marker and
co—located non—
directional beacon
(N.D.B.) for centerline
guidance

Present I.L.S. coverage

I.C.A.O. guidance area
15° deep, 80° wide (±40°)
with continuous D.M.E.
coverage to 20,000 ft.

2,000 ft roll
out and
missed
approach

No
unique
approach
path

Overshoot guidance
40° wide (±20°)

Range 20 n.m.
FAA and ICAO.

15°

20°   20,000 ft.

20°   20,000 ft.

5,000 ft.

5 n.m.

20 n.m.

FAA preferred
guidance 20° deep,
120° wide (±60°)
coverage to 20,000 ft.

Future M.L.S. coverage

FIGURE 5.5   MLS landing system.

give guidance along one alignment only, so that all aircraft must align themselves
with the runway axis from many miles out. This forces them to form a single
"queue" to the final approach, with a corresponding restriction on landing
rates.

Microwave landing systems, which overcome most of the problems associated
with ILS, are at the testing stage. The much higher frequencies would allow
the use of smaller transmitting aerials; and with much relaxed restrictions on
beam forming and propagation, constraints now imposed by terrain, building,
and ground activity would be eliminated. Equally important is the continuous
information on distance, absent in the ILS system, which gives only point
locations over the markers. MLS systems with continuous information to the

cockpit are ideal for "hands-off" landings. Also important, however, is the multipath approach facility provided by MLS systems (Figure 5.5). Since international agreement on the form of MLS to be used has only recently been reached, the depth and width of approach coverage is not yet known. However, it is clear that there is no need for a unique approach path. There can be multiple paths, which may add to runway approach capacity.

There is still much to be achieved before MLS systems can be universally adopted. Clearly the implications of a changeover, not only of ground equipment, but of airborne facilities, are substantial. The ICAO has indicated that present ILS systems will be current at least until 1995. Even if some MLS facilities are introduced in the late 1980s, it will be many years before the full potential of this form of approach aid is achieved.

5.6   AIR TRAFFIC CONTROL FACILITIES

Air traffic control facilities are the basis for ground communication and control of aircraft, and for the relay and clearance of flight plans for air traffic. There are four basic types of manned facility: air route traffic control centers, approach controls, air traffic control towers, and flight service stations.

Air Route Traffic Control Center (ARTCC)

The air route traffic control centers control the movement of aircraft along the airways; each center has control of a definite geographical area and is concerned primarily with the control of aircraft operating under instrument flight rules. At the boundary points marking the limits of the control area of the center, the aircraft is released either to an adjacent center or to an approach control. At present, aircraft separation is maintained primarily by radar. With radar, off-airways vectors can be utilized, allowing the ARTCCs to maintain positive control of the aircraft and accommodate more aircraft.

Each ARTCC is broken down into sectors to increase the efficiency of operation. Sectors are smaller geographic areas, and air traffic is monitored in each sector by remote radar units at that geographic location. Aircraft flight plans are transferred between sectors within a single air route traffic control center and between ARTCCs when center boundaries are crossed.

With continuous improvement of communications, it has been possible to reduce the number of these centers by enlarging their areas of responsibility. Increases in aircraft speed have also contributed to this reduction. Jets were found to be passing through control areas in half the time that had been required for piston aircraft. This general speeding up has produced the need for control coordination at a flow control center, located in Washington, D.C., during periods of very heavy traffic.

Approach Control

Approach control is responsible for handling all instrument flight within its area of responsibility, which is from the boundary of the airport traffic control tower area to the area of jurisdiction of ARTCC. Approach control, which may operate over a terminal area containing one or more airports, exercises

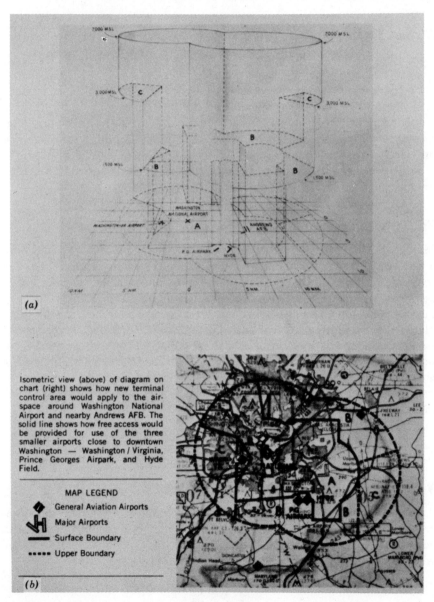

Isometric view (above) of diagram on chart (right) shows how new terminal control area would apply to the airspace around Washington National Airport and nearby Andrews AFB. The solid line shows how free access would be provided for use of the three smaller airports close to downtown Washington — Washington / Virginia, Prince Georges Airpark, and Hyde Field.

MAP LEGEND

◆ General Aviation Airports

⚓ Major Airports

▬ Surface Boundary

▪▪▪▪▪ Upper Boundary

(b)

FIGURE 5.6 Example of a terminal control area at a major hub. (a) Perspective view. (b) Terminal control area in vicinity of Washington D.C. (*Source:* FAA, Aviation News.)

control over all traffic in the area, sequencing aircraft from the holding areas into the final approach. At about 5 mi from the threshold, control is handed over to the airport traffic control tower. Around major aviation hubs, terminal control areas (TCAs) have been designated to impose special operating requirements on all flights in this airspace. Figure 5.6 indicates the extent of the terminal control area in Washington, D.C.

Airport Traffic Control Towers

Control on the final approach, which is usually considered to be the last 5 mi, emanates from the airport traffic control tower. In many cases, the control tower has the dual function of ensuring separation of IFR aircraft in the terminal area (approach control) and monitoring the final approach. Control towers without approach control facilities accept aircraft from approach control after they have started their landing approach. It is normal for the control tower to provide the air traffic control function over a radius of 5 to 15 mi from the airport, the distance depending on adjacent control facilities and utilization of adjacent airspace.

Flight Service Stations

More than 300 flight service stations are located along the airways. They have a variety of functions, including relaying traffic control messages between en route aircraft and the ARTCCs; briefing pilots on weather, airports out of commission, and changes in procedures before and during flights; locating missing VFR aircraft and helping lost aircraft; accepting and closing flight plans; and monitoring navigational aids. At some locations, flight service stations offer specialized services such as taking weather observations, administering written examinations to pilots, and advising customs and immigration authorities of transborder flights. To improve the services and to cut down on manpower requirements, flight service stations in the United States are becoming increasingly automated.

5.7   AIRPORT LIGHTING

Visual Approach Slope Indicator System

An important visual aid to final approach to the runway threshold is the visual approach slope indicator system (VASIS),* which is frequently supplied in addition to other visual and non-visual approach aids. VASIS is usually installed where one or more of the following conditions exist (4):

---

* In FAA literature these systems bear the reference acronym VASI.

1. The runway is used by turbojet aircraft.
2. The pilot may have difficulty in judging the final approach because of inadequate visual reference over water or featureless terrain, or because of deceptive surrounding terrain or misleading runway slopes.
3. There are serious hazards in the approach area that would endanger the aircraft if it sank below the normal approach path.
4. Serious hazard would occur in the event of undershooting or overshooting.
5. Turbulence is found to exist because of terrain or meteorological conditions.

A VASIS installation basically consists of three wing bars of lights on either side of the runway. Figure 5.7a gives the locations of these bars: one set 500 ft from the runway end (downwind bars) and a second set of bars 1200 ft from the runway end (upwind bars). Each light bar in the system produces a split beam of light; the upper segment is white and the lower segment red. If the aircraft is above the glide path on approach, the pilot sees both light bar sets white; if the aircraft is too low, both sets appear red. While on the glide path, the upwind bar appears red and the downwind bar white. A number of different configurations of VASIS-type systems are recognized by the FAA and the ICAO.

A variation of the basic VASIS configuration is necessary for large aircraft such as the 747 or the Concorde. VASIS gives an insufficient margin of safety for undershoot because of the great distance between the pilot's eye and the main landing gear in the approach; thus the three-bar VASIS configuration (Figure 5.7b) is used. Pilots of large aircraft ignore the downwind bar and are guided by the center and upwind bars only; small aircraft can use either the upwind-center or center-downwind combination.

A more elaborate visual system is provided by the T-VASIS configuration (Figure 5.7c), consisting of one wing bar on either side of the runway, 920 ft from the threshold (4). Six "fly up" and six "fly down" lights are located either side of the runway. When the pilot is above the glide slope, the wing bar appears white, and the higher the aircraft the more fly down units are seen.

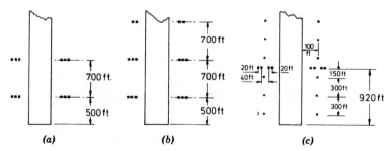

FIGURE 5.7 (a) Layout of a VASIS system. (b) Layout of a three-bar VASIS system. (c) Layout of a T-VASIS system. (*Source:* Reference 4.)

On the correct approach slope, the pilot sees only the white wing bar. Below the correct approach path, the wing bar is white and the fly up units appear white. The more fly ups that are visible, the lower the approach. When the aircraft is well below the correct approach slope, the wing bar and all fly up units appear red. Figure 5.8 shows the arrangement of the split light beams for three-bar VASIS and T-VASIS.

Precision Approach Path Indicator System. Although VASIS AND T-VASIS gives pilots considerable visual assistance on final approach, experience indicates that they are not without criticism. VASIS especially tends to give rise to an oscillatory approach as the pilot moves between the upper and lower limiting approach planes. Both VASIS and T-VASIS are imprecise below 60 m (200 ft), and are not suitable for a nonstandard approach. The three-bar VASIS has an approach corridor which is 20 ft steeper than the lower corridor, and both two and three bar configurations require extensive maintenance and flight checking to keep them operational. Also, in bright sunlight, the pink transition zone is difficult to differentiate from red. All these factors tend to

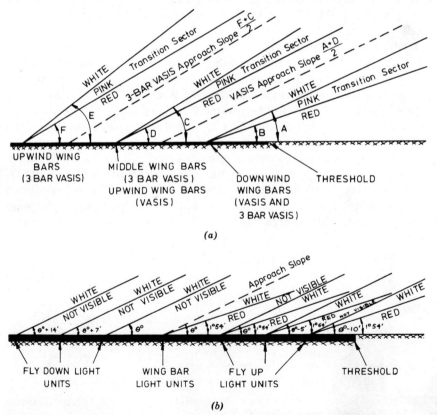

FIGURE 5.8 Light beams and angle of elevation settings. (a) VASIS and three-bar AVASIS. (b) T-VASIS. (*Source:* Reference 4.)

result in a large touchdown scatter. T-VASIS overcomes some of the problems of VASIS; for example, T-VASIS is more suited to multipath approaches and does not rely on color change except in the case of severe underflying. However, it is more complex to site and maintain. It is also important to note that there is no failsafe indication if the downwind "fly-up" lights fail.

The PAPI system shown in Figure 5.9 overcomes most of these disadvantages. It is a two-color light system using sealed units, giving a bicolored split beam: white above, red below. These sealed units are much more easily sited, set, and maintained, and are capable of multipath interpretation. The units are high powered and visible for up to 7 km from the threshold. The approach has been found under tests in the United States, Great Britain, France, and Russia to be more precise and more flexible than VASIS. PAPI systems are expected to replace VASIS at large airports in the late 1980s and early 1990s.

Runway End Identifier Lights (REIL)

Sometimes lights are placed at runway ends to assist in the rapid and positive identification of the approach end of the runway. The system consists of two synchronized flashing lights, one at each end of the runway threshold. Not normally provided where sequenced flashers are incorporated in the approach lighting system, REIL systems are used to distinguish the threshold in locations characterized by numerous ground lights such as neon signs and other lights that could confuse or distract the pilot.

Approach Lighting Systems (ALS) (4, 5)

Approach lighting systems are used in the vicinity of the runway threshold as adjuncts to electronic aids to navigation for the final portions of IFR precision and nonprecision approaches, and as visual guides for night flying during VFR conditions. The approach lighting system supplies the pilot with visual cues relative to aircraft alignment, roll, horizon, height, and position with respect to the threshold. Since the use of lighting systems relies on the brain's rapid action on visual information leading to decision and action, a visual system is ideal for guidance during the last few critical seconds of movement down the glide path.

Approach light systems have been developed on the basis of the glide path angle, visual range, cockpit cutoff angle, and aircraft landing speeds. It is essential that pilots be able to identify ALS and to interpret the system without confusion. Thus, approach lighting systems have been standardized internationally so that longitudinal rows of lights indicate the extended alignment of the runway, with transverse crossbars of lights at standard distances from the threshold for roll and position guidance. In most aspects, the U.S. approach lighting systems are virtually identical to ICAO standards; where differences occur they are of minimal importance.

Approach lighting systems are classified under two basic categories: high intensity systems and medium intensity systems.

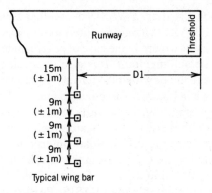

Typical wing bar

Indications to pilot:

a) The distance D_1 shall ensure that the lowest height at which a pilot will see a correct approach path indication will give for the most demanding aircraft a wheel clearance over the threshold of not less than:

   1) 9 m where the code number is 3 or 4; and

   2) 3 m or the aircraft eye-to-wheel height in the approach attitude, whichever is the greater, where the code number is 1 or 2.

b) In addition, when the runway is equipped with an ILS, to make the visual and nonvisual glide paths compatible, the distance D_1 shall:

   1) equal the distance between the threshold and the effective origin of the ILS glide path where the code number is 1, 2 or 3; or

   2) be at least equal to, but not more than 120 m greater than, the distance between the threshold and the effective origin of the ILS glide path where the code number is 4.

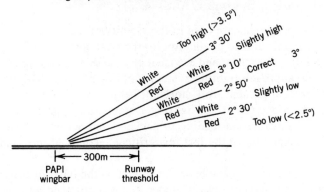

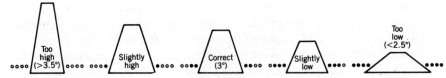

FIGURE 5.9 PAPI—location of lights and visual indication to pilot.

124

FAA High Intensity Systems.   Designed for operation with ILS approaches categories I, II, and III, the FAA high intensity systems come in two standard layouts (Figure 5.10).

1. *ALSF-II.*   This 3000 ft high intensity ALS is composed of barrettes of five white lights along the extended runway centerline, with sequenced flashing lights on the outer 2000 ft centerline. The effect of the bright sequenced flashers gives the appearance of a fast moving ball of light traveling toward the runway. The inner 1000 ft of the approach is additionally lit by barrettes of red lights on either side of the centerline, with crossbars of white lights at 1000 and 500 ft from the threshold. The threshold itself is marked by a threshold bar of green lights. This

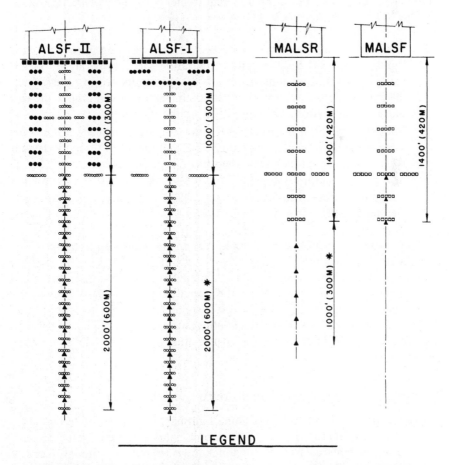

FIGURE 5.10   FAA approach light systems. (*Source:* Reference 5.)

configuration also conforms to ICAO standards for category II and III approach instrument runways.

2. *ALSF-I.*   These configurations are used for category I approach runways. U.S. standards state that where glide path angles exceed 2.75°, the length of the configuration is 2400 ft only, with 3000 ft being used only for lower glide slope angles. To conform with the standard ICAO requirements, 3000 ft configurations are specified at a number of U.S. airports that serve international carriers.

FAA Medium Intensity Systems.   Three types of medium intensity ALS are specified for U.S. airports; MALSR, MALSF, and MALS configurations. These systems, which are used mainly for utility airports catering to general aviation aircraft, meet the minimum requirements of the *Simple Approach Lighting System* specified by ICAO.

1. *MALSR.*   A medium intensity ALS with runway alignment indicator lights. It is the U.S. standard configuration for ILS operations during category I visibility minima. Eight flashing units are installed along the extended runway centerline, at 200 ft spacings extending to the end of the configuration, from 1400 ft from the threshold.

2. *MALSF.*   Medium intensity ALS with sequenced flashers at the outer three barrettes of centerline lights. This and the MALSR configuration is used where approach area identification problems exist.

3. *MALS.*   A medium intensity ALS similar to MALSF, except for the absence of sequenced flashing lights. This is the simplest of the U.S. standard configurations.

Where airports must be designed with "economy approach lighting aids," the FAA recommends the use of MALS or MALSF.

Another system used widely in the United Kingdom, Europe, and some other parts of the world, particularly those that have traditionally been in the British sphere of influence, is the Calvert system. This system is distinguished by six transverse lines of lights of variable length at right angles to the axis of approach. The length of the transverse bars diminishes as the pilot approaches the threshold.

Runway Centerline and Touchdown Zone Lighting

Runway centerline and touchdown zone lighting systems facilitate landings, rollouts, and takeoffs (6). The touchdown zone lights are primarily for landing, and centerline lights assist in after touchdown rollout and furnish primary takeoff guidance. Both systems are designed for use in conjunction with the electronic precision aids and the standard approach lighting systems under limited visibility.

Runway Centerline Lighting. Runway centerline lights are semiflush units set into the pavement and offset by a maximum of 2 ft to clear centerline paint marking. Centerline lights are white, except for the last 3000 ft. From 3000 to 1000 ft from the runway end, the lights are alternately red and white; they are red for the final 1000 ft. All lights are bi-directional, therefore red lights in the 3000 ft zone show white toward the runway end for approaches from the other direction. Light spacing is set at 50 ft centers.

ICAO requirements for centerline lights are generally similar to those of the FAA. Centerline lights are required for precision runways categories II or III and are recommended for category I and other runways with specified visibility operational requirements. Spacing is specified at 50 ft for category III runways and permitted at 100 ft centers for others.

To prevent pilots from losing orientation after passing over the threshold bar, airports install touchdown zone lighting. For example, if an aircraft were still a substantial height above an airport that did not have transverse bars, the pilot would lack roll guidance, given only the longitudinal runway edge lights. Added to this would be a "black hole" effect after passing out of the zone of high intensity approach and threshold lighting. Flush-mounted transverse pavement light bars for the first 3000 ft of the runway ensure continuous visual roll guidance. Rows of light bars are set symmetrically about the centerline, each bar consisting of three unidirectional lights, the first row mounted 100 ft from the threshold. A standard FAA touchdown zone configuration appears in Figure 5.11. ICAO requirements are again generally similar to those of the FAA, except that the maximum bar spacing is set at 100 ft for category II and III runways only. For other installations this dimension is merely advisory.

Runway Edge, Threshold, and Runway End Lighting (7)

Lighting at the runway edges gives pilots locational information in both the landing and takeoff operations. The FAA specifies three types of runway edge

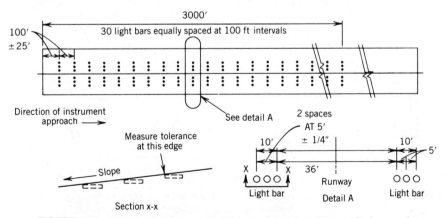

FIGURE 5.11 FAA touchdown zone lighting configuration. (*Source:* Reference 6.)

lighting: low, medium, and high intensity. Low intensity lights are intended for use on VFR airports having no planned approach procedures. Medium intensity edge lights are used on runways having a nonprecision IFR procedure for circling or straight-in approaches. High intensity edge lights are used on runways with IFR approach procedures.

Edge lights are white, except that the last 2000 ft of an instrument runway has bi-directional yellow/white lights, with the yellow pointing toward a departing pilot, indicating a caution zone. The FAA requires a maximum spacing of 200 ft, each unit located not more than 10 ft from the runway edge. ICAO requirements are less stringent, permitting spacing up to 100 m on noninstrument runways. Edge lights are normally elevated single lights, although semi-flush installations are permitted. Semi-flush units are installed at the intersections of runways and taxiways.

Bi-directional lights at the runway ends indicate red in the direction of the runway and green in the direction of the approach. Figure 5.12 shows an arrangement for a medium intensity edge lighting system. For noninstrument runways, six bi-directional threshold lights are used; for an instrument runway, eight lights are used. For category I and greater precision runways, the threshold bar is a continuous line of green lights in the direction of the approach; some of the lights are bi-directional red to indicate the runway end to aircraft on rollout.

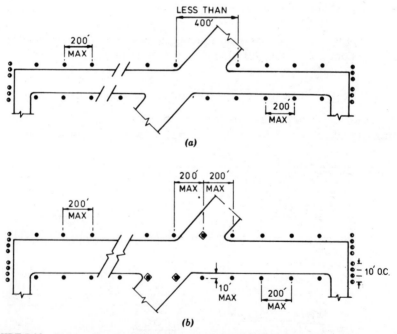

FIGURE 5.12 FAA medium intensity runway and threshold lighting system: solid circles 360° white, except for last 2,000 ft of the instrument runway; half solid circles, red 180°, green 180°; circle in square, semi-flush bidirectional. (a) Application of single elevated lights. (b) Application of single elevated lights and semi-flush lights. (*Source:* Reference 6.)

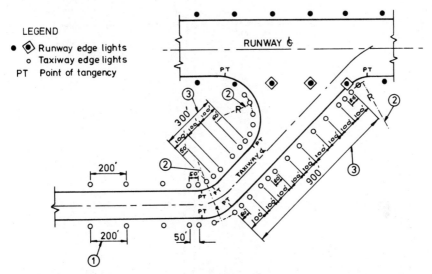

FIGURE 5.13   Typical FAA taxiway lighting configuration. (*Source:* Reference 7.)

For ICAO requirements, which are generally similar, the reader is referred to Annex 14 (4).

Taxiway Edge and Centerline Lights

In the interests of safety and efficiency, the locations and limits of taxiways must be indicated clearly. This is achieved principally by the use of taxiway edge and centerline lights.

Taxiway edge lights are blue, to differentiate them from runway edge lights. They are elevated fixtures, extending (under FAA specifications) to a maximum height of 14 in above finished grade (7), set at a maximum distance of 10 ft from the taxiway edge. On long tangents, spacing can be up to 200 ft centers (Figure 5.13). On shorter tangents, spacings are kept below 200 ft. Figure 5.14 indicates the required spacing of lights for curved taxiway edges. In setting out taxiway edge lighting systems, it is essential to eliminate all possibilities of confusing a portion of a taxiway with a runway, either from the air or the ground.

In new construction, taxiway centerline lights may be installed instead of taxiway edge lights, or, where operations occur in low visibility or taxiing confusion exists, the centerline lights may supplement the edge lights. Lights for taxiway centerlines consist of single semi-flush units inset into the taxiway pavement along the centerline. These lights are steady burning and are standard aviation green.

ICAO Annex 14 specifies the use of taxiway centerline lights on high speed exit taxiways and other exit taxiways, taxiways, and aprons when the runway visual range (RVR) is less than 1200 ft, except where only low traffic volumes are encountered. On long tangents, the maximum spacing is 200 ft varying

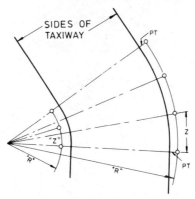

FIGURE 5.14   FAA spacing of lights on curved taxiway edges: PT, point of tangency. (*Source:* Reference 7.)

down to 50 ft maximum at lower RVRs. Spacings down to a maximum of 25 ft are indicated on curved taxiway sections. For further details of the recommendations of the international agency, the reader is referred to the pertinent sections of the ICAO document.

Obstruction Lighting and Airport Beacons

Obstruction lights must be placed on towers, bridges, and other structures that may constitute a hazard to air navigation. Single and double obstruction lights, flashing beacons, and rotating beacons are used to warn pilots of the presence of obstructions during darkness and other periods of limited visibility. These lights are standard aviation red and high intensity white. The number, type, and placement of obstruction lights depends principally on structure height. FAA standards for the lighting obstructions are given in the advisory circular *Obstruction Marking and Lighting* (8).

The location and presence of an airport at night is indicated by an airport beacon. In the United States, a 36 in. beacon is typically used rotating at 6 rpm and equipped with an optical system that projects two beams of light 180° apart. One light is green and the other white. A split white beam giving a double white flash denotes a military airport.

5.8   RUNWAY AND TAXIWAY MARKING

Markings are applied to the paved areas of runways and taxiways to identify clearly the functions of these areas and to delimit the physical areas for safe operation. We can cover this topic only briefly; for a complete discussion the reader is referred to ICAO Annex 14 and Reference 9. Our description relates to the FAA specifications, which are generally similar in function and form to the international standards; where differences occur, they are not sufficiently great to cause confusion.

Runways

Three types of runway marking can be provided: *basic* or *visual, nonprecision instrument*, and *precision instrument*. This categorization conforms with that outlined in Chapter 4. Figure 5.15 shows the standard patterns of markings for each type.

1. *Basic Runways.* These unpaved runways have runway stop markers only. Paved basic runways are marked with the runway number and centerline.
2. *Nonprecision Instrument Runway.* Marking consists of basic runway marking plus threshold markings. Where considered necessary, additional elements of the precision instrument pattern may be added.
3. *Precision Instrument Runways.* These are marked like nonprecision runways but with the additions of touchdown zone markings, fixed distance markings, and side strips.

All runway markings are normally in white to differentiate them from yellow taxiway and apron markings. The runway number given to all paved runways is the number nearest one-tenth the magnetic azimuth of the runway centerline. For example, a runway oriented N10° E would be numbered 1 on the south end and 19 on the north end. Additional information is needed when two or three parallel runways are used, and the designations L, C, and R are added to identify the left, center, and right runways, respectively. Where four or five parallel runways are numbered, two of the runways are assigned numbers of the next nearest one-tenth magnetic azimuth to avoid confusion. Figure 5.15 gives marking dimensions.

Taxiways

Taxiway markings are set out in yellow. They consist of 6 in. wide continuous stripe centerlines and holding lines at 100 ft minimum from the runway edge. Where runways are operating under ILS conditions, special holding lines must be marked to clear glide slope and localizer critical areas to prevent interference between the navigational signal and ground traffic.

Markings in the form of diagonal yellow stripes 3 ft wide are also applied to runway and taxiway shoulders and blast pad areas to indicate that those areas are not for aircraft support.

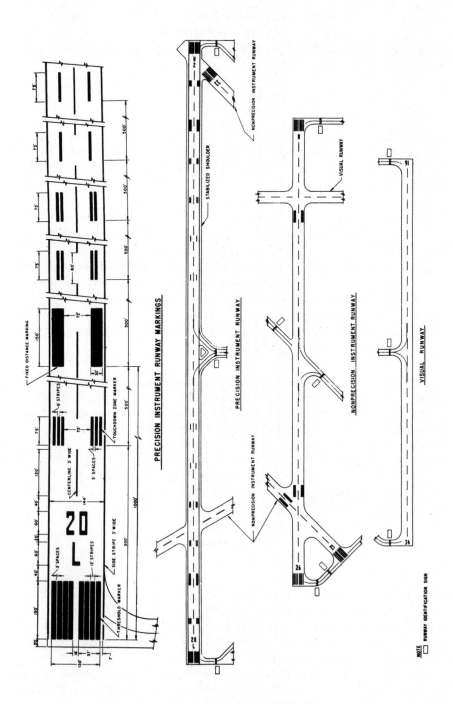

PRECISION INSTRUMENT RUNWAY MARKINGS

PRECISION INSTRUMENT RUNWAY

NONPRECISION INSTRUMENT RUNWAY

VISUAL RUNWAY

NOTE ▢ RUNWAY IDENTIFICATION SIGN

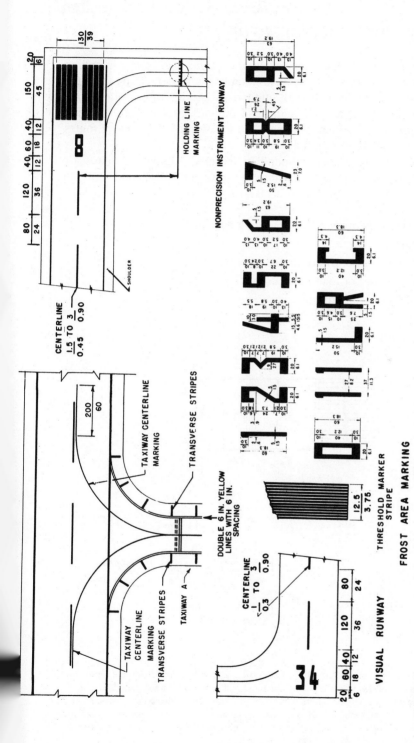

FIGURE 5.15 Typical FAA runway markings. In detail A, all runway centerline spacing should be laid out from both ends toward the center, and the holding line should be 100 ft from the edge of the runway, or 150 ft from the edge of runways where "heavy" jets operate. With respect to the frost area marking, all stripes and spaces are to be of equal width: maximum 6 in., minimum 4 in. All dimensions of numerals and letters, (detail C) are in feet and inches. The numerals and letters must be horizontally spaced 15 ft apart, except the numerals in "11" (as shown); work is to be done to dimensions, not to scale. (*Source:* Reference 9.)

133

5.9 TAXIWAY GUIDANCE SIGNING (10)

Signs are placed along the edges of taxiways and aprons to aid pilots in finding their way when taxiing and to help them comply with instructions from the ground traffic controller. The signs fall into two categories: *destination signs*, indicating paths to be taken by inbound and outbound taxiing aircraft, and *intersection signs*, which either designate the location of intersecting routes or indicate category II ILS critical areas.

Destination signs are either outbound or inbound. Outbound routes are identified by signs indicating the directions to runway ends. Inbound signs are standardized to give the following information:

RAMP or RMP: general parking, servicing and loading areas.

PARK: aircraft parking.

FUEL: areas where aircraft are fueled or serviced.

GATE: gate position for loading or unloading.

VSTR: area for itinerant aircraft.

DISPLAY UNIT

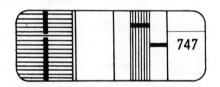

DOCKING SAMPLE

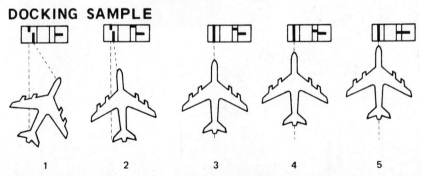

FIGURE 5.16 BOLD Nose-in aircraft self-docking system as used at Schiphol Airport Amsterdam. Docking proceeds as follows: Position 1—Pilot turns and proceeds toward gate; Position 2—aligns lower vertical bar with upper datum bar, horizontal stop cue bar comes into view; Position 3—maintains centerline alignment, horizontal bar moves down right bar; Position 4—25 ft to stop and horizontal bar moving downward; Position 5—horizontal bar in line with right stop-cue bar. This is perfect alignment. (*Source:* Jeppesen Sanderson Inc., Denver, Colorado.)

MIL: area for military aircraft.

CRGO: area for freight and cargo handling.

INTL: area for international flights.

HGR: hangar area.

ILS: ILS critical area.

For some time, guidance signs have been standardized into three categories:

Type 1: Illuminated and reflective, with a white legend on a red background; used to denote holding positions.

Type 2: Illuminated with a black legend on a yellow background; used to indicate a specific location or destination on the aircraft movement area.

Type 3: Nonilluminated with a black legend on a yellow background; adequate for airports without operations in poor weather.

Good experience has been obtained in recent years with retro-reflective signs, which are easier to see and less expensive in cost and energy than illuminated or non-illuminated signs. It is likely that, in the long term, the use of retro-reflective signs will become more widespread. The maximum height of signs above grade is 42 in. and the minimum distance of signs from the apron or taxiway edge is specified at 10 ft. Both these dimensions depend on the size of the sign.

5.10   AIRCRAFT SELF-DOCKING SYSTEMS

A number of aircraft nose-in self-docking systems are available to cut down the required apron manpower and to reduce human error in the final positioning of aircraft on the apron.

The Burroughs optical lens docking system (BOLD: Figure 5.16) is a visual system for parking and guidance. Two display units have been installed at Schiphol Airport, Amsterdam, one on top of the other. The upper display serves the 747, for example, and the lower display serves other aircraft (e.g., DC-10, DC-8, L-1011). The elements for centerline guidance and determination of the stop position are mounted in one unit. The centerline guidance is obtained from two vertical light bars: a fixed bar indicating the centerline, and below it a bar indicating the observer's position (e.g., left or right, or on the centerline). Stop position is determined by a horizontal light bar (stop bar) that moves down from the top of the display when the aircraft approaches the stand; showing simultaneously is a fixed bar with the type designation of the aircraft attempting to dock.

Azimuth guidance for nose-in stands (AGNIS; Figure 5.17) is a system that allows the pilot to park the aircraft accurately on stands served by the air jetty. The centerline guiding system consists of a light unit that emits red and/or

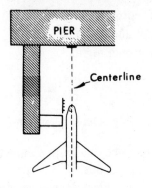

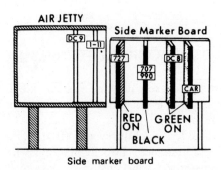

Side marker board

FIGURE 5.17 Nose-in aircraft self docking system used at Brussels and London Heathrow airports, consisting of centerline guidance system AGNIS and side marker boards, as described in text. (*Source:* Jeppesen Sanderson Inc., Denver Colorado.)

green beams through two parallel vertical slots; it is mounted on the face of the pier and aligned with the left-hand pilot's position. The signals are interpreted as follows:

1. *Two Greens.*   On centerline.
2. *Left Slot Red, Right Slot Green.*   Left of centerline, turn right toward green.
3. *Left Slot Green, Right Slot Red.*   Right of centerline, turn left toward green.

The side marker board is a white base board with vertical slats mounted at specific intervals; it is erected on the pier side of the air jetty. The edge of each slat is painted black, the side toward the taxiway is green, and the side toward the pier is red. Each slat bears a name tab to indicate the aircraft type(s) to which the slat applies. When entering the stand the pilot sees the green side; when the correct STOP position is reached, only the black edge is visible. If the correct STOP position is passed, the red side of the slat comes into view. BAC 1-11 and DC-9 aircraft are not served by the side marker board; a mark on the air jetty itself shows the correct stopping position.

REFERENCES

1. *En Route Low Altitude Charts*, U.S. Series L-1 to L-28, National Ocean Survey, Riverdale, Md.: National Oceanic and Atmospheric Administration, 1978.

2. *Airman's Information Manual*, Washington, D.C.: Federal Aviation Administration, 1984.

3. Paquette, R. J., N. Ashford, and P. H. Wright, *Transportation Engineering*, 2nd Ed., New York: Wiley, 1982.

4. *Aerodromes*, Annex 14 to the Convention on Civil Aviation, 8th Ed., Montreal: International Civil Aviation Organization, 1983.

5. *Visual Guidance Lighting Systems*, 6850.2, Washington, D.C.: Federal Aviation Administration, May 1969 as amended to Change 8.

6. *Installation Details for Runway Centerline and Touchdown Zone Lighting Systems*, FAA Advisory Circular AC 150/5340-4C, June 6, 1975 as amended to Change 2.

7. *Runway and Taxiway Edge Lighting System*, FAA Advisory Circular AC 150/5340-24, September 3, 1975, including Change 1, November 25, 1977.

8. *Obstruction Marking and Lighting*, FAA Advisory Circular AC 707/7460-1F, September 27, 1978.

9. *Marking Paved Areas on Airports*, FAA Advisory Circular AC 150/5340-1E, November 4, 1980.

10. *Taxiway Guidance Sign System*, FAA Advisory Circular, AC 150/5340-18A, June 2, 1980.

6

AIRPORT CAPACITY
AND CONFIGURATION

6.1 INTRODUCTION

Chapter 2 covered airport demand. Here we turn to the supply side of the equation, with a discussion of airport capacity and configuration.

Airport capacity analyses are undertaken for two purposes: (1) to measure objectively the capability of various components of an airport system of handling projected passenger and aircraft flows, and (2) to estimate the delays experienced in the system at different levels of demand (1). Thus capacity analyses make it possible for the airport planner to determine the number of required runways, to identify potentially suitable configurations, and to compare alternative designs.

This chapter defines airport capacity, assesses the various factors that influence capacity, and describes approaches to performing airport capacity analyses. In addition, we discuss airport configuration, which, from the viewpoint of the airport planner, is the most important determinant of the capacity of an airport system.

It should be recognized that bottlenecks and delays can result from inadequacies in any component of the airport system—airside or landside. However, this chapter is restricted to the capacity of airside facilities: the runway, taxiway, and apron-gate components. Particular emphasis is given to the runway component of the system.

6.2 CAPACITY, DEMAND, AND DELAY

The term "capacity" refers to the ability of a component of the airfield to accommodate aircraft. It is expressed in operations (i.e., arrivals, departures) per unit of time, typically in operations per hour. Thus, the hourly capacity of the runway system is the maximum number of aircraft operations that can be accommodated in one hour under specified operating conditions. Capacity depends on a number of prevailing conditions such as ceiling and visibility, air traffic control, aircraft mix, and type of operations. To determine the capacity, the prevailing conditions must be specified.

The FAA previously recommended (2, 3) the concept of a "practical capacity" measure that corresponds to a "reasonable" or "tolerable" level of delay (e.g., delays to departing aircraft average 4 min during the normal two peak adjacent hours of the week.) The preferred measure (4) and that employed in this chapter, is the *ultimate* or *saturation* capacity, the maximum number of aircraft that can be handled during a given period under conditions of continuous demand.

Capacity should not be confused with demand. Capacity refers to the physical capability of an airfield and its components. It is a measure of supply, and it is independent of both the magnitude and fluctuation of demand and the amount of delay to aircraft (5). Delay, however, is dependent on capacity and the magnitude and fluctuation in demand. One can reduce aircraft delays by increasing capacity and by providing a more uniform pattern of demand (i.e., by reducing the peaks in demand). These relationships are illustrated by Figure 6.1.

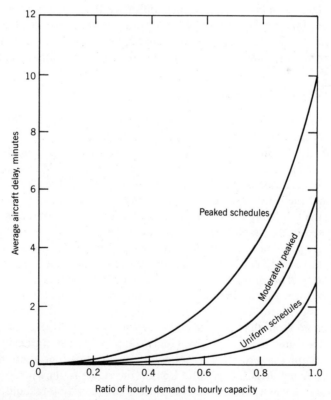

FIGURE 6.1   Relationship of demand-capacity ratio and demand fluctuation to average hourly aircraft delay. (Adapted from Reference 5.)

As demand approaches capacity, delays to aircraft increase sharply. Because of the congestion that may be associated with these increases in delay, planners should exercise caution when planning for airports where the level of airport demand is expected to approach capacity for more than short periods of time. Furthermore, estimating the magnitude of delays and their economic impact are more important in justifying airport improvements than a determination of capacity.

Runway Capacity

Runway capacity is normally the controlling element of the airport system capacity. In succeeding sections, various aspects of this key element of capacity are examined: (1) factors that affect runway capacity, (2) procedures for estimating hourly and annual capacities, and (3) procedures for estimating delays.

6.3 FACTORS THAT AFFECT CAPACITY

There are a large number of factors that influence the capacity of a runway system. These factors can be grouped into four classes, those related to: (1) air traffic control, (2) characteristics of demand, (3) environmental conditions in the airport vicinity, and (4) the layout and design of the runway system.

Air Traffic Control Factors

As was discussed in Chapter 5, the FAA specifies minimum vertical, horizontal, and lateral separations for aircraft in the interests of air safety. In the vicinity of an airport, the minimum allowable horizontal separation is typically 2 to 5 nautical mi, depending on the aircraft size, availability of radar, and the sequencing of operations. Since no two airplanes are allowed on the runway at the same time, the runway occupancy time may also influence the capacity.

Consider the following hypothetical example. A runway serves aircraft that land at a speed of 165 mph while maintaining the minimum separation of 3 nautical mi as specified by the FAA. The average runway occupancy time for landing aircraft is 25 sec. Let us examine the effect of these factors on the runway capacity. The minimum spacing is (3 × 6076 ft/nautical mi) = 18,228 ft. In terms of time, the minimum arrival spacing is 18,228 ft ÷ (165 × 5280/3600) ft/sec = 75 sec. The maximum rate of arrivals that can be served by the runway is no more than 3600 sec/hr ÷ 75 sec/arrival = 48 arrivals/hr.

Figure 6.2 is a time-distance diagram for two approaching aircraft maintaining the 3 nautical mi separation. The solid line on the left represents the first arrival. The second arrival (the solid line on the right) is shown at a point 3 nautical mi away when the first arrival crosses the runway threshold. As the figure illustrates, if the runway is used for arrivals only, it will remain unoccupied two-thirds of the time. In capacity calculations, it is usually necessary to compute the percentage of all aircraft operations that are arrivals or the arrival-to-departure ratio and to make allowance for this effect.

Arrivals on final approach are generally given absolute priority over departures. Departures are released when suitable gaps occur in the arrival stream.

The capacity of a runway can be substantially increased by inserting a departure between pairs of arrivals, as illustrated by the dashed line in Figure 6.2. One limiting feature of this sequencing pattern is the FAA regulation requiring a minimum separation of 2 nautical mi between the insertion of a departure and the next arrival.

Separation is the dominant air traffic control factor affecting capacity. Other factors are as follows:

1. The length of the common path from the ILS gate to the threshold, normally 4 to 8 mi.

2. The strategy employed by controllers in sequencing aircraft traveling at different speeds (e.g., first come–first served, speed-class sequencing).

3. The allowable probability of violation of the separation rule, recognizing that it is not possible to maintain the allowable separation with perfect precision at all times.

4. The sophistication of the air traffic control system, which affects the precision with which aircraft can be delivered to the ILS gate and the ability to monitor aircraft speeds and detect aircraft positions and movements.

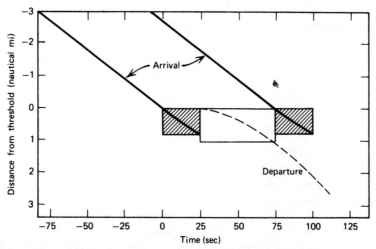

FIGURE 6.2 Time-distance diagram for two approaching and one departing aircraft: open box, runway occupied by departure; cross-hatched box, runway occupied by arrival.

Characteristics of Demand

The capacity of a runway depends on aircraft size, speed, maneuverability, and braking capability, as well as pilot technique. The effect of aircraft size is reflected both in the wing tip vortex phenomenon and in differences in approach and touchdown speeds. As indicated in Chapter 3, heavy jet aircraft generate wing tip vortices that create problems of maneuverability and control for smaller aircraft operating in their wake. In the interest of safety, the FAA has introduced air traffic control rules that increase the separation between small aircraft following a heavy jet to 5 nautical mi. This regulation decreases the capacity of runways that serve significant numbers of heavy jets and small aircraft.

Unlike the situation illustrated by Figure 6.2, the speeds at which different aircraft approach a runway are neither equal nor constant along the approach path. Frequently, separations longer than the minimum allowed by air traffic rules must be tolerated to accommodate a mixture of slow and fast aircraft. Because of variations in approach speeds, a margin of safety must be allowed to ensure that the minimum separation is not violated at any point along the approach path. Touchdown speed, braking capability, and ground maneuverability affect the runway occupancy time for landing, which, in turn, determines the time that a departing aircraft can be released.

Many general aviation airports have a great deal of pilot training activities that involve "touch-and-go" operations. The term refers to an aircraft that lands and takes off without coming to a complete stop. Such operations, which are counted as two aircraft movements, may significantly affect runway capacities. Studies have shown that "one aircraft performing touch and go operations can generate up to 16 movements per hour: one takeoff, seven 'touches' (14 movements), and one final landing" (6). In capacity calculations, empirical correction factors are applied to allow for the presence of touch-and-go traffic.

Another characteristic of demand that can significantly affect the capacity of a runway is the percentage of all aircraft operations that are arrivals. That is, a runway used exclusively for arrivals will have a capacity different from one used for departures or mixed operations.

Environmental Factors

The most important environmental factors influencing runway capacity are visibility, runway surface conditions, winds, and noise abatement requirements.

Under conditions of poor visibility, pilots and air traffic controllers become more cautious. Longer separations and greater runway occupancy times result, and runways with marginal crosswinds are less likely to be used. When the visibility or ceiling falls below certain prescribed values, instrument flight rules are employed and the responsibility for safe separation between aircraft passes from the pilots to air traffic control personnel. A runway or runway system may be closed to traffic when visibility is extremely limited. Similarly, wet or slippery runway surface conditions may cause longer deceleration distances and greater runway occupancy times. Heavy snow and ice accumulations warrant the closing of a runway.

For safety reasons, the wind speed component perpendicular to the aircraft path should not exceed 15 knots, and the component in the direction of the aircraft's movement must not exceed 5 knots (7). Objectionable crosswinds and tail winds occasionally impose restrictions on the use of one or more runways, and calculations of runway capacity should include appropriate allowances for such restrictions.

Noise abatement regulations affect the capacity of a runway system by limiting or restricting the use of one or more runways during certain hours of the day.

Design Factors

For the airport planner, layout and design features comprise the most important class of factors that affect runway capacity. When quantum increases in airport capacity are needed to serve future demand, the airport planner considers improvements in the layout and design of the runway and taxiway system. The principal factors in this class are as follows:

1. The number, spacing, length, and orientation of runways.
2. The number, locations, and design of exit taxiways.
3. The design of ramp entrances.

Further discussion of these factors and their relationship to capacity is given later in this chapter and in Chapter 7.

6.4 DETERMINATION OF RUNWAY CAPACITIES AND DELAYS

A number of different approaches may be employed to estimate runway capacities and delays, including:

1. Empirical approaches.
2. Queuing models.
3. Analytical approaches.
4. Computer simulation.

The simplest approach is to base capacity and delay estimates on the results of extensive traffic surveys performed at existing airports. Such surveys may serve as the sole basis for graphs and tables from which estimates may be directly made, see, for example, Reference 6. Empirical surveys are also a vital component in the development and validation of both analytical and simulation models (8).

Examples of simple queuing models are given in Section 6.5. Queuing models may be used to estimate queue lengths and average delays to aircraft in simple systems. Such estimates may serve as a component or building block of a computer simulation model.

The runway capacity models described in Section 6.6 are examples of analytical models. These models are based on the concept that aircraft can be represented as attempting to arrive at points in space at particular times (5).

A computer simulation model was used to produce estimates of aircraft delays for Reference 8. This approach is discussed more fully in Section 6.10.

6.5 QUEUING THEORY APPROACHES

It has long been recognized that a simple runway system can be described by mathematical models or formulas of queuing theory. In 1948, Bowen and Pearcey (9) made an empirical study of aircraft arriving at the Kingsford-Smith Airport in Sydney and found that arrivals could be satisfactorily described by the Poisson probability distribution. Since flights on civil airlines are scheduled, one would intuitively suspect that aircraft arrivals are regular; however it was found that the difference between the expected and actual times of arrival was large and that the process was more random than regular.

A runway serving landings only can be described as a single-channel queuing system with first come–first served services. The "service time" is the "length of time the most recent arrival blocks the runway from receiving any subsequent arrival" (10). It depends on the runway occupancy time, or more commonly, the minimum separation necessitated by air traffic rules.

Assuming Poisson arrivals and constant service times, Bowen and Pearcey derived an equation for average (steady state) landing delay:

$$W = \frac{\rho}{2\mu(1 - \rho)} \tag{6.1}$$

where

ρ = the load factor = λ/μ
λ = arrival rate (aircraft/unit time)
μ = service rate (aircraft/unit time) = $1/b$
b = mean service time

In a more general form, this equation is known as the Pollaczek-Khinchin formula:

$$W = \frac{\rho(1 + C_b^2)}{2\mu(1 - \rho)} \tag{6.2}$$

where

C_b = coefficient of variation of service time = σ_b/b
σ_b = standard deviation of service time

These equations can also be applied to runways serving departures only. A more complicated formula has been developed to calculate the average delay to departures in mixed operations.

Although mathematical equations such as these help us to understand delay-capacity relationships, they do not provide accurate estimates of average delay, except for extremely simple situations. The equations have at least two major shortcomings:

1. They account for the effects of only a few of the many factors known to influence runway capacity and delays.
2. They give "steady state" solutions. As Harris (10) has demonstrated, many hours may be required to achieve steady state conditions.

6.6 DETERMINATION OF RUNWAY CAPACITIES—ANALYTICAL APPROACH

During the past several years, researchers have developed a number of analytical models for the calculation of runway capacity. The simplest model of this type is a landing intervals model that accounts for the effects of the following factors:

1. Length of the common approach path.
2. Aircraft speeds.
3. Minimum aircraft separations as specified by air traffic regulations.

The simplest model assumes error-free approaches. That is, it is assumed that controllers are able to deliver aircraft to the entry gate exactly at scheduled times, and pilots are able to precisely maintain the required separations and speeds.

Two situations are considered: (1) the overtaking case, in which the trailing aircraft has a speed equal to or greater than the lead aircraft; and (2) the opening case, in which the speed of the lead aircraft exceeds that of the trailing aircraft. Harris (10) has shown that for the error-free case the following minimum separation function applies:

$$m(v_2, v_1) = \frac{\delta}{v_2} \quad \text{for } v_2 \geq v_1 \qquad (6.3)$$

$$m(v_2, v_1) = \frac{\delta}{v_2} + \gamma\left(\frac{1}{v_2} - \frac{1}{v_1}\right) \quad \text{for } v_2 < v_1 \qquad (6.4)$$

where

v_i = speed of aircraft i
γ = length of common approach path
δ = minimum safety separation
$m(v_2, v_1)$ = error-free minimum time separation over threshold for aircraft 2 following aircraft 1

Time-space diagrams for the overtaking and opening situations, shown as Figures 6.3 and 6.4. With the aid of these figures, the reader is advised to develop equations 6.3 and 6.4.

In computing the saturation capacity, it is suggested that the various aircraft be grouped into n discrete speed classes (v_1, v_2, . . . , v_n) and that a matrix of minimum intervals be formed.

$$M = [m(v_i, v_j)] = \begin{Bmatrix} \text{matrix of minimum intervals,} \\ m_{ij}, \text{ for speed class } i \\ \text{following speed class } j \end{Bmatrix}$$

Associated with each of the n speed classes is a probability of occurrence [p_1, p_2, . . . , p_n]. These probabilities are the percentages of the various speed classes in the mix divided by 100.

The expected minimum landing interval (or weighted mean service time) can be approximated by

$$\bar{m} = \Sigma_{ij} P_i m_{ij} P_j \tag{6.5}$$

The hourly saturation capacity is the inverse of the weighted mean service time.

$$C = \frac{1}{\bar{m}} \tag{6.6}$$

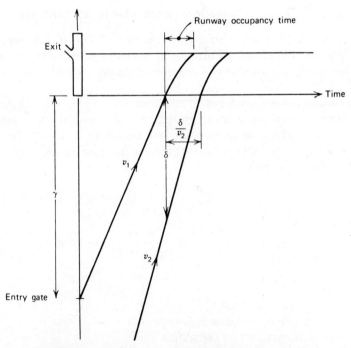

FIGURE 6.3   Time-space diagram for the overtaking situation.

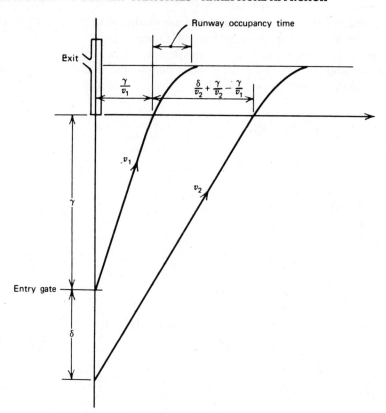

FIGURE 6.4 Time-space diagram for the opening situation.

Consider the following example, which has been adopted from Reference 10.

Example 6.1 Ultimate Runway Capacity with Error-Free Landings

Given a length of common approach path $\gamma = 6$ nautical mi and a minimum separation of 3 nautical mi, calculate the ultimate capacity for the following population of aircraft landing on a single runway, assuming error-free approaches.

Percentage of Aircraft	Approach Speed (knots)
20	100
20	120
60	135

Assume that the runway occupancy times are smaller than the time separations during approach and have no effect on the capacity.

From equations 6.3 and 6.4, it is possible to calculate the minimum time separation over the threshold for various combinations of speeds. Consider the situation $v_i = 100$, $v_j = 120$. Since $v_j > v_i$, the minimum separation is

$$m(v_j, v_i) = \frac{\delta}{v_j} = \frac{3}{120} \text{ hr} = 90 \text{ sec}$$

For $v_i = 135$, $v_j = 100$, we have

$$m(v_j, v_i) = \frac{\delta}{v_j} + \gamma\left(\frac{1}{v_j} - \frac{1}{v_i}\right)$$

$$= \frac{3}{100} + 6\left(\frac{1}{100} - \frac{1}{135}\right) = 0.0456 \text{ hr} = 164 \text{ sec}$$

The complete matrix M is as follows:

		Speed of leading aircraft, v_i			Probability, P_j
		100	120	135	
Speed of trailing	100	108	144	164	0.2
aircraft, v_j	120	90	90	110	0.2
	135	80	80	80	0.6
Probability,		0.2	0.2	0.6	
			P_i		

This shows the minimum time separation for each combination of approach speeds.

The next step is to compute a weighted average separation, by equation 6.5, based on the probabilities associated with each pair of aircraft speeds.

$$\begin{aligned}
\bar{m} = &(108 \times 0.2 + 90 \times 0.2 + 80 \times 0.6)0.2 + \\
&(144 \times 0.2 + 90 \times 0.2 + 80 \times 0.6)0.2 + \\
&(164 \times 0.2 + 110 \times 0.2 + 80 \times 0.6)0.6 = 98.16
\end{aligned}$$

Finally, the ultimate capacity is computed by equation 6.6:

$$c = \frac{1}{\bar{m}} = \frac{1}{98.16} = 0.0102 \text{ arrivals/sec} = 36.7 \text{ arrivals/hr}$$

In an effort to provide more realism, Harris (10) postulated normally distributed errors in aircraft interarrival times at the approach gate and at the threshold. Ultimate capacity models were developed that allowed time separation buffers to account for such errors. As Figure 6.5 illustrates, these buffer times are a function of the probability the buffer zone will be violated.

In the overtaking case ($v_2 \geq v_1$), the buffer zone

$$b(v_2, v_1) = \sigma_0 q(p_v) \tag{6.7}$$

where

σ_0 = standard deviation of the normally distributed buffer zone
$q(p_v)$ = the value for which the cumulative standard normal distribution function has the value $(1 - p_v)$
p_v = probability that the buffer zone is violated

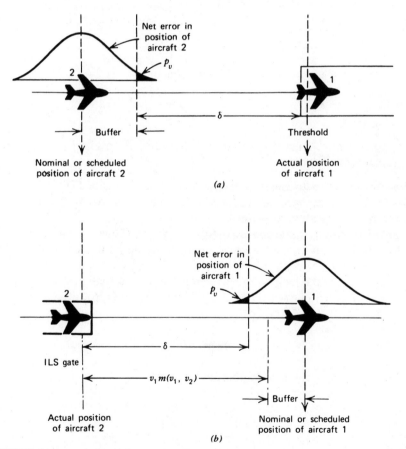

FIGURE 6.5 Error distribution and separation buffering. (a) Overtaking, $v_2 \geq v_1$. (b) Opening, $v_2 < v_1$. (*Source:* Reference 10.)

In the opening situation ($v_2 < v_1$), the buffer zone is also a function of the separation and the relative aircraft speeds

$$b(v_2, v_1) = \sigma_0 q(p_v) - \delta\left(\frac{1}{v_2} - \frac{1}{v_1}\right) \tag{6.8}$$

With this model the minimum interval of time between the arrival of a leading aircraft traveling at a speed v_1 and the trailing aircraft traveling at a speed v_2 is

$$l(v_2, v_1) = m(v_2, v_1) + b(v_2, v_1) \tag{6.9}$$

Using matrix notation,

$$B = [b(v_i, v_j)] = \left\{\begin{array}{l}\text{matrix of buffer zones,} \\ b_{ij}, \text{ for speed class } i \\ \text{following speed class } j\end{array}\right\}$$

The matrix of scheduled landing intervals becomes

$$L = M + B \tag{6.10}$$

Example 6.2   Ultimate Runway Capacity Allowing for Approach Errors

Compute the ultimate capacity for the conditions described in Example 6.1 allowing a buffer zone that has a standard deviation $\sigma_0 = 20$ sec. Use a probability of violation $p_v = 0.05$.

To obtain $q(p_v)$, consult a statistics table that shows the area under the normal curve from $q(p_v)$ to infinity. In such a table, corresponding to $p_v = 0.05$, $q(p_v) = 1.65$.

Then compute the lengths of buffer zones b_{ij} (in seconds) for various combinations of speed classes. For example, from equation 6.7, the buffer zone for $v_2 = 100$ and $v_1 = 100$ is

$$b(v_2, v_1) = \sigma_0 q(p_v) = 20 \times 1.65 = 33 \text{ sec}$$

Similarly, by equation 6.8, the buffer zone for $v_2 = 100$, $v_1 = 135$ is

$$b(v_2, v_1) = \sigma_0 q(p_v) - \delta\left(\frac{1}{v_2} - \frac{1}{v_1}\right)$$

$$= 20 \times 1.65 - 3\left(\frac{1}{100} - \frac{1}{135}\right)3600 = 5 \text{ sec}$$

The complete matrix of buffer zones

$$B = \begin{bmatrix} 33 & 15 & 5 \\ 33 & 33 & 23 \\ 33 & 33 & 33 \end{bmatrix}$$

Adding this matrix to matrix M from Example 6.1, we obtain the landing interval matrix

$$L = \begin{bmatrix} 141 & 159 & 169 \\ 123 & 123 & 133 \\ 113 & 113 & 113 \end{bmatrix}$$

The weighted average separation is

$$
\begin{aligned}
\bar{m} = & (141 \times 0.2 + 123 \times 0.2 + 113 \times 0.6)0.2 + \\
& (159 \times 0.2 + 123 \times 0.2 + 113 \times 0.6)0.2 + \\
& (169 \times 0.2 + 133 \times 0.2 + 113 \times 0.6)0.6 = 125.88 \text{ sec}
\end{aligned}
$$

and the ultimate capacity

$$c = \frac{1}{\bar{m}} = \frac{1}{125.88} \text{ arrivals/sec} = 28.6 \text{ arrivals/hr}$$

More complex models have been published (10) that account for speed errors along the approach or variations in times required to fly the common path. Such models, which are conceptually similar to those given above, are available for exclusive arrival and departure runways, as well as for mixed operations runways. Analytical models have also been developed for multiple runway configurations using the ultimate capacity concept (1, 11).

6.7 DETERMINATION OF RUNWAY CAPACITIES—HANDBOOK APPROACH

In 1976, the FAA published a comprehensive handbook (8) that contains procedures for the determination of ultimate airfield capacities and aircraft delays for purposes of airport planning. The handbook and its companion reports (5, 12, 13) were based on an extensive four-year study by the FAA and a project team composed of Douglas Aircraft Company in association with Peat, Marwick, Mitchell and Co., McDonnell Douglas Automation Company, and American Airlines, Inc.

The handbook contains 62 graphs, exemplified by Figure 6.6, for the estimation of hourly capacities. Based on analytical models, the graphs account for the effects of the following variables:

1. Aircraft mix.
2. Runways serving both arrivals and departures.
3. Touch-and-go operations.
4. Different exit taxiway configurations.
5. Environmental conditions (VFR, IFR).
6. A variety of runway configurations and uses.

In the handbook, the aircraft mix is expressed in terms of four aircraft "classes":

Class A: small single-engine aircraft, 12,500 lb or less.
Class B: small twin-engine aircraft, 12,500 lb or less and Learjets.
Class C: large aircraft, more than 12,500 lb and up to 300,000 lb.
Class D: Heavy aircraft, more than 300,000 lb.

The graphs employ a "mix index," which is determined by the percentages of aircraft in classes C and D:

mix index = (% aircraft in class C) + 3 × (% aircraft in class D)

Many of the capacity diagrams from the handbook have been published by the FAA as an Advisory Circular (4).

Consider the following example, taken from Reference 8.

Example 6.3   Ultimate Runway Capacity, Using Figure 6.6

Determine the hourly capacity of a single runway (10,000 ft long) in VFR under the following conditions:

Aircraft mix: 35% A, 30% B, 30% C, and 5% D.
Percent arrivals: 50%.
Percent touch and go: 15%.
Exit taxiway locations: 4500 and 10,000 ft from arrival threshold.

The mix index for the assumed aircraft mix is

percentage (C + 3D) = 30 + (3 × 5) = 45

From Figure 6.6, the hourly capacity base C^* in VFR conditions is 65 operations/hr. Also from Figure 6.6, for 15% touch and go, the touch-and-go factor T is 1.10. With one exit taxiway located between 3000 and 5500 ft from the arrival runway threshold, the exit factor E is 0.84.

Therefore the hourly capacity of the runway is

65 × 1.10 × 0.84 = 60 operations/hr

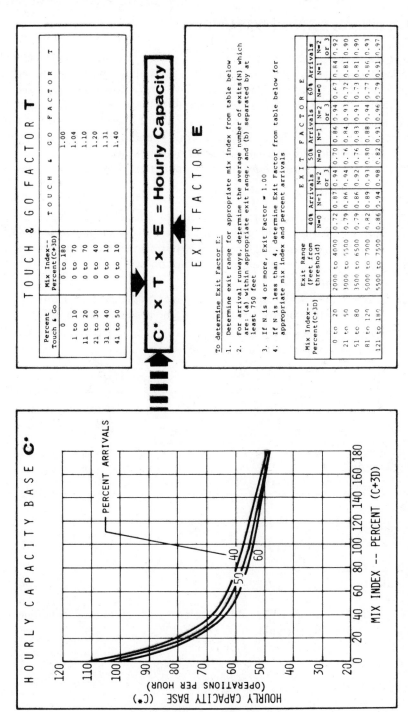

HOURLY CAPACITY BASE C*

(chart: HOURLY CAPACITY BASE (C*) (OPERATIONS PER HOUR) vs MIX INDEX -- PERCENT (C+3D), with PERCENT ARRIVALS curves labeled 40, 50, 60)

TOUCH & GO FACTOR T

Percent Touch & Go	Mix Index-- Percent(C+3D)	TOUCH & GO FACTOR T
	0 to 180	1.00
1 to 10	0 to 70	1.04
11 to 20	0 to 70	1.10
21 to 30	0 to 40	1.20
31 to 40	0 to 10	1.31
41 to 50	0 to 10	1.40

C* x T x E = Hourly Capacity

EXIT FACTOR E

To determine Exit Factor E:

1. Determine exit range for appropriate mix index from table below
2. For arrival runways, determine the average number of exits(N) which are: (a) within appropriate exit range, and (b) separated by at least 750 feet
3. If N is 4 or more, Exit Factor = 1.00
4. If N is less than 4, determine Exit Factor from table below for appropriate mix index and percent arrivals

Mix Index-- Percent(C+3D)	Exit Range (Feet from threshold)	40% Arrivals			50% Arrivals			60% Arrivals		
		N=0	N=1	N=2 or 3	N=0	N=1	N=2 or 3	N=0	N=1	N=2 or 3
0 to 20	2000 to 4000	0.72	0.87	0.94	0.70	0.86	0.94	0.67	0.84	0.92
21 to 50	3000 to 5500	0.79	0.84	0.94	0.76	0.84	0.93	0.72	0.81	0.90
51 to 80	3500 to 6500	0.79	0.86	0.92	0.76	0.83	0.91	0.73	0.81	0.99
81 to 120	5000 to 7000	0.82	0.89	0.93	0.80	0.88	0.94	0.77	0.86	0.93
121 to 180	5500 to 7500	0.86	0.94	0.98	0.82	0.91	0.96	0.79	0.91	0.97

FIGURE 6.6 Hourly capacity diagram for a single-runway in VFR conditions. (*Source*: Reference 8.)

153

6.8 ANNUAL SERVICE VOLUME

The concept of annual service volume has been proposed as an alternative to practical annual capacity as a reference in preliminary planning. As annual aircraft operations approach annual service volume, the average aircraft delay throughout the year tends to increase rapidly with relatively small increases in aircraft operations, causing a deterioration in the level of service. Annual service volume is the level of annual aircraft operations that will result in an average annual aircraft delay on the order of 1 to 4 min.

The recommended procedure for the calculation of annual service volume is outlined below (8).

1. Identify the various operating conditions (e.g., VFR, dual runways; IFR, single runway) under which the runway system may by used during a year, and determine the percentage of time that each condition occurs. Determine the hourly capacity of the runway component for each operating condition.

2. Identify the hourly capacity for the operating condition that occurs the greatest percentage of the year (i.e., the predominant capacity).

3. Determine the weight to be applied to the capacity for each operating condition from the following table:

	Weight			
	Mix Index in VFR	Mix Index in IFR		
Percentage of Predominant Capacity	0–180	0–20	21–50	51–180
91 or more	1	1	1	1
80–90	5	1	3	5
66–80	15	2	8	15
51–65	20	3	12	20
0–50	25	4	16	25

4. Calculate weighted hourly capacity C_w of the runway component by the following formula:

$$C_w = \frac{\sum_{i=1}^{n} C_i W_i P_i}{\sum_{i=1}^{n} W_i P_i} \tag{6.11}$$

where

P_i = the proportion of the year with capacity C_i
W_i = the weight to be applied to capacity, chosen from the table accompanying item 3.

5. Determine the ratio of the annual aircraft operations to average daily aircraft operations during the peak month (i.e., the daily ratio). If data are not available for determining the daily ratio, use the following typical values:

Mix Index	Daily Ratio
0–20	280–310
21–50	300–320
51–180	310–350

6. Determine the ratio of average daily aircraft operations to average peak hour aircraft operations of the peak month (i.e., the hourly ratio). If data are not available for determining the hourly ratio, use the following typical values:

Mix Index	Hourly Ratio
0–20	7–11
21–50	10–13
51–180	11–15

7. Compute annual service volume ASV from the following formula:

$$ASV = C_w \times D \times H \qquad (6.12)$$

where

C_w = weighted hourly capacity
D = daily ratio
H = hourly ratio

Example 6.4   Annual Service Volume for Runways (8)

Determine the annual service volume of a dual parallel runway configuration under the following operation conditions:

	Operating Condition				
No.	Ceiling and Visibility	Runway Use	Mix Index	Percentage of Year	Hourly Capacity
1	VFR		150	70%	93
2	VFR		150	20%	72
3	IFR		180	10%	62

Based on historical traffic records,

$$
\begin{aligned}
\text{Total annual operations} &= 367{,}604 \\
\text{Average daily operations} &= 1{,}050 \\
\text{Average peak hour operations, peak month} &= 75
\end{aligned}
$$

The predominant capacity occurs in Operating Condition No. 1 and is 93 operations per hour. From the table in paragraph 3, the following weights for each operating condition are determined:

Operating Condition Number	Hourly Capacity, Operations per Hour	Percent of Predominant Capacity	Weight
1	93	100	1
2	72	77	15
3	62	67	15

By Equation (6.11), the weighted hourly capacity,

$$
C_w = \frac{(0.70 \times 93 \times 1) + (0.20 \times 72 \times 15) + (0.10 \times 62 \times 15)}{(0.70 \times 1) + (0.20 \times 15) + (0.10 \times 15)}
$$

$C_w = 72$ operations per hour

For the assumed conditions:

$$
\text{Daily ratio} = \frac{367{,}604}{1{,}050} = 350
$$

$$
\text{Hourly ratio} = \frac{1{,}050}{75} = 14
$$

By Equation 6.12, the annual service volume

$$ASV = 72 \times 350 \times 14 = 352,800 \text{ operations per year}$$

6.9 PRELIMINARY CAPACITY ANALYSES

The FAA (8) has published approximate estimates of hourly capacity and annual service volumes for a variety of runway configurations. These estimates, exemplified by Table 6.1, are suitable only for preliminary capacity analyses. In addition to runway configuration, the capacities in Table 6.1 account for differences due to weather (VFR and IFR conditions) and aircraft mix. IFR conditions exist when the cloud ceiling is less than 1000 ft and/or the visibility is less than 3 mi. Runway capacity is normally less under IFR conditions than under VFR conditions.

To utilize Table 6.1, it is necessary to group the aircraft being served into four aircraft classes and to express aircraft mix as a mix index. (See Section 6.7.)

The capacities in the table are based on the following assumed conditions:

1. Availability of sufficient airspace to accommodate all aircraft demand.
2. Availability of a radar environment with at least one ILS-equipped runway.
3. Availability of sufficient taxiways to expedite traffic on and off the runway system.
4. Touch-and-go operations ranging from 0 to 50%, depending on the mix index.

Reference 8 provides additional information on the performance of preliminary capacity analyses.

6.10 DETERMINATION OF HOURLY DELAYS

Capacity analyses, though useful for initial screening of alternative proposals, should not be used as the sole criterion for evaluating and phasing airfield improvements. Detailed and objective analyses should be made of alternative improvements and, to the extent possible, the costs and benefits of each solution should be quantified. A major requirement for such analyses is the estimation of the magnitude of aircraft delays.

Aircraft delay is defined as the difference between the time required for an aircraft to operate on an airfield or airfield component, and the normal time it would require to operate without interference from other aircraft (5).

TABLE 6.1 Guidelines for Preliminary Capacity Analysis

Configuration	Runway Configuration Diagram	Mix Index—Percent (C + 3D)	Hourly Capacity (Operations per Hour) VFR	IFR	Annual Service Volume (Operations per Year)
A Single Runway		0–20	98	59	230,000
		21–50	74	57	195,000
		51–80	63	56	205,000
		81–120	55	53	210,000
		121–180	51	50	240,000
B Dual Lane	700' to 2,499'	0–20	197	59	355,000
		21–50	145	57	275,000
		51–80	121	56	260,000
		81–120	105	59	285,000
		121–180	94	60	340,000
C Independent IFR Parallels	4,300' or more	0–20	197	119	370,000
		21–50	149	114	320,000
		51–80	126	111	305,000
		81–120	111	105	315,000
		121–180	103	99	370,000

D				
Parallels plus Crosswind R/W	0–20	197	62	355,000
2,500' to 3,499'	21–50	149	63	285,000
	51–80	126	65	275,000
	81–120	111	70	300,000
	121–180	103	75	365,000
E				
Four Parallels	0–20	394	119	715,000
700' to 2,499' 3,500' or more 700' to 2,499'	21–50	290	114	550,000
	51–80	242	111	515,000
	81–120	210	117	565,000
	121–180	189	120	675,000
F				
Open V Runways	0–20	150	59	270,000
	21–50	108	57	225,000
	51–80	85	56	220,000
	81–120	77	59	225,000
	121–180	73	60	265,000
G				
Parallels plus Crosswind R/W	0–20	295	59	385,000
700' to 2,499'	21–50	210	57	305,000
	51–80	164	56	275,000
	81–120	146	59	300,000
	121–180	129	60	355,000

Source: Techniques for Determining Airport Airside Capacity and Delay, FAA Report No. FAA-RD-74-124, June 1976.

A number of Monte Carlo simulation models have been developed to estimate aircraft delays. With such a model, a team of researchers produced a series of graphs published in Reference 8, by which aircraft delays can be estimated for various runway configurations and operating conditions. The model operates by tracing the path of each aircraft through space and time on the airfield. The airfield is represented by a series of links and nodes depicting all possible paths an aircraft could follow. The traces of the paths of all aircraft on the airfield are made by continually advancing clock time and recording the new location of the aircraft. The records of aircraft movement are then processed by the model to produce desired outputs, including delays and flow rates (5).

The following graphical procedure is recommended (4, 8) for the estimation of hourly delays:

1. Calculate the ratio of hourly demand to hourly capacity, D/C, for the runway component.

2. Determine the arrival delay index, ADI, and the departure delay index, DDI, from graphs such as those shown in Figure 6.7. These delay indices reflect the ability of a runway use to process aircraft operations under specified conditions of aircraft mix, arrival/departure ratio, and demand. Reference 4 provides 32 sets of delay index graphs to account for differences in runway configuration and use conditions.

3. Calculate the arrival delay factor, ADF, by the following formula:

$$ADF = ADI \times [D/C] \qquad (6.13)$$

4. Calculate the departure delay factor, DDF, by the following formula:

$$DDF = DDI \times [D/C] \qquad (6.14)$$

5. Determine the demand profile factor, defined as the percent of hourly demand occuring in the busiest 15-minute period.

6. Estimate the average hourly delay for arrival and departure aircraft from Figure 6.8.

7. Compute the total hourly delay to aircraft, DTH, by the following formula:

$$DTH = HD\{[PA \times DAHA] + [(1 - PA) \times DAHD]\} \qquad (6.15)$$

where

HD = hourly demand on the runway component
PA = percent of arrivals/100
$DAHA$ = average hourly delay per arrival aircraft on the runway component
$DAHD$ = average hourly delay per departure aircraft on the runway component

This procedure is applicable only when the hourly demands on the runways, taxiways, and gates do not exceed the capacities of these components. If the

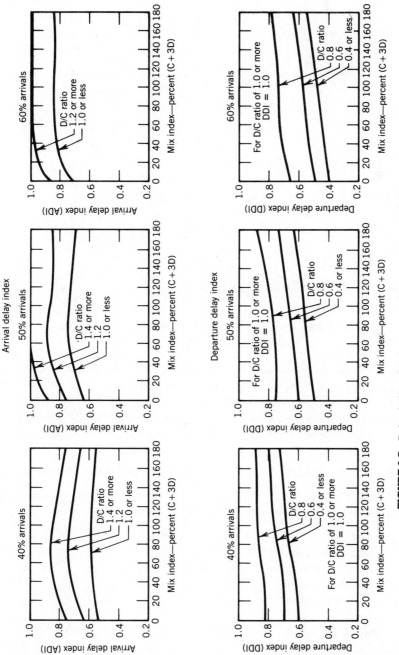

FIGURE 6.7 Delay indices for runway use diagrams. (*Source:* Reference 8.)

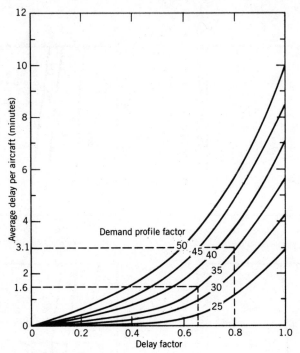

FIGURE 6.8 Average aircraft delay in an hour. (*Source:* Reference 8.)

demand on one or more components exceeds its capacity, delays to aircraft for a period of more than one hour should be considered. The recommended procedure for such analyses is not covered here, but see Reference 8.

Consider the following example that is modeled after one from the capacity and delay handbook (8).

Example 6.5   Hourly Delay to Aircraft on a Single Runway, VFR

Determine the total hourly delay to aircraft under VFR conditions using a single 10,000-foot runway with:

$$
\begin{aligned}
\text{Hourly demand} &= \text{59 operations per hour} \\
\text{Peak 15-minute demand} &= \text{21 operations} \\
\text{Hourly capacity} &= \text{65 operations per hour} \\
\text{Percent arrivals} &= \text{50\%} \\
\text{Mix index} &= \text{45}
\end{aligned}
$$

The ratio of hourly demand to hourly capacity is 59/65 = 0.91.

From Figure 6.7, for a mix index of 45, the arrival delay index is 0.71, and the departure delay index is 0.88.

By equations 6.13 and 6.14, the arrival delay factor is 0.71 × 0.91 = 0.65, and the departure delay factor is 0.88 × 0.91 = 0.80.

For the given peak 15-minute demand, the demand profile factor is (21/59) × 100 = 36. Therefore, from Figure 6.8, the average hourly delay to arrival aircraft on the runway is 1.6 min, and the average hourly delay to departure aircraft is 3.1 min.

By equation 6.15, the total hourly delay to aircraft on the runway is:

$$DTH = 59\{[0.50 \times 1.6] + [(1 - 0.50) \times 3.1]\} = 139 \text{ min}$$

6.11 ESTIMATION OF ANNUAL AIRCRAFT DELAY

The annual delay to aircraft on runways, gates, and the airfield depends on a number of factors including: the overall magnitude of demand, the hourly and daily patterns of demand, the hourly capacities for various operating conditions (e.g., runway use, ceiling and visibility), and the pattern of occurrence of various operating conditions throughout the year. The computation of annual delay to aircraft must therefore account for the seasonal, daily, and hourly variations in demand and capacity throughout the year.

Ideally, annual delay could be obtained by determining the delays for each day of the year and summing the 365 daily delays. That approach, however, is likely to require a prohibitive amount of data, time, and effort.

The FAA recommends that the demand conditions in each of the 365 days of the year be characterized by those in a much smaller number of representative days. The delay for each representative day can be determined, and then multiplied by the number of days "represented" to determine the total delay associated with each representativ daily demand. The annual delay can be estimated by summing the total delay for all representative daily demands.

For example, in the capacity and delay handbook (8), each representative daily demand corresponds to the typical demands in the days of one month. Since daily demand usually varies in VFR and IFR conditions, 24 representative daily demands are assumed.

A manual procedure for computation of annual delay to aircraft can involve a time-consuming calculation process. For this reason, computer programs have been developed to facilitate the estimation of annual delays (5, 8).

Reference 8 also presents a simplified procedure for obtaining annual delay to aircraft when an approximate estimate is all that is needed.

6.12 GATE CAPACITY

The term "gate" designates an aircraft parking space, adjacent to a terminal building and used by a single aircraft for the loading and unloading of passengers, baggage, and mail. Gate capacity refers to the ability of a specified number of gates to accommodate aircraft loading and unloading operations under conditions of continuous demand. It is the inverse of the weighted average gate occupancy time for all the aircraft served.

Gate occupancy time depends on the following variables:

1. The type of aircraft.
2. Whether the flight is an originating, turnaround, or through flight.
3. The number of deplaning and enplaning passengers.
4. The amount of baggage and mail.
5. The efficiency of apron personnel.
6. Whether each gate is available to all users or is allocated for exclusive use of one airline or class of aircraft.

Example 6.6 Gate Capacity: Each Gate Available to All Users

Determine the capacity of 10 gates that serve three classes of aircraft, given the following aircraft mix and average gate occupancy times:

Aircraft Class	Mix (%)	Average Occupancy Time (min)
1	10	20
2	30	40
3	60	60

Assume that each gate is available for all aircraft.
   The gate capacity for a single gate is given by

$$c = \frac{1}{\text{weighted service time}} = \frac{1}{(0.10 \times 20) + (0.3 \times 40) + (0.6 \times 60)}$$

$$= 0.02 \text{ aircraft/min/gate}$$

If G = the total number of gates, the capacity for all gates is

$$C = Gc = 10 \times 0.02 = 0.2 \text{ aircraft/min} = 12 \text{ aircraft/hr}$$

Example 6.7 Gate Capacity with Exclusive Use

Suppose the 10 gates in the preceding example are assigned for exclusive use of the three classes of aircraft as follows:

Aircraft Class	Gate Group	Number of Gates	Mix (%)	Mean Service Time (min)
1	A	1	10	20
2	B	2	30	40
3	C	7	60	60

If the effect of mix is ignored, the capacity of group A would be the inverse of the service time: $C_A = 1/T_A = 3.0$ aircraft/hr. Similarly, $C_B = 1.5$ and $C_C = 1.0$. One might (incorrectly) conclude that the total capacity of these gates is the sum of the capacities of the three groups or $(1 \times 3) + (2 \times 1.5) + (7 \times 1.0) = 13$ aircraft/hr. When mix is taken into consideration, an overall demand of 13 aircraft/hr would result in excessive demand for gate groups B and C:

Gate Group	Demand (aircraft/hr)	Capacity (aircraft/hr)
A	$0.10 \times 13 = 1.3$	$3.0 \times 1 = 3.0$
B	$0.30 \times 13 = 3.9$	$1.5 \times 2 = 3.0$
C	$0.60 \times 13 = 7.8$	$1.0 \times 7 = 7.0$

The capacity of the gate system is

$$C = \min_{\text{all } i} \left[\frac{G_i}{T_i M_i} \right] \tag{6.16}$$

where

G_i = the number of gates that can accommodate aircraft of class i
T_i = mean gate occupancy time of aircraft of class i
M_i = fraction of aircraft class i demanding service

For the given example

$$C_1 = \frac{1}{20 \times 0.10} = 0.5 \text{ aircraft/min}$$

or 30 aircraft/hr. Similarly, $C_2 = 10$ and $C_3 = 11.67$ aircraft/hr. The capacity is therefore 10 aircraft/hr.

Reference 8 gives a graph that makes it possible to estimate the hourly gate capacity in operations per hour.*

6.13 TAXIWAY CAPACITY

Empirical studies have shown that the capacity of a taxiway system generally far exceeds the capacities of either the runways or the gates (11). There is one notable exception, namely, taxiways that cross an active runway. For such a situation, the taxiway capacity depends on the runway operations rate, the

---

* One aircraft using a gate represents two operations, an arrival and a departure.

aircraft mix, and the location of the taxiway relative to the departure end of the runway. Graphical solutions for capacities of taxiways that cross active runways, omitted from this book, are given in Reference 11.

6.14 AIRPORT CONFIGURATION

It was stated earlier that a major determinant of airport capacity is the overall layout and design of the system. Foremost in this class of factors is airport configuration, which is the general arrangement of the various parts or components of the airport system.

6.15 PRINCIPLES OF AIRPORT LAYOUT

The layout of an airport must be suitable for the shape and acreage of available land. It must contain enough runways to meet air traffic demand, and the runways must have adequate separation to ensure safe air traffic movements. Runways should be oriented to take advantage of prevailing winds and should be directed away from fixed air navigation hazards. An airport layout should include suitable parking areas for aircraft and automobiles, as well as space for freight and baggage handling and storage, and for aircraft maintenance and service. The configuration should facilitate safe and expeditious movements of aircraft and ground transportation vehicles.

6.16 RUNWAY CONFIGURATION

A wide variety of runway configurations exist; however most runway systems are arranged according to some combination of four basic configurations: (1) single runways, (2) parallel runways, (3) open-V runways, and (4) intersecting runways. Examples of runway configurations appear in Table 6.1.

The simplest runway configuration is a single runway system, illustrated as configuration A, Table 6.1. Although capacity varies widely with aircraft mix, the hourly capacity is 51 to 98 operations per hour under VFR conditions, and 50 to 59 operations per hour under IFR conditions (8).

Since only one aircraft may occupy a runway at any time, it is frequently necessary for a departing airplane to wait for a landing airplane to clear the runway before beginning the takeoff maneuver. Significant increases in capacity could be utilized if departing airplanes were permitted to enter the runway by way of an acceleration ramp during the arrival rollout (10). However such a procedure is not considered to be safe. A similar scheme has been recommended that would utilize a *dual-lane* runway consisting of two parallel runways spaced at least 700 ft between centerlines. Such a scheme (configuration B) would increase capacity without introducing undue hazard.

The attractiveness of the dual-lane approach stems from the fact that an over 50 percent increase in (saturation) capacity might be achieved without going to the construction of a fully separated independent parallel runway. In situations where land costs are very high (as at many major "landlocked" hub airports), the savings in land may yield an extremely high benefit/cost ratio for the dual-lane configuration (10).

The dual-lane configuration would operate in the following way. The upper runway in Figure 6.9 would have high speed exits and would be used for arrivals. The lower runway in Figure 6.9 would be used for departures, which would be released as arrivals touched down. Departing airplanes would taxi across the end of the arrival runway in groups interspersed between arrivals. For arrival rates greater than 60/hr, it would probably be necessary for controllers to periodically open an arrival gap to allow departing aircraft to taxi across (14). To achieve maximum capacity capability, the FAA has suggested a minimum centerline spacing of 1000 ft for dual-lane runways (15).

Layout B is an "IFR-dependent" configuration: that is, under instrument flight rules, an operation on one runway is dependent on the operation on the other runway. In effect, simultaneous operations are permitted under VFR conditions, but not under IFR conditions. Therefore this layout provides nearly twice the capacity of a single runway under VFR conditions, but only a slight improvement over a single runway under IFR conditions.

Layout C in Table 6.1, with a spacing of 4300 ft, is an independent IFR configuration. With this layout, simultaneous precision instrument approaches are permitted.

Other variations of the parallel configuration result from differences in the location of the terminal building relative to the runways. A common arrangement is to place the terminal facilities to one side of a pair of runways. This layout has the objectionable feature of causing aircraft to taxi across an active runway. This disadvantage is overcome by an *open parallel* runway system in which the terminal building, apron, and taxiways are placed between the two runways.

Where prevailing winds are from one direction a large percentage of the time, parallel runways may be staggered or placed in tandem, with the runway lengths overlapping. In the tandem-parallel configuration, the terminal facilities are located between the runways. This makes it possible to reduce taxiing distances by using one runway exclusively for takeoff operations and the other

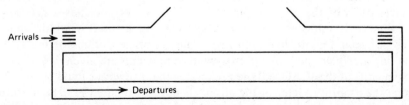

FIGURE 6.9 Dual-lane runway concept; departures are released on departure runway after arrival touchdown; parallels are spaced at less than 1000 ft, centerline to centerline. (*Source:* Reference 10.)

runway for landings. This configuration, however, requires a great deal of land.

A common approach to increasing airport capacity is to provide one or more additional parallel runways. The effect of an additional runway on capacity depends on the runway spacing, weather conditions (VFR or IFR), runway use, and the type of air traffic control system. More detailed information on the required separation of parallel runways is given in Section 7.6.

Frequently, a second runway is added in a different direction to take advantage of a wider range of wind directions. The runways may or may not intersect. Layout D illustrates dual parallel runways with an intersecting crosswind runway. An example of the nonintersecting configuration, termed "open-V," is shown as layout F. Parallel runways plus a crosswind runway is illustrated as layout G.

The capacities of open-V and intersecting runway configurations depend to a great extent on the direction of operations and the amount of wind. Both runways can be used simultaneously when winds are light. In conditions of high winds and poor visibility, these configurations operate as single-runway systems.

Large airports may require three or more runways. The best configuration for a multiple-runway system depends on the minimum spacing required for safety, the prevailing wind directions, the topographic features of the airport site, the shape and amount of available space, and the space requirements for aprons, the terminal, and other buildings.

The world's airports are characterized by varied configurations, ranging from virtually unimproved landing strips or fields to complex runway-taxiway-apron configurations accommodating more than 2000 aircraft movements each day and serving 20 to 30 million passengers each year.

6.17 RUNWAY ORIENTATION

Because of the obvious advantages of landing and taking-off into the wind, runways are oriented in the direction of prevailing winds. Aircraft may not maneuver safely on a runway when the wind contains a large component at right angle to the direction of travel. The point at which this component (called the crosswind) becomes excessive will depend upon the size and operating characteristics of the aircraft. The FAA (15, 18) recommends a maximum crosswind of 12 miles per hour for runways less than 100 ft in width, and 15 miles per hour for all other runways. The recommendations of the ICAO regarding maximum permissible crosswind components are given in Table 6.2.

Standards of the ICAO and the FAA agree that runways should be oriented so that the usability factor of the airport is not less than 95%. (The usability factor is the percentage of time during which the use of the runway system is not restricted because of an excessive crosswind component.) Where a single runway or set of parallel runways cannot be oriented to provide a usability factor of at least 95%, one or more crosswind runways should also be provided.

TABLE 6.2   ICAO Maximum Permissible Crosswind Components

Reference Field Length	Maximum Crosswind Component
1500 m or over[a]	37 km/h (20 kt)
1200 m to 1499 m	24 km/h (13 kt)
<1200 m	19 km/h (10 kt)

Source: *Aerodromes*, Annex 14 to the Convention on International Civil Aviation, including Amendment 36, July 23, 1982.

[a] When poor runway braking action owing to an insufficient coefficient of friction is experienced with some frequency, a crosswind component not exceeding 24 km/h (13 kt) should be assumed.

Wind Rose Method.   A graphical procedure utilizing a wind rose typically is used to determine the "best" runway orientation insofar as prevailing winds are concerned. (See Figure 6.10.)

A wind analysis should be based on reliable wind distribution statistics that extend over as long a period as possible, preferably at for least five years. Suitable wind data are often available from the national weather agency. For example, in the United States, wind data are usually available from the National Oceanic and Atmospheric Administration, Environmental Data Service, National Climatic Center, Ashville, North Carolina.

If suitable weather records are not available, accurate wind data for the area should be collected. (Another alternative would be to form a composite wind record from nearby wind-recording stations.) The wind data are arranged according to velocity, direction, and frequency of occurrence as shown by Table 6.3. This table indicates the percentage of time that wind velocities within a certain range and from a given direction can be expected. For example, the table indicates that for the hypothetical site, northerly winds in the 4–15 mph range can be expected 4.8% of the time.

These data are plotted on wind rose by placing the percentages in the appropriate segment of the graph. On the wind rose, the circles represent wind velocity in miles per hour, and the radial lines indicate wind direction. The data from Table 6.3 have been plotted properly on Figure 6.10.

The wind rose procedure makes use of a transparent template on which three parallel lines have been plotted. The middle line represents the runway centerline and the distance between it and each of the outside lines is equal to the allowable crosswind component (e.g., 15 mph).

The following steps are necessary to determine the "best" runway orientation and to determine the percentage of time that orientation conforms to the crosswind standards.

1. Place the template on the wind rose so that the middle line passes through the center of the wind rose.
2. Using the center of the wind rose as a pivot, rotate the template until the sum of the percentages between the outside lines is a maximum.

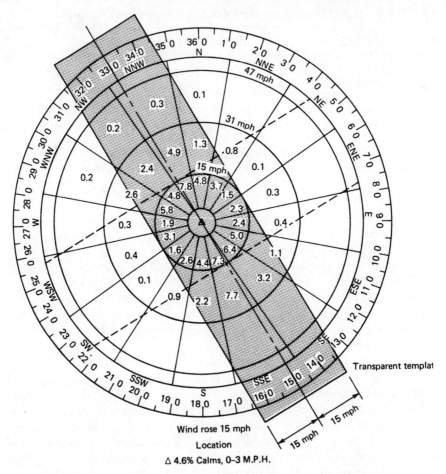

FIGURE 6.10   A typical wind rose for an allowable crosswind of 15 miles per hour.

When the template strip covers only a fraction of a segment, a corresponding fractional part of the percentage shown should be used.

3. Read the true bearing for the runway on the outer scale of the wind rose beneath the centerline of the template. In the example, the best orientation is 150°–330° or S 30° E, true.

4. The sum of percentages between the outside lines indicates the percentage of time that a runway with the proposed orientation will conform with crosswind standards.

It is noted that wind data are gathered and reported with true north as a reference, while runway orientation and numbering are based on the magnetic azimuth. The true azimuth obtained from the wind rose analysis should be changed to a magnetic azimuth by taking into account the magnetic variation*

---

* The magnetic variation can be obtained from aeronautical charts.

TABLE 6.3   Typical Wind Data

Wind Direction	Percentage of Winds			
	4–15 mph	15–31 mph	31–47 mph	Total
N	4.8	1.3	0.1	6.2
NNE	3.7	0.8	—	4.5
NE	1.5	0.1	—	1.6
ENE	2.3	0.3	—	2.6
E	2.4	0.4	—	2.8
ESE	5.0	1.1	—	6.1
SE	6.4	3.2	0.1	9.7
SSE	7.3	7.7	0.3	15.3
S	4.4	2.2	0.1	6.7
SSW	2.6	0.9	—	3.5
SW	1.6	0.1	—	1.7
WSW	3.1	0.4	—	3.5
W	1.9	0.3	—	2.2
WNW	5.8	2.6	0.2	8.6
NW	4.8	2.4	0.2	7.4
NNW	7.8	4.9	0.3	13.0
Calms	0–4 mph			4.6
Total				100.0%

for the airport location. An easterly variation is subtracted from the true azimuth, and a westerly variation is added to the true azimuth.

A more refined breakdown of wind data than that shown in the example (Table 6.3 and Figure 6.10) should be used. The FAA recommends that 36 wind directions and the standard speed groupings of the Environmental Data Service (EDS) be used. The standard wind speed groupings used by EDS are: 0-3, 4-6, 7-10, 11-16, 17-21, 22-27, 28-33, 34-40 knots, and so forth.

6.18   OBSTRUCTIONS TO AIRSPACE: FAA AND ICAO STANDARDS

Airports must be sited in areas where airspace is free from obstructions that could be hazardous to aircraft turning in the vicinity or on takeoff or approach paths. It is also necessary to maintain the surrounding airspace free from obstacles, preventing the development and growth of obstructions to airspace that could cause the airport to become unusable. The regulations on the protection of airspace in the vicinity of airports are laid down by the definition of a set of imaginary or obstacle limitation surfaces, penetration of which represents an obstacle to air navigation. In the United States, the layout of the imaginary surfaces is governed by the FAA regulations set out in FAR Part 77 (16). A somewhat similar set of international standards is promulgated by the ICAO in Annex 14. In FAA terms, protected airspace around airports is made up of five principal imaginary surfaces. These are illustrated in Figure 6.11; Table 6.4 lists the dimensions corresponding to the drawings.

1. *Primary Surface.* A surface that is longitudinally centered on the runway, extending 200 ft beyond the threshold in each direction in the case of paved runways.

2. *Approach Surface.* An inclined plane or combination of planes of varying width running from the ends of the primary surface.

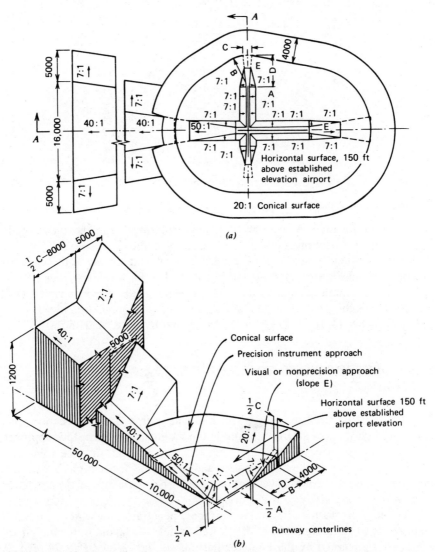

FIGURE 6.11 FAA imaginary surfaces for civil airports. (a) Plan view. (b) Isometric view of A–A. (*Source:* Reference 16.)

TABLE 6.4　Dimensions of FAA Imaginary Surfaces for Civil Airports

Dimensions[a]	Item	Dimensional Standards (ft)					
		Visual Runway		Non-precision Instrument Runway			Precision Instrument Runway
					B		
		A	B	A	C	D	
A	Width of primary surface and approach surface width at inner end	250	500	500	500	1,000	1,000
B	Radius of horizontal surface	5,000	5,000	5,000	10,000	10,000	10,000

		Visual Approach		Non-precision Instrument Approach			Precision Instrument Approach
					B		
		A	B	A	C	D	
C	Approach surface width at end	1,250	1,500	2,000	3,500	4,000	16,000
D	Approach surface length	5,000	5,000	5,000	10,000	10,000	—[b]
E	Approach slope	20:1	20:1	20:1	34:1	34:1	—[b]

Source: *Objects Affecting Navigable Airspace*, Federal Aviation Regulations, Part 77, January, 1975.

[a] Key to dimensions: A—Utility runways; B—Runways larger than utility; C—Visibility minima greater than ¾ mi.; D—Visibility minima as low as ¾ mi.

[b] Precision instrument approach slope is 50:1 for inner 10,000 ft and 40:1 for an additional 40,000 ft.

3. *Horizontal Surface.*　A horizontal plane 150 ft above the established airport elevation. As Figure 6.11 indicates, the plan dimensions of the horizontal surface are set by arcs of specified dimensions from the end of the primary surfaces, which are connected by tangents.

4. *Transition Surface.*　An inclined plane with a slope of 7:1 extending upward and outward from the primary and approach surfaces, terminating at the horizontal surface where these planes meet.

5. *Conical Surface.*　An inclined surface at a slope of 20:1 extending upward and outward from the periphery of the horizontal surface for a horizontal distance of 4000 ft.

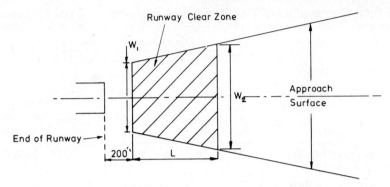

FIGURE 6.12   FAA clear zone proportions.

The dimensional standards are determined by the runway classification, (visual, non-precision instrument, or precision instrument runways). A *visual* runway is a facility designed for operation under conditions of visual approach only. A *non-precision instrument* runway has limited instrument guidance in the form of azimuth or areawide navigation equipment. A *precision instrument* runway is fully equipped for instrument landing procedures with ILS (instrument landing system) or PAR (precision approach radar) equipment.

The federal government additionally requires the establishment of *clear zones* at the ends of runways when federal funds are to be expended on new or existing airports. Figure 6.12 is a schematic view of the clear zone; the dimensions appear in Table 6.5. The airport owner must have positive control

Table 6.5   FAA Clear Zone Dimensions

Category[a]	Dimensions (ft)		
	W_1	W_2	L[b]
1. Precision instrument	1,000	1,750	2,500
2. Non-precision instrument for larger than utility with visibility minimums as low as ¾ mi	1,000	1,510	1,700
3. Non-precision instrument for larger than utility with visibility minimum greater than ¾ mi	1,000	1,425	1,700
4. Visual approach for larger than utility	1,000	1,100	1,000
5. Non-precision approach for utility	500	800	1,000
6. Visual approach utility	250	450	1,000

Source: *Reference* 16.

[a] Categories described in Section 6.17.

[b] Length of clear zone is determined by distance required to reach a height of 50 ft for the appropriate approach surface.

over development within the clear zone by long term easements or by ownership in fee simple; this gives long term positive assurance that there will be no encroachment of airspace within the critical portions of the inner approach surface.

The international recommendations on obstacle limitation surfaces set by ICAO are generally similar to these contained in FAR, Part 77; however, there are some significant differences.

1. The horizontal projection of the conical surfaces varies by runway type in the ICAO standards; it is fixed at 4000 ft by FAR Part 77.

2. The slope of the transition surface varies by runway type in Annex 14; it is fixed at 7:1 by FAR, Part 77.

3. For all but Category 1 Precision Approach Runways of Code Numbers 1 and 2, the approach surface is horizontal beyond the point where the 2.5% slope intersects the horizontal plane 150 m above the threshold elevation.

4. The ICAO takeoff and approach surfaces are different; the FAA approach surfaces are the same.

Tables 6.6 and 6.7 show the ICAO dimensions and slopes for obstacle limitation surfaces for approach and takeoff runways (17).

Table 6.6 Takeoff Runways: Dimensions and Slopes of Obstacle Limitation Surfaces

Surface and Dimensions[a]	Code Number		
	1	2	3 or 4
(1)	(2)	(3)	(4)
Takeoff climb			
Length of inner edge	60 m	80 m	180 m
Distance from runway end[b]	30 m	60 m	60 m
Divergence (each side)	10%	10%	12.5%
Final width	380 m	580 m	1,200 m
			1,800 m[c]
Length	1,600 m	2,500 m	15,000 m
Slope	5%	4%	2%

Source: Aerodromes, Annex 14 to the Convention on International Civil Aviation, including Amendment 36, July 23, 1982.

[a] All dimensions are measured horizontally unless specified otherwise.

[b] The takeoff climb surface starts at the end of the clearway if the clearway length exceeds the specified distance.

[c] 1800 m when the intended track includes changes of heading greater than 15° for operations conducted in IMC, VMC by night.

Table 6.7 Approach Runways: Dimensions and Slopes of Obstacle Limitation Surfaces

Runway Classification	Non-Instrument Code Number				Non-Precision Approach Code Number			Precision Approach Category I Code number		Precision Approach Category II or III Code number
Surface and Dimensions[a]	1	2	3	4	1,2	3	4	1,2	3,4	3,4
(1)	(2)	(3)	(4)	(5)	(6)	(7)	(8)	(9)	(10)	(11)
Conical										
Slope	5%	5%	5%	5%	5%	5%	5%	5%	5%	5%
Height	35 m	55 m	75 m	100 m	60 m	75 m	100 m	60 m	100 m	100 m
Inner Horizontal										
Height	45 m	45 m	45 m	45 m	45 m	45 m	45 m	45 m	45 m	45 m
Radius	2,000 m	2,500 m	4,000 m	4,000 m	3,500 m	4,000 m	4,000 m	3,500 m	4,000 m	4,000 m
Inner Approach										
Width								90 m	120 m	120 m
Distance from threshold								60 m	60 m	60 m
Length								900 m	900 m	900 m
Slope								2.5%	2%	2%
Approach										
Length of inner edge	60 m	80 m	150 m	150 m	150 m	300 m	300 m	150 m	300 m	300 m
Distance from threshold	30 m	60 m	60 m	60 m	60 m	60 m	60 m	60 m	60 m	60 m
Divergence (each side)	10%	10%	10%	10%	15%	15%	15%	15%	15%	15%

	Col 1	Col 2	Col 3	Col 4	Col 5	Col 6	Col 7	Col 8	Col 9	Col 10
First section										
Length	1,600 m	2,500 m	3,000 m	3,000 m	2,500 m	3,000 m	3,000 m	3,000 m	3,000 m	3,000 m
Slope	5%	4%	3.33%	2.5%	3.33%	2%	2%	2.5%	2%	2%
Second section										
Length						3,600 m[b]	3,600 m[b]	12,000 m	3,600 m[b]	3,600 m[b]
Slope						2.5%	2.5%	3%	2.5%	2.5%
Horizontal section										
Length						8,400 m[b]	8,400 m[b]		8,400 m[b]	8,400 m[b]
Total length						15,000 m	15,000 m	15,000 m	15,000 m	15,000 m
Transitional										
Slope	20%	20%	14.3%	14.3%	20%	14.3%	14.3%	14.3%	14.3%	14.3%
Inner Transitional										
Slope								40%	33.3%	33.3%
Balked Landing Surface										
Length of inner edge								90 m	120 m	120 m
Distance from threshold								[d]	1,800 m[c]	1,800 m[c]
Divergence (each side)								10%	10%	10%
Slope								4%	3.33%	3.33%

Source: *Aerodromes*, Annex 14 to the Convention on International Civil Aviation, including Amendment 36, July 23, 1982.

[a] All dimensions are measured horizontally unless specified otherwise.
[b] Variable length.
[c] Or end of runway, whichever is less.
[d] Distance to the end of strip.

6.19   THE TAXIWAY SYSTEM

A key component in the airport layout is the taxiway system, which connects the runways to the terminal building and service hangars. In taxiway layout and design, major emphasis is given to providing smooth and efficient flow of aircraft along the taxiways.

Where air traffic warrants, the usual procedure is to locate a taxiway parallel to the runway centerline for the entire length of the runway. This makes it possible for landing aircraft to exit the runway more quickly and decreases delays to other aircraft waiting to use the runway.

At smaller airports, air traffic may not be sufficient to justify the construction of a parallel taxiway. In this case, taxiing is done on the runway itself, and a cul-de-sac or *turnaround* must be provided at the ends of the runway.

Consideration should be given to constructing a partial parallel taxiway when construction of a full parallel taxiway is not practicable (18).

Whenever possible, taxiways should be designed so that they do not cross active runways. Ideally, at busy airports, separate taxiway routes to and from the terminal area should be constructed, to provide one-way flow.

Specific criteria for the design of runways, taxiways, and aprons are given in Chapter 7.

REFERENCES

1. Hockaday, Stephen L. M. and Adib K. Kanafani, "Developments in Airport Capacity Analysis," *Transportation Research*, Vol. 8, pp. 171–180.

2. *Airport Capacity Criteria Used in Long-Range Planning*, FAA Advisory Circular AC 150/5060-3A, December 24, 1969.

3. *Airport Capacity Criteria Used in Preparing the National Airport Plan*, FAA Advisory Circular AC 150/5060-1A, July 8, 1968.

4. *Airport Capacity and Delay*, FAA Advisory Circular AC 150/5060-5, September 23, 1983.

5. *Technical Report on Airport Capacity and Delay Studies*, prepared for the FAA by Douglas Aircraft Company et al., Report No. FAA-RD-76-153, June 1976.

6. *Airport Capacity Handbook*, 2nd Ed., prepared for the FAA by Airborne Instruments Laboratory, Report No. AD 690470, June 1969.

7. Hauer, E., "Runway Capacity," in *Readings in Airport Planning*, Toronto: University of Toronto, Centre for Urban and Community Studies and Department of Civil Engineering, 1972.

8. *Techniques for Determining Airport Airside Capacity and Delay*, prepared for the FAA by Douglas Aircraft Company et al., Report No. FAA-RD-74-124, June 1976.

9. Bowen, E. G., and T. Pearcey, "Delays in the Flow of Air Traffic," *Journal, Royal Aeronautical Society*, Vol. 52, p. 251, 1948.

10. Harris, Richard M., "Models for Runway Capacity Analysis," Report No. FAA-EM-73-5, McLean, Va.: Mitre Corporation, May 1974.

11. *Procedures for Determination of Airport Capacity*, prepared for the FAA by Douglas Aircraft et al., Interim Report No. FAA-RD-73-111, Vols. 1 and 2, April 1973.

12. Ball, Carl T., *Model Users' Manual for Airfield Capacity and Delay Models*, Books 1 and 2, Federal Aviation Administration, Report No. FAA-RD-76-128, November 1976.

13. *Supporting Documentation for Technical Report on Airport Capacity and Delay Studies*, prepared for the FAA by Douglas Aircraft Company et al., Report No. FAA-RD-76-162, June 1976.

14. Astholtz, Paul T., David J. Sheftel, and Richard M. Harris, "Increasing Runway Capacity," *Proceedings of the IEEE*, Vol. 58, No. 3, March 1970.

15. *Airport Design Standards—Transport Airports*, FAA Advisory Circular AC 150/5300-12, Washington, D.C.: February 28, 1983.

16. *Objects Affecting Navigable Airspace*, Federal Aviation Regulations, Part 77, January, 1975.

17. *Aerodromes*, Annex 14 to the Convention on International Civil Aviation, including Amendment 36, Montreal: International Civil Aviation Organization, July 23, 1982.

18. *Utility Airports—Air Access to National Transportation*, FAA Advisory Circular AC 150/5300-4B, including Changes 1–6, February 24, 1983.

7

GEOMETRIC DESIGN OF THE AIRSIDE

7.1 INTRODUCTION

This chapter contains material of fundamental importance to the airport designer. It includes specific design standards and procedures that are required for the preparation of plans and specifications for an airport. Topics covered include determination of runway lengths, longitudinal grade design for runways, and geometric design of the runway and taxiway system.

The design criteria presented here have been prepared by the International Civil Aviation Organization, the U.S. Federal Aviation Administration, the U.S. Navy, and the U.S. Air Force. There is some variation in the rigidity of these criteria. Unless otherwise indicated, the ICAO criteria are *recommended practices*, as distinguished from compulsory standards. Although ICAO member countries endeavor to conform to these practices in the interests of air safety and efficiency, conformity is not mandatory. Similarly, the FAA criteria are recommended standards rather than absolute requirements. Design standards for military airports must accommodate the characteristics and peculiarities of high performance aircraft and tend to be more rigidly enforced.

Because of local conditions and requirements, designers may find it necessary to deviate from a particular standard to improve another aspect or feature of the airport design. In such cases, they should be prepared to justify any decision to deviate from the recommended standards.

Chapter 1 describes how airports are grouped into classes according to the type of air service provided. Clearly, the design requirements for a given airport must reflect the numbers, types, and operating characteristics of the aircraft to be served.

The ICAO (1) relates the recommended runway dimensions and clearances to a "reference code." This code takes into account key lateral dimensions of the critical aircraft, as well as the runway length requirements of the critical aircraft for sea level and standard atmospheric conditions. Section 7.4 further describes the ICAO reference code.

The FAA provides design criteria for six groups of transport airports, four classes of general aviation airports, and special criteria for heliports and STOL ports. Aircraft are grouped according to approach speed and wingspan width. Section 7.5 describes the FAA's airplane design group concept.

The U.S. Air Force employs a "use" category as an indication of the principal function of its bases: heavy bomber, fighter, trainer, and so on. However, most of the design criteria normally remain constant for airfields of all types, regardless of use categories (2). The U.S. Navy has one set of design standards for all of their station facilities and makes no differentiation on the basis of use.

7.2 RUNWAY LENGTH

Selecting a design runway length is one of the most important decisions an airport designer makes. To a large degree, the runway length determines the size and cost of the airport, and controls the type of aircraft it will serve. Furthermore, it may limit the payload of the critical aircraft and the length of journey it can fly.

The runway must be long enough to allow safe landings and takeoffs by current equipment and by future aircraft expected to use the airport. It must accommodate differences in pilot skill and a variety of aircraft types and operational requirements.

The following factors most strongly influence required runway length:

1. Performance characteristics of aircraft using the airport (see Chapter 3).
2. Landing and takeoff gross weights of the aircraft.
3. Elevation of the airport.
4. Average maximum air temperature at the airport.
5. Runway gradient.

Other factors causing variations in required runway length are humidity, winds, and the nature and condition of the runway surface.

Aircraft performance curves of individual airplanes have been developed and published by the FAA (3) as a design and planning tool. These curves, which are based on actual flight test and operational data, make it possible to determine precisely required landing and takeoff runway lengths for almost all the civilian aircraft in common use, both large and small. The curves vary in format and complexity.

The FAA performance curves appearing in Figures 7.1 and 7.2 indicate the required runway lengths for the Boeing 727-00 and the Douglas DC-9-30 series, respectively.

Performance curves for takeoff are based on an *effective runway gradient* of 0%. Effective runway gradient is the maximum difference in runway centerline elevations divided by the runway length. The FAA specifies that the runway lengths for takeoff be increased by the following rates for each 1% of effective runway gradient:

1. For piston and turboprop airplanes, 20%.
2. For turbojet airplanes, 10%.

In the case of turbojet aircraft landing on wet or slippery runways, it may be necessary to increase the required landing length from 5.0 to 9.5%, depending on aircraft series (3). No correction is required for piston or turboprop airplanes.

Example 7.1 demonstrates the use of Figure 7.1. The curves in Figure 7.2 are explained in the figure itself.

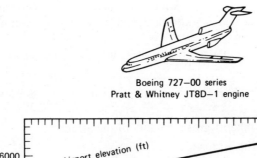

Boeing 727—00 series
Pratt & Whitney JT8D—1 engine

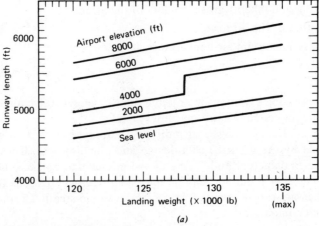

(a)

FIGURE 7.1   Aircraft performance curves for Boeing 727-00 series aircraft. (a) Landing.

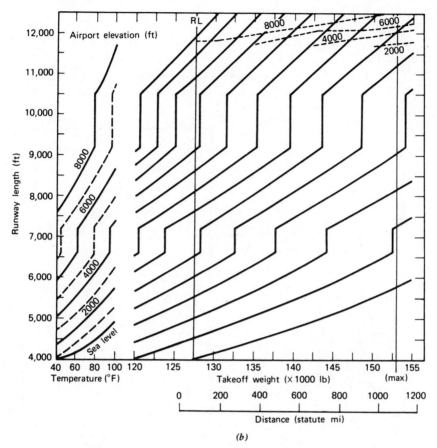

FIGURE 7.1 (continued)   (b) Takeoff. (*Source:* Reference 3.)

Example 7.1   Runway Length Requirement for a Boeing 727-00 Series Aircraft

What length of runway is required for a Boeing 727-00 series aircraft, given the following conditions?

1. Maximum landing weight, 135,000 lb.
2. Allowance for slippery pavement, 7.0%.
3. Normal maximum temperature, 80°F.
4. Airport elevation, 4000 ft.
5. Flight distance, 1000 mi.
6. Takeoff weight, 147,500 lb.
7. Effective runway gradient, 0.5%.

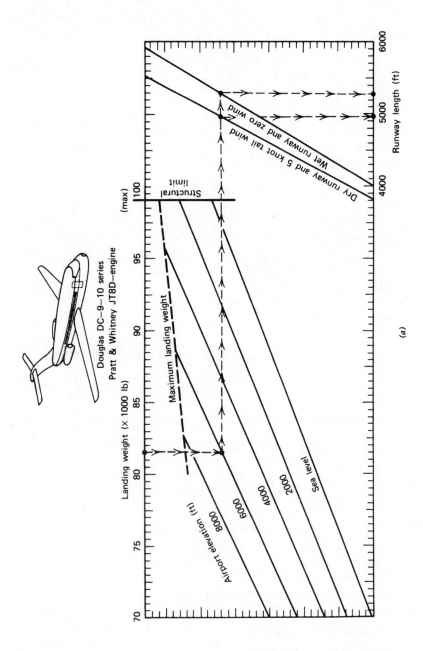

Douglas DC–9–10 series
Pratt & Whitney JT8D–engine

Landing weight (× 1000 lb)

Structural limit

Maximum landing weight

Airport elevation (ft)

8000
6000
4000
2000
Sea level

Dry runway and 5 knot tail wind
Wet runway and zero wind

Runway length (ft)

(a)

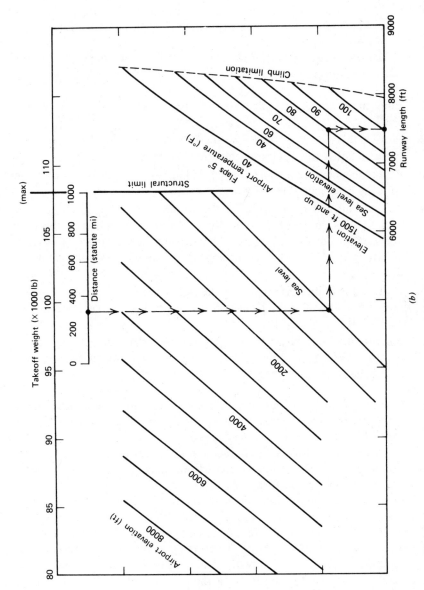

FIGURE 7.2 Aircraft performance curves for a Douglas DC-9-30 aircraft. (a) Landing. (b) Takeoff. (*Source:* Reference 3.)

185

Runway Length Required for Landing.   Enter Figure 7.1a on the abscissa axis at the maximum landing weight (135,000 lb) and project this point vertically to intersect with the 4000 ft airport elevation line. Extend this point of intersection horizontally to the right ordinate scale, where a runway length required for landing of 5650 ft is read. If this figure is increased by 7.0% to allow for slippery pavement, the required runway length for landing is 6045 ft.

Runway Length Required for Takeoff.   The following steps are required to determine from Figure 7.1b the runway length required for takeoff:

1. Enter the temperature scale on the abscissa axis at the given temperature (80°F).
2. Project this point vertically to the intersection with the slanted line corresponding to the airport elevation (4000 ft).
3. Extend this point of intersection horizontally to the right until it coincides with the reference line (RL).
4. Proceed up and to the right or down and to the left, parallel to the slanted lines, to the intersection of the elevation limit line (in this case, 4000 ft), or until reaching a point directly above the aircraft's takeoff weight (e.g., 147,500 lb) or distance (e.g., 1000 mi), whichever occurs first.
5. Project this point horizontally to the right and read the required runway length for takeoff at the right ordinate scale. In this example, a length of 9200 ft is required for takeoff.
6. Increase this runway length for effective gradient. The resulting runway length is 9660 ft, and this value, being the larger of the two, is taken as the design runway length.

Recently, the FAA has begun to publish aircraft performance data in tables from which planners can determine runway length by interpolation.

For general aviation airports, it may be possible to determine runway length without referring to performance characteristics curves for a specific aircraft. This is made possible by grouping aircraft into general classes according to function and referring to performance curves for the various aircraft groups. Such procedures are appropriate for the planning of general aviation airports and can be used for design where a specific aircraft for a location is not known.

The FAA (4) has published a family of curves (Figure 7.3) that gives recommended runway lengths for basic utility and general utility airports. Figure 7.3 gives runway lengths for elevations up to 9000 ft. Since some aircraft cannot operate at such high elevations without modification, it is advisable to examine the aircraft performance curves of individual airplanes for operations at higher elevations.

At utility airports where a crosswind runway is planned, the FAA recommends that it be 80% of the length required for the main runway (4). This length will

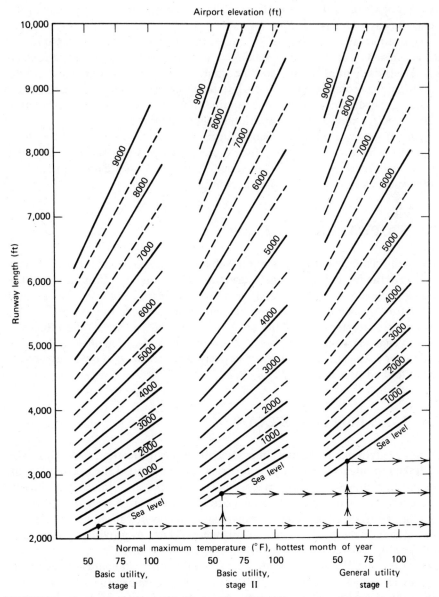

FIGURE 7.3 Runway length curves for basic and general utility airports. (*Source:* Reference 4.)

accommodate the average small aircraft when the crosswind component of the main runway exceeds 12 mph.

To use the curves in Figure 7.3, enter the appropriate family of curves on the abscissa axis at the normal maximum temperature.* From this point, extend a line vertically until it intersects the slanted line corresponding to the airport elevation, interpolating if necessary. Extend the point of intersection horizontally to the right ordinate, and read the required runway length there. No correction is required for runway gradient or other such factors.

Similar generalized performance curves have been published (4) for small airplanes which accommodate 10 or more passengers and for small turbojet airplanes. These curves were developed by the FAA with data from airplane flight manuals and assumed loading condition.

7.3 STOPWAYS AND CLEARWAYS

In certain instances, it is possible to substitute stopways and clearways for a portion of the full depth pavement structure. The decision to provide a stopway and/or a clearway as an alternative to an increased length of runway will depend on the nature of the area beyond the end of the runway and on the operating characteristics of the airplanes expected to use it. The effects of aircraft characteristics on stopway, clearway, and runway lengths are discussed in Chapter 3. Recommended uses of stopways and clearways at transport airports are described in Reference 5.

7.4 ICAO REFERENCE CODE

Runway length, being the most important airside design feature, should logically be linked to other physical characteristics of the airport. Like runway length, the physical dimensions, clearances, and separations are a function of the size and operating characteristics of the critical aircraft. We have seen, however, that large differences in required runway length may be caused by local factors that influence the performance of airplanes. Thus, to provide a meaningful relationship between field length† and other physical characteristics of the airside, the actual runway length must be converted to standard sea level conditions by removing the local effects of elevation, temperature, and gradient. When these local effects are removed, the airplane reference field length remains.

To facilitate the publication of quantitative specifications for the physical characteristics of airports, the ICAO employs an *aerodrome reference code* consisting of two elements. As Table 7.1 indicates, the first element is a

---

* The normal maximum temperature is the arithmetical average of the daily highest temperature during the hottest month. This information is usually available from the nearest National Weather Service office.

† The field length includes the runway length plus the stopway and/or clearway lengths, if provided.

Table 7.1   ICAO Reference Code

Code Element 1		Code Element 2		
Code Number	Aeroplane Reference Field Length	Code Letter	Wing Span	Outer Main Gear Wheel Span[a]
(1)	(2)	(3)	(4)	(5)
1	Less than 800 m[b]	A	Up to but not including 15 m	Up to but not including 4.5 m
2	800 m up to but not including 1200 m	B	15 m up to but not including 24 m	4.5 m up to but not including 6 m
3	1200 m up to but not including 1800 m	C	24 m up to but not including 36 m	6 m up to but not including 9 m
4	1800 m and over	D	36 m up to but not including 52 m	9 m up to but not including 14 m
		E	52 m up to but not including 60 m	9 m up to but not including 14 m

Source: *Aerodromes*, Annex 14 to the International Convention on Civil Aviation, 7th Ed., including Amendment 36, Montreal: International Civil Aviation Organization, July 23, 1982.

[a] Distance between the outside edges of the main gear wheels.

[b] 1 m = 3.2808 ft.

number based on the aerodrome reference field length and the second element is a number based on the aircraft wing span and outer main gear wheel span. The code number or letter selected for design purposes is related to the critical airplane characteristics for which the facility is provided. For a given airplane, the reference field length can be determined from the flight manual provided by the manufacturer. It is noted that the airplane reference field length is used only for the selection of a code number. It is not intended to influence the actual runway length provided.

In certain instances, it may be desirable to convert an existing or planned field length to the reference field length. The reference field length is computed by dividing the planned or existing length by the product of three factors representing local elevation F_e, temperature F_t, and gradient F_g conditions.

$$\text{reference field length} \ = \ \frac{\text{planned or existing field length}}{F_e \times F_t \times F_g} \qquad (7.1)$$

The required field length increases at a rate of 7% per 1000 ft elevation above mean sea level. Thus, the elevation factor F_e can be computed by the following equation:

$$F_e \ = \ 0.07 \times E \ + \ 1 \qquad (7.2)$$

where E = airport elevation (thousands of feet)

The field length that has been corrected for elevation should be further increased at a rate of 1% for every 1°C by which the airport reference temperature exceeds the temperature in the standard atmosphere for that elevation. The airport reference temperature T is defined as the monthly mean of the daily maximum temperatures (24 hr) for the hottest month of the year. It is recommended that the airport reference temperature be averaged over a period of years. The temperature in the standard atmosphere is 15°C at sea level, and it decreases approximately 1.981 degrees for each 1000 ft increase in elevation. The equation for the temperature correction factor becomes:

$$F_t = 0.01[T(°C) - (15 - 1.981E)] + 1 \qquad (7.3)$$

It is recommended that the runway length that has been corrected for elevation and temperature be further increased at a rate of 10% for each 1% of effective runway gradient G. This recommendation is applicable for takeoff conditions when the runway code number is 2, 3, or 4. Thus for takeoff conditions for runway code numbers 2, 3, or 4, the gradient factor is

$$F_g = (0.10G + 1) \qquad (7.4)$$

The relationships between planned and reference field lengths given in this section are generally applicable to military airports; however the recommended corrections for nonstandard conditions are not the same as for civilian airports. References 6 and 7 give recommended corrections for nonstandard conditions of altitude, temperature, and effective gradient for military runways.

7.5 THE FAA AIRPLANE DESIGN GROUP CONCEPT

In 1983 the FAA (4, 5) introduced a new concept for airport classification and design. With this system, airports are grouped into two broad categories and nine design groups.* According to the FAA concept, there are two broad airport classes: utility airports and transport airports. Utility airports serve the general aviation community and commonly accommodate small aircraft (i.e., those with maximum certificated takeoff weights of 12,500 lb or less). Transport airports can accommodate the smaller airplanes but are designed to serve the larger ones.

The FAA defines five aircraft approach categories. These categories group airplanes on the basis of an approach speed of 1.3 V_{so}. (V_{so} is the aircraft stall speed at the maximum certificated landing weight.) See Table 7.2. Utility airports serve the less demanding approach category A and B airplanes, that is, those with approach speeds of less than 121 knots. Transport airports are

---

* In the design of utility airports, subgroups are used to account for differences in airplane weight (i.e., small airplanes only) and air traffic control procedures (visual, nonprecision, and precision instrument runways).

Table 7.2   FAA Aircraft Approach Category Classification

Approach Category	Approach Speed, Knots	Airport Category
A	Less than 91	Utility Airport
B	91–120	Utility Airport
C	121–140	Transport Airport
D	141–165	Transport Airport
E	166 or greater	Transport Airport

Source: Utility Airports—Air Access to National Transportation, FAA Advisory Circular AC 150/5300-4B, including Change 7, September 23, 1983.

usually designed, constructed, and maintained to serve airplanes with approach speeds of 121 knots or greater.

FAA geometric design standards are linked to the wingspan of the critical aircraft. Definitions of each Airplane Design Group are given in Table 7.3 along with a list of typical aircraft for each group. The chart shown in Figure 7.4 provides guidance in selecting the proper airplane design group and airport dimensional standards.

7.6   SEPARATION OF PARALLEL RUNWAYS

The overriding consideration in the determination of parallel runway separation is safety. Where simultaneous operations will be permitted to occur under favorable weather conditions (VFR operations), the ICAO permits, for Code Number 1, parallel runway centerlines to be placed as close as 400 ft (1). ICAO specifies a minimum separation for simultaneous visual operations of 500 ft for Code Number 2 and 700 ft for Code Numbers 3 and 4.

For simultaneous landings and takeoffs under visual flight rules, the FAA specifies a minimum separation between centerlines of parallel runways of 700 ft (5). However, the minimum centerline separation distance for Airplane Design Group V is 1200 ft.

Table 7.3   FAA Airplane Design Groups for Geometric Design of Airports

Airplane Design Group	Wing Span (ft)	Typical Aircraft
I	Less than 49	Beech Bonanza A36, Learjet 25
II	49 up to 79	DeHavilland DHC-6, Gulfstream II
III	79 up to 118	Boeing 737, Martin-404
IV	118 up to 171	Boeing 757, Lockheed 1011
V	171 up to 197	Boeing 747
VI	197 up to 262	Lockheed C5A

Source: Utility Airports—Air Access to National Transportation, FAA Advisory Circular AC 150/5300-4B, including Change 7, September 23, 1983.

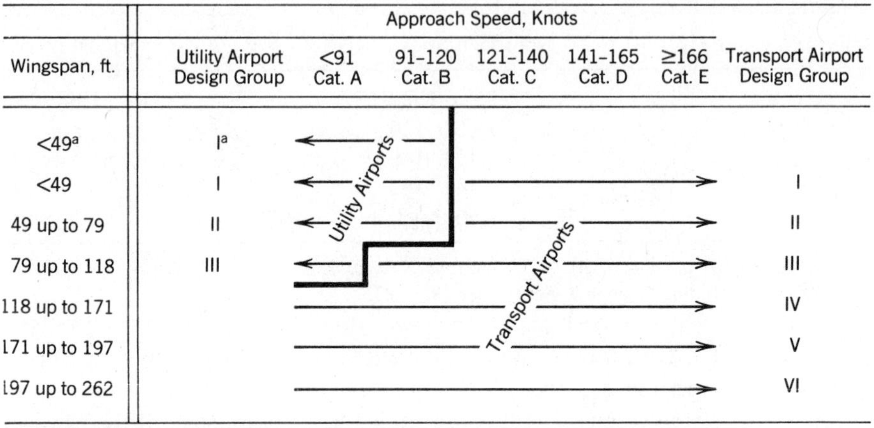

Wingspan, ft.	Approach Speed, Knots						
	Utility Airport Design Group	<91 Cat. A	91–120 Cat. B	121–140 Cat. C	141–165 Cat. D	≥166 Cat. E	Transport Airport Design Group
<49ᵃ	Iᵃ						
<49	I						I
49 up to 79	II						II
79 up to 118	III						III
118 up to 171							IV
171 up to 197							V
197 up to 262							VI

ᵃApplies to airports that are to serve only small airplanes.

FIGURE 7.4   FAA airplance design group concept. (Adapted from Reference 4.)

The Navy (7) and Air Force (8) specify a minimum clearance of 1000 ft between the centerlines of parallel runways for simultaneous VFR operations. Where an intervening taxiway is to be provided, the Air Force recommends a clearance of 2000 ft.

Criteria for minimum separation of parallel instrument runways is based on empirical data from special flight tests and studies of ground track recordings for actual flights. Such studies have provided data on lateral deviations from the ILS centerline and the effect of speed and intercept angle (9). Research in the 1960s indicated that a minimum separation of parallel runways of 5000 ft was required for simultaneous instrument approaches. However, the FAA (5) now specifies a minimum separation of 4300 ft for simultaneous precision instrument approaches, provided specific electronic navigational aids and monitoring equipment, air traffic control, and approach procedures are used. A minimum separation of 3500 ft is required for simultaneous departures and is also suitable for simultaneous arrivals and departures, provided radar air traffic control is exercised and the thresholds are not staggered (5). When the thresholds are staggered, the 2500 ft separation may be reduced if the approach is to the nearer threshold but must be increased if the approach is to the farther threshold. Specific recommendations with respect to the effect of staggered thresholds are given in Reference 5. It will be necessary to observe wake turbulence avoidance procedures when centerline spacings under 2500 ft are used. The Navy (7) specifies a minimum separation of parallel runways of 5000 ft for simultaneous instrument approaches.

7.7   RUNWAY AND TAXIWAY CROSS SECTION

In the early days of aviation, all aircraft operated from relatively unimproved landing fields, maneuvering along unpaved paths called *landing strips*. Later, to meet the requirements of more advanced aircraft, it became necessary to improve or pave the center portion of the landing strip. The term "landing strip" came to refer to the graded area on which the load-bearing surface was placed. The function of the landing strip changed to that of a safety area bordering the runway. The FAA (4) now refers to the entire graded area between the side slopes as the *runway safety area*, as Figures 7.5 and 7.6 illustrate. In its literature, the ICAO refers to a comparable area as the *runway strip*.

The border areas immediately adjacent to the runway pavement are referred to as shoulders. Shoulders are usually paved or otherwise stabilized in order to resist jet blast erosion and/or to accommodate maintenance equipment. The portion of the runway safety area abutting the edges of the shoulders is cleared, drained, graded, and usually turfed. At airports serving small aircraft, the entire border area abutting the paved runway may be a natural surface, such as turf.

Runway safety areas range in width from 120 ft at the smallest utility airports to 500 ft or wider for all categories of transport airports (4, 5). Similar widths of runway strips are recommended by the ICAO (1).

Runways and Shoulders

The runway is a paved load-bearing area that varies in width from about 60 ft at the smallest general aviation airports to 150 ft or more at the largest air carrier airports. Studies have shown that the distribution of wheel load applications occurring during landings and takeoffs approximates a normal distribution centered about the runway centerline. Virtually all the load applications are concentrated in a central width of about 100 ft. The additional 50 ft of width on major runways protects jet aircraft engines from ingestion of loose material and also provides an added measure of safety for errant aircraft.

The FAA recommends shoulder widths ranging from 10 ft to 40 ft for transport airports (5). The ICAO recommends that the overall width of the runway plus its shoulders be not less than 60 m or approximately 200 ft (1).

Airports serving military aircraft may require runways and runway safety areas wider than those provided at civilian airports. For example, the Air Force (6) requires a runway width of 150 ft for runways serving fighter and trainer aircraft, but a width of 300 ft for those serving heavy bombers. A graded area bordering the runway 200 ft in width is uniformly specified. The Navy (7) specifies a 200 ft runway and a 500 ft runway safety area width.

Shoulders are not designed for frequent applications of aircraft or vehicular loads. Rather, they are intended to minimize the probability of serious damage

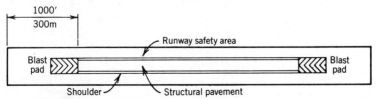

FIGURE 7.5 Plan view of runway elements. (*Source:* Reference 5.)

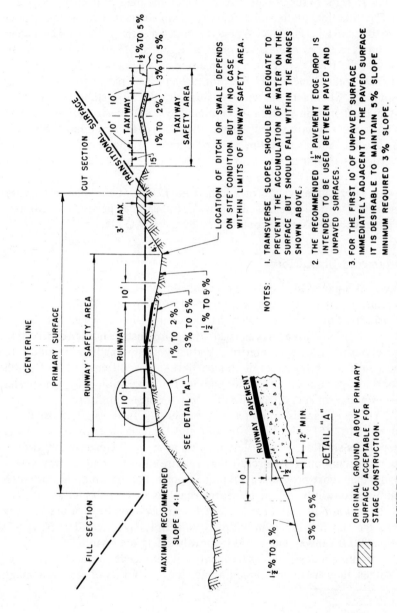

FIGURE 7.6 Transverse grade limitations for utility airports. (*Source:* Reference 4.)

NOTES:

1. TRANSVERSE SLOPES SHOULD BE ADEQUATE TO PREVENT THE ACCUMULATION OF WATER ON THE SURFACE BUT SHOULD FALL WITHIN THE RANGES SHOWN ABOVE.

2. THE RECOMMENDED 1½" PAVEMENT EDGE DROP IS INTENDED TO BE USED BETWEEN PAVED AND UNPAVED SURFACES.

3. FOR THE FIRST 10' OF UNPAVED SURFACE IMMEDIATELY ADJACENT TO THE PAVED SURFACE IT IS DESIRABLE TO MAINTAIN 5% SLOPE MINIMUM REQUIRED 3% SLOPE.

to aircraft or injury to the crew or passengers in the event that an aircraft suddenly veers from the runway. At civilian airports, shoulders are most commonly constructed of stabilized earth with a turf cover. The Air Force (6) recommends that the first 10 ft of shoulder beyond the runway edge be constructed with a select base material having a California bearing ratio (CBR) of 10, and paved with a double bituminous surface treatment, or with 6 in. of soil cement topped with a single bituminous treatment.

Consideration should be given to constructing runway blast pads at the ends of runways that accommodate frequent jet operations. These pads should extend across the full width of the runway plus shoulders and should be marked as nontraffic areas. Blast pads vary in length from 100 ft to 400 ft depending on the airplane group served.

Taxiways

In cross section, a taxiway is similar in appearance to a runway. The dimensions are, of course, much smaller. The taxiway structural pavement is typically 20 to 60 ft wide at general aviation airports and 50 to 125 ft at air carrier airports. Both the Air Force and the Navy specify a standard taxiway width of 75 ft.

In the interests of safety and good aircraft maneuverability, adequate separations must be provided between runways and taxiways, along with ample clearances to buildings and other obstacles. Tables 7.4 to 7.7 summarize these and other minimum dimensional standards. To use the ICAO dimensional standards, first determine the reference field length, the wing span, and the outer main gear wheel span for the critical aircraft. The standards are keyed to the reference code defined in Table 7.1.

FAA's dimensional standards for runways and taxiways at transport airports are given by Tables 7.5 and 7.6, respectively. These standards are given by Airplane Design Group. (Refer to Table 7.3 and Figure 7.4.) Similar standards are given in Table 7.7 for utility airports.

Table 7.4a ICAO Minimum Dimensional Recommended Practices

	ICAO Code Number			
	1	2	3	4
Width of runway strips				
Precision approach runway (m)[a]	75	75	150	150
Nonprecision approach runway (m)	75	75	150	150
Noninstrument runway (m)	30	40	75	75
Width of cleared and graded area				
Instrument runway (m)	40	40	75	75
Noninstrument runway (m)	30	40	75	75

[a] 1 m = 3.2808 ft.

Table 7.4b   ICAO Recommended Practices—Width of Runways

	Code Letter				
Code Number	A	B	C	D	E
1[a]	18 m[b]	18 m	23 m	—	—
2[a]	23 m	23 m	30 m	—	—
3	30 m	30 m	30 m	45 m	—
4	—	—	45 m	45 m	45 m

[a] The width of a precision approach runway should be not less than 30 m where the code number is 1 or 2.

[b] 1 m = 3.2808 ft.

Transverse Grades

As shown in the typical section (Figure 7.6), runways are crowned or sloped away from the centerline to facilitate drainage. As a general rule, transverse runway slopes should be kept to a minimum consistent with drainage requirements. Normally, to prevent the accumulation of water on the surface, transverse grades of at least 1.0% are required; however, when rigid pavements are used, the Air Force (8) permits slopes as small as 0.5%. Maximum transverse slopes are specified to facilitate operational safety. Slopes up to 2.0% are permitted for runways that serve the smaller classes of aircraft (utility runways, and for ICAO code letters A and B). For all other runways, the maximum grade is 1.5%.

Beyond the runway edge, steeper slopes are employed to expedite the removal of surface water. Most agencies permit shoulder slopes up to 5.0% for the first 10 ft beyond the pavement edge. Beyond that point, slopes of 1.5 to 3.0%

Table 7.4c   ICAO Recommended Practices—Width of Taxiways

Code Letter	Taxiway Width
A	7.5 m[a]
B	10.5 m
C	15 m if the taxiway is intended to be used by airplanes with a wheel base less than 18 m;
	18 m if the taxiway is intended to be used by airplanes with a wheel base equal to or greater than 18 m.
D	18 m if the taxiway is intended to be used by airplanes with an outer main gear wheel span of less than 9 m;
	23 m if the taxiway is intended to be used by airplanes with an outer main gear wheel span equal to or greater than 9 m.
E	23 m

[a] 1 m = 3.2808 ft.

Table 7.4d   ICAO Recommended Practices—Taxiway Minimum Separation Distances

Code Letter	Distance between Taxiway Center Line and Runway Center Line (m)[a]								Taxiway Center Line to Taxiway Center Line (m)	Taxiway, Other Than Aircraft Stand Taxilane, Center Line to Object (m)	Aircraft Stand Taxilane Center Line to Object (m)
	Instrument Runways Code Number				Non-instrument Runways Code Number						
	1	2	3	4	1	2	3	4			
(1)	(2)	(3)	(4)	(5)	(6)	(7)	(8)	(9)	(10)	(11)	(12)
A	82.5	82.5			37.5	47.5			21	13.5	12
B	87	87			42	52			31.5	19.5	16.5
C			168				93		46.5	28.5	24.5
D			176	176			101	101	68.5	42.5	36
E				180				105	76.5	46.5	40

Note: The separation distances shown in columns 2 to 9 represent ordinary combinations of runways and taxiways. The basis for development of these distances is given in the Aerodrome Design Manual, Part 2.

[a] 1 m = 3.2808 ft.

Table 7.5 FAA Runway Dimensional Standards for Transport Airports

Design Item	Airplane Design Group					
	I	II	III	IV	V	VI
Runway safety area Width (ft)[a,b]	500	500	500	500	500	500
Runway safety area Length (ft)[c]	1000 ft beyond each runway end					
Runway width (ft)	100	100	100[d]	150	150	200
Runway shoulder width (ft)	10	10	20	25	35	40
Runway blast pad width (ft)	120	120	140[d]	200	220	280
Blast pad length (ft)	100	150	200	200	400	400
Runway centerline to:						
Taxiway centerline (ft)	400	400	400	400	Varies[e]	600
Aircraft parking area (ft)	500	500	500	500	500	500
Property/building restriction line (ft)	750	750	750	750	750	750

Source: Airport Design Standards—Transport Airports, FAA Advisory Circular AC 150/5300-12, February 28, 1983.

[a] 1 ft = 0.3048 m.

[b] For airplanes in Approach Category C, the safety area width increases 20 ft for each additional 1000 ft of airport elevation greater than 8200 ft above sea level. For airplanes in Approach Category D, it increases 20 ft for each 1000 ft of airport elevation above sea level.

[c] For a runway with a stopway over 1000 ft in length, the runway safety area extends to the end of the stopway.

[d] For airports serving airplanes with maximum certificated weight greater than 150,000 pounds, increase dimension by 50 ft.

[e] Dimension varies with airport elevation. See Reference 5.

Table 7.6. FAA Taxiway Dimensional Standards for Transport Airports

Design Item	Airplane Design Group					
	I	II	III	IV	V	VI
Taxiway safety area width (ft)[a]	49	79	118	171	197	262
Taxiway width (ft)	25	35	50[b]	75	75	100
Taxiway edge safety margin (ft)[c]	5	7.5	10[d]	15	15	20
Taxiway shoulder width (ft)	10	10	20	25	35	40
Taxiway centerline to:						
Parallel taxiway centerline (ft)	69	103	153	225	251	340
Fixed or movable object and to property line (ft)	44	64	94	139	153	205
Fixed or movable object (ft)	39	54	80	118	131	172

Source: *Airport Design Standards—Transport Airports*, FAA Advisory Circular AC 150/5300-12, February 28, 1983.

[a] 1 ft = 0.3048 m.

[b] For Airplane Design Group III taxiways intended to be used by airplanes with a wheelbase equal to or greater than 60 ft, the standard taxiway width is 60 ft.

[c] The taxiway edge safety margin is the minimum acceptable distance between the outside of the airplane wheels and the pavement edge.

[d] For airplanes in Design Group III with a wheelbase equal to or greater than 60 ft, the taxiway edge safety margin is 15 ft.

Table 7.7 FAA Minimum Dimensional Standards for Utility Airports

Design Item	Nonprecision and Visual Runways Airplane Design Group			Precision Instrument Runways Airplane Design Group			
	I[b]	I	II	I[b]	I	II	III
Runway safety area width (ft)[a]	120	120	150	300	300	300	300
Runway width (ft)	60	60	75	75	100	100	100
Runway safety area length beyond runway end (ft)[c]	240	240	300	600	600	600	600
Taxiway safety area width (ft)	49	49	79	49	49	79	118
Taxiway width (ft)	25	25	35	25	25	35	50
Runway centerline to:							
Taxiway centerline (ft)	150	225	240	200	250	300	350
Building restriction line and aircraft tiedown area (ft)	125	200	250	Refer to AC 150/5300-4B			
Taxiway centerline to:							
Taxiway centerline	69	69	103	69	69	103	153

Source: *Utility Airports—Air Access to National Transportation*, FAA Advisory Circular AC 5300-4B, including Change 7, September 23, 1983.

[a] 1 ft = 0.3048 m.

[b] These dimensional standards are for facilities expected to serve only small airplanes.

[c] These distances may need to be increased to keep the stopway within the runway safety area.

are commonly used, depending on the type of shoulder surface. The FAA (5), for example, specifies transverse gradients of at least 3.0% for turf shoulders. The FAA further recommends a 1.5 in. drop from the paved surface to the graded shoulder surface. For taxiways, most agencies specify the same transverse gradient criteria recommended for runways.

7.8 LONGITUDINAL GRADE DESIGN FOR RUNWAYS AND STOPWAYS

From the standpoint of aircraft operational efficiency and safety, a level runway is ideal. However this ideal is seldom achievable in practice. A runway safety area encompasses a vast expanse, and its preparation may involve the excavation and movement of great quantities of earth. The cost of such earthmoving will generally rule out the attainment of a totally level runway gradient. Nevertheless, to facilitate smooth, comfortable, and safe landings and takeoffs, longitudinal runway grades should be as flat as practicable, and grade changes should be avoided. It should also be remembered that needless gradients have the effect of increasing the required runway length, thereby raising the construction costs.

As Table 7.8 and Figure 7.7 indicate, a maximum longitudinal grade of 1.25 to 1.50% is generally specified for runways that serve the largest classes of aircraft. Much flatter slopes should be used in the first and last quarters of such runways. Maximum grades of 2.0% are permitted at utility airports. The FAA (4, 5) recommends that longitudinal grade changes be not greater than 1.5% at air carrier airports and no more than 2.0% at general aviation airports. Similar criteria have been given by the ICAO (1).

Note from Tables 7.8 and 7.9 that agencies specify the minimum distance between the points of intersection of two successive grade changes. This distance is based on the sum of the absolute values of corresponding grade changes.

Example 7.2

A −0.5% runway longitudinal grade intersects a −1.2% grade, which in turn intersects a +0.3% grade. Based on the specification for ICAO code number 3, what minimum distance should be used between the points of intersection for these grades?

Solution. The absolute value of the grade change for the first point of intersection is given by

$$A = -0.5\% - (-1.2\%) = 0.7\%$$

Similarly, the absolute value of the grade change for the second point of intersection is given by

$$B = -1.2\% - (+0.3\%) = 1.5\%$$

Table 7.8 Runway Longitudinal Grade Design Criteria for Civilian Airports[a]

	Maximum Longitudinal Grade (%)	Maximum Grade, First and Last Quarter (%)	Maximum Effective Grade (%)	Maximum Change (%)	Distance Between Points of Inter-section (ft)[d]	Length of Vertical Curve[b] (ft/1% grade change)
FAA						
Transport airports	1.5	0.5	1.0	1.5	1000(A + B)	1000
Utility airports	2.0	—	—	2.0	250(A + B)	300
ICAO						
Code number 4	1.25	0.8	1.0	1.5	984(A + B)	984
Code number 3	1.5	0.8[c]	1.0	1.5	492(A + B)	492
Code number 2	2.0	—	1.0	2.0	164(A + B)	246
Code number 1	2.0	—	2.0	2.0	164(A + B)	246

Sources: *Utility Airports*, FAA Advisory Circular AC 150/5300-4B including Changes 1–7, September 23, 1983; *Airport Design Standards—Transport Airports*, FAA Advisory Circular AC 150/5300-12, February 28, 1983; and *Aerodromes*, Annex 14 to the Convention on International Civil Aviation, Montreal: ICAO including Amendment 36 (proposed), July 23, 1982.

[a] Runway grade changes shall also conform to sight distance criteria described in Section 7.8.

[b] No vertical curve is required when grade change is less than 0.4%.

[c] For precision approach runway category II or III.

[d] 1 ft = 0.3048 m.

202

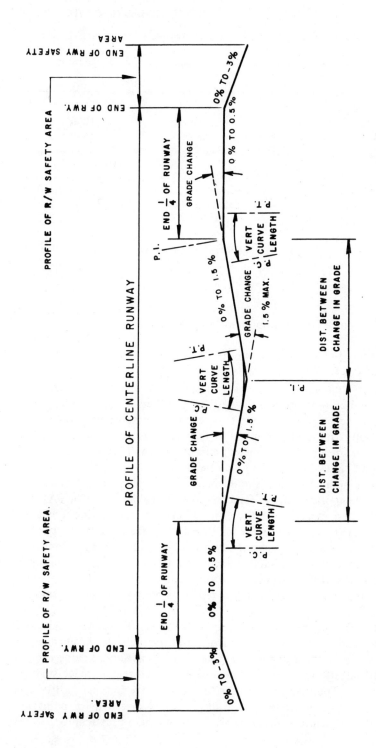

MINIMUM DISTANCE BETWEEN CHANGE IN GRADE = 1000' (300m) x SUM OF GRADE CHANGES (IN PERCENT).

MINIMUM LENGTH OF VERTICAL CURVES = 1000' (300m) x GRADE CHANGE (IN PERCENT).

FIGURE 7.7 Longitudinal grade criteria for transport airports: P.I. = point of intersection; P.T. = point of tangency; P.C. = point of curvature. (*Source*: Reference 5.)

Table 7.9   Runway Longitudinal Grade Design Criteria for U.S. Navy and Air Force Airports

Design Item	Value
1. Maximum longitudinal grade (%)	1.0
2. Minimum distance between points of intersection (ft)[a]	1000[b]
3. Minimum length of vertical curve (ft/1% change)	600
4. Maximum grade change criteria near runway ends	No grade change within 3000 ft of ends

Sources: *Design Manual—Communications, Navigation Aids, and Airfield Lighting*, NAVFAC DM-21, including Changes 1,2, Naval Facilities Engineering Command, August, 1978, and *Airfield and Airspace Criteria*, Air Force Manual 86-8B, May 3, 1967.

[a] 1 ft = 0.3048 m.

[b] The Navy specifies that no two successive distances between points of intersection shall be the same.

The minimum distance between points of intersection,

$$D = 492(A + B) = 492(0.7 + 1.5) = 1082 \text{ ft}$$

When there is a change in grade as great as 0.4%, a transition from one slope to another should be provided. The FAA recommends that the length of the transition curve be at least 300 ft for each 1% grade change at utility airports and 1000 ft for each 1% grade change at transport airports. Similar criteria for minimum lengths of vertical curves for the ICAO, the FAA, the U.S. Navy, and U.S. Air Force are given in Tables 7.8 and 7.9.

Sight distance along runways should be as unrestrictive as possible and must adhere to the applicable requirements given in Table 7.10. The FAA (4, 5) has also published special visibility criteria between intersecting runways.

Longitudinal grade design criteria for that part of the runway safety area between the runway ends are generally the same as the comparable standards for the runway. Some deviations may be required because of taxiways or other runways in the area. In such cases, the longitudinal grades of the runway safety area should be modified to the extent feasible by the use of smooth curves.

For the first 200 ft of the runway safety area beyond the runway ends, the FAA (5) recommends that the slope be downward from the ends and not steeper than 3%. For the remainder of the safety area, the longitudinal slope should be such that no part of the runway safety area penetrates the approach surface or clearway plane. The maximum negative grade is 5% for that part of the safety area. A maximum grade change of ± 2% is specified for points of intersection, and vertical curves are recommended where practical (5).

Table 7.10 Runway Sight Distance Requirements

Runway grade changes shall be such that any two points Y ft above the runway centerline will be mutually visible for a minimum distance of X ft.

Airport Category	Y (ft)[a]	X (ft)
Utility and transport		
without 24-hr traffic control	5	Entire runway length[b]
with 24-hr traffic control		See footnote c
ICAO code letter A	5	Half runway length
ICAO code letter B	7	Half runway length
ICAO code letter C, D, E	10	Half runway length
U.S. Air Force	10	5000 ft
U.S. Navy	8	5000 ft

Sources: Airport Design Standards—Transport Airports, FAA Advisory Circular AC 150/5300-12, February 28, 1983; and Utility Airports—Air Access to National Transportation, FAA Advisory Circular AC 150/5300-4B, including Changes 1–7, September 23, 1983.

[a] 1 ft = 0.3046 m.

[b] If full length parallel taxiway is provided X = half the runway length.

[c] Adherence to runway longitudinal gradient standards will provide adequate line of sight. However, care should be taken to insure that the tower will remain in 24-hr operation and that visibility requirements from the tower to airport surface areas used for aircraft ground movements will not be violated.

7.9 LONGITUDINAL GRADE DESIGN FOR TAXIWAYS

Since aircraft movements along taxiways are relatively slow, longitudinal grade design standards for taxiways are not as rigorous as for runways. Operationally, level taxiways are preferred. But there is also a need for taxiway gradients to harmonize with associated parallel runway gradients.

At the highest functional airport classes the maximum taxiway gradient of 1.5% is generally specified. This includes taxiways for all FAA air carrier airports, ICAO code letters C, D, and E, and military jet bomber bases. Maximum longitudinal taxiway gradients of 3.0% are permitted for ICAO code letters A and B and for Air Force bases other than jet bomber bases.

Agencies generally agree that taxiway vertical curves should be at least 100 ft long for each 1% grade change. The ICAO permits taxiway vertical curves as short as 83 ft for each 1% grade change where the code letter of the longest runway served is A or B. The FAA further recommends that at transport airports, the distance between points of intersection of vertical curves be kept to a minimum of 100 times the sum of the grade changes (in percent) associated with the two vertical curves. That is, using the terminology of the previous section, the minimum distance between vertical points of intersection should be $100(A + B)$.

The FAA has no specific line of sight requirements for taxiways, but recommends that special analyses be made of sight distance where taxiways and runways intersect. The Air Force recommends a minimum taxiway sight distance of 1000 ft measured from any two points 10 ft above the pavement. The ICAO recommendations (1) are as follows:

Where slope changes on taxiways cannot be avoided, they should be such that, from any point:

1. Ten feet above the taxiway, it will be possible to see the whole surface of the taxiway for a distance of 1000 ft from that point, where the code letter is C, D, or E.

2. Seven feet above the taxiway, it will be possible to see the whole surface of the taxiway for a distance of 660 ft from that point, where the code letter is B.

3. Five feet above the taxiway, it will be possible to see the whole surface of the taxiway for a distance of 500 ft from that point, where the code letter is A.

7.10 TAXIWAY DESIGN

The design of the taxiway system is determined by the volume of air traffic, the runway configuration, and the location of the terminal building and other ground facilities. The ICAO (9) and the FAA (5) have published general guidelines for taxiway layout and design, which are summarized below.

Taxiway routes should be direct, straight, and uncomplicated. Where curves cannot be avoided, their radii should be large enough to permit taxiing speeds on the order of 20 to 30 mph. Radii corresponding to taxiing speeds of 20, 30, and 40 mph are, respectively, 200, 450, and 800 ft. The taxiway pavement should be widened on curves and at intersections to lessen the likelihood of an aircraft's wheels dropping off the pavement. Table 7.6 shows recommended taxiway edge safety margins, the minimum distance between the outside of the airplane wheels and the pavement edge. The dimensions given in Table 7.11 are suitable for the design of intersections, entrance taxiways, and other areas where low speed movements are anticipated. These standards should give adequate taxiway edge safety margins for the aircraft in each design group. The symbols for these dimensions are keyed to those shown in Figure 7.8. Where these standard fillet designs are not appropriate (e.g., because of space limitations or because a particular type of airplane does not have the minimum taxiway edge safety margin), the pavement fillet may be custom designed using equations given in Reference 5.

The minimum separations between centerlines of parallel taxiways are based on a minimum wingtip clearance of 0.25 times the wingspan of the most

Table 7.11 Taxiway Fillet Dimensions

Design Item	Dimension[a]	Airplane Design Group					
		I	II	III	IV	V	VI
Radius of taxiway turn (ft)	R	75	75	100	150	150	170
Length of lead-in to fillet (ft)	L	50	50	150	250	250	250
Fillet radius for judgmental oversteering symmetrical widening (ft)	F	62.5	57.5	68	105	105	110
Fillet radius for judgmental oversteering one side widening (ft)	F	62.5	57.5	60	97	97	100
Fillet radius for tracking centerline (ft)	F	60	55	55	85	85	85

Source: Airport Design Standards—Transport Airports, FAA Advisory Circular AC 150/5300-12, February 28, 1983.

[a] 1 ft = 0.3048 m.

[b] Letters are keyed to those shown as dimensions on Figure 7.8.

[c] For Airplane Design Group III taxiways intended to be used by airplanes with a wheelbase equal to or greater than 60 ft, a fillet radius of 50 ft should be used.

demanding airplane plus a 7 ft (2 m) margin of safety. The same wingtip clearance is recommended for taxiway to obstacle separation (5). In the immediate terminal area where taxiing is accomplished at slow speeds and with special guidance procedures and devices, a wingtip clearance of approximately one-half of that required for an apron taxiway is recommended. Assuming these wingtip clearances, the required separations, expressed in feet, for taxiway design become:

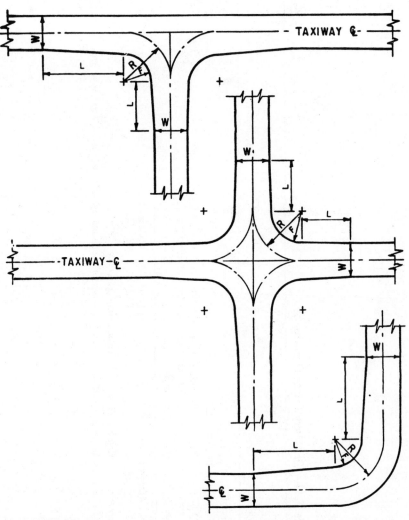

FIGURE 7.8 Typical taxiway intersection details. (*Source:* Reference 5.)

Taxiway centerline to taxiway centerline	$1.25\ W\ +\ 7$
Taxiway centerline to obstacle	$0.75\ W\ +\ 7$
Taxiway centerline to obstacle	$0.63\ W\ +\ 7$

where W = wingspan of the most demanding aircraft.

In most instances, the clearance and separation distances given in Table 7.6 will satisfy the minimum wing tip clearances. However, at high density airports where higher taxiing speeds are desired, larger clearances and separations should be used.

At large and busy airports, the time an average aircraft occupies the runway frequently determines the capacity of the runway system and the airport as a whole. This indicates that exit taxiways should be conveniently located so that landing aircraft can vacate the runway as soon as possible.

Figure 7.9 illustrates three common types of exit taxiways. Perpendicular exit taxiways may be used when the design peak hour traffic is less than 30 operations per hour. To expedite the movement of landing aircraft from the runway, most modern air carrier airports provide exit taxiways that are oriented to an angle to the runway centerline. The exit taxiway angled 45° to the runway centerline is recommended for small aircraft. It will accommodate an exit speed of 40 mph. The exit configuration Figure 7.9c (30° angle of intersection) permits runway turnoff speeds up to 60 mph.

The number and location of exit taxiways depends on the type and mix of aircraft using the runway. At utility airports, three exit taxiways are generally sufficient: one at the center and one at each end of the runway. A modern air carrier runway may have three angled exit taxiways for each landing direction, plus several 90° exit taxiways.

For a given class of aircraft, the desired location of a high speed exit taxiway can be calculated, based on the following factors.

1. Distance from the threshold to touchdown.
2. Touchdown speed.
3. Initial exit speed (turnoff speed at the P. C.).
4. Rate of deceleration.

The distance from the threshold to touchdown averages about 1500 ft for turbojet aircraft (categories C and D)* and approximately 1000 ft for other aircraft (category B). Typical touchdown speeds are 164, 202, and 237 ft/sec, respectively, for category B, C, and D aircraft. Initial exit speeds are generally

---

* The categories here refer to groupings of airplanes in U.S. Standard for Terminal Instrument Procedures (TERPS). These categories, which are made on the basis of approach speed and maximum landing weight, should not be confused with those mentioned in Sec. 6-4 for the ICAO categories designated by the same letters.

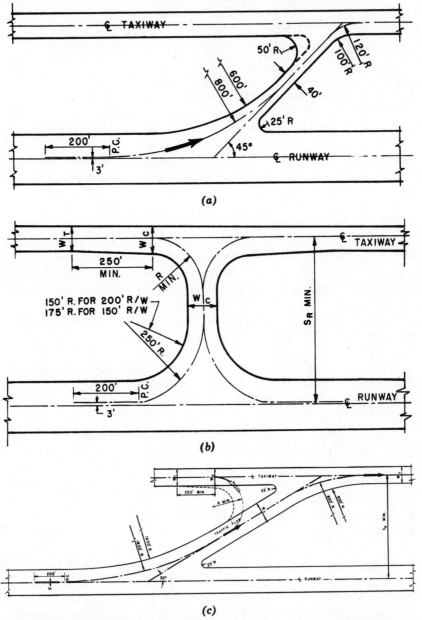

FIGURE 7.9 Common types of exit taxiways. (a) Angled exit taxiway for small airplanes. (b) 90 degree exit taxiway. (c) Angled exit taxiway for large airplanes. (*Source:* Reference 5.)

taken to be 40 mph (59 ft/sec) for small aircraft and 60 mph (88 ft/sec) for large aircraft. The ICAO (10) recommends a deceleration rate of 1.25 m/sec^2 (4.1 ft/sec^2), and the FAA has utilized 5 ft/sec.^{2}

The distance from touchdown to ideal exit location can be determined by the following formula:

$$D = \frac{(S_1)^2 - (S_2)^2}{2a} \qquad (7.5)$$

where

$S_1 = $ runway touchdown speed (ft/sec)
$S_2 = $ runway initial exit speed (ft/sec)
$a = $ deceleration (ft/sec^2)

The distance from the threshold to the P. C. of the exit curve is determined by adding to D a distance of 1000 or 1500 ft, as appropriate. Normally it is necessary, however, to correct this distance for local altitude and temperature conditions. It is suggested that exit taxiway distances from the threshold be increased 3% per 1000 ft of altitude over that required for standard sea level and 1.5% per 10°F above 59°F.

7.11 HOLDING APRONS

A holding apron is an area contiguous to the taxiway, near the runway entrance, where aircraft park briefly before taking off while cockpit checks and engine runups are made. The use of holding aprons reduces interference between departing aircraft and minimizes delays at this portion of the runway system.

In the case of utility airports, the FAA (4) recommends the installation of holding aprons when air activity reaches 30 operations per normal peak hour. Space to accommodate at least two, but not more than four, is recommended for small airports.

General space requirements may be approximated by applying factors to the wingspans of the aircraft that will be using the facility. These factors will provide a guide for space requirements for maneuvering and wingtip clearance. Studies of aircraft equipped with *dual-wheel undercarriages* reveal that the diameter of the space required to maneuver and hold such aircraft may be closely approximated by multiplying the wingspan by factors varying between 1.35 and 1.50. Similar investigations for dual-tandem gear aircraft reveal that factors of between 1.60 and 1.75 will suffice. This factor for small aircraft with a conventional single-wheel gear varies between 1.50 and 1.65 (10).

7.12 TERMINAL APRONS

Airport designers must provide paved areas where aircraft may be parked while fueling, light maintenance, loading and unloading of passengers and cargo, and similar operations are performed. Perhaps the most important such area is the terminal apron, which is located adjacent to the terminal building. Individual loading positions along the terminal apron are known as "gate positions" or "stands." This section discusses approaches to determining the size and design of gate positions. Chapter 8 covers methods of forecasting the number of required gate positions and of determining the total area of the terminal apron.

The design of the airport apron area depends on four factors:

1. The configuration of the terminal (linear, inboard pier, satellite, etc.) and the clearances required for safety and the protection of passengers from propeller wash, blast, heat, noise, and fumes.

2. The movement characteristics of the aircraft to be served (e.g., turning radius), whether it moves into and out of the apron under its own power, and the angle at which it parks with respect to the building.

3. The physical characteristics of the aircraft (i.e., its dimensions and service points and their relationship to the terminal and its appendages).

4. The types and sizes of ground service equipment and the maneuvering, staging, and operational practices employed in their use.

As indicated previously, wing tip clearance requirements in the immediate terminal area are about half those for an aircraft moving along a taxiway or apron taxiway. Thus, the following minimum wing tip clearances are needed for the terminal apron:

Twin-engine turboprop	20 ft
Two- and three-engine turbojet	25 ft
Three- and four-engine turbojet	30 ft
High capacity turbojet	35 ft
Next generation airplanes	40 ft

For aircraft with wing spans less than 75 ft, clearances on the terminal apron of 10 to 15 ft may be sufficient (9).

Aircraft usually taxi into the apron area, but they either taxi out or are pushed from the apron area by a tractor. The taxi-out arrangement is normally employed at low volume locations where smaller aircraft may maneuver with few restrictions on space or operation, but the push-out procedure is often used for large jet aircraft (11).

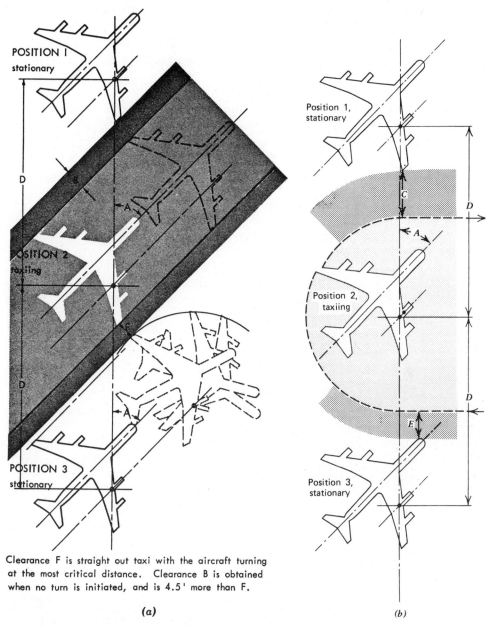

POSITION I
stationary

D

B

A

POSITION 2
taxiing

F

D

POSITION 3
stationary

Position 1,
stationary

C

D

A

Position 2,
taxiing

D

F

Position 3,
stationary

Clearance F is straight out taxi with the aircraft turning at the most critical distance. Clearance B is obtained when no turn is initiated, and is 4.5' more than F.

(a)

(b)

FIGURE 7.10 Methods of taxiing out from a parked position. (a) Plane taxis straight out. (b) Plane turns, then taxis out. (*Source:* Reference 9.)

Consider two methods of taxiing out from a parked position:

1. The aircraft pulls straight out between two parked aircraft (Figure 7.10a).
2. The aircraft turns until it is aligned perpendicular to the parking line, then pulls out (Figure 7.10b).

For straight-out taxiing, the wing tip clearance B may be computed as follows:

$$B = D \sin A - S \qquad (7.6)$$

where

D = spacing between parking positions (ft)
A = parking angle (degrees), as shown in Figure 7.10a
S = airplane wing span (ft)

Clearance F occurs when a swept wing aircraft turns at the most critical distance (i.e., when immediately adjacent to the neighboring aircraft). It is computed by the equation

$$F = D \sin A - (a + R) \qquad (7.7)$$

where

a = the distance perpendicular to the centerline of the airplane from the pivot point to the wing tip (ft)
R = wing tip radius (ft)

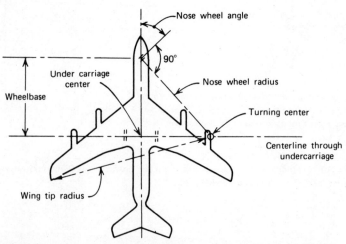

FIGURE 7.11   Geometry of minimum aircraft parking turns. (*Source:* Reference 9.)

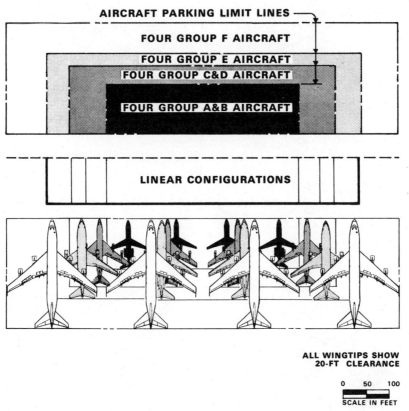

AIRCRAFT PARKING LIMIT LINES

FOUR GROUP F AIRCRAFT

FOUR GROUP E AIRCRAFT

FOUR GROUP C&D AIRCRAFT

FOUR GROUP A&B AIRCRAFT

LINEAR CONFIGURATIONS

**ALL WINGTIPS SHOW
20-FT CLEARANCE**

0 50 100

SCALE IN FEET

FIGURE 7.12 Scaled sketches showing apron space requirements for six groups of aircraft. (*Source:* Reference 12.)

The area required for an airplane negotiating a turn is governed by the size of nose wheel angle that is used. Thus, under turn and taxi-out conditions, the minimum size of gate position is determined by the maximum nose wheel angle. The geometry of minimum aircraft parking turns is illustrated by Figure 7.11. To locate an aircraft's turning center, a line is extended along the nose wheel axle to intersect a line drawn through the center of the aircraft undercarriage. This point of intersection is the turning center about which the aircraft rotates in a turn.

The FAA (10) has published graphs and equations that may be used to determine clearances for aircraft turning and taxiing out of a parking position for parking angle values ranging from 40 to 90°. The FAA recommended clearances allow 10 ft forward roll for nose wheel alignment prior to turn for taxiing out and another 10 ft forward roll prior to stopping. A design procedure for determining the separation of aircraft parking stands that utilizes polar coordinate graph paper has been described by the ICAO (9).

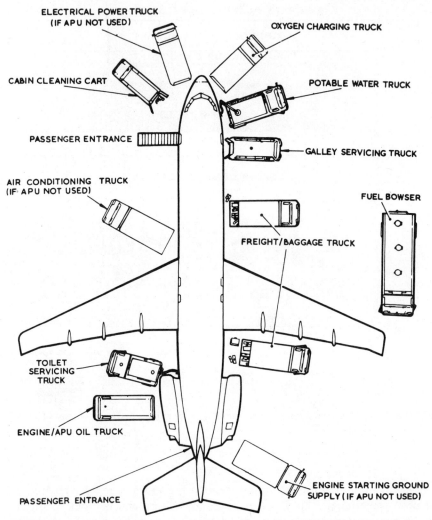

FIGURE 7.13   Ground servicing arrangement for model BAC 111 series aircraft. (*Source:* Reference 12.)

One method of designing stand spacing and depth is to obtain accurate scaled outlines or silhouettes of all aircraft that may use the stand and a similarly scaled outline of the apron area (9). The outline of each aircraft that is to use the gate position is traced on the sketch, with the main wheels on a common stop line and the line through the undercarriage passing through the turning center. The sketches are drawn so that the aircraft turning centers are located at a common stand turning center. From these outlines, the maximum wing tip radius for that particular group of aircraft becomes readily apparent, as do the nose wheel paths. Nose wheel guidelines painted on the pavement are commonly used to aid pilots in terminal apron maneuvers. These lines must be designed to accommodate all the aircraft that will use the apron. The sketches also reveal the angle of parking that will give the most economical use of the space in both width and depth of the gate position. A slight variation of this procedure involves the use of plastic models or templates of the various aircraft in plan view.

Table 7.12 Ground Servicing Equipment Summary: Dimensions of Ground Equipment

Item	Width (ft,in.)[a]	Length (ft,in.)	Height (ft,in.)
Passenger Stairs			
Self-propelled	7,6	20,3	13,0
Truck mounted	8 to 14,10	25 to 35,0	12,8 to 21,3
Baggage Equipment			
Containers (wide body)	5,0	6,7	5,4
Containers (narrow body)	3,6	7,10	3,4
Dolly (self-propelled)	7,2	10,2½ to 13,7½	1,8
Dolly (truck-mounted)	4,0	8,6 to 12,9	1,11
Small tug	4,8	8,6	6,10
Typical cart	4,10	10 to 14,0	6,9
Transporter (single container)	9,3	13,8½	5,10½
Transporter (double container)	8,3	19,7	5,10
Container loader (wide body)	8,0	24,6	9,9 to 11,0
Container loader (narrow body)	6,0	14,9	7,11
Loading conveyor	7,0	10,8	10,0 to 13,0
Cabin Service			
High-lift catering	8,0	26,0	11 to 18,0
Lavatory service	7,11	23,6	5,10 to 13,8
Cabin service	8,0	31,8	12,7 to 25,10
Typical Aircraft Tugs			
Wide body	10,0	30,0	5,2
Narrow body	8,0	20,0	7,4
Fuel Trucks			
Tanker	10,0	41,8	9,0
Hydrant truck	7,5	20,6	8,6 to 22,2
Miscellaneous			
Ground power (truck-mounted)	8,0	21,3	11,1
Ground power (dolly-mounted)	4,10	10 to 14,0	7,0
Pneumatic power	8,0	21,9	8,4
De-icing unit	8,0	28,4	12,0
Reel cart for fixed utilities	3,0	4,6	6,0

Source: The Apron and Terminal Building Planning Report, prepared for the FAA by Ralph M. Parsons Company, Report FAA-RD-75-191, July 1975 (rev. March 1976).

[a] 1 ft = 0.3048 m.

Table 7.13 Comparative Parking Envelopes: Push-out[a]-Versus Taxi-out[b]

Aircraft Group	Push-out (ft,in.)[c] L^d	W^d	Area (yd²)	Taxi-out (ft,in.) L^d	W^d	Area (yd²)
A						
FH-227	103,1	115,2	1319	148,10	140,2	2318
YS-11B	106,3	124,11	1474	171,0	149,11	2850
BAC-111	123,6	113,6	1557	130,0	138,6	2001
DC-9-10	134,5	109,5	1634	149,2	134,5	2228
B						
DC-9-21,30	149,4	113,4	1880	149,0	138,4	2290
727 (all)	173,2	128,0	2463	194,0	153,0	3298
737 (all)	120,0	113,0	1507	145,4	138,0	2228
C						
B-707 (all)	172,11	165,9	3188	258,0	190,9	5468
B-720	156,9	150,10	2627	228,0	175,10	4454
DC-8-43,51	170,9	162,5	3081	211,10	187,5	4411
D						
DC-8-61,63	207,5	168,5	3882	252,4	193,5	5423
E						
L-1011	188,8	175,4	3676	263,6	200,4	5865
DC-10	192,3	185,4	3959	291,0	210,4	6801
F						
B-747	241,10	215,8	5795	328,0	240,8	8771

Source: *The Apron and Terminal Building Planning Report*, prepared for the FAA by Ralph M. Parsons Company, Report FAA-RD-75-191, July 1975 (rev. March 1976).

[a] Including clearances of 20 in. wing tip to wing tip; nose to building: 30 ft, groups A and B; 20 ft, groups C and D; 10 ft, groups E and F.

[b] Including clearances of 20 ft to other aircraft and GSE, 45 ft.

[c] 1 ft = 0.3048 m.

[d] Length and width are based on the largest dimension in the group of aircraft.

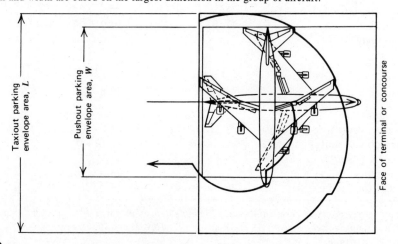

An apron and terminal planning report (11) prepared for the FAA provides scaled outlines for six groups of aircraft that comprise the bulk of the United States fleet. The report gives general guidance for planning airport apron-terminal complexes. It includes scaled sketches showing apron space requirements for various combinations of aircraft group, terminal configuration, parking arrangement, and operational procedures (taxi-out, push-out). Figure 7.12 gives an example.

The designer of terminal aprons must also consider the need for apron space and vertical clearances for service equipment. A wide variety of equipment is required to service modern aircraft, as Figure 7.13 illustrates. Table 7.12 lists the dimensions of various pieces of ground service equipment. Generally, a minimum of 10 ft should be added to the depth of the apron to permit service access to the aircraft. When nose-in parking is used, as much as 30 ft additional depth may be required for operation of the push-out tractor. Table 7.13 shows recommended parking envelopes for six aircraft groups for push-out and taxi-out conditions.

A service road, typically 20 to 30 ft wide, must be provided either adjacent to the terminal or on the airside of the gate positions. If the road is placed next to the terminal building, it may be necessary to segregate passengers and service vehicles by use of nose loading bridges. This calls for a clearance under the bridges of about 15 ft. If the service road is located on the airside of the parked aircraft, special precautions may need to be taken to minimize conflicts between ground vehicles and aircraft and to prevent collisions.

The effects of jet blast should also be considered in determining gate position size and location (5). It is sometimes necessary to install jet blast deflector screens or fences to protect workers and possibly passengers.

Finally, to facilitate taxiing, towing, and servicing activities, apron slopes should be kept to a minimum consistent with the need for good drainage. Apron slopes should not exceed 1.0%, and in aircraft fueling areas, a maximum slope of 0.5% is preferred. The apron should slope downward from the face of the terminal for proper drainage and safety in case of fuel spillage.

REFERENCES

1. *Aerodromes*, Annex 14 to the International Convention on Civil Aviation, Seventh Edition including Amendment 35, Montreal: International Civil Aviation Organization, November 26, 1981.

2. *Airfield and Airspace Criteria*, Air Force Manual AFM 86-8B, May 3, 1967.

3. *Runway Length Requirements for Airport Design*, FAA Advisory Circular AC 150/5325-4, including Change 14, September 27, 1978.

4. *Utility Airports—Air Access to National Transportation*, FAA Advisory Circular AC 150/5300-4B, including Changes 1–7, September 23, 1983.

5. *Airport Design Standards—Transport Airports*, FAA Advisory Circular AC 150/5300-12, February 28, 1983.

6. *Civil Engineering Programming Standard Facility Requirements*, Air Force Manual AFM 86-2, including Changes 1–8, July 7, 1980.

7. *Design Manual—Communications, Navigation Aids and Airfield Lighting*, NAVFAC DM-21, Naval Facilities Engineering Command, June 1973.

8. *General Provisions for Airfield Design, Chapter 1*, Air Force Manual AFM 88-6, April 1, 1977.

9. *Aerodrome Design Manual*, 1st Ed. Part 2, Montreal: International Civil Aviation Organization Document 9157, 1977.

10. *Airport Aprons*, FAA Advisory Circular AC 150/5355-2, January 27, 1965.

11. *The Apron and Terminal Building Planning Report*, prepared for the FAA by Ralph M. Parsons Company, Report FAA-RD-75-191, July 1975 (rev. March 1976).

8

PASSENGER TERMINAL

8.1 THE FUNCTION OF THE AIRPORT PASSENGER TERMINAL

The airport passenger terminal constitutes one of the principal elements of infrastructure cost at the airport. Many terminals have been built as architectural monuments to the progress of regional or national aviation, and air travelers have become accustomed to lavish visual displays of design that have little to do with the functions the terminal is intended to perform. As this chapter points out, the functional design of the terminal can be made subservient to architectural design considerations only at the expense of the proper functioning of the component parts of the design. The passenger terminal performs three main functions:

1. *Change of Mode.* Few air trips are made direct from origin to destination. By their nature, "air" trips are mixed-mode trips, with surface access trips linked at either end to the line haul air trips. In changing from one mode to the other, the passenger physically moves through the airport terminal according to a prescribed pattern of movement. These movement patterns are accommodated by *passenger circulation areas*.

2. *Processing.* The terminal is a convenient point to carry out certain processes associated with the air trip. These may include ticketing and checking in the passengers, separating them from and reuniting them with their baggage, and carrying out security checks and governmental controls. This function of the terminal requires *passenger processing space*.

3. *Change of Movement Type.* Although aircraft move passengers in discrete groups in what is termed batch movements, the same passengers access the airport on an almost continuous basis, arriving and departing in small groups mainly by bus, auto, taxi, and limousine. The terminal therefore functions on the departure side as a reservoir that collects passengers continuously and processes them in batches. On the arrivals

side the pattern is reversed. To perform this function the terminal must provide *passenger holding space*.

Thus, the primary function of the terminal is to provide circulation, processing, and holding space. To function smoothly and to ensure the premium level of service that should be associated with air travel, numerous facilities are necessary in these primary and support areas, which are more fully detailed in Section 8.3.

8.2   THE TERMINAL USER

The successfully designed air terminal facility must perform satisfactorily to meet the needs of those who can be expected to use it. The passenger terminal has three principal user classes: the passenger and those who accompany him or her, the airline, and the airport operator (1). Most current terminal designs emphasize passenger needs. The volume of passengers is large in comparison with the number of airline and airport staff, and as the prime reason for having the facility, the passenger is seen as a major source of airport income during the time that he or she spends in the terminal. Thus, the maximum accommodation of passenger needs is the chief objective of terminal design (2).

Airlines are another prime source of airport revenue, as well as constituting one of the principal functional areas of airport operations. Satisfactory terminal design must provide a high level of service to the airline. In some airports, airlines are also a source of initial investment capital. In such cases they can be expected to have a substantial role in terminal design decision making.

Design for the needs of the airport operator requires a balance: facilities for the staff and operational areas must be adequate, but the overhead of unnecessarily luxurious installations should be avoided. Passenger terminals at larger airports are the work place of a large number of individuals, and terminal design should ensure that this environment is acceptable for its workers, even under peak flow conditions. Within the category of airport operator should be included all concessionaires who may be regarded as carrying out part of the operator's function on a commercially delegated basis.

8.3   FACILITIES REQUIRED AT THE PASSENGER TERMINAL

The airport terminal acts as the transfer point between the landside and airside portions of the mixed-mode "air trip" made by the air passenger. The level at which the terminal functions is crucial in the passenger's evaluation of the level of service provided by air travel, and it is in the interest of both the airport operator and the airline to have the terminal designed to permit a maximum level of service for passengers and visitors, the airlines, and the airport operator (3). The facilities can be categorized as follows: access (including the landside interface), passenger processing areas, passenger holding areas, internal circulation and airside interface, and airline and support areas (4).

Access and the Landside Interface

Within the passenger terminal area, access facilities should ease a transfer of passenger flows from the available access modes to, from, and through the terminal itself, and vice versa. These facilities include curbside loading and unloading, curbside baggage check-in, shuttle services to parking lots and other terminals, and loading and unloading areas for buses, taxis, limousines, and rapid surface modes.

Processing

Areas are designated for the formalities associated with processing passengers. The usual facilities include airline ticketing and passenger check-in, baggage check-in and seat selection, gate check-in where desirable, incoming and outgoing customs, immigration control, health control, security check areas, and baggage claim.

Holding Areas

A very large portion of the passenger's time at the airport is spent outside the individual processing areas (see Section 8.7). Of nonprocessing time, the largest portion is spent in holding areas where passengers wait, in some cases with airport visitors, between periods occupied by passing through the various processing facilities. It is in these holding areas that significant portions of airport revenue are generated. Consideration of revenue generation (Section 8.8) and a care for the level of service supplied by these necessary facilities warrants careful design of holding areas. The following are among the facilities that may be required:

1. *Passenger Lounges.*   General, departure, and gate lounges.
2. *Passenger Service Areas.*   Wash rooms, public telephone, nurseries, post office, information, first aid, shoeshine, valet service, storage, barber shop, beauty parlor.
3. *Concessions.*   Bar, restaurants, newsstands, novelties, duty-free shops, hotel reservations, banks and currency exchange, insurance, car rental, automatic dispensing machines.
4. *Observation Decks and Visitors' Lobbies.*   Including V.I.P. and C.I.P.* facilities.

* CIP: Commercially Important Persons.

Internal Circulation and Airside Interface

Passengers move physically through the terminal system using the internal circulation system, which should be simple to find and follow and easy to negotiate. The airside interface is designed for secure and easy boarding of the aircraft.

Internal circulation is handled by corridors, walkways, people movers and moving belts, ramps, and tramways.

Airside interface requirements include loading facilities such as jetways, stairs, nose bridges, and mobile lounges. At international facilities, transit passenger lounges may be necessary.

Airline and Support Activities

Although airline terminals are designed primarily for airline passengers, most of whom will be quite unfamiliar with the surroundings, the design must also cater for the needs of airline, airport, and support personnel working in the terminal area. Frequently, the following facilities must be provided (5, 6):

1. Airline offices, passenger and baggage processing stations, telecommunications, flight planning documentation, crew rest facilities, airline station administration, staff and crew toilets, rest and refreshment areas.
2. Storage for wheelchairs, pushcarts, etc.
3. Airport management offices and offices for security staff.
4. Governmental office and support areas for staff working in customs, immigration, health, and air traffic control; bonded storage and personal detention facilities.
5. Public address systems, signs, indicators, flight information.
6. Maintenance personnel offices and support areas, maintenance equipment storage.

8.4 PASSENGER AND BAGGAGE FLOW

An adequately designed airport terminal is the work of a designer who understands the various flows of passengers and baggage at a terminal. Figure 8.1 is the flow diagram for passengers and baggage at an airport catering to mixed international and domestic flights. Where domestic flights only are anticipated, the routing is significantly less complex, since customs, immigration, and health controls can be omitted and transfer passengers can move between flights without baggage and untroubled by governmental controls (7, 8).

The usual enplaning pattern is to pass through the general concourse into the airlines checking area. From there, no longer encumbered by baggage, the passengers move into the general departure lounge and finally into the gate lounge. On international flights, entry into the departure lounge may be preceded by customs control. (In many countries airports must have customs space for outbound passengers, although such areas may be used quite infrequently.) Passengers then pass to the departure gate, which may consist of a small gate lounge for final holding purposes. If personal security control is not centralized, passengers may undergo a gate security check before entering the aircraft. International passengers may also have to await some form of departing passport control. The layout shown also permits gate check-in at the gate lounge; this of course is not found at many airports. Gate check-in necessitates decentralized security checks, since these must be performed at the gates themselves.

Deplaning domestic passengers proceed directly to the baggage claim and pass immediately into the general departures concourse; international arrivals must first pass through health and immigration controls and proceed through customs inspection before entering the general concourse. In many European airports, those who have goods to declare and those who have nothing to declare pass along red and green channels, respectively. This innovation has significantly speeded flow through the customs area with no apparent increase in serious smuggling offenses.

International deplaning passengers en route to yet a third country normally pass into a holding transit lounge without officially entering the country of transit. Therefore they are not subject to health, immigration, and customs formalities, and their baggage is transferred directly to their outgoing flight without passing through baggage claim and customs. Deplaning international passengers transferring to domestic flights must pass through all governmental controls, then recheck their baggage for the domestic leg of the flight. This is handled with differing levels of efficiency at different airports. In some airports, passengers must traverse significant distances between connections. Since departing customs controls are usually far less stringent, the domestic/international passenger usually does not face the same problem.

8.5 TERMINAL DESIGN CONCEPTS (9)

The design of a terminal depends on the nature of the air traffic to be handled at an airport. The design concept chosen is a function of a number of factors, including the size and nature of traffic demand, the number of participating airlines, the traffic split between international, domestic, scheduled, and charter flights, the available physical site, the principal access modes, and the type of financing.

The most fundamental choice is that of *centralized* or *decentralized* processing. With centralized concepts, all the elements in the passenger processing sequence are conducted as far as feasible in one localized area. Processes normally included are ticketing, check-in, customs and immigration, baggage checking and claim, and possibly security. All concessions and ancillary facilities are also grouped in the central terminal area. Decentralization involves a

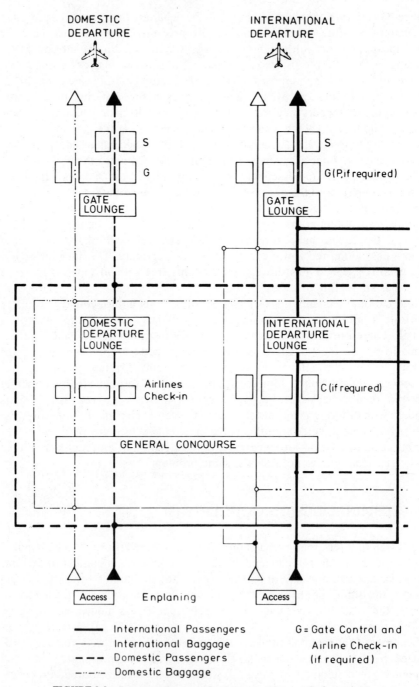

FIGURE 8.1 Passenger/baggage flow system. (*Source:* Reference 4.)

226

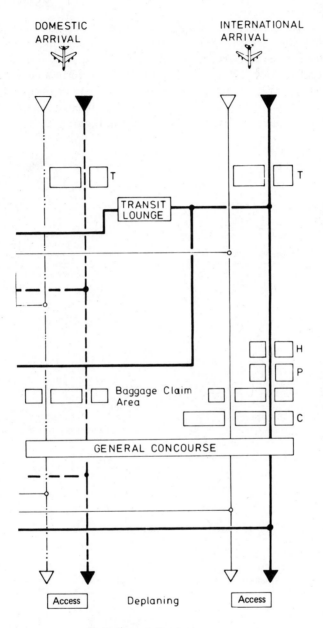

DOMESTIC
ARRIVAL

INTERNATIONAL
ARRIVAL

T

T

TRANSIT
LOUNGE

H

P

Baggage Claim
Area

C

GENERAL CONCOURSE

Access   Deplaning   Access

P = Passport Control
C = Customs Control
H = Health Control (if required)
T = Transfer Check-in
S = Security Control

spreading of these functions over a number of centers in the terminal complex; the concept embraces the range of possibilities, from using independent terminals for various airlines (the unit terminal concept) to simply providing facilities at the aircraft for the lightly loaded traveler to perform a complete check-in (the gate check-in concept). In practice, many design solutions fall between the extremes of completely centralized and decentralized operation (2). Examples of the airport types discussed below appears in Figure 8.2.

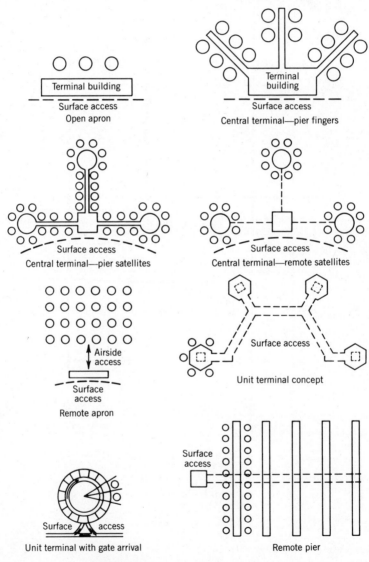

FIGURE 8.2   Terminal configurations.

Open Apron or Linear Concept

The most centralized of all arrangements is the simple open apron or linear arrangement, which can be operated with a single terminal, with passenger access to the aircraft directly across the apron, or by direct connection to the main terminal building. Operation can be with or without specific gate assignment to particular airlines on a permanent basis. Since this type of arrangement gives a small length of airside interface in relation to the size of the terminal, it is frequently used for low volume airports where the number of gates required would not necessitate an inconveniently long terminal. An extension of the open apron concept is the *gate arrival* concept, as exemplified by the Kansas City airport, where the terminal is arranged in such a manner that the traveler can park at a point opposite his departure gate, thereby minimizing walking distances. Part of the Seattle terminal operates on the open apron concept.

Central Terminal with Pier Fingers

Centralized terminal operation can be achieved with a large gate requirement by effectively increasing the airside periphery of the terminal with the construction of pier fingers. In this way, centralized processing can be achieved, even with a very large number of gates. The piers can also be designed to have limited holding and assembly facilities, and possibly even gate check-in facilities. Frequently, gates are assigned to individual airlines on a long term basis, to assist in orderly operation of the necessary apron equipment. This type of design, of which the international airport at Chicago O'Hare is an example, can be very economic to build; however, passengers may be required to walk long distances between the check-in area and the aircraft gate, and for interlining passengers the situation is often exacerbated.

Central Terminal with Pier Satellites

The pier satellite terminal represents a move toward decentralization of the pier finger concept. Examples of this design are provided by the terminals at Frankfurt, Stuttgart, some parts of Kennedy, in New York, at Tullamarine in Melbourne and at Dublin.

In the simplest designs, the satellites simply provide decentralized holding areas for passengers adjacent to their gates. Decentralization can be increased by offering gate check-in, limited concessions and servicing facilities for refreshment, and so on. Unsurprisingly, this modification of the pier finger design has similar problems related to walking distances. As the facilities of the satellites become more elaborate, the economies of the design disappear and the system tends to operate more as a series of unit terminals.

Central Terminal with Remote Satellites

Remote satellites of a central terminal are connected by some mechanized form of transport, either above (e.g., Tampa International Airport) or below the apron (e.g., Los Angeles). In the latter case, there is no surface interference by the connection to the main terminal, and aircraft gates can be sited all around the satellites. Depending on the degree of centralization desired, the satellites can be designed with more elaborate facilities as more decentralized operation is envisaged. In the Tampa airport example, all ticket purchase, baggage check and reclaim facilities, and other main passenger services are provided in the central terminal area; only holding lounges and supplementary check-in facilities for passengers not carrying baggage are located in the satellites.

Remote Apron or Transfer or Transporter

Perhaps the most significant examples of the remote apron type of design are Dulles International Airport, in Washington, D.C., and Mirabel International Airport, in Montreal. The servicing of remote stands by buses is common, both in the United States and Europe. The transporter concept is distinguished by the use of mobile lounges or buses, totally centralized processing, and gates that usually are not assigned permanently to any particular airline. The principal advantages accrue from the separation of the aircraft servicing apron from the terminal, giving greater flexibility on the airside to changes in the size and maneuvering characteristics in aircraft; in addition, less time is required for taxiing on the ground. The principal disadvantages seem to be the poor level of service given by the mobile lounges and buses, which delays passengers in the loading and unloading processes. Equally important are the difficulties associated with maneuvering the mobile lounges, and the increased traffic on the aprons caused by bus or mobile lounge operation (11). In concept, a layout known as the Pipe airport system is similar in functioning to the transporter system, except that the apron is linear and passengers are moved airside by a more conventional rapid transport system (10).

Unit Terminal

The unit terminal concept is defined by IATA (4) as two or more separate, self-contained buildings, each housing a single airline or group of airlines, and each having direct access to ground transportation. Kennedy International Airport in New York is a good example of the unit terminal layout, as is London's Heathrow. Usually justified at high volume airports, where walking distances become excessive with pier finger operation, this concept can cause severe problems for interlining passengers. More modern designs have attempted to provide a high level of interline connection service by surface connection systems (e.g., Dallas–Fort Worth International Airport). Unit terminal systems can be designed to operate gate check-in facilities, which is the conceptual design of the Kansas City airport and the Rio de Janeiro facility opened in 1977.

Central Terminal with Remote Piers

A fairly recent innovation in terminal layout is the central terminal linked under the apron to remote piers. This is a good layout for high volume airports, especially where there is a great amount of domestic transfer and interlining. The large apron area can suitably fit between the twin parallel runways of a high capacity facility. Parallel alignment of the piers assures efficient use of apron space. The sub-apron corridor connecting the terminals and piers is suited to automated movement of both passengers and baggage. Atlanta Hartsfield Airport is an example of this form of design.

8.6 VERTICAL DISTRIBUTION OF ACTIVITIES

In small airport terminals, for example, the passenger and baggage flows described can be accommodated on a single level. Where passenger flows are relatively small and there are few transfer passengers, the complexity and expense of multilevel terminal facilities is unwarranted. However, unilevel terminals can be most difficult to extend in the face of growing passenger demand, and the intermingling of growing enplaning, deplaning, and transfer flows presents significant problems. Figure 8.3 illustrates the major approaches to the problems associated with the vertical distribution of acitivities.

The most common solution adopted to the separation of flows is the adoption of two-level operation. Typical flow arrangements separate enplaning passengers on the upper level from deplaning passengers, who enter the terminal, then

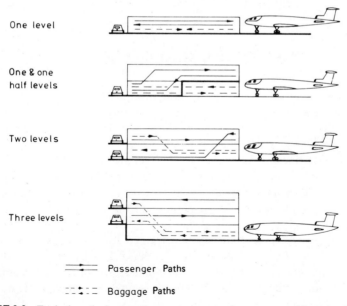

FIGURE 8.3 Typical vertical separation arrangements of passenger and baggage flows.

descend to the lower level for governmental controls where necessary and for baggage reclaim. Usually, arriving and departing passengers are separated on the landside access with two levels of bus and car curbside pickup and set down; design solutions in the past have used single-level access at the landside interface. Two-level operation has the advantage of maximum site utilization and can provide good flow characteristics with a minimum of conflicting flows suitable for high traffic volumes.

A variation of two-level design is *one-and-a-half-level* operation. This form of design offers the advantages of two-level apron operation, but passengers usually change level after entering the building. This design allows better service than the unilevel layout, but there can be serious conflicts of flow at the landside access interface.

The one-and-a-half-level arrangement works well at lower volume airports because departing passengers require more facilities than arriving passengers. Many domestic designs place arrival facilities and baggage handling on the lower level and departure facilities at the upper level. Where piers are used at multilevel terminals, single-level operation of the piers is the general rule, with the public operational level being above the airport and airline functions at apron level.

Three-level designs are also possible. The most usual form of separation is departures, arrivals, and baggage flow; a less usual separation is international, domestic, and baggage flow. The former arrangement seems to give the best separation of possibly conflicting flows, but the expense of the third floor of operations may not be warranted, even for relatively high flows. Some designs use the latter form of separation, but these layouts tend to have undesirable conflicts between enplaning and deplaning flows.

8.7   PASSENGER BEHAVIOR IN THE TERMINAL (7, 12, 13)

Air passengers consider time spent in the terminal to be an important portion of the overall air journey, even though the terminal's function is of modal transfer rather than part of the mode of carriage. It is therefore essential that airports convey the same image of being part of the premier mode that is presented by airlines in their efforts to market air travel. This being the case, airport terminals have been constructed in a more lavish manner than bus or railway stations. This is especially true in the United States; European air terminals tend to be less spacious and more utilitarian than those in the United States (2).

Terminal design is customarily constrained by the needs of passengers, workers, and visitors, as discussed in Section 8.2. Of these three classes of user, the passengers are considered to be the most important. The comfortable accommodation of the passenger can be a reasonable and economic objective, since expenditures in the terminal area are a substantial proportion of the overall revenue of any passenger airport operation (Section 8.8).

It has been stated that terminal design should reflect awareness of passenger needs and behavior. However, passenger behavior varies according to the purpose of the trip, the flight logistics, and the type of flight. *Air travel purpose* is normally divided into leisure and business categories. Business travelers tend to use the airlines more frequently, and consequently are more familiar with the workings of the terminal and the reliability of the access mode. Such travelers usually spend less time in the terminals and less money in areas of nondeductible business expenses (e.g., duty-free and novelty shops); however, areas such as restaurants and bars are patronized by these travelers. Business trips encourage few airport visitors as senders or greeters.

It is a general rule that the longer the distance traveled, the greater the time allowed by passengers prior to time of scheduled departure. Figure 8.4a plots cumulative arrivals for passengers on transatlantic and European flights from a British airport, It can be seen that, for the intercontinental flights, the average arrival time was 17 min earlier than for an international European flight. Almost all passengers had arrived a full hour before scheduled time of departure.

Equally important is the logistics of the flight—whether it is a scheduled flight or a special charter flight. Because of the special difficulties encountered in charter flight (e.g., long processing times at passenger and baggage check-in, and the nonavailability of alternate flights if the booked flight is missed), charter passengers tend to spend even more time in the passenger terminal than passengers on scheduled international flights. Figure 8.4b shows the cumulative distribution for chartered and scheduled passengers at a European airport.

Since the introduction of advanced purchase excursion tickets (APEX) and standby fares, the development of charter operations has been inhibited. However, the terminal dwell times of all these types of "nonstandard" passengers tends to be much greater than for passengers holding transferable tickets on scheduled flights.

Design of any terminal cannot proceed without knowledge of the mix of passenger traffic envisaged. Clearly, the design of a terminal that serves mainly business domestic travel is the simplest, requiring the least range of facilities. The most complicated terminals must cater to a mix of business and leisure traffic, operating on a mixture of chartered and scheduled flights, traveling over domestic, short haul international, and intercontinental distances. Modifications and extensions to the terminals take into account variations in traffic mix across these variables.

The initial design of a terminal ideally must take into account anticipated changes in traffic volume resulting from increases over the long term and from short term fluctuations throughout the year due to holiday peak periods. These considerations lead to design concepts that are *modular and flexible*. Modularity permits sections of the terminal to be added at times of traffic increase, or

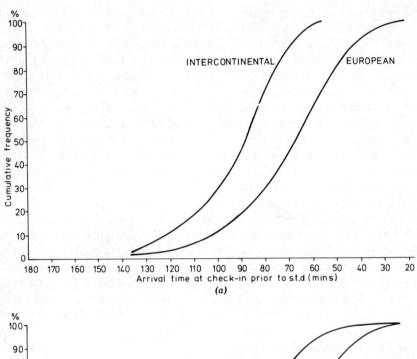

(a)

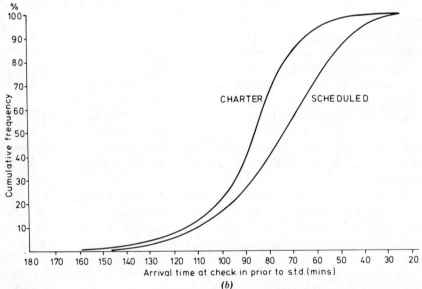

(b)

FIGURE 8.4 Relationship of arrival time for enplaning passengers and type of flight. (a) Short and long haul, international, (b) charter and scheduled. (*Source:* Reference 12.)

withdrawn during annual off-peak periods to conserve labor. Flexibility of design permits easy change of use of existing floor space as passenger traffic needs change. Both modular and flexible designs often increase initial construction costs, but in the long term, they can be extremely cost effective in an industry where terminal alteration may be necessary at five-year intervals, and complete obsolescence of terminal infrastructure is common over a 20-year period.

8.8 IMPORTANCE OF PASSENGER TERMINAL EXPENDITURES

Although departing passengers spend a considerable amount of time in holding and waiting areas in the terminal, a very small portion of the terminal time is in fact spent in the processing sequence. Consequently, terminal facilities are designed to attract passengers to patronize concessionary areas such as restaurants, shops, and bars. The financial implications of nonaviation-related terminal concessions should not be underestimated, for in practice these facilities can contribute substantially to an airport's total revenue structure. As already seen in Chapter 1 (Table 1.3), with increasing airport size, terminal revenues supplant landing fees as the principal source of operational revenues, which normally account for approximately 95% of total revenues. Clearly, the designer must consider passenger services, not merely from a viewpoint of supplying reasonable facilities; the terminal must be also capable of providing a high level of fiscal support to the airport operation.

8.9 SPACE REQUIREMENTS FOR INDIVIDUAL FACILITIES

To assure orderly and smooth functioning of the terminal, the individual facility areas that form the constituent parts should be designed to accommodate the level and type of passenger loading they are expected to experience. This process ideally requires the following steps:

Determination of peak hour design demand.
Statement of passenger traffic by type.
Identification of individual facility volumes.
Calculations of space requirements.

Determination of Peak Hour Design Demand

Although knowledge of annual passenger movements is important for the estimation of potential revenues, the demand that is manifested in the peak hours determines facility size. The most widely relied-on design parameter is the TPHP (typical peak hour passenger) used by the FAA. This is not the absolute peak demand that can occur, but an estimate of a figure that will be exceeded

Table 8.1   FAA Recommended Relationships for TPHP Computations from Annual Figures

Total Annual Passengers	TPHP as a Percentage of Annual Flows
20 million and over	0.030
10,000,000-19,999,999	0.035
1,000,000-9,999,999	0.040
500,000-999,999	0.050
100,000-499,999	0.065
Under 100,000	0.120

Source: Aviation Demand and Airport Facility Requirement Forecasts for Medium Air Transportation Hubs Through 1980, Federal Aviation Administration, January 1964.

only for very short periods. In concept, it is similar to the thirtieth highest hour used in the design of highways. Some European designers still use the Standard Busy Rate (SBR), which is, in fact, the thirtieth highest hour of the year. The British Airports Authority now uses a slightly different measure, the Busy Hour Rate (BHR), which is the hourly rate above which only 5% of the traffic is handled.

To compute the TPHP from annual passenger volumes, the FAA recommends the relationships shown in Table 8.1.

Statement of Passenger Traffic by Type

Studies of passenger movements in airport terminals have indicated that different types of passengers place different demands on the facilities in terms of space. It is therefore desirable to be able to categorize peak hour passengers according to flight type, trip purpose, trip type, and access mode. Ideally, estimates of passenger volumes could be categorized into domestic or international, scheduled or charter, transfer or transit, business or leisure, intercontinental or short haul, and by access mode.

Identification of Individual Facility Volumes and Area Computations

The movement of the various categories of passengers through the terminal identifies the level of usage placed on the various facilities in the peak hour. Based on the number of passengers processed in each facility, areas can be computed so that reasonable levels of service can be furnished.

Calculations of Space Requirements

In the past, the space requirement criteria used for the design of air terminals have varied capriciously. However, the FAA and other bodies have set down guidelines that, if related to the TPHP figures, will give adequate and comfortable levels of service to the terminal user. Table 8.2 indicates FAA standards in conjunction with those recommended by IATA and others derived from ergonomic research.

The ergonomic criteria show a range of values. The higher space recommendations are applicable where level of service requirements are necessarily high (e.g., in areas where passengers will spend a long period of time or where

Table 8.2   Various Terminal Space Design Standards

FAA Standards (14)	
Domestic Terminal Space Facility	Space Required per 100 TPHP, (1000 ft^2 or 100 m^2)
Ticket lobby	1.0
Airline operational	4.8
Baggage claim	1.0
Waiting rooms	1.8
Eating facilities	1.6
Kitchen and storage	1.6
Other concessions	0.5
Toilets	0.3
Circulation, mechanical, and maintenance, walls	11.6
Total	24.2
International Terminal Space Facility	Additional Space Required per 100 TPHP, (1000 ft^2 or 100 m^2)
Public health	1.5
Immigration	1.0
Customs	3.3
Agriculture	0.2
Visitor waiting rooms	1.5
Total	7.5
Circulation, baggage assembly, utilities, walls, partitions	7.5
Total	15.0
IATA (4)	
Passenger requirements	Space Required per 100 TPHP, (1000 ft^2 or 100 m^2) in each facility
Standing passengers	1.0
Seated passengers	1.5
Plus 10% additional circulation and airline requirements space at lounges	

(*Table continues on p. 238.*)

Table 8.2 (continued)

Ergonomic Criteria (15)	
Area Function	Space Required per 100 TPHP, (1000 ft^2 or 100 m^2 in each facility)
Processing	0.9–1.1
Circulation	1.35–3.15
Holding	0.35–1.1

Overall Standards FAA (24)	
Overall passenger terminal area per annual enplanement:	0.08–0.12 ft^2 (0.007–0.011 m^2)
Overall passenger terminal area per design hour passenger:	150 ft^2 or 14 m^2

ease of movement is essential, such as in corridors where luggage is being carried). These ergonomic criteria do not, in general, differentiate for the majority of passenger categories discussed earlier. Until more specific space requirement recommendations are developed, the designer must modify the standards above to account for differing needs (12).

It is very likely that a designer will find that the FAA overall gross floor area recommendations given in Reference 24 are not suitable for terminals with any appreciable international traffic. Such terminals are likely to require 220–270 ft^2 per peak hour passenger.

Other Recommendations (5)

More specific recommendations on terminal buildings were made in the mid-1970s by the Ralph M. Parsons Company, which developed spatial requirements for the various functions and facilities accommodated at the airport passenger terminal. Figure 8.5a–j shows relationships between passenger volumes and the requisite areas for the ticket lobby, the waiting lobby, departure lounges, the outbound baggage hall, the baggage claim area, food and beverage services, and the concessions and building services. Example 8.1 indicates how these charts may be used in the design of a domestic terminal.

Example 8.1

Design of Domestic Terminal Using Ralph M. Parsons Charts

Assumptions

1. Annual passenger throughput in design year = 5 million. This is assumed to equate with 2000 design hour passengers; 60% of arrivals or departures maximum imbalance of flow, 80% passengers terminate.

2. Aircraft mix in peak hour.

Type of Aircraft	No. of Aircraft	Seat Range	Equivalent Aircraft Factor	Column 1 × Column 3
A	—	Up to 80	0.6	—
B	10	81–110	1.0	10
C	3	111–160	1.4	4.2
D	2	161–210	1.9	3.8
E	1	211–280	2.4	2.4
F	2	281–420	3.5	7.0
G	1	421–500	4.6	4.6

Total Equivalent Aircraft Factor = 32

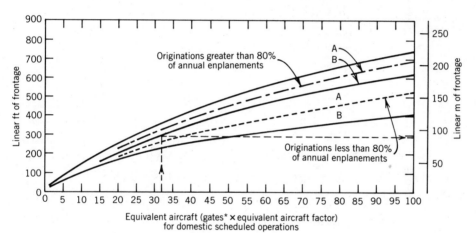

FIGURE 8.5 Space planning charts for the passenger terminal. (a) Terminal counter frontage. (b) ATO office and support space.

(*Figure 8.5 continues on p. 240.*)

Computation of Overall Areas

Overall gross area:

2000 passengers/peak hr $\times$ 14 m^2/peak hr
passenger = 28,000 m^2

Estimated Breakdown by Functional Areas (Gross):

Airline	Other	Public	Services
ATO	Concessions	Circulation	Mechanical
Administration	Food and beverage	Waiting areas	Shafts
Operations	Airport administration	Restrooms	Tunnels
Baggage	Miscellaneous	Exits	Stairs
			Shops
			Electrical
			Communication
38% $\times$ 28,000 = 10,640	17% $\times$ 28,000 = 4760	30% $\times$ 28,000 = 8400	15% $\times$ 28,000 = 4200

Rentable and airport administration: Nonrentable:
55% $\times$ 28,000 = 15,400   45% $\times$ 28,000 = 12,600

Computation of Individual Areas

1. *Airline Ticket Counters* (see Figure 8.5a):
   Linear meters of counter = 87
   Assuming depth of area = 3 m, Area = 87 $\times$ 3 =   261 m^2
2. *Airline Ticket Offices and Support* (see Figure 8.5b):
   Area required =   590 m^2
3. *Outbound Baggage Room* (see Figure 8.5c):
   Area required =   1300 m^2
4. *Bag Claim:*
   Assume 60% arrivals: 32 EQA $\times$ 0.6
                            = 19.2 EQA
   Assume 50% occur in peak 20 minutes = 9.6 EQA
   With 80% terminating passengers, Figure 8.5d
   gives 107 lineal meters of claiming frontage
   Assuming oval sloping bed devices (Type D), from
                            Figure 8.5e, area = 1000 m^2
5. *Airline Operations and Support Areas:*
   Use 2 $\times$ ATO/Support area = 2 $\times$ 590 m^2 = 1180 m^2

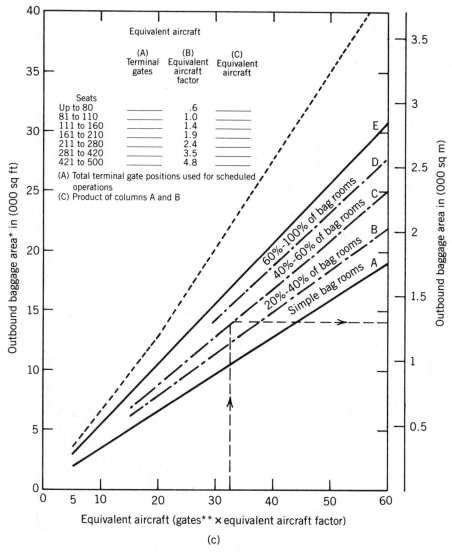

FIGURE 8.5 (continued) (c) Outbound baggage area.

(Figure 8.5 continues on p. 242.)

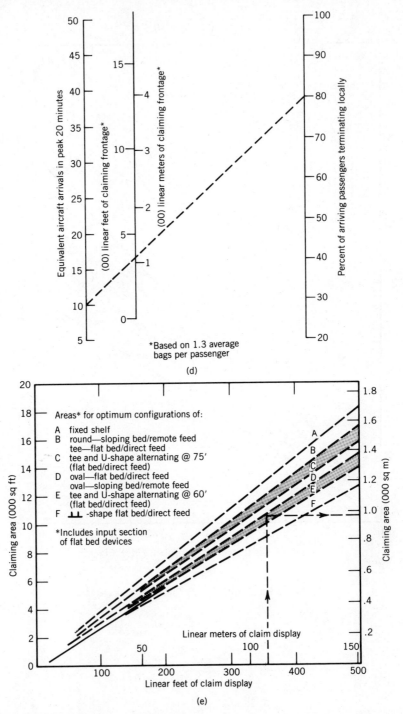

FIGURE 8.5 (*continued*) (d) Inbound baggage claim frontage. (e) Baggage claim area.

Aircraft Type Model	Seat Capacity Range	Average Departure Lounge Size
CV-580: DC-9 -10; BAC-111; YS-11-B; M-404; F-227B	40–80 Av. 60	640 sq ft 60 sq m
B-737; B-727 -100; DC-9 -30; CV-880	90–110 Av. 100	1080 sq ft 100 sq m
DC-8 -50; DC-8 -62; B-727 -200; B-727 -300; B-707 (all); B-720	120–160 Av. 140	1500 sq ft 140 sq m
DC-8 -61, B-757	170–210 Av. 190	2050 sq ft 190 sq m
DC-10, L-1011, A300, B-767	220–280 Av. 250	2690 sq ft 250 sq m
B-747	300–420 Av. 360	3870 sq ft 360 sq m
High capacity Wide body	420–500 Av. 460	4950 sq ft 460 sq m

(f)

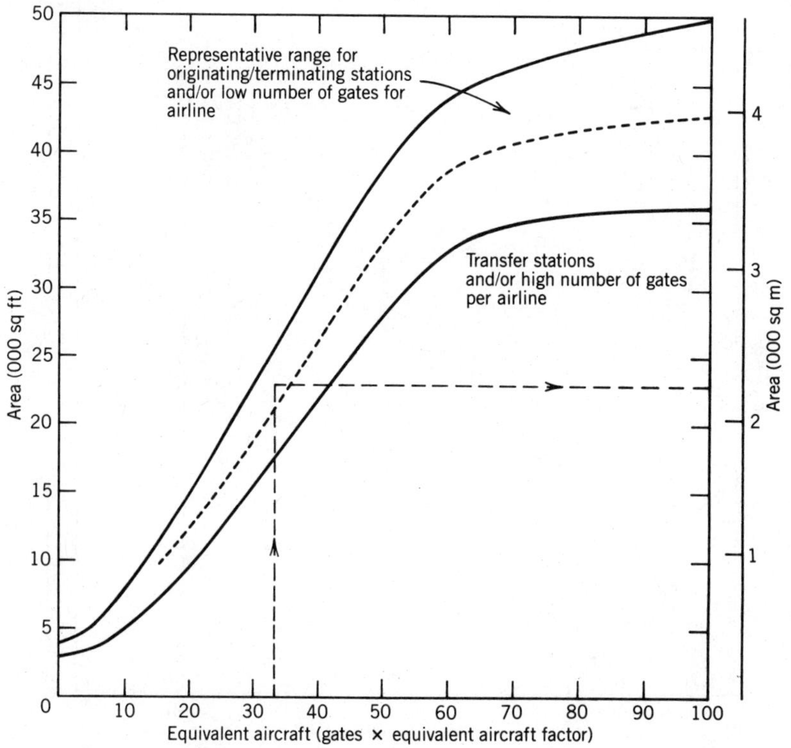

(g)

FIGURE 8.5 (continued)   (f) Departure lounge area—type of aircraft served. (g) Ticket lobby and counter area.

(*Figure 8.5 continues on p. 244.*)

6. *Departure Lounges* (see Figure 8.5f):

Type of Aircraft	No. of Gates	Area/Gate	Area
A	0	60 m^2	0
B	10	100 m^2	1000
C	3	140 m^2	420
D	2	190 m^2	380
E	1	250 m^2	250
F	2	360 m^2	720
G	1	460 m^2	460

$$= 3230 \text{ m}^2$$

7. *Other Airline Space:*
    Use 20% of item 5 $= 236 \text{ m}^2$

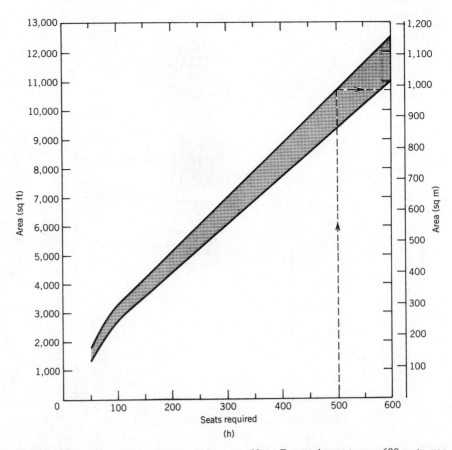

FIGURE 8.5 *(continued)* (h) Waiting lobby area. (Note: For requirements over 600 seats, use multiples of 200 or more. Graph includes primary circulation areas from counters to concessions, connector, etc.)

8. *Lobby & Ticketing* (see Figure 8.5g):

$$\begin{aligned}\text{Area from graph} &= 2300 \text{ m}^2\\ \text{less ticket counters (item 1)} &= \underline{261 \text{ m}^2}\\ &= 2039 \text{ m}^2\end{aligned}$$

9. *Lobby Waiting Area (Departure)* (see Figure 8.5h):
    Assume seating for 25% design peak flow. Remainder
    in concessions, and so on, and departure lounges.
    Seating for 500 pass/hr. $= 1000 \text{ m}^2$

10. *Lobby Bag Claim*:
    Estimated two greeters/passenger plus one passenger.
    Assume average waiting time 30 minutes, space
    requirement of 1.5 m^2/person and 60% of design peak
    flow arriving.
    $3 \times 1.5 \text{ m}^2 \times 0.5 \text{ hr} \times 0.60 \times 2000$ $= 2700 \text{ m}^2$

11. *Food and Beverage* (See Figure 8.5i):

    Assume 40% usage factor $= 2700 \text{ m}^2$

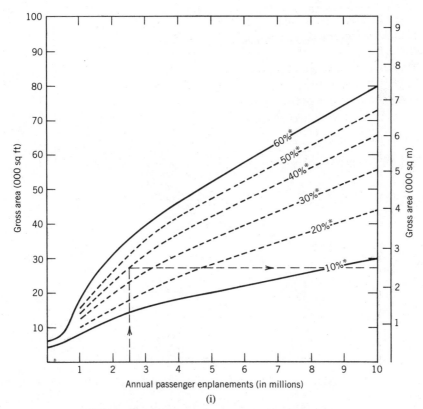

FIGURE 8.5 (continued)   (i) Food and beverage services.

(*Figure 8.5 continues on p. 246.*)

12. *Other Concessions and Terminal Services*
    (See Figure 8.5j):

    Area from graph $= 3000 \ m^2$

13. *Other Rental Areas*:

    Assume 50% item 12 $= 1500 \ m^2$

14. *Other Circulation Areas*:

    Assume 0.7 × (total items 1 through 7) $= 5458 \ m^2$

15.

    Sub-total   26,198 m^2

16. *Heating, Ventilating, Air Conditioning and Other Mechanical Areas*:

    15% × item 15   3,929 m^2

17.

    Sub-total   30,127 m^2

18. *Structure*:

    5% × item 17   1,506 m^2

    Total =   31,633 m^2

This amounts to 15.8 m^2/peak hr passenger.

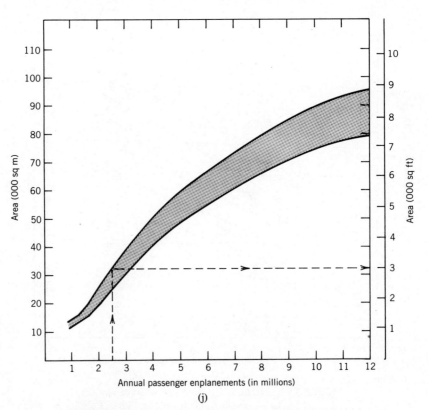

(j)

FIGURE 8.5 (*continued*) (j) Concessions and building services.

8.10 BAGGAGE HANDLING

Unlike most other modes, in air transport it is customary to separate passengers from their baggage during the line haul portion of the trip. This adds substantially to the complexity of handling the air trip and seriously complicates the design of passenger terminals, since it is essential that the separation and reuniting of passenger and baggage be carried out with maximum efficiency and at an extremely high level of reliability. Figure 8.6 diagrams the possible baggage flows from pickup and check-in through to the reclaim area. The most complex portion of baggage handling is the departures portion of the journey. Prior to arrival in the departures baggage hall, baggage may be checked at the car park, at curbside, at the town or satellite terminal, or at the terminal itself. Baggage also arrives from long and short term storage and by way of transfer baggage facilities. Depending on the size and nature of the terminal function, all or some of these facilities will be present.

Sorting for the individual flights in the baggage sortation area depends greatly on the size of the airport and the number of flights with baggage requirements at any one time. At small airports, where only one flight is being checked in at any one time, baggage moves directly from check-in to the baggage hall, usually on a belt. It is then manually off-loaded to carts, which are pulled by tractor to the apron stand. Where a number of flights are dealt with simultaneously, baggage can be sorted manually from a carousel in the baggage hall.

Because manual sorting becomes difficult when there are many people on a flight, and to minimize labor costs, mechanical sorting systems are operated at high baggage volumes. As the baggage comes by belt from check-in to the sortation area, the destination label is visually inspected by a sorter. This employee mechanically sorts the baggage by pressing a control button that activates the appropriate diversion arm along the length of the belt. Baggage is either packed on baggage carts, which are driven to the airplane baggage hold for individual baggage storage, or is placed directly into baggage containers, which can be mechanically loaded and unloaded from the airplane.

The treatment of arrivals baggage is simpler, although requiring more elaborate equipment in the passenger baggage claim unit. The aircraft is unloaded, either manually or, if container pods are used, semi-mechanically. The baggage is brought to the airside baggage hall, where it is unloaded into the passenger claim system. Again, the form of system used is dependent on the volume of traffic the baggage claim hall handles and the size of aircraft unloaded. Figure 8.7 depicts five different forms of delivery. The simplest system is the linear counter: here baggage carts are unloaded manually, directly onto a counter, where the passengers are waiting. A simple mechanized system is the linear track, where the carts are unloaded onto a moving belt, which carries the baggage on to a roller track. The more elaborate carousel and racetrack designs are necessary to handle the volume of baggage delivered by the large, wide-bodied aircraft.

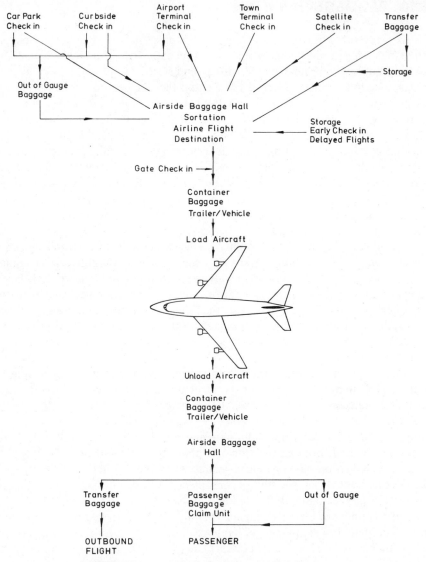

FIGURE 8.6 Baggage loading and unloading sequence.

It is important to ensure, in the design of the inbound baggage claim hall, that not only is the overall size of the facility adequate to cope with the design peak baggage flow, but also that th͟e i͟ndividual claim devices are matched to the size of aircraft anticipated.

8.11 ANALYSIS OF FLOWS THROUGH TERMINALS

As Figure 8.1 indicates, the pattern of flows through airports can be extremely complex. A knowledge of daily and even hourly flows is insufficient for detailed

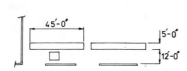

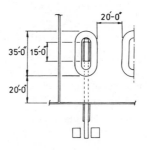

Claim length available 45'-0"
Area per unit: 225 sq.ft.
Max. bags per unit: 69 (at 1'-4" per 2 bags)
Alternate: 2-level counters at single depth.

Linear Counter

Claim length available 45'-0"
Area per unit: 218 sq.ft.
Max bags per unit: 36 (at 2'-6" per 2 bags presented lengthwise)

Linear Track

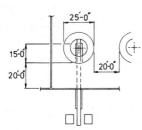

Claim length available: 78'-6"
Area per unit: 491 sq.ft.
Max bags per unit: 60 (at 1'-4" per bag)

Carousel

Claim length available: 90'-0"
Area per unit: 547 sq.ft.
Max bags per unit: 69 (at 1'-4" per bag)

Oval Carousel/Racetrack

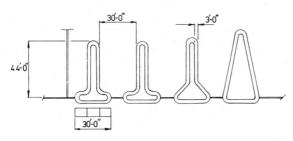

Claim length available: 115'-0"
Area per unit: 576-1020 sq.ft.
Max. bags per unit: 120 (at 1'-4" per bag) 88 bags on track, 32 bags inside track.

Various Racetrack Designs

FIGURE 8.7 Examples of baggage delivery systems. (*Source:* Reference 4.)

design of some facilities, since flows are of a varying and stochastic nature rather than uniform, even during peak design periods. To be able to examine the detailed behavior of passenger and baggage flows, the interaction of the design of one facility on another, three principal methods of analysis are used:

1. Network analysis.
2. Queuing theory.
3. Simulation.

Network Analysis

In network analysis, the time sequence of various activities is examined and structured to establish patterns of temporal interrelationships. Figure 8.8 is a very simplified critical path network, showing the interrelationships of the various activities associated with the enplanement of a domestic air passenger. This systems analysis technique can be used to identify the critical path of time through a network by assigning duration times to each activity. Applied to terminal planning, the analysis is a tool for scheduling terminal activities, hence for determining equipment and labor requirements within the terminal and on the apron (16). Airport designers also make use of PERT (program evaluation and review technique) in arriving at such decisions.

Queuing Theory

In a system composed of one or more processes that can be described in terms of the patterns of the arrivals of the individuals undergoing processing and the service times during processing, queuing theory can be applied to predict delays. Typically, queuing theory analysis gives outputs of overall system delays, delays at individual facilities, time in the system, and average numbers of passengers in the system or in any facility. Figure 8.9 shows the structure of a chain of probabilistic queuing models that was used to model flow at an

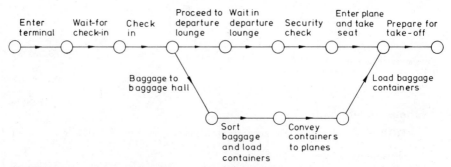

FIGURE 8.8 Simple network analysis of the enplanement of a domestic passenger. (*Source:* Reference 15.)

Node	Description	Model Used
1	Disembarkation	Dummy node
2	Immigration - Domestic	Random arrivals/exponential service/ n channels
3	Immigration - Alien	Random arrivals/exponential service/ m channels
4	Baggage Reclaim	Random arrivals/exponential service/ ∞ channels
5	Customs-Red Channel	Random arrivals/exponential service/ k channels
6	Customs- Green Channel	Random arrivals/ exponential service/ ∞ channels
7	Leaving terminal	Dummy node

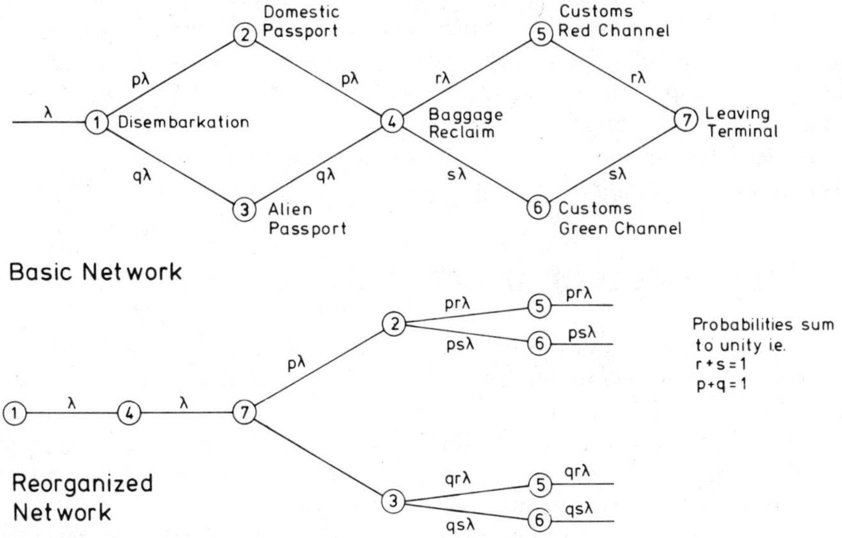

Basic Network

Reorganized Network

FIGURE 8.9 Queueing theory model for disembarkation with red and green channel customs operation. (*Source:* Reference 15.)

international airport. The average queuing time for the network can be shown to be equal to the weighted contributions from the activities comprising each route through the network (17):

$$\text{Prob}(\text{delay} > \tau)_{1234567} = pr \times \text{Prob}(\text{delay} > \tau)_{14725} + ps \times \text{Prob}(\text{delay} > \tau)_{14726} + qr \times \text{Prob}(\text{delay} > \tau)_{14735} + qs \times \text{Prob}(\text{delay} > \tau)_{14736}$$

Chief among the many difficulties associated with the use of analytical models when they are linked in chains, as required by airport terminal networks, is the need to incorporate random arrivals and exponential servicing in all models, if the mathematics is not to become intractable (18). The great advantage of queuing model analysis is that once the difficult mathematics has been handled, the amount of computing time required for general sizing of facilities may be quite small.

Simulation Procedures

The vast majority of analyses of passenger and baggage flows through terminals has been carried out by simulation methods, which are usually too complex to be performed without the aid of computers. As with queuing theory, simulation requires a detailed knowledge of the characteristics of the arrival and service patterns at each process. Using random generating techniques, the computer can simulate a large number of arrivals and services, enabling the computation of anticipated delays, length of time in the system, and number in the system at any one time. Since simulation models are microscopic in their treatment of the activity, they are excellent for detailed design of individual facilities and especially useful for determining the sensitivity of system parameters to minor changes in design.

There are a number of commercially available simulation programs that are either specifically designed for airport use or are easily adapted for this purpose.

8.12   THE NUMBER OF AIRCRAFT GATES

The final configuration of the airside interface depends largely on the number of aircraft gates. First principles would lead the designer to the conclusion that the number of gates is a function of the design peak hour aircraft movements, the length of time that the individual aircraft spend at the gates, and some utilization factor to account for the impossibility of filling all gates for 100% of the peak time, because of maneuvering and taxiing.

A formula by Horonjeff for computing the required number of gates (n) reflects this reasoning (19):

$$n = \frac{vt}{u}$$

where

v = design hour volume for arrivals *or* departures (aircraft/hr)
t = weighted mean stand occupancy (hr)
u = utilization factor, suggested to be 0.6 to 0.8 where gates are shared

From empirical observation, Piper suggests another formula of somewhat similar form, based on the arrival rate of aircraft (20):

$$n = mqt$$

where

m = design hour volume for arrivals and departures (aircraft/hr)
q = proportion of arrivals (total movements)
t = mean stand occupancy (hr)

Experience at some European airports, where stand occupancy times may be longer than is typical in the United States, indicates that a considerably larger number of gates is required according to the following formula:

$$n = 1.1m$$

where m = design hour volume for arrivals and departures (aircraft/hr)

Simulation programs have also been used to model stand usage and to predict stand requirements. The number of aircraft gates required is a function of:

Aircraft type and mix

percent of arrivals

total arrivals and departures

type of flight: (through or turnaround), (based or nonbased)

stand discipline: (method of sharing gates)

8.13 PARKING CONFIGURATIONS

The form of the airside interface and the design dimensions of the apron depend on the number of gates and the parking configuration chosen. In many airports, aircraft come to the nose-in parking position immediately next to the terminal under their own power and are towed out by tractors. The two principal advantages to this design are that passenger loading can be carried out by loading bridges, thereby protecting passengers from the elements, and that apron dimensions can be minimized. The main disadvantage of power-in push-out designs is the added manpower and equipment requirement (i.e., the tractor and its driver).

Power-in power-out designs have five basic configurations (Figure 8.10). Usually the choice of any of these configurations means exposure of passengers to the weather conditions on the apron. The main difference between the nose-in and nose-out configurations is that with the former there is the convenience of having the main passenger doors near the terminal, whereas the latter configuration normally minimizes noise and jet blast because the aircraft is lighter and has more momentum when turning immediately after taxiing. Often the

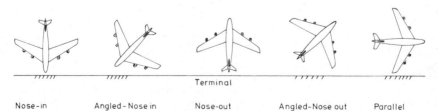

| Nose-in | Angled-Nose in | Nose-out | Angled-Nose out | Parallel |

FIGURE 8.10 Aircraft parking configurations.

latter configurations have less overall apron area requirements. For passenger
flow, under power-in power-out conditions, the best position is the parallel
parking configuration, but this requires the greatest apron space, and blast and
high frequency noise are directed at adjacent gate positions at breakaway.

8.14   APRON LAYOUT

The aircraft is unloaded, loaded, and serviced in the terminal apron, which is
usually in close proximity to the passenger airside gates. The spacing of aircraft
on the apron, therefore the layout of the apron itself, is determined by the
physical characteristics of the aircraft, the choice of parking configuration,
the effect of jet blast, and the manner in which aircraft will maneuver into
parking position.

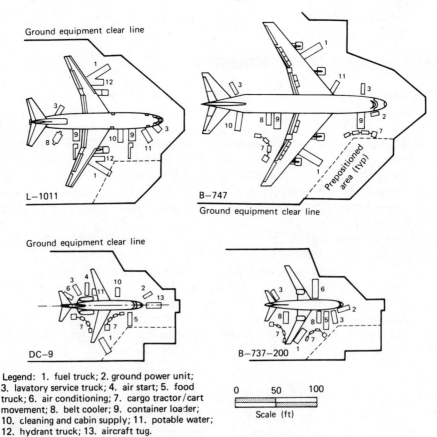

Legend: 1. fuel truck; 2. ground power unit;
3. lavatory service truck; 4. air start; 5. food
truck; 6. air conditioning; 7. cargo tractor/cart
movement; 8. belt cooler; 9. container loader;
10. cleaning and cabin supply; 11. potable water;
12. hydrant truck; 13. aircraft tug.

FIGURE 8.11   Examples of aircraft and ground servicing equipment maneuvering for pushout
and taxiout angle configurations. The parking angle, normally 30° and 60° or 45°, will be at the
discretion of the airline unless physical or other constraints dictate otherwise. Note that the

Aircraft can either move into and out of parking positions under their own engine power ("power-in, power-out") or use the "power-in, push-out" configuration just discussed. The former method, though requiring no special equipment or apron personnel to move the aircraft out, fails to place the nose of the aircraft in the most desirable position, since it does not permit the loading and unloading of passengers with jetways. Because jetways are needed only at the largest facilities, most airports are still designed without them; their aprons and gate positions must have dimensions that permit the aircraft to maneuver with adequate clearances (5).

The apron dimensions are determined on the basis of the aircraft parking configuration (21). Figure 8.11 gives examples of the maneuvering requirements for push-out and taxi-out angle configurations of parking. Angle parking is normally used at apron stations where traffic is relatively light and manpower is to be conserved. Less ramp frontage is required than for the parallel parked

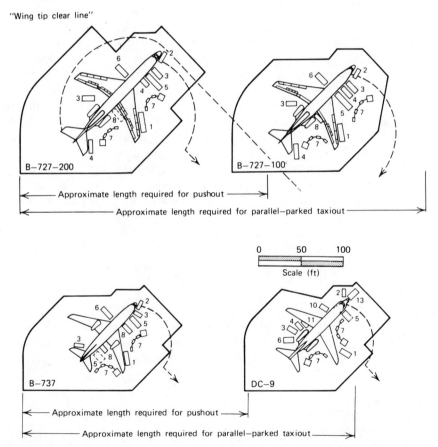

illustration of the B-747 shows equipment staging before aircraft positioning. (*Source:* Reference 5.)

arrangement but more than for push-out parking. Figure 8.11 indicates the comparative length requirements for the three arrangements.

For design purposes, commercial passenger transport aircraft may be designated as belonging to one of six categories (5). Table 7.11 gave the required dimension ranges of their parking envelopes, indicating the extreme requirements of push-out and parallel taxi-out parking configurations. For detailed discussion of apron design dimensions, see Section 7.11 and other standard references (22, 23). When detailed geometrics are not necessary—in master planning, for example—the following apron areas are suggested for various aircraft classes (14):

Wide-bodied, four-engine jet aircraft and SST	15,000 m^2
Four-engine narrow-bodied jet aircraft	6,000 m^2
Three-engine narrow-bodied jet aircraft	4,000 m^2
Two-engine narrow-bodied jet aircraft	3,000 m^2

In determining apron dimensions, it is customary to predict the aircraft mix for the peak design hour. There must be enough gates to accommodate the number of aircraft expected, and at least as many gates capable of parking the longest aircraft as there are expected aircraft in this category in the design hour. If gates are permanently assigned to individual airlines, the requirement for maximum sized gates is larger than if there is a nondesignated system of gate assignment. Pavement markings on the apron furnish guidance to maneuvering aircraft. The guideline, usually yellow, traces out the track to be followed by the nose wheel of the largest aircraft that can use the gate position. Since this is the critical vehicle, smaller aircraft can follow the pavement marking while maintaining adequate clearance from other parked aircraft and buildings.

8.15 APRON FACILITIES AND REQUIREMENTS

The apron serves two functions: it is an area for parking airplanes and for performing servicing and minor maintenance work. The dimensions and strength of the apron are determined by the first function. The facilities supplied on the apron and their location are set by the servicing function. The principal services to be supplied are:

Aircraft fueling facilities.
Electrical supply.
Aircraft grounding facilities.
Apron roadways.

Fueling Facilities

There are three methods by which aircraft are refueled: from an apron hydrant system, from fuel pits, and by mobile fuel trucks.

In the hydrant system, pipes beneath the apron are connected to a central fuel storage. Flush-mounted hydrant valves are provided at the gate positions. The aircraft is refueled using small mobile hydrant dispensers, each equipped with a pump filter, an air eliminator, and a meter. Fuel can be rapidly pumped into the parked airplane by attaching the dispenser to the closest hydrant valve.

A variation on the hydrant system is the fueling pit, which is similarly connected to a central fuel storage. But since each pit is fitted with hose, reel, filter, and air eliminator, there is no need for mobile dispensers on the apron. However, the fuel pits must be much larger than hydrant boxes, as well as more substantial, to withstand rolling apron wheel loads. Additionally, there is an inevitable redundancy of refueling equipment, which is avoided by the hydrant valve system.

At most small airports, the conventional system of refueling is by fueling trucks, which carry their own pumps, reels, meters, filters, and air eliminators. These trucks, carrying very large fuel loads (up to 8000 U.S. gal), are specially designed for operation on the apron. They are low-slung vehicles with very high axle loadings, and thus are unsuitable in most countries for operation on highways.

Opinions on the best system of refueling are sharply divided. Apron operators have conflicting views on the relative suitability of mobile and fixed systems. The disadvantages of using fueling trucks are obvious. Very large aircraft such as the Boeing 747 can require four large tankers for a complete fuel load. At a large airport, the apron traffic generated by fuel trucks alone can be unacceptably high and a potential source of accidents. Moreover, aircraft may be delayed if fuel trucks are not available because of insufficient supply or industrial strike action. Consequently, many of the new major airports in the United States have installed hydrant systems.

In the past, however, hydrant systems have been found to lack flexibility in adapting to new airplanes. With the introduction of wide-bodied large aircraft, for example, it became apparent that hydrant valves located for smaller aircraft are unsuitably positioned for the new aircraft. Where gates are not exclusively used by one airline, but must accommodate a number of airlines and a range of aircraft, hydrant positions can present large operational problems. IATA recommends modular apron design, which permits acceptance of both conventional and wide-bodied aircraft (4). Therefore many European airport operators still use fueling trucks extensively.

Electrical Supply

Electricity must be supplied to the aircraft during the period that its engines are shut off, to run lighting and other equipment, and, frequently, to start the engines. Supply can be arranged either by flush-mounted supply points from sub-apron conduits, sufficiently separated from any fuel hydrant valves, or by mobile units. In the United States, power usually comes from apron supply points. This arrangement may be less successful where the range of aircraft types to be accommodated is very wide because requirements for voltages, and even for alternating or direct current, may be different (25).

Grounding Facilities

Grounding facilities must be supplied to prevent fire hazard on the apron. Aircraft undergoing high speed refueling are especially likely to generate high static charges, which could cause explosion and fire in the presence of volatile aviation fuels.

Airside Roadways

Airside roadways are necessary to permit the servicing, cleaning, and refueling of aircraft. As the size of aprons increases, the number of potential conflicts between surface apron vehicles becomes very large, requiring careful layout of airside surface routes to ensure reasonable safety for personnel walking on the apron. If passenger access to aircraft is permitted across the apron, the layout becomes even more critical.

8.16   SECURITY CONSIDERATIONS

The development of aerial hijacking as a means of political terrorism or criminal extortion has caused airports all over the world to introduce personal security checks and other security measures to discourage and prevent hijackers from boarding aircraft. There appears at the moment to be no general agreement on the best method of carrying out personal security checks. In some airport terminals (e.g., Atlanta), the security check is performed in the central terminal, leaving large areas of interconnecting piers security "clean" and "airside." No further security check is carried out at the point of loading. Many airports do their security checks at the gate immediately before boarding. The former method uses less security staff and is advantageous insofar as if the security checkpoint is rushed, a considerable interception distance may remain before the attacker can reach an aircraft. Gate checks require more security staff, but provide a greater measure of certainty that there has been no evasion of security on the piers and at the airside interface.

The choice of system depends greatly on the concept used in terminal design. Clearly, for example, where a gate arrival terminal has been designed, security cannot be centralized and must be carried out at the gate itself. The introduction of secure aprons at existing airports has been extremely troublesome. For example, at Heathrow Airport in London, there are more than 20 points of vehicular access to the apron that must be manned on a 24 hr basis.

REFERENCES

1. Boothby, J., and N. Ashford, *Construction of a Dynamic Airport System*, Report No. TT7408, Loughborough: Loughborough University of Technology, August 1974.

2. de Neufville, Richard, *Airport Systems Planning*. London: Macmillan, 1976.

3. *Airport Landside Capacity*, Special Report No. 159. Washington, D.C.: Transportation Research Board, 1976.

4. *Airport Terminals Reference Manual*, 6th Ed. Montreal: International Air Transport Association, 1976.

5. *The Apron Terminal Building*, FAA Report No. FAA-RD-75-191, July 1975.

6. *The Apron Terminal Complex, Analysis of Concepts for Evaluation of Terminal Buildings*, prepared for the FAA by the Ralph M. Parsons Company, AD-771 186, September 1973.

7. Horonjeff, R., "Analysis of Passenger and Baggage Flows in Airport Terminal Buildings," *Journal of Aircraft*, American Institute of Aeronautics and Astronautics, Vol. 5, No. 5, 1969.

8. *Heathrow Passenger and Baggage Survey*, London: Metra Consulting Group, 1973.

9. Ashford, N., et al., *The Design of the Passenger Processing System for Airport Terminals*, Report No. TT7407, Loughborough: Loughborough University of Technology, August 1974.

10. Fischer, Hans, *Pipe Airport Systems*, Rome: Alitalia, 1975.

11. de Neufville, R., R. Moore, and J. Yaney, *Optimal Use of Transporters in the Design of Airport Terminals*, DOC 7204-TEC/20, Paris: International Civil Airports Association, July 1972.

12. Ashford, N., et al., *Passenger Behavior and the Design of Airport Terminals*. Washington, D.C.: Transportation Research Board Record No. 588, 1976.

13. Perrett, J. D., "The Capacity of Airports—Planning considerations," *Proceedings of the Institution of Civil Engineers*, Vol. 50, 1971.

14. *Aviation Demand and Airport Facility Requirement Forecasts for Medium Air Transportation Hubs Through 1980*, Federal Aviation Administration, January 1969.

15. Ashford, N., "Passengers in Airport Terminals," *Airports International*, March 1976.

16. Moder, J. J., and C. R. Phillips, *Project Management with CPM and PERT*, 2nd Ed., New York: van Nostrand Reinhold, 1970.

17. Ashford, N., M. O'Leary, and P. D. McGinity, "Stochastic Modelling of Passenger and Baggage Flows Through an Airport Terminal," *Traffic Engineering and Control*, May 1976.

18. O'Leary, "Stochastic Modelling of Airport Passenger Terminals," Master's thesis, Loughborough University of Technology, 1975.

19. Horonjeff, R., and Francis X. McKelvey, *Planning and Design of Airports*, 3rd Ed., New York: McGrawHill, 1983.

20. Piper, H. P., "Design Principles for Decentralized Terminals," *Airport Forum*, Vol. 3, October 1974.

21. *Airport Design Standards—Airports Serviced by Air Carriers—Taxiways*, FAA Advisory Circular AC/5335-1A, including Changes 1, 2, 3, May 15, 1970.

22. *Aerodrome Design Manual—Part 2, Taxiways, Aprons, and Holding Bays*, Montreal: International Civil Aviation Organization, 1977.

23. *Airport Aprons*, FAA Advisory Circular AC 150/5335-2A, January 1965.

24. *Planning and Design Considerations for Airport Terminal Building Development*, FAA Advisory Circular AC 150/5360/7, October 1976.

25. Ashford, N., H. P. M. Stanton and Clifton E. Moore, *Airport Operations*, New York: Wiley–Interscience, 1984.

9

AIR CARGO FACILITIES

9.1 THE IMPORTANCE OF AIR CARGO

In order to prevent unnecessary and undesirable interference between surface freight and passenger traffic, cargo operations are ideally separated from the passenger terminal area. Therefore, even the frequent air traveler tends to regard the passenger terminal as the hub of all the important comings and goings in the daily activities of the airport. The airport designer, however, cannot overlook air cargo, for this is an important and fast growing area of civil aviation. During the period 1960–69, overall growth rates in tonne km. carried averaged 19%, a rate that consistently exceeded passenger growth rates. By 1982, these very high growth rates had disappeared. As Table 9.1 indicates, the rate of growth fluctuated significantly, averaging 9.1% between 1971 and 1980. This compares closely with the figure of 8.7% for the annual growth rate for passenger tonne km carried. The table shows that there is strong evidence that the freight market has stabilized to a predictable share of the overall market for air transport, and that the very dramatic growth rates of the early 1960s are unlikely to reappear in the absence of dramatic technological innovations. However, while air freight represents only the small fraction of 1% of all freight transported by all modes, its importance to civil aviation should not be underrated. Accounting for approximately 22% of the total combined passenger and freight tonne km, the revenue generated is approximately 14% of total revenues. These revenues generally far outweigh even allocated costs, and the freight operations are seen to be highly profitable when examined on a marginal basis.

The air cargo area of civil aviation is the area of fastest technological change. This is partly because the freight distribution industry in general is undergoing conversion to unitization of loads (containerization), and partly because of the rapid introduction of wide-bodied aircraft capable of accepting large unit loads. The air cargo industry presents the image of still being in a period of rapid change and flux. Consequently, the design of air cargo terminals is susceptible to rapid changes in parameters because of technological advances. Design flexibility, therefore, is felt to be imperative (1).

260

Table 9.1 World Total International and Domestic Revenue Traffic 1971–80

Year	Freight (tonnes)		Freight (tonne km)		Total Freight and Passenger (tonne km)		Freight as a Percentage of Total tonne km
	Millions	Annual Increase (%)	Millions	Annual Increase (%)	Millions	Annual Increase (%)	
1971	6.7	9.6	13,230	9.6	60,470	6.7	21.9
1972	7.3	9.2	15,020	13.6	68,170	12.7	22.0
1973	8.2	12.9	17,530	16.7	75,790	11.2	23.1
1974	8.7	5.2	19,020	8.5	80,700	6.5	23.5
1975	8.7	0.7	19,370	1.8	84,780	5.1	22.8
1976	9.3	7.4	21,540	11.2	93,270	10.0	23.1
1977	10.0	7.5	23,630	9.7	100,440	7.7	23.5
1978	10.6	6.0	25,940	9.8	113,540	13.0	22.8
1979	10.9	5.7	27,970	7.8	125,950	10.9	22.2
1980	11.0	0.9	29,050	3.9	129,320	2.7	22.4

Source: *World Air Traffic Statistics 1980.* Montreal: International Civil Aviation Organization, 1981.

9.2   THE FUNCTIONS OF THE CARGO TERMINAL

In many ways, the functions performed by the cargo terminal are very similar to those that take place in the passenger terminal, even though the aspects of the two areas are strikingly different. The cargo terminal serves four principal functions: *conversion*, *sorting*, *storage*, and *facilitation and documentation*.

In *conversion*, the size of a load is changed by combining a number of small loads into a larger unit, such as a pallet or container, which can be more easily handled airside. A conversion also almost certainly takes place in flow patterns. The landside flow is characterized by the continual arrivals or departures of small loads, which may form either the entire load or part of the load of a truck. These loads are batched into individual aircraft loads.

The *sorting* function occurs as the terminal accepts loads consisting of cargo bound for a number of different destinations, combining them, and forming aircraft loads for individual destinations.

Storage is necessary to permit load assembly by conversion and sorting, since flow rates and patterns on the landside and airside are quite dissimilar.

Finally, *facilitation and documentation* is conveniently carried out at the cargo terminal, where frequently a physical transfer takes place between the surface and air carriers, and governmental controls such as customs are normally performed. The efficient operation of a large, modern cargo terminal is vitally dependent on modern documentation procedures. The application of electronic computer data processing techniques to a large cargo terminal is described in Section 9.7.

9.3   FACTORS AFFECTING THE SIZE AND FORM OF THE CARGO TERMINAL

Although most airports are capable of handling air freight in some capacity, the size and form of the cargo terminal facilities vary substantially. The degree of sophistication provided depends on the following factors:

The mix and flow characteristics of the cargo.
The characteristics of the surface and air vehicles.
Materials handling, documentation, and communication techniques.
Degree of capitalization.

The Mix and Flow Characteristics of the Cargo

Air cargo can arrive at the terminal in two forms: as a large number of small consignments that require sorting, storing, and batching before transfer to the aircraft, or as containerized large unit loads, requiring far less handling at the cargo terminal itself. The mix of large and small consignments has strong design implications. In the mid-1960s, the containerization revolution was underestimated by many involved in air cargo planning. Until that time, air cargo had been composed of a large number of heterogeneous consignments that required significant handling in the air cargo terminal.

Some of the major cargo terminals being planned at that time (1965) were designed around the assumption that the nature of the traffic would remain relatively unchanged. Therefore, these terminals were designed to mechanize and automate the handling of numerous small consignments. However, starting in the late 1960s, there was a rapid move toward containerization. Terminals such as Cargocentre Europe became obsolete even as they were put into operation. More flexible but more labor intensive systems were found to be better adaptable to the changing nature of traffic. Figure 9.1 shows how air freight has become increasingly containerized since 1965, and indicates that technological improvements will promote wider use of intermodal containers. This innovation will itself generate further changes in cargo terminal handling procedures, which must be accommodated in future designs.

Automation and mechanization have been introduced successfully in the area of transfer vehicles (TV) and elevated transfer vehicles (ETV). These systems deal with the individual container as the unit to be moved and stored within the terminal. Modern ETV systems can produce very efficient utilization of terminal floor area by the use of multilevel container storage, and can also dramatically decrease expensive container damage that inevitably results from handling with mobile units such as forklift trucks.

In addition to the mix, the planner must consider total volume and the peaking characteristics of the flow. The total volume of cargo moved is the prime determinant of revenues, hence implying the level of investment that can be made. Monthly, weekly, and daily volumes have scheduling implications setting in part the overall level of storage that the facility must normally supply for the design peak period. Peaking of flow is the major parameter of storage requirements and materials handling, since systems throughput cannot economically be made equal to peak demand throughout the whole system. Figures

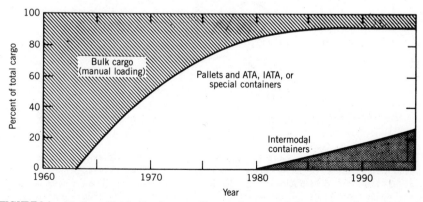

FIGURE 9.1   Air Cargo Unitization forecast. (*Source:* Aerospace Industries Association of America, 1979.)

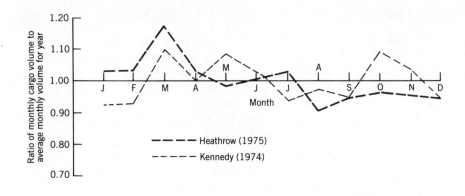

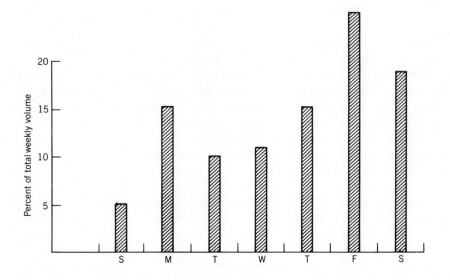

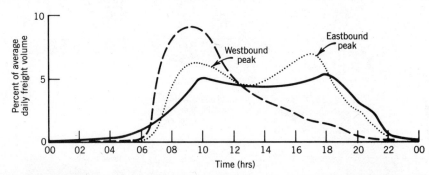

FIGURE 9.2 Peaking characteristics of air freight flows. (a) Annual peaking characteristics. (*Source:* FAA and CAA.) (b) Daily peaking characteristics. (c) Hourly peaking characteristics. (*Source for (b) and (c):* British Airways, London Heathrow.) (Note: Solid line indicates landside freight received; dashed line, airside freight inbound; dotted line, airside freight outbound.)

9.2a, b, and c plot examples of the peaking of cargo flows on an annual, daily, and hourly basis.

It is very important to be aware that each terminal will have its own characteristic peaking graphs. Variations throughout the year will depend on seasonal variations of commodities carried and industrial output. Daily variations relate to shipper and receiver preferences on clearing and receiving material. Hourly variations of throughput vary according to the variable used (landside received, landside dispatch, airside outbound, or airside inbound). These are affected by shipper and receiver operating preference, location of airport relative to eastbound and westbound traffic, aircraft schedules, noise curfews *in situ* and at destination airports.

Although the designer can expect to spread the peaks by the use of terminal storage, prudence must be exerted in the choice of storage time. If system throughput is too slow and cargo is delayed too long in storage, the premium level of service supplied by air cargo is vulnerable to severe deterioration, certainly in the short haul. Typically, dwell time will be less than one day outbound and less than four days inbound. It may be necessary for the operator to set storage charges at a punitive level beyond 72 hours in order to encourage rapid clearance of inbound freight.

Cargo is normally categorized into three groups: *emergency* demand, where speed is essential to the usefulness of the commodity (e.g., blood plasma), *regular* demand, where the commodity has limited commercial life (e.g., flowers or newspapers), and *planned* demand, where air freight is selected after analysis of distribution costs. Each may require different treatment within the terminal.

Aircraft and Surface Vehicle Characteristics

The size and type of anticipated aircraft will affect the materials handling procedures adopted in the cargo terminal; the various aircraft types have differing requirements of standard containers, low containers, igloos, and pallets. Aircraft of the same family have strikingly different requirements when used as all freight or mixed payload craft. The most successful terminal design is that which is best adopted to the mix of aircraft it receives over its working life. This implies a level of optimal fit and a degree of flexibility to adapt to technological change in the short and long term.

Degree of Capitalization

Potentially heavy capitalization of air freight terminals seems like a highly attractive way to decrease labor costs, which can form a major portion of terminal handling costs. However, high capitalization and automation is economic only at relatively high load factors (i.e., when throughput is sustained at a reasonably high level) and the traffic mix conforms to expectations. If either of these conditions is not met, overmechanization can lead to poor economic performances and unsatisfactory operation. Equally necessary is the ability to eliminate labor on the scale anticipated, which requires both union cooperation and a precise knowledge of what is feasible in the area of industrial relations.

Three basically different types of freight terminal can be identified:

Low Technology. These are often, but not necessarily, low volume terminals. Where manpower is both available and cheap, freight is moved by manhandling over extensive layouts of roller beds and transfer tables.

Medium Technology. Containers are moved by mobile lifting and transfer equipment, for example, forklift trucks. The vast majority of existing medium and high volume facilities still operate with this level of sophistication.

High Technology. Involving TVs and ETVs, these facilities use single or multiple level storage of containers, which are moved within the terminal mainly by the railed transfer vehicles. ETV operations produce high throughputs per square meter, with minimum container damage and minimum labor requirements. There is, however, a very high level of capitalization required. Figures 9-3a and b show two modern freight terminals that have extensive container storage areas served by ETVs.

Materials Handling, Documentation, and Communications

Although automated cargo handling had a disappointing early history due to an undue concentration on uncontainerized bulk cargo, automation of documentation through the application of electronic computer data processing (ECDP) has proved remarkably successful. Since cargo cannot move without its documentation, the use of on-line computers to pinpoint the progress of a shipment through the complex cargo handling process has offered substantial benefits to shippers, forwarders, carriers, and customs. First introduced in London for Customs and Excise purposes, computerized documentation and expediting is now commonplace.

9.4   FLOW THROUGH THE AIRPORT CARGO TERMINAL

Figure 9.4 illustrates how import and export flows of cargo move through the airport terminal (2). Incoming cargo for export passes through the reception area, is moved through the documentation area (where it undergoes count checks, weighing, measuring, and labeling), and either is passed directly into a pre-flight assembly lineup or is placed in a short term storage area, from which it eventually transfers into preflight assembly. Next the cargo is moved into the flight assembly area, the nature of which depends on whether the freight is to be carried by a passenger-cargo or by all-cargo aircraft. From the

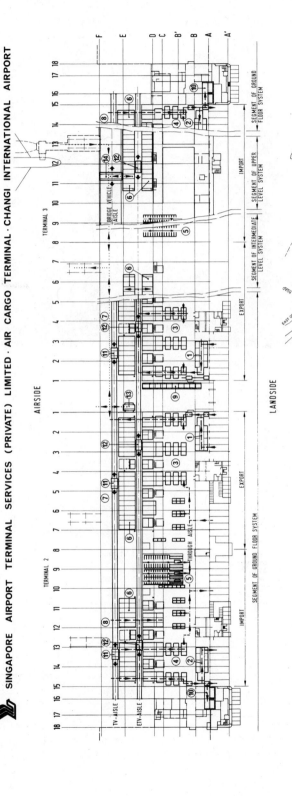

SINGAPORE AIRPORT TERMINAL SERVICES (PRIVATE) LIMITED · AIR CARGO TERMINAL · CHANGI INTERNATIONAL AIRPORT

① OUTBOUND TRUCK DOCK SUBSYSTEM
② INBOUND TRUCK DOCK SUBSYSTEM
③ BUILD UP AREA
④ BREAK DOWN AREA
⑤ BOX STORAGE SYSTEM
⑥ CONTAINER STORAGE SYSTEM
⑦ RAMP VEHICLE UNLOADING ZONE
⑧ RAMP VEHICLE LOADING ZONE
⑨ DIRECT DELIVERY LINE
⑩ CHILLER AND COOLER ROOM

⑪ 20" TRANSFER VEHICLE   QTY 4
⑫ 10-ft ELEVATING TRANSFER VEHICLE QTY 4
⑬ 20-ft ELEVATOR   QTY 1
⑭ BRIDGE VEHICLE   QTY 2

FLOW SYMBOLS

——   10 ft CONTAINER
—·— 8x8 STORAGE BOXES
—··— 4x4 AND 4x8 STORAGE BOXES
······ 20 ft CONTAINER

FIGURE 9.3 (a) SATS Air Cargo Terminal, Chang: International Airport, Singapore. (*Source:* Mannesmann Demag.)

FIGURE 9.3 (*continued.*) (b) Lufthansa cargo center Frankfurt. (*Source:* Lufthansa German Airlines.)

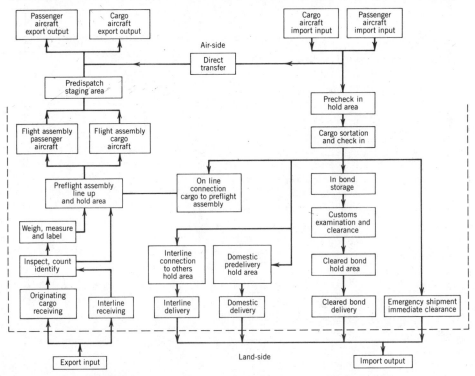

FIGURE 9.4 Flow through cargo terminal. (*Source:* Reference 2.)

flight assembly area, flight loads of freight move to the final staging area, then across the cargo or passenger apron to their outbound flight.

Incoming or import cargo can similarly arrive on mixed payload or all-cargo flights. On arrival it passes through an initial holding area before sorting and check-in. After sorting, cargo requiring customs clearance goes to in-bond storage, from there by way of customs clearance to a cleared bond storage area, and eventually to the receiver via import delivery. Domestic cargo, on the other hand, requires no customs clearance and proceeds directly from the check-in area to a pre-delivery hold area, where it remains pending arrangement of delivery.

Figure 9.4 also points up the need for interline transfers to other carriers, and across the apron movements for intracarrier transfers between flights. The latter type of movement is extremely important in some European cargo gate airports, where transfer freight can account for a large proportion of the incoming traffic. At the Frankfurt Lufthansa terminal, more than half of all incoming freight is transferred to outgoing flights; the terminal design reflects this specialized need.

9.5 PALLETS, CONTAINERS, IGLOOS, AND OTHER UNITIZED SYSTEMS

Until the early 1960s, air cargo was generally loose loaded into combination and freight aircraft. As freight traffic increased, paralleling growth in aircraft size, economic operation could be maintained only by limiting the turnaround time of freight-carrying aircraft on the apron. Rapid loading and unloading can be achieved by unitizing loads. Various unit load devices are currently in use: containers, pallets and igloos.

Containers

Rigid-bodied *containers* are used to protect air cargo and ease the handing of numerous small, individual consignments of air cargo. Wide-bodied freight aircraft such as the Boeing 747F are capable of taking modular ISO* 8 × 8 ft containers in 10, 20, and 40 ft lengths. These containers are not intermodal, however, since tare weight considerations limit their structural strength; ISO aircraft containers can be rolled but not lifted. Special low height containers are built for the lower holds of wide-bodied freight and combination aircraft. Figure 9.5 shows the container loading arrangements. Typically, lower hold containers have dimensions of 60.4 × 61.5 in. and 60.4 × 125 in.

---

* International Standards Organization.

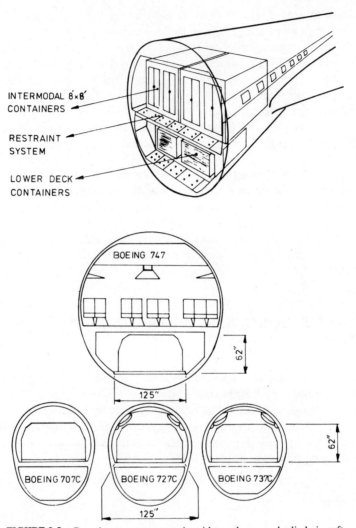

INTERMODAL 8´×8´
CONTAINERS

RESTRAINT
SYSTEM

LOWER DECK
CONTAINERS

BOEING 747

62″

125″

BOEING 707C   BOEING 727C   BOEING 737C

62″

125″

FIGURE 9.5   Container arrangements in wide- and narrow-bodied aircraft.

Pallets

Pallets are devices with integral rolling surfaces on which cargo can be loaded.
The load is held in place by nets, and the complete load can be manhandled,
forklifted, or moved mechanically as a unit (Figure 9.6). For narrow-bodied
aircraft, standard pallet dimensions are 88 × 125 in. for all-freight craft, and
88 × 108 in. where there is necessity to move through the cargo hold for
access, to passenger areas. Wide-bodied craft also can accept pallets to 96 ×
117.75 in. in the upper hold. In the lower hold, 96 × 125 in. pallets can be
accommodated, as well as the pallets normally taken by narrow-bodied craft.

Igloos

Igloos are rigid-bodied pallets, used primarily to prevent damage to cargo or to the inside of the aircraft, where passenger cabins are converted to freight usage. A *structural igloo* is a fully enclosed shell, constructed integrally with a pallet to ensure that cargo conforms to required contours. The shell and the pallet of the igloo form a single structural unit. A *nonstructural igloo* is a bottomless shell that fits over the pallet to give a shape to loaded cargo. The shell is used in conjunction with the pallet but adds no structural strength.

IATA Unit Load Devices

The IATA system of classifying ULDs is shown in Figure 9.7. Each container type is identified by a multi-alphanumeric code in which each alphanumeric identifies a particular category, (3).

Alphanumeric 1:
- A. Certified container
- B. Noncertified container
- P. Aircraft pallet.
- R. Thermal certified aircraft container
- U. Nonstructural igloo

Alphanumeric 2: Base dimensions

Alphanumeric 3: Contour and aircraft compatability

FIGURE 9.6 Palletized unit being transferred to an aircraft.

Figure 9.7 Air freight unit load devices. (Source: IATA.)

Type	Owner	Corresponding IATA container classification		Cubic capacity	External dimensions and cubic displ.	Weight		Handling features for shippers
						Minimum chargeable pounds	Maximum gross weight	
M-1	Airline provided (available at 747F cities)	Type 2	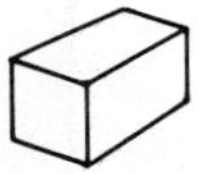	572 cu ft	L 125 W 96 H 96 cu displ 666 cu ft	4,400	15,000	Picked up or delivered on conventional truck trailer chassis
M-2	Airline provided (available at 747F cities)	Type 1	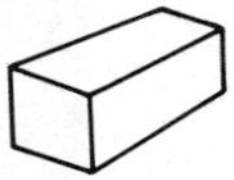	1077 cu ft	L 240 W 96 H 96 cu displ 1280 cu ft	12,363	25,000	Picked up or delivered on conventional truck trailer chassis
L-6	Airline provided		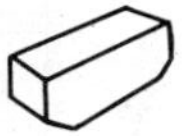	310 cu ft	L 160 W 60 4 H 64	2,800	7,000	Dolly transporters available
LD-7	Airline provided (available at 747DC-10 and L1011 cities)	Type 5	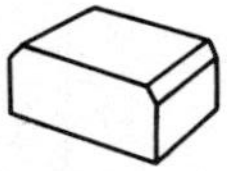	cu capacity 355 cu ft	L 125 W 88 H 63 cu displ 401 cu ft	2,800	10,400	Dolly transporters available
L-11 L-5	Airline provided (available at 747DC-10 and L1011 cities)	Type 6	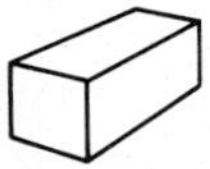	cu capacity 265 cu ft	L 125 W 60 H 64 cu displ 277 cu ft	1,800	7,000	Dolly transporters available

	Provided by	Type		Cu capacity	Dimensions		Max wt	Remarks
L-10	Airline provided	Type 6		varies	L 125 W 60 4 H 63 cu displ 242 cu ft	1,694	6,500	Dolly transporters available
A-1	Airline provided (available at Freighter cities)	CO1 CO2		cu capacity 393 cu ft	L 88" W 125" H 87" cu displ 425 cu ft	3,000	13,300	Dolly transporters available / Can be pallet & net
A-2 A-3	Airline provided (available at Freighter cities)	CO1 CO2		cu capacity 440 cu ft	L 88" W 125" H 87" cu displ 475 cu ft	3,200	12,500	Dolly transporters available / Can be pallet & net / Forkable
		CO3 CO4 CO5 CO6	(Insert for A)		L 84" W 58" H 76"-45" cu displ 197 70 cu ft			
B	Shipper provided			varies		1,800	5,000	
L-W	Airline provided			varies	L 98 W 42 2 H 41 6 cu displ 76 cu ft	500	1,200	Dolly transporters available
L-3	Airline provided (available at 747DC-10 and L1011 cities)	Type 8		cu capacity 150 cu ft	L 79 0 L 62 0 W 60 0 H 64 0 cu displ 166 0 cu ft	1,100	3,500	Dolly transporters available

(*Fig. 9.7 continued on p. 274.*)

Type	Owner		Corresponding IATA container classification	Cubic capacity	External dimensions and cubic displ.	Weight		Handling features for shippers
						Minimum chargeable pounds	Maximum gross weight	
B-2	Shipper provided	(Insert for A) 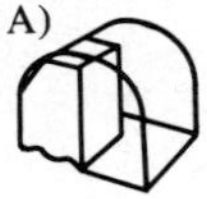	none	varies	L 42" W 58" H 76"-45" cu displ 98 85 cu ft	900	2,500	Forkable
D	Shipper provided	(Insert for A) 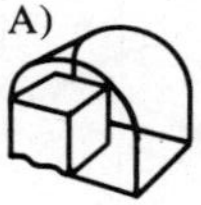	CO8, CO9, COJ	varies	L 58" W 42" H 45" cu displ 63 44 cu ft	500	2,000	Forkable
L-N	Shipper provided	(Insert for LD-3) 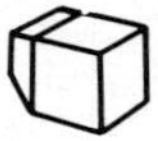	CO7	varies	L 56 W 55 H 57 cu displ 101 6 cu ft	900	3,160	Forkable
E	Shipper provided		COS	varies	L 42 W 29 H 25 5 cu displ 17 97 cu ft	130	500	Side handles recommended
E-H	Shipper provided		COS(E)	cu displ. 9.03 cu ft	L 35 4" W 21" H 21"	100	250	Consult air carrier
Q	Shipper provided		none	varies	L 39 5 W 27 5 H 21 cu displ 120 cu ft	100	11,400	Side handles recommended

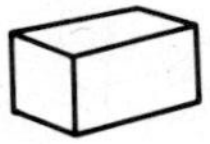

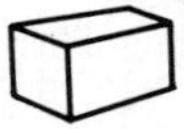

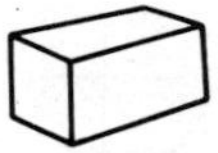

FIGURE 9.7 (continued.)

9.6 FREIGHT-CARRYING AIRCRAFT

Freight can be carried by aircraft in a number of ways; in the lower compartments of narrow-bodied aircraft, in the lower holds of wide-bodied aircraft, or in all-freight aircraft. Narrow-bodied aircraft have only small holds for cargo and baggage, and they must be loaded with loose cargo. Small amounts of cargo are carried in this way, but the vast majority of freight is carried by all-freight aircraft or in the lower holds of the wide-bodied vehicles.

Until the early 1970s, there was an increasing trend to use all-freight aircraft, including passenger aircraft that could be converted rapidly from passenger use—the so-called QC (quick change) models. The introduction of wide-bodied aircraft in the early 1970s appears to have altered this pattern in some market areas (4). The cargo hold capacity of the 747 is very large (6190 ft^3), even when compared with the all-freight 707 (8074 ft^3). The rapid introduction of wide-bodied aircraft over many long distance routes, has made spare cargo capacity available. This space can utilize reasonably large containers, thus affording to the carrier the advantages of modern materials handling in the terminal. The use of the wide-bodied belly compartments for freight therefore is economic, and this option has been extensively chosen. Whether the trend to all-freight operation will be reasserted is not yet clear, but it appears that in the long term, the separation of passenger and freight traffic is likely to be desirable. Table 9.2 shows the freight capacities of a number of freight and combination aircraft.

Table 9.2 Freight Capacities of a Typical Freight and Combination Aircraft

Aircraft Model	Maximum Freight Payload (lb)
B-707-320C	91,390
B-747-200F	254,640
B-747-200C	237,110
B-737-200QC	33,350
B-727-100D	44,000
DC-8F	95,282
DC-8-63F	118,583
DC-10 (Series 30F)	155,700
L-100-30	51,402
Merchantman 953-C	37,400
Hawker-Siddley Argosy	31,009
Caravelle 11R-SE210	20,000
Fokker F27-600	12,511
BAC-111-475	21,223
L-1011 TriStar	86,002

Source: *Janes All the World's Aircraft*, 1981–1982. London: McDonald and Janes, 1981.

9.7   DOCUMENTATION AND CONTROL

Electronic data processing has become essential in the control of cargo flow through large terminals. Since cargo cannot move without documentation, the rapid movement of large volumes of cargo requires the rapid processing of large amounts of documentation, with a high level of accuracy and reliability. In addition, the documentation must be available to a large number of persons who are separated in the system both spatially and temporally. Figure 9.8 outlines in simplified form a typical documentation and flow control system for the export side of an air cargo terminal.

Reservations of space are made by checking computer records of the current status of space available on individual flights. Then freight can be scheduled to arrive in time for the outgoing flight. At reception, the freight is weighed and checked, an airway bill is produced, then computerized from an on-line terminal, and an on-line manifest is printed out. In conjunction with flight data, the individual consignment information is aggregated into the flight tally for loading purposes.

The freight is sorted at reception into small, heavy, and special or out-of-gauge freight and is temporarily stored in the terminal stacks. Cargo is moved into the flight assembly area in accordance with the flight tally. Pallets and containers are packed or "stuffed" after passing through the live lanes in the flight assembly area, data on pallet contents are transmitted to the computer for information and location purposes during flight and on arrival. In this way the locations of individual pieces are known, and stray consignments can be traced more easily than is possible with noncomputerized techniques.

9.8   APRON CARGO HANDLING

Unlike the passenger apron, where the passenger payload can move itself, the cargo apron must be highly mechanized to carry out the transfer of the freight

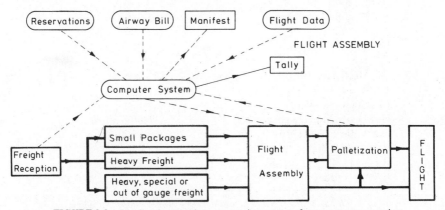

FIGURE 9.8   Idealized cargo data processing system for an export operation.

FIGURE 9.9 Nose dock system.

from the terminal to the aircraft. Since short aircraft turnaround time is essential to profitability, apron cargo handling systems must be capable of rapid unloading and loading times while achieving high payload densities. The type of equipment used depends on the exact nature of the cargo.

The palletized and igloo units comprise the most common cargo form. After the pallets have been assembled and rolled to the preflight holding area in the terminal, they must be transferred across the apron. This is frequently achieved by rolling the pallets onto roller mat dollies, which are pulled to the aircraft by a ramp tractor. The pallets are rolled onto a cargo lift that raises them to the level of the aircraft floor, onto which they are rolled. Movement along the aircraft can be by simple manhandling, or in the case of large aircraft by powered floor roller mats. At some airports, dolly and tractor systems have been replaced by ramp transporters, which perform much the same function.

Where containers are used, very similar loading strategies can be employed. A more sophisticated loading device is the mechanized nose dock system (Figure 9.9). The nose dock consists of two rows of container stacks with a transfer vehicle running between the two rows. Containers are moved on roller mats onto the transfer vehicle, which moves to the aircraft loading bridge. A second transfer is made across the powered roller floor loading bridge to the deck of the aircraft.

Loose cargo can be transferred across the apron by dollies and loaded either by cargo lift or small cargo conveyors, which handle light loads. Out-of-gauge and nonpalletized cargo can be handled in this way, but this can become uneconomic in large volumes because of poor aircraft turnaround time at the cargo apron.

The choice of apron handling devices depends chiefly on the air vehicle to be loaded. Combination wide-bodied aircraft and narrow-bodied cargo aircraft can take igloos, pallets, and low containers. They are normally side loaded using cargo lifts and transporters or dollies. Wide-bodied all-cargo craft can take large 8 ft by 8 ft containers, in modular lengths up to 40 ft, and can be loaded by nose docks. Narrow-bodied combination aircraft, which have low cargo capacity, must be loose loaded in the belly holds.

9.9 ELEMENTS TO BE CONSIDERED IN DESIGN OF AIR FREIGHT TERMINALS

1. Market Demand Forecast

Domestic/international volumes.

Inbound/outbound transfer volumes.

Cargo/mail.

Bypass traffic (freight already containerized in flight ready containers).

Nature and amount of material requiring special handling:

　　Heavy/oversized freight.

　　Perishables.

　　Very great urgency material.

　　High value.

　　Dangerous goods.

　　Livestock

Seasonal, daily, and hourly fluctuations of flows.

2. Forecast of Aircraft Fleet and Flight Activity

Fleet mix.

Type of operation: all cargo, combination, belly loads only.

Frequency of operations.

Number of aircraft to be handled simultaneously on the apron.

Air vehicle type: 747, DC-10, L1011, A300, A320, 757, 767, 707, 727, DC-9, DC-8, and so on.

3. Main Capacity Constrained Elements of Design

Overall area.

Build-up positions.

Pallet storage area.

Bins.

Airside and landside doors.

4. Cargo Handling Concept Choice

Low mechanization, high manpower.

Low manpower, mobile lifting, and loading equipment.

High mechanization with transfer vehicles (TVs) and elevating transfer vehicles (ETVs).

5. Site Selection Factors

Dimensions of terminal, apron and landside access areas.

Layout of road access and degree of separation of commercial freight vehicles from passenger terminal traffic.

Proximity and ease of airside access to the passenger apron.

Layout and capacity of airside service roads.

Availability of utilities.

6. Architectural Decisions

Main floor level.

Landside and airside dock levels.

Clear height (later installation of ETVs should be considered).

Construction materials.

Expandability for future traffic growth.

Flexibility for changes of freight type and handling methods.

7. Other Areas to Be Included

In all cases, the dimensions of the space allotted as well as of the doors must be suitable for the function of the area.

Maintenance and Support Facilities: For the maintenance and repair of ULD's and their handling devices. Space will include facilities for washing and welding, compressor and vehicle hoist.

Customs: Inspection areas, offices, toilets, secure storage areas.

Livestock: Storage areas, cages, feeding, watering, and cleaning facilities. Environmental control.

Dangerous goods: Facilities dependent on nature of goods; Secure storage.

Cold Room: Areas for high value and fragile cargo, human remains, and radioactive material.

8. General Design Considerations

Security: Ease of general access into the freight terminal area, location of space for security personnel, use of closed-circuit TV.

Health and Safety: Design to observe local and national industrial health and safety laws that govern workers and working conditions. Noise levels, operating procedures predicted by design, and surface finishes.

Insurance: Sprinkler systems, smoke detectors, fire ratings of building materials.

Suitability of Building Materials: Material used must reflect the handling methods within the terminal. Potential damage should be minimized and repair of damaged material should be easy.

9.10 EXAMPLE OF THE DESIGN OF MIDDLE TECHNOLOGY FREIGHT TERMINAL

Project

To design the layout and areal requirements for a freight terminal to meet the following annual demand profile:

	Total	Percent Received at Terminal Already Containerized and Therefore Bypassable
Domestic		
In ($\times$ 1000 kg)	18,000	40
Out ($\times$ 1000 kg)	18,000	20
Export ($\times$ 1000 kg)	12,000	NIL
Import ($\times$ 1000 kg)	16,000	NIL

Peak month domestic: 10% annual domestic traffic
Peak month import: 15% annual import traffic
Peak month export: 8% annual export traffic

$$\text{Peak day traffic} = 0.05 \times \text{peak month traffic}$$
$$\text{Bypass peak hour traffic} = 30\% \text{ peak day traffic}$$
$$\text{Non-bypass peak hour traffic} = 25\% \text{ peak day traffic}$$
$$\text{Import peak hour traffic} = 20\% \text{ peak day traffic}$$

Dwell times:

Domestic out and export: 1½ days
Domestic in and import: 6 days

A. Assumptions

Extensive containerization

Containers and loose bulk freight moved by mobile lifting equipment, for example, forklift trucks.

No fixed transfer vehicles (TVs and ETVs).

B. Design Criteria*

	Domestic and Export	Import
Throughput per unit floor area: (Kg/m²/yr)	13500–22500 (use 13500)	5500
Landside truck loading and unloading doors: (Kg/door/hr)	2500–4500 (use 3500)	1800
Airside door capacity:		
Bypass pallets/door/hr	15	—
Processed pallets/door/hr	20	20
Average pallet/container weight (kg)	1800	1800
Average bin weight (kg)	225	225
Build-up/breakdown floor area (kg/building unit/hr)	2000	1800

C. Traffic Structure

	Total	Bypass	Processed
	(Kg × 1,000)	(Kg × 1,000)	(Kg × 1,000)
Domestic			
In	18,000	7,200	10,800
Out	18,000	3,600	14,400
Sub-total	36,000	10,800	25,200
Export	12,000	—	12,000
Import	16,000	—	16,000
Total	64,000	10,800	53,200

	Bypass	Non-Bypass	Import
	(Kg × 1,000)	(Kg × 1,000)	(Kg × 1,000)
Peak month	1,080	3,480	2,400
Peak day traffic = 0.05 × peak month	54	174	120
Peak hour traffic	16.2	43.5	24

* *Source:* R. Brawner, Flying Tiger Airlines.

D.   Facility Requirements

1. *Bypass Facilities*

$$\text{Pallets processed} = \frac{\text{peak hour flow (kg)}}{1,800 \text{ kg/pallet}} = \frac{16,200}{1,800}$$

$$= 9 \text{ pallets/peak hr, or 1 bypass door}$$

2.   *Domestic and Export Non-Bypass Facilities*

a. Gross meter ^{2} required $= \dfrac{\text{annual volume}}{13,500 \text{ kg/m}^2\text{/yr}} = \dfrac{37.2 \text{ mill.kg}}{13,500} = 2756 \text{ m}^2$

b. Landside truck doors $= \dfrac{\text{peak hr flow (kg)}}{3500 \text{ kg/door/hr}} = \dfrac{43,500 \text{ kg}}{3500}$

$$= 12.4, \text{ say 13 truck doors}$$

c. Build-up/breakdown positions $= \dfrac{\text{peak hour flow}}{2000} = \dfrac{43,500}{2000}$

$$= 21.75, \text{ say 22 positions}$$

d. Assuming 70% of peak day flow loaded on to pallets and staged,

Pallet staging racks $= \dfrac{\text{peak day flow} \times 70\%}{1800 \text{ kg/pallet}} = \dfrac{174,000 \times 0.7}{1800}$

$$= 68 \text{ racks}$$

e. Assuming 30% of peak day flow to go to bin storage,

Bins $= \dfrac{\text{peak day flow} \times 30\%}{225 \text{ kg/bin}} = \dfrac{174,000 \times .30}{225} = 232 \text{ bins}$

f. Airside doors:

$$\frac{\text{peak hr flow}}{\text{Pallet wt} \times \text{pallets/door/hr}} = \frac{43,500}{1800 \times 20} = 1.2 \text{ (not critical)}$$

3.   *Import Facilities*

a. Gross meter^2 required $= \dfrac{\text{annual volume}}{5500} = \dfrac{16 \text{ mill.kg}}{5500} = 2910 \text{ m}^2$

b. Landside truck doors $= \dfrac{\text{peak hr flow (kg)}}{1800 \text{ kg/door/hr}} = \dfrac{24,000}{1800}$

$$= 13.3, \text{ say } 14 \text{ truck doors}$$

c. Build-up/breakdown positions $= \dfrac{\text{peak hour flow}}{1800 \text{ kg/hr}} = \dfrac{24,000}{1800}$

$$= 13.3, \text{ say } 14 \text{ positions}$$

d. Pallet staging racks (75% of flow into pallet racks): Assume pallet positions required in-bond and customs cleared. This will give a duplication factor between 1 and 2. Allow 1.5.

Pallet staging racks $= \dfrac{\text{peak day flow (kg)} \times 1.5 \times 0.75}{1800 \text{ kg/pallet}}$

$$= \dfrac{120,000 \times 1.5 \times 0.75}{1800} = 75 \text{ racks}$$

e. Bins: Assume 25% of flow into bin racks with duplication of in-bond and custom cleared racks. This will give a duplication factor of between 1 and 2. In this case allow 2.

Bins $= \dfrac{\text{peak day flow (kg)} \times 2 \times 0.25}{225}$

$$= \dfrac{120,000 \times 2 \times 0.25}{225}$$

$$= 267$$

$$= 267 \text{ bins}$$

f. Airside doors: Not critical.

E. Summary Design Requirements

1. *Overall Requirements*

		Domestic/Export	Import	Total
a.	Total area (m²)	2756	2910	5666
b.	Landside truck doors	13	14	27
c.	Build-up/breakdown positions	22	14	36
d.	Pallet staging rack	68	75	143
e.	Bins	232	267	499
f.	Bypass doors	1	—	1

2. *Space Breakdown*

Facility	Area (m^2)
a. Cold room	20
b. Strong room	20
c. Radioactive	20
d. Human remains	20
e. Toilets	20
f. Changing rooms/staff facilities	40
g. Fragile cage	50
h. Reception and dispatch/office	450 ≃ 8% total
i. Customs clearance	450
j. ULD breakdown and build	900
h. Maintenance	300 ≃ 5% total
i. Circulation and storage	3460
	5700

A typical layout of the above areas is shown in Figure 9.10.

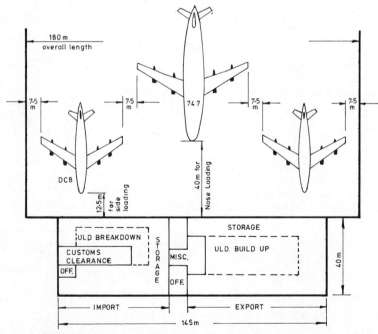

FIGURE 9.10 Example of layout of cargo apron and terminal.

F. Comparison with IATA Recommended Standards (?)

Frequently, even less rigorous methods of cargo terminal sizing are used, with the overall area being computed from annual tonnage throughout. IATA recommends 1.0 ft^2 per ton per year for the export area, and 1.1 ft^2 per ton per year for import area calculations. General experience indicates that most designs have overall areas somewhere in the region of 0.1 m^2/ton for both the export and import sides, although this can increase substantially to 0.2 m^2 where cargo moves slowly through the terminal. Using the flows in the above problem, a designer would arrive at the following overall areas:

Export: 30,000 tonnes = 33042 tons   Requires: 3070 m^2
Import: 34,000 tonnes = 37478 tons   Requires: 3824 m^2

Total area required: 6894 m^2

9.11 CONCLUSION

The planning of high volume, special purpose air cargo terminals is a complex procedure. Since the high volume terminals are often owned and operated by the airlines, the design of these terminals may well be carried out internally by airline staff. The most satisfactory design procedure is likely to be a simulation study based on a knowledge of the mix and flow characteristics of the cargo, the airline's predicted fleet mix, and surface transport procedures. The designer can simulate the functioning of the terminal under different assumptions of internal materials handling procedures reflecting different levels of capitalization and mechanization.

Experience in cargo terminal design indicates that serious errors in the underlying assumptions of the nature and flow of cargo consignments are not unusual. Given the present well-defined tendency toward increasing containerization, it appears that the prediction problems remaining involve the extent to which unitization of surface load will proceed, and the aircraft mix of the freight aircraft themselves. For the foreseeable future, designs of cargo facilities should provide a large degree of flexibility, recognizing that the industry is still in its infancy, and therefore still subject to large changes in both traffic and technology (5).

REFERENCES

1. Smith, P., *Air Freight: Operators, Marketing and Economics*, London: Faber and Faber, 1974.
2. *Airport Terminal Reference Manual*, 6th Ed., Montreal: International Air Transport Association, 1976.
3. *Janes Freight Containers, 1982*, London: Sampson, Law and Marston, 1982.
4. *Janes All the World's Aircraft, 1981–82*, London: McDonald and Janes, 1981.
5. Ashford, N., H. P. M. Stanton and C. A. Moore, *Airport Operations*, New York: Wiley-Interscience, 1984.

10

AIRPORT DRAINAGE AND PAVEMENT DESIGN

This chapter discusses two subjects of fundamental importance to the airport engineer: airport drainage and structural pavement design.

AIRPORT DRAINAGE

10.1 Introduction

A well-designed airport drainage system is a prime requisite for operational safety and efficiency, as well as pavement durability. Inadequate drainage facilities may result in costly damage due to flooding, as well as constituting a source of serious hazards to air traffic. Furthermore, inadequate drainage systems may cause unsightly erosion of slopes, and saturated and weakened pavement foundations.

In many respects, the design of an airport drainage system is similar to street and highway drainage design. However, airports often have special drainage problems and challenges. Characterized by vast expanses of relatively flat areas and a critical need for the prompt removal of surface and subsurface water, airports usually require an integrated drainage system. Such a system must provide for the removal of surface water from runways, taxiways, aprons, automobile parking lots, and access roads. The runoff then must be removed from the airport by means of surface ditches, inlets, and an underground storm drainage system. Some of the more important airport drainage design principles and procedures, described in the following subsections, include the following:

1. Estimation of runoff.
2. Design of a basic system for collection and disposal of runoff.
3. Provision for adequate subsurface drainage.

For a more complete treatment of this important subject, the reader is referred to the FAA advisory circular *Airport Drainage* (1), and the other references listed at the end of this chapter.

10.2 Estimation of Runoff

A number of formulas and analytical procedures have been developed for the estimation of surface runoff. However, all the available estimation techniques are fraught with imprecision and require the judicious employment of engineering judgment. The method most commonly used for airport drainage design is the rational method. To introduce this technique, we describe briefly the factors that influence the magnitude of surface runoff.

Coefficient of Runoff. Only a part of the precipitation that falls on a watershed flows off as free water. Some of the precipitation evaporates, and some of it may be intercepted by vegetation. A portion of the precipitation may infiltrate the ground or fill small depressions or irregularities in the ground surface. Therefore the storm runoff, for which airport drainage channels and structures must be designed, is the precipitation minus the various losses that occur.

These losses are strongly related to the various characteristics of the watershed, such as the slope, soil condition, vegetation, and land use. The designer should keep in mind that certain of these factors, especially vegetation and land use, are likely to change with time. It is especially important to consider possible effects of planned future airport development on the quantity of runoff from the airport area.

Table 10.1 Value of Factor C

Type of Surface	Factor C
For all watertight roof surfaces	.75–.95
For asphalt runway pavements	.80–.95
For concrete runway pavements	.70–.90
For gravel or macadam pavements	.35–.70
For impervious soils (heavy)[a]	.40–.65
For impervious soils, with turf[a]	.30–.55
For slightly pervious soils[a]	.15–.40
For slightly pervious soils, with turf[a]	.10–.30
For moderately pervious soils[a]	.05–.20
For moderately pervious soils, with turf[a]	.00–.10

[a] For slopes from 1 to 2%.

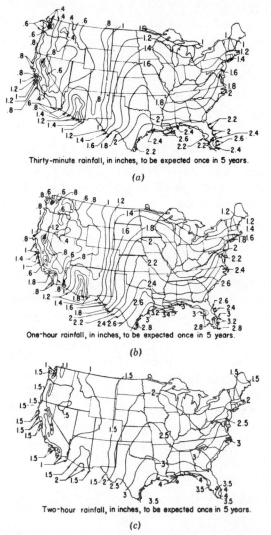

Thirty-minute rainfall, in inches, to be expected once in 5 years.

(a)

One-hour rainfall, in inches, to be expected once in 5 years.

(b)

Two-hour rainfall, in inches, to be expected once in 5 years.

(c)

FIGURE 10.1   Rainfall frequency maps. (*Source:* Reference 2.)

Most analytical procedures for estimating runoff involve the use of a coefficient of runoff or factor to account for the hydrologic nature of the drainage area. As used in the rational method, the coefficient of runoff is the ratio of the quantity of runoff to the total precipitation that falls on the drainage area. Table 10.1 gives recommended values of the runoff coefficient C for use in the rational formula. If the drainage area under consideration consists of several land use types, for which different runoff coefficients must be assigned, the runoff coefficient for the entire area should be a weighted average of the coefficients of the individual areas. For example, if a drainage area consists of 2 acres of concrete pavement having a runoff coefficient of .8, and 5 acres of impervious soil with turf with a coefficient of .4, the weighted average coefficient for the overall area is [(2 × .8) + (5 × .4)] ÷ (2 + 5) or .51.

Rainfall Intensity, Duration, and Frequency.   Rainfall intensity is the rate at which rain falls, typically expressed in inches per hour. Because of the probabilistic nature of weather, the intensity of rainfall must be discussed in the context of its frequency and duration.

For many years the National Weather Service (formerly U.S. Weather Bureau), the Department of Agriculture, and other agencies have collected rainfall data in the United States. Based on these data, the National Weather Service has published a series of technical papers that contain rainfall-frequency (isopluvial) maps and empirical relationships that are useful in airport drainage design. Technical Paper No. 40 (2) gives such data for the conterminous United States. Similar data can be obtained for Puerto Rico, the Virgin Islands, Hawaii, and Alaska. Local rainfall data may also be available from the National Weather Service, the City Engineer's Office, the State Highway Department, and possibly drainage districts or utility companies.

Procedures for the construction of rainfall intensity-duration curves have been published by the FAA (1). Suppose we want to construct a rainfall intensity-duration curve for a storm frequency of 5 years. By spotting the airport location on the charts like those of Figure 10.1, we can determine the amount of rainfall that can be expected once every 5 years for rainfalls lasting 30 min, 1 hr, and 2 hr. For example, Figure 10.1a indicates a 30 min, 1.37 in. rainfall can be expected to occur in Chicago once every 5 years. Similarly, rainfalls of 1.73 and 2.10 in. would be expected with durations of 1 and 2 hr, respectively. To plot a rainfall intensity-duration curve in terms of inches per hour, these values must be expressed in a 1 hour basis; conversion is achieved by multiplying the scaled values by the ratio between 1 hr and the durations shown on the chart. Thus, for example, the rainfall intensities are as follows:

Duration (min)	Chart Value	Intensity (in./hr)
30	$1.37 \text{ in.} \times \dfrac{60}{30}$	$= 2.74$
60	$1.73 \text{ in.} \times \dfrac{60}{60}$	$= 1.73$
120	$2.10 \text{ in.} \times \dfrac{60}{120}$	$= 1.05$

To obtain values for short duration rainfalls, the following relationships between a 30 min rainfall and 5, 10, 15 min amounts may be used:

Duration (min)	Ratio
5	0.37
10	0.57
15	0.72

In the Chicago example, the 30 min rainfall of 1.37 in. would be multiplied by the ratios given yielding rainfalls of

0.51 in.	in 5 min
0.78 in.	in 10 min
0.99 in.	in 15 min

These values must be converted to inches per hour for curve plotting purposes:

Duration (min)	Chart Value	Intensity (in./hr)
5	$0.51 \text{ in.} \times \dfrac{60}{5}$	$= 6.12$
10	$0.78 \text{ in.} \times \dfrac{60}{10}$	$= 4.68$
15	$0.99 \text{ in.} \times \dfrac{60}{15}$	$= 3.96$

These six values may now be used to plot a 5 year rainfall intensity-duration curve (Figure 10.2). Similar curves for 2 years, 10 years, and other return periods may be plotted by referring to appropriate isopluvial maps published by the National Weather Service (2).

To use a tool like Figure 10.2, the designer must choose the right curve, which involves weighing the physical and social damages that might result from a flood of a given frequency against the additional costs of designing a drainage system to decrease the risk of such damages. As Figure 10.2 discloses, the choice of the 10 year curve instead of the 5 year curve would mean designing for a more severe storm but at a higher cost. On the other hand, the choice of a 2 year frequency would result in a less costly drainage system but would involve the risk of more frequent runoffs exceeding the capacity of the system. A return period of 5 years is commonly used for the design of drainage systems at civil airports. However, the design should be checked to determine the consequences of less frequent but more severe storms.

As Figure 10.2 indicates, rainfall intensity decreases nonlinearly with increases in the rainfall duration.

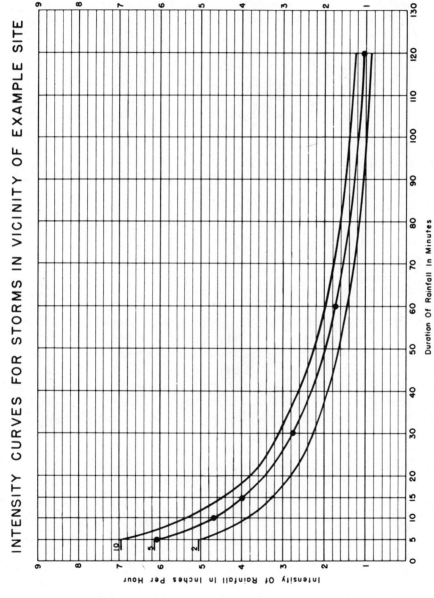

FIGURE 10.2 Intensity-duration curves for storms in vicinity of example site. (*Source: Airport Drainage,* FAA Advisory Circular AC 150/5320-5A, 1965.)

Time of Concentration.   In the design of airport drainage facilities, a rainfall duration equal to the *time of concentration* is chosen. The time of concentration is the time required for a particle of water to flow from the most remote point* in the drainage area to the point being investigated. It consists of two components: the time of surface flow (sometimes referred to as the "inlet time" or time of overland flow), and the time of flow within the structural drainage system.

The surface flow time varies with land slope, type of surface, size and shape of the drainage area, and other characteristics of the watershed. Many empirical studies have been made relating the time of surface flow to the slope, dimensions, and other characteristics of a drainage area.

Figure 10.3 plots some values found using the following formula, recommended by the FAA (1):

$$T \approx \frac{1.8(1.1 - C)(D)^{\frac{1}{2}}}{(S)^{\frac{1}{3}}} \tag{10.1}$$

where

T = surface flow time (min)
C = the runoff coefficient
S = slope (%)
D = distance to most remote point (ft)

The time of flow within the structural system can be determined by dividing the structure length (in feet) by the velocity of flow (in feet per minute).

Maximum flow through a given section of an airport drainage system should occur when the duration of rainfall equals the time of concentration for the tributary area. Although rainfalls of greater intensity than that corresponding to the time of concentration can be expected to occur, these rainfalls will be of such short duration that only a portion of the tributary area will contribute to the flow.

The Rational Method.   The rational method is recommended for the calculation of runoff from airport surfaces. The method is expressed by the equation:

$$Q = CIA \tag{10.2}$$

where

Q = runoff (cfs)
C = the runoff coefficient (typical values are given in Table 10.1)

---

* Strictly speaking, the "most remote point" is the point from which the time of flow is greatest. For practical reasons, the greatest linear distance from the point under investigation is sometimes used as the most remote point.

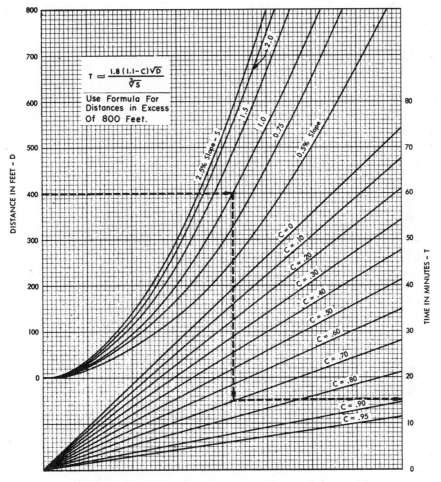

FIGURE 10.3 Surface flow time curves. (*Source:* Reference 1.)

I = intensity of rainfall (in./hr for the estimated time of concentration)

A = drainage area (acres); the area may be determined from field surveys, topographical maps, or aerial photographs

Example 10.1, which follows the subsection on underground pipes, illustrates the use of the rational method.

10.3 Collection and Disposal of Runoff

The hydraulic design of a system for the collection and disposal of surface runoff is discussed in the framework of four subtopics:

1. Layout of the drainage system.
2. Design of underground pipe system.

3. Design of open channels.

4. Design of inlets, manholes, and other appurtenances.

Layout of the Drainage System. As a first step in the layout and design of the drainage system, a generalized topographical map showing existing 2 ft ground contours should be obtained or prepared. This map should show all the natural and man-made features that could affect (or be affected by) the overall layout and design of the drainage system (e.g., existing watercourses and outfalls, canals, irrigation ditches, drainage structures, railroads, highways, and developed areas).

In addition, a more detailed map or grading and drainage plan, which shows the runway-taxiway system and other proposed airport features, should be prepared. This plan, which normally indicates the finished grading surfaces by 1 ft interval contours, can serve as a working drawing for the proposed drainage system. Each drainage subarea should be outlined on the plan, and pipe sizes, lengths, and slopes should be shown. It is customary to identify drainage structures and pipelines by numbers or letters for easy reference in design computations. Figure 10.4 is an example of a portion of a grading and drainage plan.

The grading plan makes it possible to select appropriate locations for drainage ditches, inlets, and manholes. Storm drain inlets are placed as needed at low points and are typically spaced 200 to 400 ft on tangents. The FAA (1) recommends that inlets be located laterally at least 75 ft from the edge of pavements at air carrier airports and 25 ft from the edge at general aviation airports. The designer should avoid placing inlets close to pavement edges; otherwise ponding may cause pavement flooding or saturation of the subgrade.

Manholes permit workers to inspect and maintain the underground system. Normally, manholes are placed at all changes in direction, grade, and pipe sizes, and approximately every 300 to 500 ft on straight segments. A typical runway safety area and runway drainage plan appears in Figure 10.5.

Design of the Underground Pipe System. After the ditches, pipes, inlets, and manholes have been generally located on the drainage plan, the size and gradient of the pipes must be determined. The underground conduits are designed to operate with open channel flow, and because pipe sections in the system are long, uniform flow can be assumed.

The Manning equation is the most popular formula for the determination of the flow characteristics in pipes. Its use is recommended by the FAA (1) in the design of underground airport pipe systems. The equation is:

$$Q = \frac{1.486AR^{2/3}S^{1/2}}{n} \tag{10.3}$$

where

Q = discharge (cfs)
A = cross-sectional area of flow (ft^2)

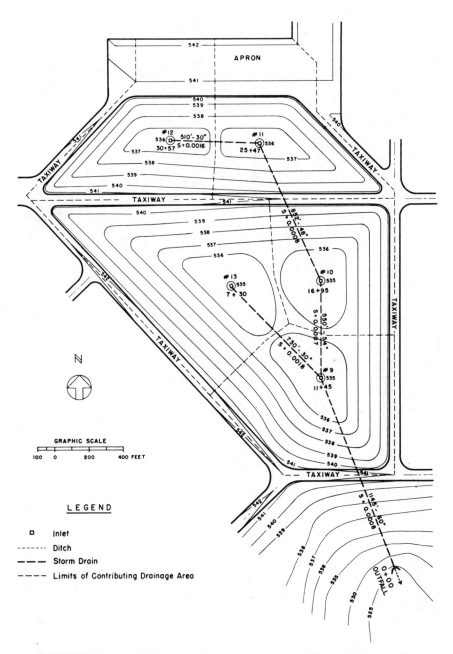

FIGURE 10.4 Portion of airport showing drainage design. (*Source:* Reference 1.)

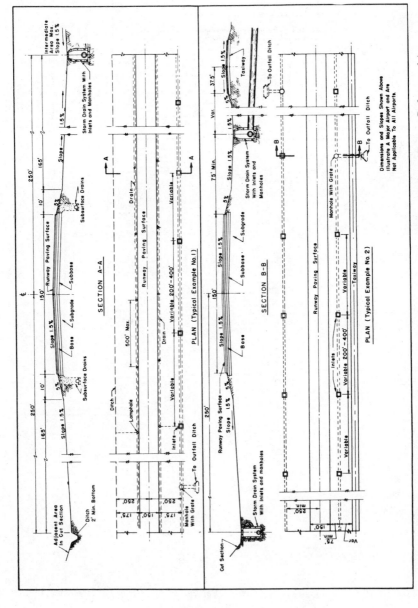

FIGURE 10.5 A typical runway safety area and runway drainage cross-section. (*Source:* Reference 1.)

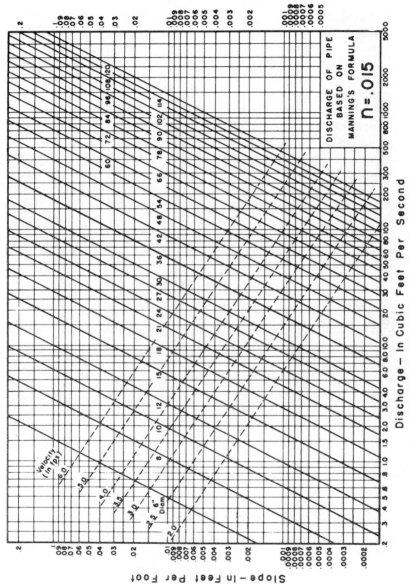

FIGURE 10.6 Design chart for uniform flow. (*Source:* Reference 1.)

297

R = hydraulic radius (ft: area of section/wetted perimeter)
S = slope of pipe invert (ft/ft)
n = coefficient of roughness of pipe

A number of agencies have prepared nomographs and charts for the solution of the Manning equation (1, 3, 4); Figure 10.6 is representative of this material. The FAA, for example, has nomographs for circular pipes flowing full with Manning roughness coefficients ranging from 0.012 to 0.031. The roughness coefficient for clay, concrete, and asbestos cement is 0.012, whereas those for corrugated metal pipes range from 0.012 to 0.031, depending on the pipe size, wall configuration, and whether the wall is paved or unpaved.

It is important that sufficient velocities be maintained to prevent the deposition and accumulation of suspended matter within the pipes.

Past experience shows that a mean velocity of 2.5 feet per second will normally prevent the depositing of suspended matter in the pipes. When lower velocities are used, special care should be taken in the construction of the system to assure good alignment, straight grades, smooth, well-constructed joints, and proper installation of structures. The pipelines and slopes should be designed, wherever possible and when topographical conditions permit, so that the velocity of flow will increase progressively or be maintained uniformly from inlets to outfall (1).

Example 10.1   Drainage Design Without Ponding

Consider, for example, the portion of an airport shown in Figure 10.4.* Given the following information, determine the size, capacity, and slope of pipe, and the invert elevation at the outer end for line segment 13-9. The 21.5 acre drainage area (approximately 9% of which is paved, and the remainder turfed) has a weighted average runoff coefficient of .35. The distances and slopes to the most remote point from the inlet (scaled from the sketch) are:

Area	Distance (ft)	Slope (%)
Over pavement	110	1
Over turf	1140	0.6

Use the 5 year curve in Figure 10.2 for determination of rainfall intensity, and assume a Manning roughness coefficient, $n = 0.015$. The invert elevation at the inlet end is 530.38.

Solution.   The time of surface flow is the sum of surface flow time over pavement from Figure 10.3 = 4 min, and the surface flow time over turf,

---

* This example constitutes a portion of an example published in Reference 1, to which the reader is referred for more detail.

$$T_t \approx \frac{1.8(1.1 - 0.3)(1140)^{1/2}}{(0.6)^{1/3}} = 58 \text{ min}$$

total time of surface flow = 62 min

Since inlet 13 is at the upper end of a drainage line, the time of surface flow is the time of concentration. Entering Figure 10.2 with a duration of rainfall of 62 min, the rainfall intensity $I = 1.76$ in/hr. The runoff $Q = (0.35)(1.76)(21.5) = 13.24$ cfs.

From Figure 10.6, we find that a 30 in. pipe will be suitable and, if installed on a 0.0018 slope, will result in a mean velocity of 3.1 ft/sec. The capacity of the pipe will be 15 cfs.

The elevation of the invert at the outlet end of line segment 13-9 will be

$$530.38 - (0.0018 \times 730) = 529.07 \text{ ft}$$

Example 10.2 Drainage Design With Ponding

When the rate of runoff inflow at a drainage inlet exceeds the capacity of the drainage structure to remove it, temporary storage or ponding occurs in the vicinity of the inlet. Excessive or prolonged ponding may create operational hazards, damage pavement subgrades, and kill grass. It is therefore wise to undertake special studies in suspected ponding areas to determine the probability of a ponding problem and its likely magnitude. Such a study involves the computation of the total volume of runoff that flows into a ponding basis over a period of time, and similarly the volume that can be removed by the drainage system.

The volume of runoff flowing into a drainage area, V_{in}, is the product of the runoff (as determined by the rational equation) and time, t:

$$V_{in} = Qt = CIAt \tag{10.4}$$

Note that the rainfall intensity is a function of time. The volume of runoff that can be removed from the ponding basin, V_{out}, is a product of the capacity of the drainage structure (as determined by the Manning equation) and time.

$$V_{out} = q_{cap}t \tag{10.5}$$

where

q_{cap} = the capacity of the drainage structure (cfs)

Since the capacity is independent of time, V_{out} varies linearly with time. When plots of those relationships are made, as Figure 10.7 illustrates, it is possible to determine the amount of ponding that occurs at various times, thus the maximum ponding. From such a graph, one can also determine the length of

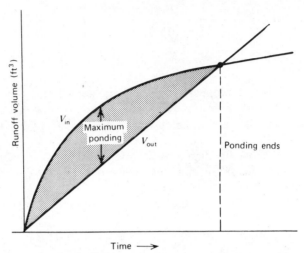

FIGURE 10.7   A cumulative runoff graph.

time that ponding will occur for the assumed conditions. Cumulative runoff graphs can be used to evaluate the ponding effects of various sizes and slopes of culverts and of different flood frequencies. An illustrative example of a ponding problem, omitted here because of limitations of space, is given in References 1 and 5.

Design of Open Channels.   Open waterways or ditches generally constitute an important part of an airport's overall drainage system. The size, shape, and slope of these channels must be carefully determined to avoid possible overflow, flooding, erosion, and siltation. As is the case with underground conduits, flow in long open channels may be assumed to be uniform, and the Manning equation (equation 10.3) may be applied. In uniform flow, a state of equilibrium exists in which the energy losses due to friction are counterbalanced by the gain in energy due to slope.

To solve the Manning equation directly, the depth and cross-sectional area of flow and the slope, shape, and frictional characteristics of the channel must be known. The more common problem of determining the depth and velocity of flow corresponding to a known discharge must be solved by repeated trials. Once the depth of flow is known for a given channel cross section, the mean velocity, V, can be easily calculated by the continuity equation, $Q = AV$. Fortunately, a wide variety of nomographs and charts for different sizes and shapes of channel cross sections have been published (1, 3, 4), making direct and repeated solution of the Manning equation unnecessary. Table 10.2 gives values of Manning's roughness coefficients for various types of channel lining.

Generally, wide, rounded, and shallow open channels are preferred. To facilitate mowing and other maintenance operations, and to enhance safety and appearance, cross-sectional channel slopes should not be steeper than

2.5:1 (horizontal to vertical). To prevent offensive and costly erosion, flow velocities should not exceed the maximum values given in Table 10.2. Where velocities greater than about 6.0 ft/sec are expected, special treatment of the ditch lining, such as soil cement or paving with asphalt or portland cement concrete, may be required.

Design of Inlets, Manholes, and Headwalls. Space limitations preclude the inclusion of a thorough discussion of the principles of design of inlets, manholes, and headwalls. Some of the most important considerations in the design of such structures are briefly treated in the following paragraphs.

Where high heads are permissible, the capacity of an inlet grating can be determined by the orifice formula:

$$Q = c\,A(2g\,H)^{1/2} \qquad\qquad (10.6)$$

where

$c = 0.6$
$A =$ waterway opening (ft^2)
$g =$ acceleration of gravity (ft/sec^2)
$H =$ head (ft)

Table 10.2 Maximum Permissible Velocities and Manning Coefficients for Various Open Channel Linings

Type of Lining	Maximum Velocity (ft/sec)	Manning Coefficient, n
Paved		
Concrete	20–30+	.011–0.020
Asphalt	12–15+	.013–0.017
Rubble or riprap	20–25	.017–0.030
Earth		
Bare, sandy silt, weathered	2.0	.020
Silt clay or soft shale	3.5	.020
Clay	6.0	.020
Soft sandstone	8.0	.020
Clean gravelly soil	6.0	.025
Natural earth, with vegetation	6.0	.030–.150[a]
Turf		
Shallow flow	6.0	.06–.08
Depth of flow over 1 ft	6.0	.04–.06

Source: *Airport Drainage*, FAA, Advisory Circular AC 150/5320-5B, July 1970.

[a] Will vary with straightness of alignment, smoothness of bed and side slopes, and whether channel has light vegetation or is choked with weeds and brush.

For low heads, the discharge conforms to the general weir equation:

$$Q = CLH^{3/2} \qquad\qquad (10.7)$$

where

$C = 3.0$
$L = $ gross perimeter of the grate opening, omitting bars (ft)
$H = $ head (ft)

With these equations, the number and size of grates needed to accommodate a given runoff and allowable headwater conditions can be readily determined. The general weir formula should be applied for aircraft servicing aprons and other areas where significant ponding depths would be unacceptable. The orifice formula normally applies to grates in turfed areas. When employing these formulas, the FAA (1) recommends the use of a safety factor of 1.25 for paved areas and 1.5 to 2.0 for turfed areas to allow for partial obstruction of the grating area with debris. The FAA coefficients are based on a model test of similar grates, with a 2:3 ratio of net width of grate opening to gross width.

Example 10.3   Capacity of a Double Inlet Grating

A double inlet grating like the one illustrated in the accompanying sketch is used to drain a paved apron area. Determine the capacity of the inlet: (a) with a head of 1.6 feet, (b) with a head of 0.4 feet.

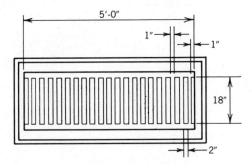

PLAN OF DOUBLE INLET GRATING

Solution to Part a.   Equation (10.6) applies for the high head situation, with $H = 1.6$ ft. There are 20 grate openings, each 2 inches by 18 inches. The total area of the opening,

$$A = 20 \times \frac{2}{12} \times \frac{18}{12} = 5.0 \text{ ft}^2$$

$$Q = cA(2gH)^{1/2} = (0.6)(5)(2 \times 32.2 \times 1.6)^{1/2} = 30.4 \text{ ft}^3/\text{sec}$$

Applying a safety factor of 1.25, the capacity is 24.4 ft^3/sec.

Solution to Part b.   For a low head of $H = 0.4$ ft, equation (10.7) applies. The gross perimeter of the grate opening,

$$L = (2 \times 5) + (2 \times 1.5) = 13 \text{ ft}$$

$$Q = CLH^{3/2} = 3.0(13)(0.4)^{3/2} = 9.9 \text{ ft}^3/\text{sec}$$

The capacity is $\dfrac{9.9}{\text{safety factor}} = \dfrac{9.9}{1.25} = 7.9 \text{ ft}^3/\text{sec}$

Inlet grates and frames such as those used for municipal storm drainage systems generally are suitable for airports in the utility and basic transport categories. At larger airports the design of inlet structures in aircraft traffic areas should be based on a careful analysis of probable aircraft loadings. As a rule, the structural strength of inlet frames and grates can be certified by the supplier. Of course, the inlet structure proper, which is normally constructed of reinforced concrete, brick, concrete blocks, and the like, must also be strong enough to support the anticipated loads. Figure 10.8 presents a typical drainage inlet.

> Manholes . . . are usually made of reinforced concrete, brick, concrete block, precast concrete, corrugated metal, or precast pipe sections [Figure 10.9]. The design will depend on the stresses to which they will be subjected. Adequate unobstructed space must be provided within the manhole to enable workmen to clean out the line when necessary. Inside barrel dimensions equivalent to a diameter of 3½ ft and a height of 4 ft are usually considered sufficient, but they can be varied to suit particular situations (1).

Suggested standard designs for headwalls have been developed by the FAA, state departments of transportation, and other public agencies. However, designers should be aware that headwalls may constitute a fixed object hazard to errant aircraft or motor vehicle traffic, and where such potential exists, the possibility of an alternative treatment should be explored.

10.4   Subsurface Drainage

Special drainage systems may be required to control and avoid the undesirable effects of subsurface moisture. Such systems are usually installed to avoid saturation and weakening of pavement foundation layers and to control or prevent damaging frost heave.*

---

* In cold climates, frost action will occur in certain subgrade soils if precautions are not taken. Interstitial water freezes in the upper soil layers, and the small ice crystals develop into large ice lenses as water is attracted upward from voids in lower strata. The resulting nonuniform "heave" of the supporting soil can be extremely harmful to the pavement structure. Reference 5 gives a more complete description of the frost heave phenomenon and measures to control it.

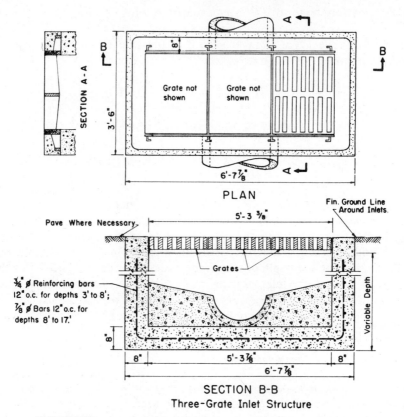

FIGURE 10.8   A typical three-grate inlet structure. (*Source:* Reference 1.)

Subsurface drainage has at least three functions: (1) to drain and upgrade wet soil masses, (2) to intercept and divert subsurface flows, and (3) to lower and control the water table.

Subsurface drains consist of small pipes (typically 6–8 in. in diameter) which are laid in trenches approximately 1.5 to 2.0 ft wide and backfilled with a pervious filter material. The pipes should be bedded in a minimum thickness of filter material. Vitrified clay, concrete, asbestos cement, bituminous fiber, corrugated steel, and corrugated aluminum alloy pipes have been used for subdrains. To allow water to enter, the pipes are normally either manufactured with gaps, slots, or perforations, or laid with open joints.

Subsurface drainage systems are most likely to be effective in sandy clays, clay silts, and sandy silts. The finer grained materials (predominantly silts and clays) are much more difficult to drain, whereas the coarser grained materials (gravels and sands) tend to be self-draining.

Careful studies of soil and water conditions are a prerequisite to the design of a subsurface drainage system. Data are available from a variety of sources including field borings and laboratory tests, topographic maps, agricultural soil surveys, and aerial photographs.

Subsurface drainage systems fall into two general classes: base and subgrade drains, and intercepting drains.

Base and Subgrade Drainage.   Normally a single line of subsurface drains installed along the edges of runways and taxiways gives adequate base and subgrade drainage (see Figure 10.5). Additional drainage lines may be required under expanses of pavement (e.g., aprons) that are wider than 75 ft (1).

The maximum rate of discharge from a saturated base course may be estimated by the following equation:

$$q = \frac{kHS}{60} \tag{10.8}$$

where

q = peak discharge (cfs/lineal ft of drain)
k = coefficient of horizontal permeability (ft/min)

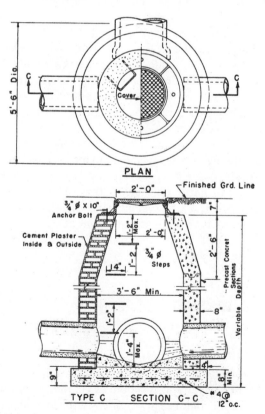

FIGURE 10.9   A suggested manhole design. (*Source:* Reference 1.)

H = base thickness (ft)
S = slope (ft/ft)

A similar but slightly more complicated formula has been published (6) for the estimation of flow from subgrades. Experience has shown that under normal conditions, a pipe 6 or 8 in. in diameter is large enough for base and subgrade drains.

Intercepting Drainage.   An intercepting drainage system intercepts and diverts groundwater flowing in a pervious shallow stratum. Although the quantity of water collected cannot be precisely computed, it depends on the amount of precipitation, the type of ground cover, the permeability of the soil, and the depth and spacing of the drain pipes. As a rule of thumb, the FAA (1) recommends that a rate of infiltration for subdrainage of 0.25 to 0.50 in./acre in 24 hr be used. With appropriate unit conversion, this corresponds to a flow rate of 0.0105 to 0.021 cfs/acre. On the basis of the estimated flow rate, the proper size of pipe can be determined from Manning curves or nomographs. The U.S. Army Corps of Engineers (6) has indicated that a 6 in. intercepting drain pipe not longer than 1000 ft generally has adequate capacity.

Slopes and Backfill.   It is recommended that subsurface drains be laid on a slope of at least 0.15 ft/100 ft. To be effective, the drain pipes must be backfilled with a carefully graded filter material. The backfill material must be pervious enough to allow free water to enter the pipe but impervious enough to prevent the pipe from becoming clogged with fine particles of soil. Specific details on the recommended gradation and permeability of backfill filter material are given in References 1 and 6.

Manholes and Risers.   Subsurface drainage systems must be inspected and maintained. To allow for this, the army recommends (6) that manholes be placed at intervals of not more than 1000 ft and at principal junction points in base and subgrade drainage systems. Inspection and flushing holes (risers) are normally placed between manholes and at dead ends. These holes are usually constructed of the same type and size of pipe as the subdrain and have a grate or cover at the surface (1).

STRUCTURAL PAVEMENT DESIGN

10.5   Introduction

An airfield pavement must be able to support loads imposed by aircraft without excessive distortion or failure. It should be smooth, firm, stable, and free from dust or other particles that might be blown or pushed up by propeller wash or jet blast (7). It must be usable in all seasons and in all weather conditions.

The ability for a pavement to perform these functions for given aircraft traffic depends on the foundation or subgrade, the quality of construction materials and workmanship, the design or proportioning of the materials in the pavement mix, and the thickness of the layers of the pavement system. This section focuses on the structural design of the pavement, that is, the determination of the thickness of the various components or layers of the pavement system.

A pavement is a structure consisting of one or more layers of processed or unprocessed materials placed on a prepared subgrade. There are two general classes of pavements, flexible and rigid.

Flexible pavements typically consist of a bituminous "surface course," a "base course," and a "subbase course." These courses or layers are carefully placed and compacted on a prepared subgrade in an embankment or excavation.

The surface course in a flexible pavement may be constructed of bituminous concrete, sand-bitumen mixtures, or sprayed bituminous surface treatments. Since it is the top layer, the surface course is subjected to the highest stresses and the most severe effects of weather and traffic. It must be able to do the following:

1. Withstand the effects of applied loads and distribute those loads to underlying layers.
2. Resist deterioration due to the environment and abrasive effects of traffic.
3. Provide a smooth, skid-resistant surface.

The base course typically consists of crushed or uncrushed aggregates, which may be untreated or treated with portland cement, asphalt, lime, or other stabilizing agents. This layer must be strong enough to fulfill its principal functions, namely, to support applied loads and to distribute the loads to the subbase or subgrade.

A subbase course, consisting of lower quality and less expensive material than that used in the base course, is sometimes employed. Subbases typically are composed of a stabilized or unstabilized granular material or a stabilized soil. Subbases distribute imposed loads to the subgrade and in certain instances may be used to facilitate subsurface drainage and prevent destructive frost action.

Rigid pavements consist of a slab of portland cement concrete that rests on a prepared subgrade or subbase. Distributed steel or tiebars and dowels are used in portland concrete pavements to control and minimize the harmful effects of cracking and to provide for load transfer between adjacent slabs. Relatively thin subbases (4–6 in.) may be placed under rigid pavements to prevent pumping (4). Subbases may also be used to improve a low strength subgrade.

A large number of methods have been proposed for the structural design of airport pavements. Most are extensions of methods that have been employed in the design of highway pavements. These methods are more or less theoretically based; however, the procedures have been modified and refined through analyses of pavement performance under service conditions. The subsections that follow briefly describe some of the most popular design methods. First, we discuss some of the significant effects on pavement performance.

Factors That Influence Pavement Performance. Airport pavements are complex structural systems, and their performance depends on a broad spectrum of variables. These variables may be classified into five groups, listed in Table 10.3.

The most important variables are those that relate to the imposed loadings. The load variables depend primarily on the sizes and numbers of airplanes that comprise the aircraft mix. The task of the pavement designer is complicated by the rapidly changing state of aircraft design technology. The introduction of larger and heavier aircraft, as well as changes in wheel loads, gear configurations, tire pressures, and other load variables significantly affect the performance of airport pavements. A pavement's performance is especially sensitive to the frequency of loadings. Areas subjected to repeated loadings due to channelization or concentration of traffic must be designed to accommodate the stress from such loadings.

The environmental variables that affect the performance of a pavement include (1) the amount and distribution of precipitation, which may weaken subgrades and contribute to pavement pumping and frost action; (2) ambient temperatures, which can cause excessive expansion of concrete slabs and asphalt

Table 10.3 Variables That Influence Pavement Performance (8)

Load Variables
    Aircraft gross load
    Wheel load
    Number and spacing of wheels
    Tire contact pressures
    Number of applications
    Duration of load application
    Distribution of lateral placement of loads
    Type of load (static or dynamic)
Environmental variables
    Amount and distribution of precipitation (especially rainfall)
    Ambient temperatures
    Aircraft blast and heat
    Fuel spillage
Structural design variables
    Number, thickness, and type of pavement layers
    Strength of materials
Construction variables
Maintenance variables

bleeding; (3) variables associated with the aircraft, such as jet blast, heat, and fuel spillage; and (4) the type of subgrade soil.

The performance of a pavement is directly related to its structural design. Structural design variables include the number and thickness of the pavement layers and the strength and behavioral characteristics of the pavement materials. It should also be obvious that performance under service conditions depends on the quality of construction workmanship and the adequacy of maintenance during its service life. Therefore the designer should make suitable allowances for probable inadequacies in quality control during construction and should consider the effects of the anticipated level of maintenance.

A further complication is the impossibility of giving a precise definition of functional pavement failure. Pavements seldom fail catastrophically; rather, they gradually wear out and suffer a loss of serviceability over time. This makes pavement performance evaluation very difficult.

Because of the complexity of the pavement structural design problem, there is no single analytical equation for its solution. Nor is it likely that such an equation will soon be developed. Nevertheless, currently available design procedures, which contain empirical factors based on pavement performance, "will give generally good designs within the limits from which the methods were developed" (9). However, the reader is cautioned that these methods "cannot be used with confidence when it becomes necessary to extrapolate the loading conditions, materials, environmental conditions, and so on, that are different from those used for the development of the methods" (9).

10.6   Flexible Pavement Design Methods (U.S. Practice)

The California Bearing Ratio Method.   The California bearing ratio (CBR) method of pavement design was developed in the late 1920s by the California Division of Highways. It was modified and adopted for airfield pavement design by the Corps of Engineers at the beginning of World War II. Since its adoption, it has been further modified on the basis of empirical and theoretical studies to account for high pressure tires and multiple-wheel landing gears.

The CBR method is based on a relatively simple test of the shear strength of the supporting soil.

> The CBR test is conducted by forcing a 2-inch diameter piston into the soil. The load required to force the piston into the soil 0.1 inch (sometimes 0.2 inch) is expressed as a percentage of the standard value for crushed stone. . . . The test can be performed on samples compacted in test molds, on undisturbed samples, or on material in place. The test must be made on material that represents the prototype condition that will be the most critical from a design viewpoint. For this reason, samples are generally subjected to a four-day soaking period. . . . Experience during the past few years has shown that CBR tests on gravelly materials in the laboratory have tended to give CBR values higher than are obtained in tests in the field. The difference is attributed to the processing necessary to test the sample in the 6-inch mold, and to the confining effect of the mold.

Therefore, the CBR test is supplemented by gradation and Atterberg limits requirements for subbases . . . (10).

The Departments of the Army and Air Force (10) recommend that the laboratory CBR test not be used in determining CBR values of base courses. Instead, selected CBR ratings have been assigned as shown below:

Type	Design CBR
Graded crushed aggregate	100
Water-bound macadam	100
Dry-bound macadam	100
Bituminous intermediate and surface courses, central plant, hot mix	100
Limerock	80
Stabilized aggregate	80

The Corps of Engineers conducted extensive full-scale tests of airport pavements during the 1950s. Analysis of the results of those tests and studies of the performance of pavements in actual service indicated that the CBR design criteria for single-wheel loads could be expressed by two parameters: thickness/(contact area)$^{1/2}$ and CBR/tire pressure (11). These parameters were shown in the form of a single curve that separates service failures and nonfailures for capacity operations (5000 coverages of the pavement). The curve is expressed mathematically as follows:

$$t = \left[\frac{P}{8.1(\text{CBR})} - \frac{A}{\pi}\right]^{1/2} \qquad (10.9)$$

where

t = design thickness (in.)
P = single-wheel load (lb)
A = measured tire contact area (in.^{2})

In 1959, the equation was modified to account for load repetitions and multiple-wheel configurations. The modified equation employed the concept of an equivalent single wheel load (ESWL):

$$t = f\left[\frac{ESWL}{8.1(\text{CBR})} - \frac{A}{\pi}\right]^{1/2} \qquad (10.10)$$

where

f = percentage of design thickness ($0.23 \log c + 0.15$)
$ESWL$ = equivalent single-wheel load, defined as that "load on a single tire

that produces the same vertical deflection on the supporting medium as that particular multiple-wheel assembly with the same single-wheel tire contact area" (11)

c = coverage, sufficient wheel passes to cover every point of a traffic land once

In the late 1960s, the Waterways Experiment Station studied pavement thickness requirements for aircraft with multiple-wheel heavy gear loads. Such aircraft were defined as those with gross loads exceeding 600 kips (e.g., the C-5A and the Boeing 747). That research indicated that equation 10.8 for low intensity traffic is adequate for all wheel-gear configurations. However, with an increase in coverages, the equation yields thicknesses that are too great. The better pavement performance for multiwheel configurations was attributed in part to "interior soil confinement afforded by a larger number of perimeter wheels" (11). Therefore the equation was further modified as follows:

$$t = \alpha_i \left[\frac{ESWL}{8.1(CBR)} - \frac{A}{\pi} \right]^{1/2} \tag{10.11}$$

where

α_i = load repetition factor, which depends on the number of wheels in each main landing gear assembly used to compute the $ESWL$

The load repetition factor allows design for any desired number of aircraft passes (i.e., operations). Table 10.4 lists representative load repetition factors.

Equation 10.9 is recommended for CBR values of 15 or less. For CBR values greater than 15, minimum pavement thickness based on durability may apply.

For a given aircraft load and wheel assembly configuration, it is possible to compute equivalent single-wheel loads for various depths based on the theory of elasticity. [Detailed procedures for making such calculations have

Table 10.4 Recommended Load Repetition Factors, α_i, for Use in Equation 10.9

Number of Passes	Number of Tires Used to Compute ESWL				
	1	2	4	12	24
1,000	0.72	0.70	0.68	0.65	0.64
5,000	0.83	0.77	0.73	0.69	0.67
10,000	0.88	0.81	0.76	0.70	0.68
100,000	1.03	0.88	0.79	0.72	0.69

Source: G. M. Hammitt II, et al., *Multiple-Wheel Heavy Gear Load Pavement Tests*, Vol. 4, Technical Report S-71-17, prepared for the U.S. Army Engineer Waterways Experiment Station, November 1971.

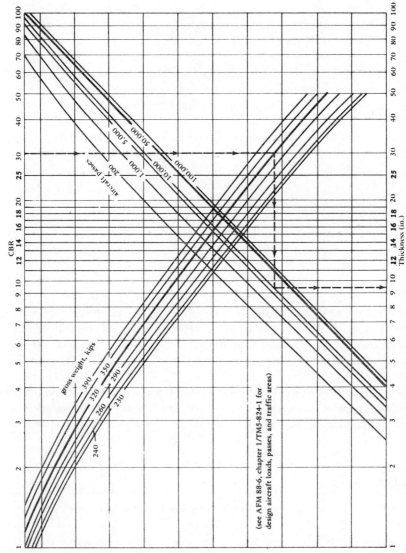

FIGURE 10.10 Example of California Bearing Ratio (CBR) design curve. *(Source: Reference 13.)*

Table 10.5 CBR Flexible Pavement Design Curves (13)

Army Class I airfield, Type B and C traffic areas
Army Class II airfield, Type B and C traffic areas
Army Class III airfield, Type B and C traffic areas
Navy and Marine Corps single–wheel aircraft, 150–psi tire pressure, Type B and C
    traffic areas
Navy and Marine Corps single–wheel aircraft, 400–psi tire pressure, Type B and C
    traffic areas
Navy and Marine Corps dual-wheel aircraft, Type B and C traffic areas
Navy and Marine Corps C–5A aircraft, Type B and C traffic areas
Air Force light-load pavement, Type B and C traffic areas and overruns
Air Force medium-load pavement, Type A traffic areas
Air Force medium-load pavement, Type B, C, and D traffic areas and overruns
Air Force heavy-load pavement, Type A traffic areas
Air Force heavy-load pavement, Type B, C, and D, traffic areas and overruns
Air Force shoulder pavement
Air Force shortfield pavement, Type A traffic areas and overruns

been described by Ahlvin (12).] By solving equation 10.9 for CBR, one may then develop a CBR versus design thickness curve for a particular aircraft.

A simple graphical procedure based on the California bearing ratio is recommended for the design of flexible pavements for military airfields. Fourteen CBR design curves, exemplified by Figure 10.10, have been published (13) for various classes of military usage and gear configurations (See Table 10.5.).

The following procedure is recommended for use of the curves:

1. Determine design CBR of subgrade.
2. Enter the top of the graph with the design subgrade CBR and follow it downward to the intersection with the appropriate gross weight curve.
3. From the point of intersection, extend a horizontal line to appropriate aircraft passes curve, then downward to required total pavement thickness above subgrade.

The thickness of surface and base course can be determined by a similar procedure and entering the graph with the design CBR of the subbase material. It may be necessary to increase the thickness of surface and base indicated by the graph to a required minimum thickness. Each of the military services specifies a minimum combined thickness of base and surface, which depends on conditions of loading, traffic, and strength of the base. The thickness of the subbase can be determined by subtracting the thickness of the surface and base from the total thickness. A minimum thickness of 6 in. is usually recommended for the subbase.

The FAA Method of Flexible Pavement Design. The FAA method (7) of flexible pavement design calls for accurate identification and evaluation of pavement foundation conditions. The recommended method requires thorough investigations to determine the distribution and physical properties of pavement foundation soils. A soil survey should be made to describe the soils that comprise the soil profile and to indicate subsurface water conditions. It is recommended that representative samples of soil be taken by means of a soil auger. Generally, borings should be taken along runway and taxiway centerlines at 200 ft intervals. One boring for every 10,000 ft^2 should be made under other pavement areas. Such borings normally are made to a depth of 10 ft below the finished grade in cut areas, and 10 ft below the existing ground surface in fill areas. Borrow areas should be adequately sampled to establish the physical characteristics of the borrow material.

The FAA (7) recommends the use of the Unified Soil Classification System. This system, which was developed by the U.S. Army Corps of Engineers and is described in ASTM D-2487, classifies soils on the basis of grain size and

Table 10.6   Classification of Soils for Airport Pavement Applications

Major Divisions	Group Symbols	Field CBR	Subgrade Modulus, k
Coarse-grained			
Soils more than 50% retained on No. 200 sieve[a]			
Gravels 50% or more of coarse fraction retained on No. 4 sieve			
Clean gravels	GW	60–80	300 or more
	GP	35–60	300 or more
Gravels with fines	GM	40–80	300 or more
	GC	20–40	200–300
Sands less than 50% of coarse fraction retained on No. 4 sieve			
Clean sands	SW	20–40	200–300
	SP	15–25	200–300
Sands with fines	SM	20–40	200–300
	SC	10–20	200–300
Fine-grained			
Soils 50% or less retained on No. 200 sieve[a]			
Silts and Clays	ML	5–15	100–200
Liquid Limit	CL	5–15	100–200
50% or less	OL	4–8	100–200
Silts and Clays	MH	4–8	100–200
Liquid Limit	CH	3–5	50–100
Greater than 50%	OH	3–5	50–100
Highly organic soils	PT		

Source: *Airport Pavement Design and Evaluation*, FAA Advisory Circular AC 150/5320-C, December 7, 1978.

[a] Based on the material passing the 3-in. (75-mm) sieve.

then further subgroups them on the basis of the Atterberg limits. Specifically, the Unified Classification System is based primarily on the following soil characteristics:

1. Percentage of material retained on No. 200 sieve.
2. Percentage of material retained on No. 4 sieve.
3. Liquid limit.
4. Plastic limit.

Fifteen soil groups comprise the Unified Classification System. The system array of soil types ranges from clean gravels, the best pavement foundation material, to peat, muck, and other highly organic materials that are unsuitable as pavement foundations.

Table 10.6 gives the criteria for classifying soils into the major divisions. Additional criteria for determining the specific soil class are given in Table 10.7. The coefficients of uniformity (C_u) and gradation (C_g) referred to in Table 10.7 are used to judge the shape of the grain-size distribution curve of a coarse grained soil. The term D_{10} means the grain size (diameter) that corresponds to 10% on a grain-size distribution curve. D_{30} and D_{60} have similar meanings.

A listing of the group symbols and an abbreviated description of each group reveals the general rationale for the Unified System:

Gravels

GW—Well graded gravels.
GP—Poorly graded gravels.
GM—Silty gravels.
GC—Clayey gravels.

Sands

SW—Well graded sands.
SP—Poorly graded sands.
SM—Silty sands.
SC—Clayey sands.

Silts and Clays

ML—Inorganic silts with liquid limit less than 50
CL—Inorganic clays with liquid limit less than 50
OL—Organic silts and silty clays with liquid limit less than 50
MH—Inorganic silts with liquid limit higher than 50
CH—Inorganic clays with liquid limit higher than 50
OH—Organic clays with liquid limit higher than 50

Table 10.7   Soil Classification Criteria for the Unified System

Group Symbols		Classification Criteria		
GW	Classification on basis of percentage of fines — Less than 5% Pass No. 200 sieve / More than 12% Pass No. 200 sieve / 5% to 12% Pass No. 200 sieve	$C_u = D_{60}/D_{10}$ Greater than 4 \ $C_g = \dfrac{(D_{30})^2}{D_{10} \times D_{60}}$ Between 1 and 3	GW, GP, SW, SP / GM, GC, SM, SC — Borderline Classification requiring use of dual symbols	
GP		Not meeting both criteria for GW		
GM		Atterberg limits plot below "A" line or plasticity index less than 4	Atterberg limits plotting in hatched area are borderline classifications requiring use of dual symbols	
GC		Atterberg limits plot above "A" line and plasticity index greater than 7		
SW		$C_u = D_{60}/D_{10}$ Greater than 6 \ $C_g = \dfrac{(D_{30})^2}{D_{10} \times D_{60}}$ Between 1 and 3		
SP		Not meeting both criteria for SW		
SM		Atterberg limits plot below "A" line or plasticity index less than 4	Atterberg limits plotting in hatched area are borderline classifications requiring use of dual symbols	
SC		Atterberg limits plot above "A" line and plasticity index greater than 7		
ML		PLASTICITY CHART. For classification of fine-grained soils and fine fraction of coarse-grained soils. Atterberg Limits plotting in hatched area are borderline classifications requiring use of dual symbols. Equation of A-line = PI = 0.73 (LL-20)		
CL				
OL				
MH				
CH				
OH				
PT	Visual-Manual Identification, See ASTM Designation D 2488			

Source: *1975 Annual Book of ASTM Standards, Part 19*, Philadelphia; American Society for Testing Materials, 1975.

Highly Organic Soils

PT—Peat, muck and other highly organic soils

Experience has shown that organic soils containing more than 3% particles finer than 0.02 mm in diameter are subject to "frost action." The harmful effects of frost action may be manifested in frost heave, the distortion of the subgrade soil or base material when prolonged severe freezing temperatures prevail. Investigations have shown that as the water in the upper soil layers of a pavement freezes, ice crystals are formed, and water may be drawn from a free water surface into the zone of subfreezing temperatures. This water then freezes, additional water may be drawn to this level, and this process continues until ice lenses of considerable thickness may be formed. The volume increase brought about by the formation of these layers of ice is the cause of frost heaving. The melting of these ice layers can result in a reduction in foundation support and even cause a failure of the pavement system.

Where the potential for damaging frost action exists, it may be necessary to include material that is not frost susceptible below the required base or subbase. The degree of frost protection required depends on the soil conditions and the usage the pavement will receive. Further guidance on the control of this problem is given in Reference 7.

The reader is cautioned that the Unified Classification System may be only roughly indicative of the behavior of the soil as a pavement foundation. A more reliable approach to predicting foundation behavior is to directly measure soil strength by the CBR or plate bearing tests. For flexible pavements, the FAA recommends the use of CBR tests. A comparison of CBR values and the various Unified Soil Classes is given in Table 10.6.

Load and Traffic Considerations.   The FAA design method is based on total gross aircraft weight, which, for design purposes, is assumed to be the maximum takeoff weight. Since the maximum landing weight is usually only about 75% of the maximum takeoff weight, traffic is expressed in departures. Pavement design curves, exemplified by Figure 10.11, have been published in Reference 7 for single, dual, and dual-tandem landing gear configurations. Separate design curves have been provided for wide bodied aircraft such as the B-747, DC-10 and L-1011.

Usually it is necessary to account for the cumulative effect of wheel loads from several classes of aircraft. This is accomplished by expressing the traffic levels in terms of "equivalent annual departures by the design aircraft." The design aircraft is the aircraft type that produces the greatest pavement thickness. To select the design aircraft, it is necessary to determine the pavement thickness required for each aircraft type in the forecast by using the appropriate design curve with the forecast number of annual departures for that aircraft.

To account for the effects of all traffic in terms of the design aircraft, convert all aircraft to the same landing gear type as the design aircraft. This

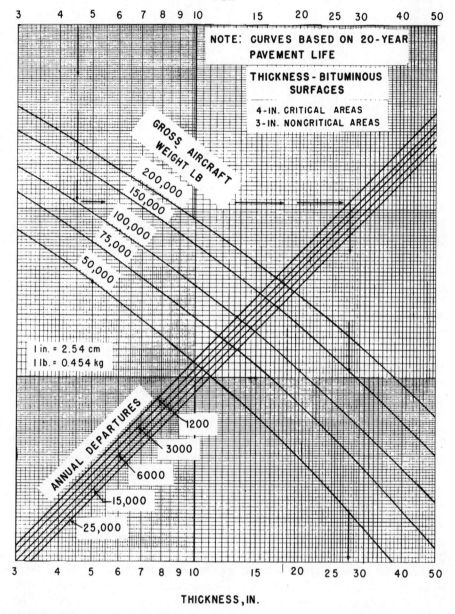

FIGURE 10.11 Flexible pavement design curves for critical areas, dual wheel gear. (*Source:* Reference 7.)

is done by multiplying the number of departures by a factor selected from Table 10.8. Then, to compute the equivalent design departures, the FAA (7) recommends the use of the following equation:

$$\log R_1 = \log R_2 \left(\frac{W_2}{W_1}\right)^{1/2} \tag{10.12}$$

where R_1 and R_2 are repetitions of loadings or departures and W_1 and W_2 are corresponding wheel loads.

Example 10.4   Equivalent Design Departures

An airport pavement is to be designed for the traffic mix tabulated below. Convert the traffic to equivalent DC-8-61 departures.

Aircraft (wheel configuration)	Departures, R	Load per Wheel, W
CV-880 (Dual-tandem)	3,100	21,800
DC-9-32 (Dual)	11,000	25,200
DC-8-61 (Dual-tandem)	3,000	39,400

For the CV-880 group,

$$\log R_1 = \log(1 \times 3,100)\left(\frac{21,800}{39,400}\right)^{1/2} = 2.5966$$

$$R_1 = 395$$

For the DC-9-32 group,

Table 10.8   Landing Gear Conversion Factors

To Convert From	To	Multiply Departures By
Single wheel	Dual wheel	0.8
Single wheel	Dual tandem	0.5
Dual wheel	Dual tandem	0.6
Double dual tandem	Dual tandem	1.0
Dual tandem	Single wheel	2.0
Dual tandem	Dual wheel	1.7
Dual wheel	Single wheel	1.3
Double dual tandem	Dual wheel	1.7

Source: *Airport Pavement Design and Evaluation*, FAA Advisory Circular AC 150/5320-6C, December 7, 1978.

$$\log R_1 = \log(0.6 \times 11{,}000)\left(\frac{25{,}200}{39{,}400}\right)^{1/2} = 3.0547$$

$$R_1 = 1134$$

For the DC-8-61 group, $R_1 = 3000$, and

total equivalent DC-8-61 departures $= 395 + 1134 + 3000 = 4529$

The designer should recognize that different parts of a runway-taxiway system are subjected to varying demands because of differences in concentrations of traffic and aircraft speeds. Heaviest traffic concentrations tend to be near the runway ends and laterally near the runway and taxiway centerlines. The demands on pavements for aprons, taxiways, and runway ends tend to be greater because traffic moves at slower speeds in those areas.

The design charts (e.g., Figure 10.11) provide a "critical pavement thickness" for use in areas where traffic is highly concentrated. In areas of dispersed traffic, thinner pavements may be used.

As a general rule of thumb the designer should specify full pavement thickness T where departing aircraft will be using the pavement; pavement thickness of $0.9T$ will be specified where traffic will be arrivals such as high speed turn-offs; and pavement thickness of $0.7T$ will be specified where pavement is required but traffic is unlikely, such as along the extreme outer edges of the runway (7).

Pavements for Lightweight Aircraft.   Some airports serving light aircraft may not require an all-weather pavement; an aggregate-turf surface may be adequate. However, it is seldom possible to provide and maintain a stable turf surface because of heavy traffic or adverse weather conditions. Bituminous pavements are generally used for pavements serving lightweight aircraft, and a high type bituminous surface course such as bituminous concrete is preferred. Figure 10.12 displays thickness design curves for pavements serving aircraft weighing less than 30,000 lb, based on the California bearing ratio. The thicknesses from the curves should not be reduced for "noncritical" areas of the runway-taxiway system.

The Asphalt Institute Method.   The Asphalt Institute Method is based on the theory that the asphalt pavement structure is a multilayer elastic system. In this approach characteristics of both the asphalt concrete and the subgrade are described by the classical terms "Poisson's ratio" and "modulus of elasticity" (14). Two critical load-induced elastic strains are separately examined in the design analysis: (1) the horizontal tensile strain, ϵ_t, at the bottom of the asphalt concrete layer (surface course), and (2) the vertical compressive strain, ϵ_c, at the top of the subgrade layer. Maximum allowable values for these two strains have been established, and thicknesses are determined to satisfy these values. The larger thickness is chosen as the design thickness. The design method is available in the form of a computer program from the Asphalt

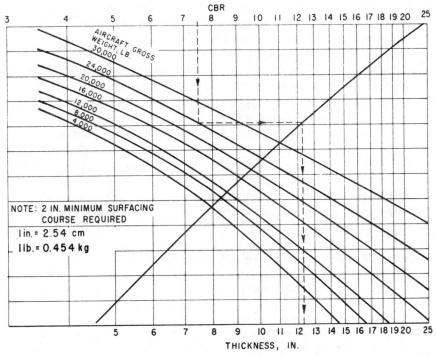

FIGURE 10.12   Design curves for flexible pavements—light aircraft. (*Source:* Reference 7.)

Institute. Space limitations preclude the inclusion of an in-depth discussion of this subject. The reader is referred to the Asphalt Institute's Manual Series No. 11 (14) for a full description of the method.

10.7   Rigid Pavement Design Methods (U.S. Practice)

Ray, Cawley, and Packard (15) have outlined significant historical milestones that led to present-day rigid pavement design procedures. They credit Dr. H. M. Westergaard with the first serious effort to develop a theoretical design procedure for airport pavements. Westergaard's research (16), which was performed for the Portland Cement Association and first published in 1939, resulted in design equations that were used during World War II for the design of many military airports.

In 1948, Westergaard published a new set of formulas for the calculation of stresses in concrete airfield pavements (17). Using Westergaard's formulas, Pickett and Ray developed influence charts for analyzing pavement stresses and published them in transactions of ASCE in 1951 (18). Westergaard's equations and Pickett's and Ray's charts have been widely used since that time. Packard developed a computer program for the design of concrete pavements that was published by the Portland Cement Association in 1967 (19).

Concrete pavement design procedures in the United States have also been influenced by full-scale pavement research conducted by the Corps of Engineers and the Navy. These agencies, as well as the FAA (earlier designated as CAA) and the Portland Cement Association, published design procedures reflecting pavement condition surveys that were made to evaluate pavement performance with respect to the thickness design procedures employed. The Portland Cement Association conducted such a survey in the late 1940s in cooperation with the CAA. PCA performed additional surveys at civilian airports in 1962 and 1963 (20), and at military airports in 1956, 1965, and 1966. During this period, the Corps of Engineers monitored pavement performance at Air Force bases, and the Navy performed pavement evaluation studies at Naval Air Stations in the United States and overseas.

Ray et al. (15) compared four methods for designing and determining the thickness of rigid airport pavements. The methods employed by the FAA, the Portland Cement Association, the U.S. Navy, and the Corps of Engineers were examined. Differences were noted in assumed loading condition, the recommended safety factor, the curing period for determination of concrete strength, the level of traffic, and the use of a saturation correction for sensitive subgrade soils. Despite these differences, the writers reported that

> [D]ifferences in design assumptions balance one another so that approximately the same slab thicknesses are obtained by the four procedures. . . . This similarity of design results is not surprising because each procedure was developed from the Westergaard analysis and coupled with safety factors or other adjustment to reflect performance experience (15).

To avoid redundancy, the rigid pavement design methods of the Navy, the Portland Cement Association, and the Corps of Engineers are not described in this chapter. For detailed information, the reader should consult the respective references (13, 21, 22) at the end of this chapter. In the following description of the FAA design method, we have drawn freely on Reference 7.

The FAA Method of Rigid Pavement Design. The FAA has published design curves for rigid pavements similar to those for flexible pavements. Separate graphs, exemplified by Figure 10.13, are given in Reference 7 for single, dual, and dual-tandem landing gear assemblies. Design curves have also been prepared for the B-747, DC-10, and L-1011 aircraft. To use the design curves, information is required on the flexural strength of the concrete, the subgrade modulus, and the gross weight and annual departures of the design aircraft. One enters the design curves with the 90-day flexural strength of the concrete as determined by the American Society for Testing Materials test method T-78.

The strength of the supporting subgrade or subbase is determined by 30 in. diameter plate bearing tests conducted in accordance with test procedures specified by the American Association of State Highway and Transportation Officials procedure T-222. It is reported as a "k-value," which is referred to

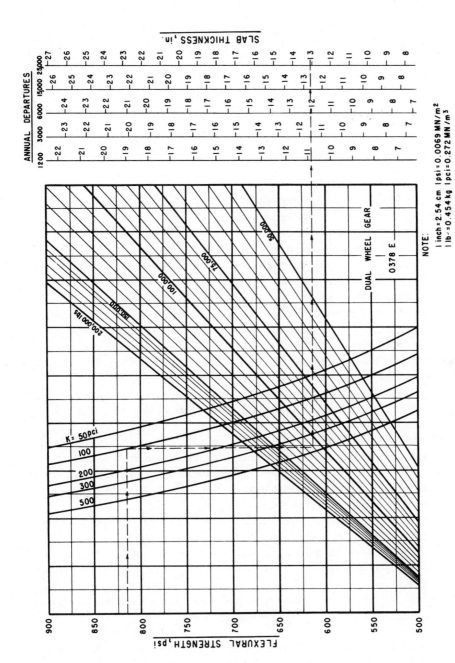

FIGURE 10.13 Rigid pavement design curves—dual wheel gear. (*Source:* Reference 7.)

NOTE:

1 inch = 2.54 cm 1 psi = 0.0069 MN/m²
1 lb = 0.454 kg 1 pci = 0.272 MN/m³

DUAL WHEEL GEAR

0378 E

SLAB THICKNESS, in.

ANNUAL DEPARTURES

FLEXURAL STRENGTH, psi

323

Table 10.9   Conditions Where No Subbase Is Required

Soil Classification	Good Drainage		Poor Drainage	
	No Frost	Frost	No Frost	Frost
GW	X	X	X	X
GP	X	X	X	
GM	X			
GC	X			
SW	X			

Source: *Airport Pavement Design and Evaluation*, FAA Advisory Circular AC 150/5320-6C, December 7, 1978.

as the modulus of subgrade reaction. The k-value is measured in pounds per square inch of loaded area, divided by the deflection in inches of the subgrade under load. If the construction and evaluation of a test section is impractical, the approximate k-values shown in Table 10.6 may be used.

As was the case in flexible pavement design, the FAA design method is based on the total gross aircraft weight (i.e., the maximum takeoff weight). The equivalent design aircraft departures must be computed as described previously.

From the left ordinate of Figure 10.13, representing the flexural strength of the concrete, a line is extended horizontally to its intersection with the foundation modulus line, vertically to the gross weight line, then horizontally to the right ordinate where the pavement thickness can be read from the appropriate annual departure line.

The thicknesses shown on the design graphs are for critical areas. For noncritical areas such as exit taxiways, a thickness of 0.9 times the critical thickness may be used.

Subbases are commonly placed under concrete slabs to provide drainage and a more stable and uniform foundation. The FAA requires that a minimum thickness of 4 inches of subbase be placed under all rigid pavements except as noted in Table 10.9. If economical, subbase thicknesses in excess of 4 inches may be used to increase the modulus of subgrade reaction and reduce the required thickness of concrete. The cost of additional subbase thickness should be weighed against the savings of reducing the concrete thickness (7). The probable increase in the k-value due to the use of a subbase depends on the thickness and type of subbase material. Some guidance on the magnitude of this increase is given by Reference 7. The FAA recommends that stabilized subbases be placed under all new rigid pavements expected to accommodate aircraft weighing more than 100,000 lb gross weight.

Reinforced Concrete Pavement.   Reinforcing steel placed in concrete pavements helps to maintain structural integrity across cracks that develop in the slab. Reinforced pavements require fewer joints and less joint maintenance, and there are fewer problems associated with joints, such as pavement pumping. It is claimed that reinforced pavements last longer than plain concrete pavements.

There are two types of reinforced concrete pavement:

1. Conventional or jointed pavements.
2. Continuously reinforced pavements.

Steel used in conventional reinforced pavements is normally in the form of welded wire fabric or bar mats distributed throughout the concrete. The quantity of steel used should be sufficient to maintain aggregate interlock along the faces of the cracked slabs. The amount of steel in conventionally reinforced pavements depends on the joint spacing, slab thickness, and other factors; typically, 0.05 to 0.30% of the cross-sectional area of the pavement is steel (21).

A continuously reinforced concrete pavement has relatively heavy continuous steel reinforcement in the longitudinal direction, and has no transverse joints except at intersections with existing pavements or structures. The amount of longitudinal steel in continuously reinforced pavements is typically 0.6% of the gross cross-sectional area of the pavement (21).

Reinforced concrete pavements have not been extensively used in the United States. Most designers here prefer to avoid the added costs for steel reinforcement and to control slab cracking by judicious design and placement of joints. However, serious consideration should be given to the use of reinforcement in situations where special cracking problems are likely to occur. For example, the Corps of Engineers (22) requires reinforcement to control cracking (1) in odd-shaped slabs, (2) at mismatched joints in adjacent pavements, and (3) in overlay pavements where it is not feasible to match the joint pattern in the lower pavement.

More detailed information on the amount, size, spacing, and strength of reinforcing steel for concrete pavements is given in the literature (7, 21, 22).

Jointing of Concrete Pavements. Variations in temperature and moisture content produce volume changes and warping of pavement slabs and cause significant stresses to occur. To reduce the effects of these stresses and to control pavement cracking, joints are installed. By this means, the pavement is divided into a series of slabs of predetermined dimensions. Various types of joints are shown in Figure 10.14; typical uses of these joints are described in Table 10.10.

There are three functional classes of pavement joints: expansion, contraction, and construction joints.

1. *Expansion joints* provide space for the expansion of the pavement and are most commonly used between intersecting pavements and adjacent to structures. Two types of expansion joints are used: those that provide load transfer across the joint (Type A, Fig. 10.14), and those that do not (Type B).
2. *Contraction joints* provide controlled cracking of the pavement that occurs because of contraction. The contraction may be caused by a

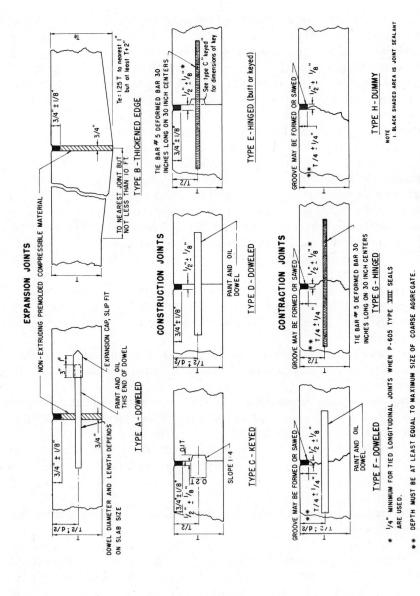

FIGURE 10.14 Details of joints in rigid pavement. (*Source:* Reference 7.)

Table 10.10 Joint Types: Description and Use

Type	Description	Longitudinal	Transverse
A	Doweled expansion joint	—	Use near intersections to isolate them
B	Thickened edge expansion joint	Use at intersections where dowels are not suitable and where pavements abut structures	Provide thickened edge (or keyway) where pavement enlargements is likely
C or D	Keyed or doweled construction joint	Use for all construction joints except where type E is used; keyed joints are not recommended for slabs <9 in. thick	Use type D where paving operations are delayed or stopped
E	Hinged construction joint	Use for all contraction joints of the taxiway and for all other contraction joints placed 25 ft or less from the pavement edge, unless wide-body aircraft are expected	—
F	Doweled contraction joint	—	Use for contraction joints for a distance of at least three joints from a free edge, for the first two joints on each side of expansion joints, and for all contraction joints in reinforced pavements
G	Hinged contraction joint	Use for all contraction joints of the taxiway and for all other contraction joints placed 25 ft or less from the pavement edge, unless wide-body aircraft are expected	
H	Dummy contraction joint	Use for all other contraction joints in pavement	Use for all remaining contraction joints in nonreinforced pavements

Source: *Airport Pavement Design and Evaluation,* FAA Advisory Circular AC 150/5320-6C, December 7, 1978.

Table 10.11   Recommended Maximum Joint Spacings for
Nonreinforced Pavements

	Spacing (ft)	
Slab Thickness (in.)	Transverse	Longitudinal
Less than 9	15	12.5
9–12	20	20
Greater than 12	25	25

Source: *Airport Pavement Design and Evaluation*, FAA Advisory Circular AC 150/5320-6C,
December 7, 1978.

decrease in moisture content, a drop in temperature, or by the shrinkage
which accompanies the curing process. Contraction joints also reduce
the stresses caused by slab warping. Details for contraction joints are
shown as Types F, G, and H in Figure 10.14.

3. *Construction joints* are required when two abutting slabs are constructed
at different times, such as at the end of work day, or between paving
lanes. Details for construction joints are shown as Types C, D, and E
in Fig. 10.14 (7).

Experience has shown that poor performance may result if keyed longitudinal
construction joints are used in pavements accommodating wide-bodied jet
aircraft when the subgrade modulus is less than 400 pci. Specific recommendations for such conditions are given in Reference 7.

Table 10.11 summarizes the recommended spacing of joints for nonreinforced
pavements. In conventionally reinforced pavements, the maximum allowable
slab length is 75 ft (7). The Portland Cement Association recommends a maximum joint spacing of 30 to 40 ft for pavements less than 12 in. thick and 50
ft for thicker pavements. With the exceptions noted earlier, continuously reinforced pavements are constructed without transverse joints.

10.8 The Load Classification Number (LCN) Design Method

Originally developed and published by the Air Ministry Directorate General
of Works, United Kingdom, the load classification number (LCN) method was
later adopted by the International Civil Aviation Organization and incorporated
in the ICAO *Aerodrome Manual*, Part 3 (23). The method is applicable to both
rigid and flexible pavements. The LCN lies on a numerical scale that represents
the severity of stresses produced by a given aircraft. A similar scale is used
to represent the strength of the supporting pavement. Based on the ratio of the
aircraft LCN and the pavement LCN, criteria have been developed that indicate
the suitability of the pavement to accommodate stated levels of aircraft movements.

The LCN method is based on an extensive series of plate bearing tests
conducted in the United Kingdom following World War II. The purpose of

these tests was to examine the relationship between the failure load and the tire contact area. The test results were generalized by expressing the load required to produce failure on each plate as a percentage of the failure load when applied through a standard plate having a contact area of 530 in.^{2} (diameter = 26 in.). This contact area was chosen as representative of heavy aircraft at the time the LCN method was developed. It was found that the following equation can be used to represent with reasonable accuracy the behavior of aircraft pavements under load:

$$\frac{W_1}{W_2} = \left(\frac{A_1}{A_2}\right)^{0.27} \tag{10.13}$$

where W_1 and W_2 are any two failure loads in pounds, and A_1 and A_2 are the respective loaded areas in square inches.

An arbitrary "standard load classification curve" was introduced as a means of expressing the load-bearing capacity of a pavement as a single number. The standard curve is produced by connecting a series of points on the load-contact area diagram. The following points, plotted in Figure 10.15, were chosen:

Tire Pressure (psi)	Wheel Loading (lb)	LCN
120	100,000	100
115	90,000	90
110	80,000	80
105	70,000	70
100	60,000	60
95	50,000	50
90	40,000	40
85	30,000	30
80	20,000	20
75	10,000	10

This standard load classification curve and equation 10.13 have been combined to produce the set of curves appearing in Figure 10.15. The curves were drawn in the following manner (23):

1. The tire contact area lines were drawn from the relationship

$$\text{contact area} = \frac{\text{load}}{\text{tire pressure}}$$

2. One point on each LCN line was taken from the standard load classification curve.

3. Other points on each LCN line were calculated from equation 10.13.

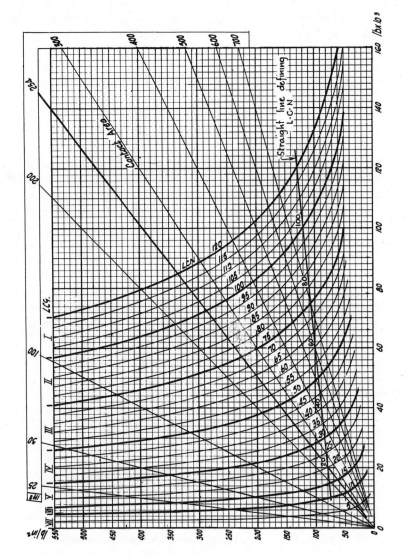

FIGURE 10.15 Load classification numbers and groups in terms of load, tire pressure, and contact area. (Courtesy of the Department of Environment, United Kingdom.)

Figure 10.15 indicates that a pavement having an LCN of 50 is capable of safely bearing a load of 50,000 lb on a contact area of 520 in.[2] or a tire pressure of 96 psi. Such a pavement would be capable of bearing any combination of load and tire pressure lying along the LCN 50 line.

It is possible to perform plate bearing tests using one size of plate and, assuming the validity of equation 10.13, to read the LCN of the pavement directly from Figure 10.15.

The LCN for an aircraft with single gear loads can be read directly from the graph. For example, a wheel load of 20,000 lb and a tire pressure of 100 psi gives a LCN value of 22. LCN values for multiple-wheel gear loads are based on an equivalent single-wheel load (ESWL). Graphs have been published (23, 24) to facilitate the determination of ESWL values for dual and dual-tandem landing gear configurations. Once the ESWL has been calculated, the LCN of the aircraft can be read from Figure 10.15. The ICAO (23) gives LCN values for specified aircraft at different operating weights. These values vary according to pavement thickness for flexible pavement systems.

Because of the variability of the properties of the materials used to construct pavements, great precision in expressing pavement strength is not warranted. For this reason, the pavement design and evaluation process may be simplified by categorizing the LCN values into broad load classification groups (LCG). These are shown by the heavy lines in Figure 10.15. For example, LCG I encompasses LCN values 101–120, LCG II includes LCN values 76–100, etc.

References 23 and 25 contain a graph that shows the relationship between the LCN (and LCG) of the aircraft, the subgrade characteristics (k-value), and the required theoretical thickness of a concrete slab. These sources also provide empirically derived charts showing recommended pavement designs for rigid and flexible pavements, as well as for composite pavements of continuously reinforced concrete with bituminous surfacing.

REFERENCES

1. *Airport Drainage*, FAA Advisory Circular AC 150/5320-5B, July 1970.

2. *Rainfall Frequency Atlas of the United States*, Technical Paper No. 40, U.S. Weather Bureau [now National Weather Service], Department of Commerce, May 1961.

3. *Drainage and Erosion Control—Surface Drainage Facilities for Airfields and Heliports*, Department of the Army, Technical Manual TM 5-820-1, August 1965.

4. *Design Charts for Open-Channel Flow*, Bureau of Public Roads, 1961.

5. *Airport Drainage*, Skokie, Il.: Portland Cement Association, 1966.

6. *Subsurface Drainage Facilities for Airfields*, Department of the Army, Technical Manual TM 5-820-2, August 1965.

7. *Airport Pavement Design and Evaluation*, FAA Advisory Circular AC 150/5320-6C, December 7, 1978.

8. Hudson, W. Ronald, and Thomas M. Kennedy, "Parameters of Rational Airfield Pavement Design System," *American Society of Civil Engineers Transportation Engineering Journal*, May 1973.

9. Hutchinson, Ronald L., and Harry H. Ulery, "Airfield Pavement Research Trends,": *Airports, Key to the Air Transportation System*, New York: American Society of Civil Engineers, 1971.

10. *Airfield Flexible Pavements—Air Force*, Departments of the Army and the Air Force, TM 5-824-2, AFM 88-6, Ch. 2, February 1969.

11. Hammitt, G. M. II, et al., *Multiple-Wheel Heavy Gear Load Pavement Tests*, Vol. 4, Technical Report S-71-17, prepared for Air Force Systems Command by U.S. Army Engineer Waterways Experiment Station, November 1971.

12. Ahlvin, R. G., "Flexible Pavement Design Criteria," *Journal of the Aero-Space Transport Division, Proceedings of the American Society of Civil Engineers*, Vol. 88, No. AT1, August 1962.

13. *Flexible Pavement Design for Airfields*, Navy DM 21.3, Army TM 5-825.2, Air Force AFM 88-6, Chapter 2, Departments of the Navy, The Army and The Air Force, August, 1978.

14. *Full-Depth Asphalt Pavements for Air Carrier Airports*, Manual Series No. 11, College Park, Md.: The Asphalt Institute, January 1973.

15. Ray, Gordon K., Martin L. Cawley, and Robert G. Packard, "Concrete Airport Pavement Design—Where Are We?" in *Airports, Key to the Air Transportation System*, New York: American Society of Civil Engineers, 1971.

16. Westergaard, H. M., "Stresses in Concrete Runways of Airports," *Proceedings*, Highway Research Board, National Research Council, Vol. 19, 1939, pp. 199–200.

17. Westergaard, H. M., "New Formulas for Stresses in Concrete Pavements of Airfields," *Transactions, American Society of Civil Engineers*, Vol. 113, 1948, p. 434.

18. Pickett, Gerald, and G. K. Ray, "Influence Charts for Concrete Pavements," *Transactions, American Society of Civil Engineers*, Vol. 116, 1949, p. 49.

19. Packard, R. G., "Computer Program for Airport Pavement Design," Skokie, Ill.: Portland Cement Association, 1967.

20. Cawley, Martin, L., "Concrete Pavement Performance at Ten Civil Airports," *Journal of the Aero-Space Transport Division, Proceedings of the American Society of Civil Engineers*, Vol. 92, No. AT2, Proceedings Paper 4981, November 1966.

21. Packard, Robert G., *Design of Concrete Airport Pavement*, Skokie, Ill.: Portland Cement Association, 1973.

22. *Rigid Pavements for Airfields Other Than Army*, U.S. Army Corps of Engineers, Document TM5-824-3, AFM 88-6, Departments of the Army and the Air Force, including Change No. 1, November 1973.

23. *Aerodrome Design Manual*, Part 3, Pavements, 1st Ed, Montreal: International Civil Aviation Organization, 1977.

24. Martin, Frederick R., Raymond F. A. Judge, and Maurice B. Chammings, "Design and Evaluation of Aircraft Pavements—1971," *Transportation Engineering Journal*, American Society of Civil Engineers, November 1973.

25. *Design and Evaluation of Aircraft Pavements 1971*, Department of the Environment, Property Services Agency, Croydon, United Kingdom: Directorate of Civil Engineering Services, 1971.

11

AIRPORT ACCESS

11.1 THE ACCESS PROBLEM

In the early days of aviation the access trip presented no substantial problem to the air traveler. The typical airport or "aerodrome" of the 1920s and 1930s was sited on the periphery of the town it served. The relatively high cost of air travel meant that only a few individuals used the mode, in comparison with the large numbers using the railroad for intercity travel. These few travelers could reach the airport by car, driving over the relatively lightly traveled roads with low traffic volumes associated with urban fringe areas before World War II. After the war, access to airports was very much affected by the separate impacts of rapid urbanization, the trend to almost universal car ownership, and the fall in real air travel costs brought about by the introduction of aircraft of an advanced technology. Currently, a typical access journey for a traveler unable to use a direct special-purpose route involves travel by either auto or bus over congested suburban roads to an airport complex that has suffered continuous encroachment of suburban development. On arrival at the airport, the traveler is confronted with a high volume interface bearing little resemblence to the informal air terminal of prewar days.

Figure 11.1, indicates the scale of changes in first-origin to final-destination times for a short haul trip over the last 35 years. It is shown that potential time savings brought about by the introduction of jet aircraft have been partially or wholly negated by increases in surface access and terminal processing time, and this is the essence of the problem. Clearly, the impact of poor access has maximum implications for short haul trips, where the proportion of access time to the overall trip time is high.

Definition of Access

There are no precise points marking where the access trip begins and where it ends. The designer cannot assume that the access trip is over once the air passenger has arrived in the general vicinity of the air terminal. Satisfactory

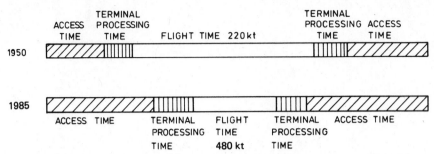

FIGURE 11.1 Comparison of short haul city-center to city-center travel, 1950–1985.

design of the access system entails integrated care for the passenger's needs from the origin point of the trip until the beginning of terminal processing. Movement during terminal processing is normally regarded as a function of terminal design, but the better terminal designs have integrated consideration of access and terminal processing to ensure smooth interfacing of the submodes of the total air journey. In preparing the design of access systems, there are usually three major areas of consideration:

1. The collection and processing of passengers and cargo in the central area of the city and other centers of high demand.
2. The movement of passengers, cargo, and service traffic to the airport by surface or air vehicles.
3. Distribution of access traffic and internal circulation traffic to terminals and gate positions.

Access for Whom?

In planning an access system, the planner should discard the misconception that airport access is for air travelers only; in fact, at many airports the travelers may be in the minority. The airport population is diverse, and any access mode must serve a number of disparate users:

Air travelers.
Senders and greeters.
Visitors.
Employees.
Air cargo access personnel.
Persons who supply services to airport.

The split of airport population between the various groups varies greatly between airports and depends on such factors as the airport size and function, the country of location, and such considerations as the number and size of based air carriers. Table 11.1 gives the estimated proportions of the various elements of the airport population for a number of facilities.

In the early 1980s, many of the world's largest airports employed very large numbers of workers: for example, London Heathrow, 48,000; San Francisco, 29,300; Atlanta, 30,000; and New York JFK, 41,000. These figures are equivalent to the entire population of a substantial town, and generate the number of work trips equivalent to the central business district of a city of close to a quarter of a million persons. A study carried out by the Los Angeles International Airport showed that the airport generated over 120,000 vehicle trips in and out of the central terminal area alone in the early 1980s. Clearly, the design of a movement system of this magnitude is a major consideration in the selection of a suitable airport site, and in the overall planning and design of any facility on the chosen location.

The Access System

The complexity of the access system and the scale of fiscal and spatial demand that system design can place on the airport planner is sketched in Figure 11.2. For the sake of simplicity, the system users considered are the "individuals" requiring access provision: passengers, visitors, and employees (air cargo is not shown). The requirements of in-town terminals, out-of-town or satellite

Table 11.1 Proportion of Passengers, Workers, Visitors, and Senders/
Greeters at Selected Airports[a]

Airport	Passengers	Senders and Greeters	Workers	Visitors
Frankfurt	0.60	0.06	0.29	0.05
Vienna	0.51	0.22	0.19	0.08
Paris–Orly	0.62	0.07	0.23	0.08
Amsterdam	0.41	0.23	0.28	0.08
Toronto	0.38	0.54	0.08	Not included
Atlanta	0.39	0.26	0.09	0.26
Los Angeles	0.42	0.46	0.12	Not included
New York–JFK	0.37	0.48	0.15	Not included
Bogota	0.21	0.42	0.36	Negligible
Mexico City	0.35	0.52	0.13	Negligible
Curaçao	0.25	0.64	0.08	0.03
Tokyo–Haneda	0.66	0.11	0.17	0.06
Singapore–Paya Labar	0.23	0.61	0.16	Negligible
Melbourne	0.46	0.32	0.14	0.08
U.S. Airports[b]	0.33–0.56	—	0.11–0.16	.31–.42 (includes senders and greeters)

[a] Derived from Institute of Air Transport Survey, July 1979.
[b] Reference (1).

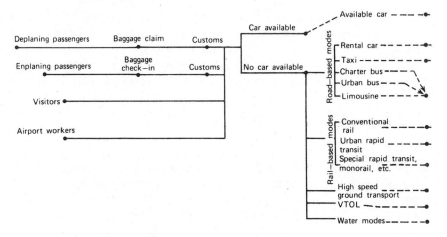

FIGURE 11.2   The access system.

terminals, and terminals at the airport are represented for a variety of modes. The infrastructure specified depends on whether a car is available to the individual. Road modes seldom cater to less than 70% of all access trips, but the airport designer should be aware that even in the United States, with the world's highest car ownership, approximately a quarter of the population has no available car. Implicitly, therefore, some public transport is necessary at all reasonably sized air carrier airports. The conventional solutions are limousine, special car, or bus service, which places minimal additional infrastructure demand on a system essentially designed for private automobile access. In very large airports, however, access by auto and limousine only is prohibitively expensive from the viewpoint of adequate access roads beyond the airport boundary, even neglecting the substantial problems that would result from the internal circulation generated. At these airports, mass transit facilities must be provided on and off the airport to permit higher density access movements, and Figure 11.2 shows that the infrastructure requirements for the higher density systems, such as conventional rail (e.g., London-Gatwick and Brussels) or urban rapid transit (e.g., Cleveland and London-Heathrow) are substantial, requiring careful site planning.

11.2   THE SYSTEMS ANALYSIS APPROACH TO ACCESS MODE SELECTION

Figure 11.3 presents a simplified conceptual model of the process by which the access mode is selected. Demand estimates over time for passengers,

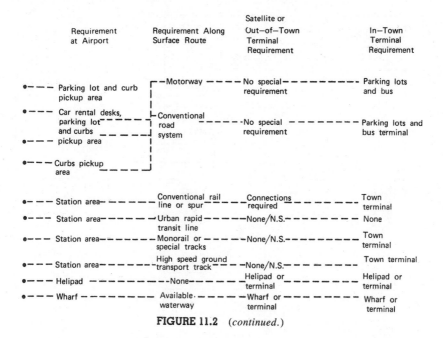

Requirement at Airport	Requirement Along Surface Route	Satellite or Out-of-Town Terminal Requirement	In-Town Terminal Requirement
Parking lot and curb pickup area	Motorway	No special requirement	Parking lots and bus
Car rental desks, parking lot and curbs pickup area	Conventional road system	No special requirement	Parking lots and bus terminal
Curbs pickup area			
Station area	Conventional rail line or spur	Connections required	Town terminal
Station area	Urban rapid transit line	None/N.S.	None
Station area	Monorail or special tracks	None/N.S.	Town terminal
Station area	High speed ground transport track	None/N.S.	Town terminal
Helipad	None	Helipad or terminal	Helipad or terminal
Wharf	Available waterway	Wharf or terminal	Wharf or terminal

FIGURE 11.2 *(continued.)*

employees, services, visitors, and freight are determined from available origin-destination data. Unless a special survey has been carried out at the airport, reliable data will be difficult to obtain. In such cases and, of course, for "green field" sites, synthetic origin–destination patterns must often be constructed.

To determine the type of access network to be assessed, some assumptions must next be made on the nature, location, and scale of the terminal interchanges to be provided, both at the airport and at other points, such as satellite access terminals or in-town access terminals (e.g., the East Side Terminal in New York, the West London Terminal in London). The next stage is to identify possible mode options, with sufficient definition to allow a reasonable estimate of modal characteristics with respect to cost and general levels of service. At this time the possible harmful effects of access modes, usually in terms of socioeconomic impact, can be enumerated for the individual options. One of the principal arguments against the expansion of London-Heathrow airport by the provision of a fifth terminal was the difficulty of absorbing the additional number of airport access trips on the existing road network, which was considered to be incapable of further expansion.

On the basis of modal split models, either calibrated on existing access data or synthesized from relevant experience elsewhere, competing mode options can be evaluated in terms of ridership and the socioeconomic implications. Normally, the most satisfactory mode option or a combination of modes is accepted for detailed planning and design. If no option or combination appears to be satisfactory, recycling (i.e., changing the network assumed for terminal interchanges and subsequent mode characteristics) is necessary. Eventually,

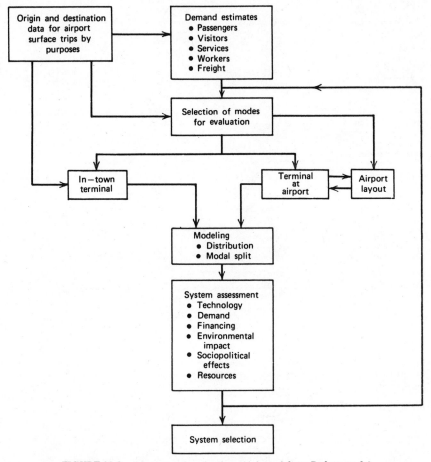

FIGURE 11.3   Access mode selection. (Adapted from Reference 2.)

at least one "optimal" solution is achieved, which meets all assessment criteria. Where several are achieved, the "best" solution is accepted.

11.3   AVAILABLE ACCESS MODES

To suit the variety of needs of airport users, and to match the various airport situations, a number of access modes are available or can be designed. Although the auto mode dominates nationally, no single mode of transport qualifies as the one most suitable access mode for the line haul air journey. It is worthwhile examining some of the advantages and disadvantages of various modes used in airport access plans.

Automobile

The most prevalent mode of airport access in the United States and in other developed countries is the personal automobile. The attractiveness of the mode stems from its great flexibility, with the strong convenience factor of direct origin-destination movement, especially where the air traveler is inconvenienced by large amounts of baggage. Overall access journey speeds are potentially high, especially where the nonairport end of the trip is not located in the central city area; when parking at the airport is required for relatively short periods, journeys can be made relatively inexpensively by auto.

The principal disadvantage of this mode of access is the high degree of surface congestion caused by individual cars on access routes, the high interaction with nonairport traffic, and the associated high level of parking infrastructure required at the airport. The mode can also be unreliable when congestion builds up, causing jams and slow moving traffic along access routes. Since airport access by auto shares the general surface transport infrastructure, this mode is vulnerable to delays caused by traffic that is not associated with the airport. Parking in the immediate vicinity of major airports is usually so expensive that most long term parkers are forced to use cheaper remote parking outside the airport boundaries. Use of such parking can materially affect access times and may seriously lower the level of convenience afforded by the overall access mode. Parking costs can be so great at airports that for some air travellers the cost will affect the choice of access mode.

The Predominance of the Automobile as the Access Mode. The vast majority of the airports that will be in use in developed countries at the end of this century are now in operation and are already closely linked with existing transport infrastructure. In the United States, some new airports will doubtless be required to serve those great metropolitan centers where population growth is substantial. These are expected to be very few in number. Other cities will increase the capacity of existing facilities at their airports rather than attempt to locate new facilities in "green field" sites. This is also very much the case in Europe, where population densities are high and airport authorities face strong local opposition to the environmental intrusion caused by the construction of an airport. Therefore, many of the access problems facing the existing airports will continue well into the future.

Possible Solutions. It is frequently suggested that high speed, dedicated rapid transit shuttles, operating between the airport and the central city, would solve the problem of airport access. Where such facilities have been provided, however, their performance often has been less than satisfactory (e.g., the monorail connecting central Tokyo with Haneda Airport). Moreover, the percentage of access trips made by way of these systems is only a small fraction of all access trips. Research has shown that even where special rail access facilities exist, in no case has more than 30% of access trips been carried, leaving 70% to be carried by road-based modes (3). Gatwick Airport (London) is an important exception to this rule.

The feasibility of high speed rail access has been studied in the United States and in Europe (4, 5). In the United States, the access situation was investigated at the 20 busiest airports. In the United Kingdom, the major regional* airports were examined, excluding the five airports serving the London area where the economic and environmental problems associated with dedicated high speed routes are so great that a solution of this type is ruled out almost automatically.

Table 11.2 gives some of the data relating to access to a number of airports in the United States and in the United Kingdom. The parameters of the access problem become clear from an examination of this table. The attractiveness of the central business district (CBD) is relatively low, increasing slowly with the size of the metropolitan area served. In general, however, the origins and destinations of access trips are found to be widely spread across the urban region, indicating that the special airport-CBD link can serve only a limited proportion of all trips. Where special public transport is provided, its usage tends to be quite limited, leaving a large proportion of trips to be made by auto and taxi. Most airports already have freeway access routes linking with either the interstate or motorway systems.

Taxicab

Taxicabs are a frequently used mode of access to airports, especially where the airport attracts a high proportion of business traffic and the distance between airport and central city is not high (e.g., Washington National Airport). Being direct from origin to destination, with easy baggage handling, the mode offers a high level of convenience. Under most conditions, the overall trip speed is high, and if several people travel together, the cost per capita can be considerably lower than for single cab occupancy.

In general, however, the taxicab mode is relatively expensive for the single traveler. Moreover, since taxis must share the existing road transport infrastructure, they are also vulnerable to surface congestion from nonairport traffic, and the trip may be slow. Taxis themselves tend to cause access congestion, since the rate of passenger loading is often quite low in comparison with the road space required.

Charter Bus

Access to many European airports is gained by specially chartered buses that serve the chartered air flights. These buses are nonstop from their origin, thus offering a reasonably high level of service. Since load factors are high, costs of access are low; costs are usually hidden in the overall charter fare. Charter buses add little to surface access congestion.

* In Europe regional airports are airports of lesser magnitude, serving noncapital or provincial cities. American usage of the word "regional" in the context of airports usually designates a remote airport serving two or more metropolitan areas.

Their chief disadvantage as a specialized access mode is that since they share the road access routes, charter buses too are vulnerable to congestion and can be delayed considerably by traffic. Also, this specialized mode serves only a portion of the total access demand and is not generally available. Depending on the length of access trip, simply getting to the charter bus may present some inconvenience and difficulty to the traveler.

Urban Bus

In some cities, the airports can be accessed by conventional urban bus services, which form part of the overall bus route structure. This mode is very cheap and adds little to the overall congestion on access routes. In being integrated with the urban network, it can provide a high level of convenience for airport staff.

From the viewpoint of the air traveler, the mode is less convenient. Routing can be difficult, especially in a strange city, and maneuvering luggage in the presence of peak loads of nonairport passengers is demanding at best. Urban buses are recognizably delayed by urban congestion; frequently the scheduling and routing of the bus system is not particularly responsive to the needs of air travelers. Overall travel speeds are usually low because of frequent stops, and in general the service is bad. The mode, however, can be very useful for access trips made by airport-based workers.

Limousine and Special Bus

One of the most common forms of access mode is the limousine or special bus, which connects a limited number of pickup areas, usually in the central city area, with the airport. This mode has two principal advantages; it is reasonably cheap for the single passenger, although not necessarily for a large party traveling together, and it offers a high level of convenience for travelers originating in or near the central area.

The disadvantages of the mode are obvious. Limousines and special buses can serve only a few central locations with nonstop service. However, having no segregated right-of-way, the mode is highly sensitive to surface congestion and tends to be unreliable. The service frequency in all but high volume airports tends to be poor, consequently increasing overall access time. A significant disadvantage is that service usually requires the user to enter the central area (e.g., a railroad station) without regard to first origin or last destination, needlessly attracting additional traffic into already heavily trafficked areas. In some cities, limousine service is extended to demand destinations outside the central area, but the cost of extended service is normally significantly higher.

Conventional Railway

A limited number of airports are served by conventional railway lines (e.g., Frankfurt, Brussels, Zurich, and London–Gatwick). As a rule, railway access links consist of special-purpose short spur lines constructed to connect with

Table 11.2 Data on Access to Airports in Cities in the United States and in the United Kingdom

Airport	Distance to	Passengers Oriented to CBD(%)	Availability of Public Transit Modes, Including Limousine	Freeway/Motorway Access	Passengers Arriving by Auto or Taxi (%)
United States					
Chicago (O'Hare)	16.5	N/A	Yes	Yes	N/A
Los Angeles	11.0	15	Yes	Yes	N/A
New York (Kennedy)	11.5	47	Yes	Yes	N/A
Atlanta	7.5	24	Yes	Yes	N/A
San Francisco	12.0	25	Yes	Yes	N/A
New York (La Guardia)	5.5	63	Yes	Yes	N/A
Miami	10.0	35	Yes	Yes	N/A
Washington D.C. (National)	2.0	25	Yes	Yes	N/A
Boston (Logan)	2.5	14	Yes	Yes	N/A
Denver (Stapleton)	7.5	30	Yes	Yes	N/A
Detroit (Wayne County)	17.5	5	Yes	Yes	N/A
Newark	10.5	61	Yes	Yes	N/A
Philadelphia	6.3	14	Yes	Yes	N/A
Pittsburgh	12.0	21	Yes	Yes	N/A
St. Louis (Lambert Field)	12.5	10	Yes	Yes	N/A
Minneapolis–St. Paul	7.3	N/A	Yes	Yes	N/A
Cleveland (Hopkins)	10.7	N/A	Yes	Yes	N/A
Seattle–Tacoma	12.0	17	Yes	Yes	N/A
Houston	15.5	38	No	Yes	N/A

United Kingdom Regional
  Airports

Airport					
Blackpool	3	19	No	No	69
Leeds/Bradford	7	27	Yes	Partially	86
Liverpool	6	37	No	Yes	82
Manchester	8	15	Yes	Yes	84
Edinburgh	5	50	Yes	Yes	72
Glasgow	6	28	Yes	Yes	76
Prestwick	28	24	Yes	No	56
Belfast	12	43	Yes	No	85
Birmingham	7	29	Yes	Yes	29
Bristol	8	47	Yes	Partially	47
Cardiff	8	22	No	Yes	22
East Midlands	12	11	No	Yes	11
Newcastle	6	21	Yes	Yes	21

the existing rail network. Under such conditions, conventional rail access can be quite inexpensive. Since it is not subject to congestion from surface road traffic, the mode is usually reliable and free of delays. Conventional rail service, often direct, offers good rapid connection with the city center, as well as overall speeds higher than those provided by urban rapid transit systems having numerous and unavoidable station stops en route. Of great benefit, however, is the availability of service that does not entail additionally obtrusive transport infrastructure.

Conventional rail systems often give relatively poor overall access time in spite of good line speeds because of the infrequency of scheduled departures. In addition, use of the service usually requires departure from the central city; therefore, only the central area is well served by this mode. Furthermore, baggage-laden air passengers encounter some difficulty at central railway stations when mixed with other passenger traffic, including commuters at peak hour periods. Finally, the rail mode satisfies the access need only partially since another trip, by taxi or other means, is frequently required to bring the traveler from the railroad station to the airport. Conventional rail systems have proved most satisfactory where the in-town terminus provides easy access to an extensive urban distribution system: taxi, bus, or urban rapid transit.

Conventional Urban Rapid Transit

At some airports there is direct access at the air terminal into the metropolitan urban rapid transit system (e.g., the Cleveland subway and, at Heathrow, the London underground). This form of access mode has several significant advantages. Usually, the rapid transit system is a coordinated part of the overall city transit system, giving the air passenger reasonable access to a large portion of the urban area. Because the mode does not suffer from delays due to the surface road transport system, the air traveler has a reliable service that does not itself add to road traffic congestion. In the situations where airport rapid transit links have been built, they have consisted of short spurs to existing systems. Consequently, an inexpensive service can be provided without constructing obtrusive transport infrastructure. The percentage of air travelers carried by this mode is small, but the urban rapid transit is most useful for the carriage of airport workers and some categories of visitors. In the case of Heathrow, this convenience was a significant factor in the decision to build the underground extension.

Because most rapid transit systems are on a radial plan, airport links of this nature tend to serve central areas best, although not exclusively. As with urban buses, urban subway trains must make frequent stops en route, leading in many cases to high overall trip times and low overall speeds. And again, perhaps the biggest objection to this mode comes from the necessary mixing of urban commuter passengers with baggage-carrying airport parties. This gives air travelers severe difficulties at crowded central rapid transit stations where station design has not considered their needs and no porters are available.

A number of urban rapid transit lines have been connected to airports yet have failed to attrack a large ridership. This has been due often to design faults that involve the baggage-laden traveler with an interchange which may be inconvenient, slow, or even physically exhausting. The two chief faults appear to be:

1. The distance from the air terminal to the rail terminal is too far to walk with baggage, for example, Washington National airport.
2. The rail terminal, which is remote, is served by a shuttle bus, constituting a slow and inconvenient interchange, for example, New York (JFK Express), Paris (Orly–Rail), Boston.

Specialized Rail Systems and High Speed Ground Transport

Despite differences in performance characteristics and in kind, specialized rail systems and high speed ground transport systems can be discussed simultaneously in terms of advantages and disadvantages. Inherently, their functional characteristics are similar as far as the airport link is concerned. For the purpose of this discussion, high speed ground transport can be regarded like any mode with overall travel speeds in excess of conventional rail speeds of 60 mph average. Specialized links (e.g., the monorail link connecting Haneda Airport with downtown Tokyo) have been widely advocated but seldom constructed. Their attraction lies in the ability to provide rapid, nonstop, reliable service between the central city and the airport terminal at a level of comfort and convenience matching the air trip itself.

On careful examination, however, the disadvantages associated with dedicated systems become manifest. Such systems are likely to be very expensive, either overtly in the form of high fares, or covertly in the form of heavily subsidized total costs. Furthermore, systems as proposed or designed serve only the central city reasonably well; they therefore attract passenger traffic by other modes into the already congested city center. Transfer between other feeder and distribution systems at the central city terminal faces the baggage-impeded traveler with linkage problems with other modes.

Possibly the overriding difficulty associated with dedicated systems is the need for segregated rights-of-way through urban areas. This involves either prohibitively expensive tunneling or the construction of less expensive but environmentally obtrusive grade separated structures, for which there is little community support. The need for a segregated right-of-way increases with the size of the urban area; concomitantly, the right-of-way costs more, either directly or in environmental terms.

VTOL Links

The most rapid and congestion-free method of linking major air passenger generators with the airport is the use of vertical takeoff and landing (VTOL) aircraft. After the late 1940s, a federal subsidy encouraged helicopter operations in New York, Chicago, and Los Angeles. Later, in 1964, operations were begun at San Francisco. Each of these enterprises had an operational history that was less than satisfactory, being plagued with accidents, financial troubles, and inadequate demand (6). More successful was the NASA–Houston link in Texas and the Heathrow–Gatwick link between the two main London airports. Experience with helicopter airport access services indicate that two conditions help to contribute to their success—first, a significant physical barrier (such as the bodies of water around San Francisco or New York, or the poor road linkage between Heathrow and Gatwick); second, the presence of a system of airports within a major transportation hub. Two helicopter access systems were initiated in 1983 in the United States. In Los Angeles, a system initially serving four off-airport origins is to expand in time to eleven origins. In San Francisco, a trans-bay system operates to cut a difficult and time-consuming road journey to minutes.

Integrated VTOL systems have the advantage in that air passengers have a minimum of inconvenience from baggage transfer at the airport and if the nonairport end of the link is close to the final destination, the overall access time can be very low. Because of high individual passenger cost, VTOL links have drawn their customer support principally from business travelers.

Although service levels of VTOL links can be excellent, the chief drawback of this mode of access is its expense; fare levels are up to 10 times those of modes such as bus and limousine. Furthermore, the nature of the service is such that only a very few nonairport locations can be served, severely limiting the area coverage available. Obviously, the noise of helicopters in congested downtown areas makes this mode extremely intrusive environmentally. In the past, the demand for such an expensive premium service was low. Indeed, services have tended to be introduced and fairly rapidly abandoned because of inadequate demand. Only when demand is fairly high will environmental intrusion become a major factor.

Waterborne Modes

Where airports have direct access to a waterfront, waterborne modes have been used to transport people to the terminal. The intrinsic attraction of the waterborne modes is the lack of competition with road-based modes, and in a few cases, waterborne modes have a special scenic attraction for passengers— as, for example, at Venice Airport, where the approach by water gives the visitor the traditional view of the city rather than a more commonplace approach to the landside by car or bus. However, the initial promise of rapid access was not fulfilled as the mode was found to be inconvenient, serving only a limited number of potential air travelers and, in the case of one hovercraft experiment, performing this service unreliably (7).

11.4 IMPLICATIONS OF MODAL CHOICE MODELS

Some studies have been carried out to determine how modal choice operates in the selection of airport access mode. One model, calibrated in conjunction with the assessment of the feasibility of a rail link with Heathrow Airport, was of the form (8):

$$Y_1 = 98 - 40X_1 + 0.17X_2 \qquad (11.1)$$

where

Y = percentage of zonal trips made by public transport
X_1 = ratio of generalized cost by public transport to generalized cost by automobile in the zone*
X_2 = percentage of zonal access origins and destinations made by nonresidents of the zone

The form of the equation indicates that modal choice can be modeled by an equation that accounts for travel cost and travel time, and by a variable that serves as a surrogate for car availability. A satisfactory model of submodal choice was obtained in the form:

$$Y_2 = 90 - 40X_3 \qquad (11.2)$$

where

Y_2 = percentage of public transport trip by road-based mode
X_3 = ratio of generalized cost by road-based public modes to generalized cost by rail

It can be seen that, where the generalized costs for alternate public modes are similar, they are equally attractive.

A more generalized modal choice model is of the form:

$$P_k = \frac{e^{L_k(X_1 \ldots X_n)}}{\sum\limits_{\text{all } j} e^{L_j(X_1 \ldots X_n)}} \qquad (11.3)$$

where

P_k = percentage of trips by mode k
L_k = some generalized cost function in terms of variables, $X_i = X_1$ to X_n
X_i = variable to which a cost function can be ascribed, e.g., travel time, fares, out-of-pocket costs, parking, fuel, taxes, maintenance, and running costs.

---

* The generalized cost of the mode in this case constituted the marginal travel costs plus travel time costs, varying from $0.25 \times$ hourly wage for leisure purposes to $2 \times$ hourly wage for business trips.

Stopher has successfully calibrated a two-mode model in the form:

$$L_k = 0.701 + 0.031\Delta C + 0.0216\Delta T \qquad (11.4)$$

where

ΔC = travel cost difference
ΔT = travel time difference

Figure 11.4 shows the general form of the linear modal choice model of equation 11.2 (9). The graph indicates the effect, for typical journey costs, of positive and negative time savings for a 10 mi access trip (a typical figure for existing metropolitan airports). We find that the access trip is not particularly sensitive to savings in access time but is highly sensitive to overall changes in cost. Clearly, public transport is viable only when out-of-pocket costs are perceived to be considerably lower than costs for private transport, since most public transport modes have a built-in element of increased time costs due to greater access and waiting times.

Examination of Figure 11.5 reveals why high speed rail systems are feasible only for relatively long distances. The time savings for short access distances are so small that passengers are unlikely to be attracted away from the auto mode. However, large access distances are necessary only for airports serving very large urban areas such as New York, London, and Tokyo. Indeed this scale of urban area is necessary to generate a corridor of demand, where the level of ridership requires a dedicated right-of-way. Cities with urban populations

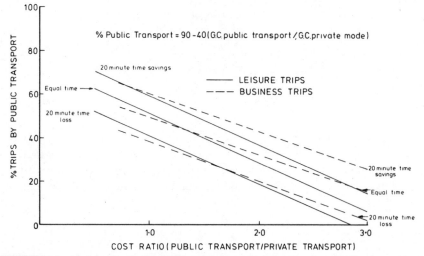

FIGURE 11.4 Modal split relationship for business and leisure trips: London Heathrow Airport. (*Source:* Reference 9.)

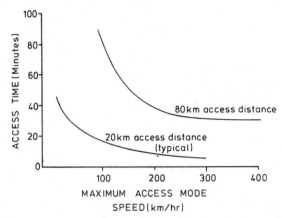

FIGURE 11.5 Comparative access times for different maximum access mode speeds. (*Source: Reference 9.*)

of 2 million or less are likely to have relatively low numbers of passengers whose prime origin or destination is the CBD itself.

Various estimates have indicated that an annual ridership of 3 to 5 million is necessary to make special access mode fares reasonably competitive with other forms of public transport or the automobile. However, the cost of providing dedicated rights-of-way from the periphery of a large metropolitan area to the CBD can be very large, and the level of urban disruption during the construction period will be severe. Cost estimates of providing rail service to Kennedy and Newark airports were in excess of $400 million for each scheme in 1973, even though existing tracks would have been used for a large part of the route in each case.

The level of social disruption that a ground-level dedicated-access rail system can cause can be inferred from an estimate that the special rail system to connect the Maplin site for the Third London Airport in the early 1970s would have required the demolition of a number of dwellings equaling two thirds of the annual number of houses built in the whole of the United Kingdom.

11.5 PARKING SPACE AT AIRPORTS

One of the greatest difficulties related to access is the determination of the location and number of parking spaces. Parking demand is a complex function of the number of persons accessing the airport, the available access modes, the type of air traveler, the parking cost, and the duration of the parking period, which is determined by the type of person making the trip, (i.e., traveler, worker, service personnel, or visitor). Demand from the travelers must be further categorized into business, leisure, long term, short term, and so on.

Table 11.3   Percentage of Total Passengers
Transferring at 14 U.S. Airports

Airport	Transfer Passengers (%)
Atlanta	73
Dallas–Fort Worth	50
Chicago	44
Philadelphia	37
Denver	43
New Orleans	32
Kansas City	32
San Francisco	17
Los Angeles	21
Miami	29
Minneapolis–St. Paul	27
Detroit	19
Boston	15
New York	21

Source: R. de Neufville, "Designing the Airport Terminal," *Airport Landside Capacity*, *Special Report No. 159*, Washington, D.C.: Transportation Research Board, 1975, and *Evidence to Heathrow–London Fifth Terminal Public Enquiry*, 1983.

It was noted earlier that air travelers may represent a minority of those entering the airport; the majority of the airport population may be visitors and workers.

Another complication in the estimation of demand arises because airports differ significantly with respect to the proportion of passengers coming into the transfer and transit category. Atlanta, for example, has a high number of annual enplanements, but Table 11.3 discloses that nearly three quarters of the passengers are transfers from other flights, requiring no landside access. On the other hand, cities such as New York and Detroit behave much more as terminals. Enplanements alone, therefore, cannot be used as a guide to parking requirements. Table 11.4, giving the relationship between availability of parking space and air passenger activity for a number of U.S. and foreign airports, indicates that there is a large variation about any normative line that could be derived for the relationship. Also shown on this graph is the FAA recommendation of 500 parking places per million annual passengers. An examination of a number of U.S. and European airports dealing with both domestic and international traffic indicated that the ratio varied between 350 and 570 parking places per million annual passengers in 1981 (10, 11).

At many large airports, the facilities can be categorized into short term parking, which is usually in the immediate vicinity of the terminal, and long term parking, which is often remote, even requiring some form of shuttle bus

Table 11.4 Magnitude of Parking Provisions—Various Airports

Airport	Total Passengers (Millions)	Total Enplane-ments (Interlines Excluded)	Places per 1000 Total Passengers	Places per 1000 Annual Enplane-ments (Interlines Excluded)
Baltimore (BWI)	3.77	1.31	1.20	3.45
Boston (BOS)	15.20	6.35	0.60	1.45
Chicago (ORD)	47.84	11.98	0.36	1.42
Dallas–Fort Worth (DFW)	22.58	8.50	0.64	1.71
New York (JFK)	26.98	9.72	0.49	1.36
New York (LGA)	18.39	8.52	0.40	0.86
Los Angeles (LAX)	34.92	13.17	0.57	1.51
Miami (MIA)	19.63	5.25	0.28	1.06
New York (EWR)	9.30	4.30	1.24	2.68
Oakland (OAK)	2.68	1.32	1.33	2.69
San Francisco (SFO)	23.05	9.74	0.43	1.03
Washington D.C. (DCA)	14.28	5.37	0.30	0.81
Charles de Gaulle Paris (CDG)	9.99	—	0.53	
Dusseldorf (DUS)	6.85	3.24	1.21	2.56
Frankfurt (FRA)	16.64	4.72	0.50	1.78
London-Gatwick (LGW)	8.70	4.08	1.24	2.65
London (LHR)	27.98	11.68	0.36	0.86
Montreal (YUL) (Dorval)	6.15	—	0.59	—
Montreal (YMX) (Mirabel)	1.53	—	2.29	—
Orly–Paris (ORY)	14.78	5.96	0.53	1.32
Tokyo (HND) (Hameda)	20.54	—	0.11	—
Tokyo (NRT) (Narita)	7.26	—	0.45	—
Toronto (YYZ)	13.71	4.92	0.62	1.73
Vienna (VIE)	2.77	1.09	0.69	1.74
Zurich (ZRH)	7.51	2.54	1.11	3.27

Source: Reference (5).

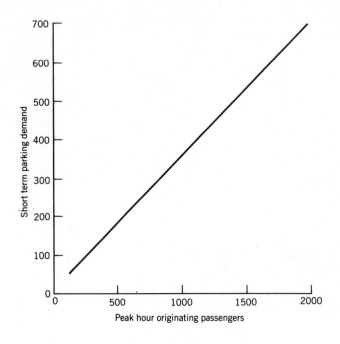

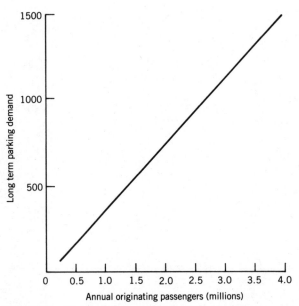

FIGURE 11.6 (a) Relationship between short term parking demand and peak hour passengers. (*Source:* Reference 12.) (b) Relationship between long term parking demand and annual passengers. (*Source:* Reference 12.)

service. Whitlock has produced design graphs that relate short term requirements to peak hourly passenger flows, and long term requirements to annual throughput, as shown in Figures 11.6 a and b (12). It is normal to price these facilities differentially in order to encourage high turnover in the short term area. The amounts of short term and long term parking provided will also depend on the geometry of the airport and the availability of land in the terminal area. Clearly, parking location will interact with the design of the internal circulation roads.

There is no single answer to the actual demand for parking facilities at an airport. Pricing policy will be a strong determinant of demand; some airports on restricted sites purposefully set charges at levels that deter parking and encourage the use of public transportation, including taxis. To ensure the adequacy of parking provision, a special study of airport access traffic must be made so that the various sectors of access traffic can be projected. Only then can a detailed plan be prepared to provide an acceptable level of parking availability.

11.6 CURBFRONT DESIGN

For space estimates in the master planning process, the length of drop-off/ pick-up curbfront can be estimated at 120 ft (35m) per million originating or destined passengers; for purposes of curbfront planning, transit and transfer passengers can be ignored (12, 13). More accurate design figures can be obtained by estimating the total demand for curbfront from a detailed breakdown of traffic type and subsequent requirements in space minutes (13). This approach can be illustrated by the following example:

Table 11.5   Curbfront Requirements at Fort Lauderdale–Hollywood Airport

Vehicle Type	Vehicle Length (ft)	Average dwell-time		Curbfront Required	
		Enplaning (min:sec)	Deplaning (min:sec)	Enplaning (ft min)	Deplaning (ft min)
Private auto	25	2:10	2:50	55	70
Taxi	25	1:15	2:10	30	55
Limousine	35	3:00	6:40	105	230
Courtesy vehicle	40	1:20	3:00	45	105
Bus	40	4:30	6:40	180	265
Other	35	6:00	3:10	210	110

Source: Reference (13).

Example 11.1

Vehicle Type	Peak Enplaning Volume	Peak Deplaning Volume
Private auto	300	350
Taxi	50	70
Limousine	20	20
Courtesy vehicle	10	10
Bus	10	10
Other	20	30

Using the figures in Table 11.5, which show the total number of foot minutes required for each vehicle type, the following can be computed:

Vehicle Type	Peak Enplaning (ft min)	Peak Deplaning (ft min)
Private auto	16,500	24,500
Taxi	1,500	3,850
Limousine	2,100	4,600
Courtesy vehicle	450	1,050
Bus	1,800	2,650
Other	4,200	3,300
	26,550	39,950

In theory, one lineal foot of curb space can provide 60 ft. min. of capacity in one hour. Cherwony and Zabawski indicate that the practical capacity of a facility is only 60% of this figure, or 42 ft min.

$$\text{Hence, the enplaning frontage required} = \frac{26,550}{42} = 632 \text{ ft}$$

$$\text{and deplaning frontage required} = \frac{39,950}{42} = 951 \text{ ft}$$

Since the enplaning and deplaning peaks are unlikely to occur in the same operational hour, where there is one level of curbfront for both pick-up and drop-off, the total required would be less than 1583 lin ft (632 + 951). For unilevel operation, the flows in both directions should be calculated for the peak enplaning hour and the peak deplaning hour. Using the same procedure as outlined above, the maximum lineal curbfront obtained from the two calculations should be used for design purposes. It must be emphasized that, in order to use this approach, the figures contained in Table 11.5 must be in general agreement with conditions found to operate at the airport under consideration, *or* the designer must generate his or her own values from observations on vehicle length and dwell time.

11.7 SUMMARY

In the medium term (5–10 years), airport planners must realize that the principal access mode will continue to be the private auto on roads serving the general urban area. The inconvenience caused by shared right-of-way is not sufficient to merit the construction of dedicated access modes. With growing volumes of access traffic over the years, it may be possible to improve access service by the use of access buses operating on reserved bus lanes, at least in peak hours. Some traffic not destined for the central business district can be served by satellite suburban terminals at convenient points on the metropolitan highway system; to avoid an undue staff burden to the airlines, these would be operated by airport authority staff, giving common facilitation for all airlines. To prevent severe congestion of surface roads, it is better to limit the capacity of available parking rather than attempt to restrict demand by means of high parking charges. Both European and North American experience indicates that for business travelers, there is little elasticity of parking demand with respect to price. This applies only to travelers requiring long term parking, for example, vacation traffic.

Where airports can be connected to existing urban rapid transit networks, such links should be provided. Connecting the airport to a network, rather than providing a point-to-point link, offers the unencumbered traveler a reasonable alternative to the car. Equally, the airport worker in the long term is more likely to locate at a point where he or she can be served by public transport.

Finally, it must be acknowledged that access potentially constitutes the most severe capacity limitation to airport operation. Some observers, for example, have indicated that such is the case for Los Angeles International Airport (1). Therefore, care is essential in siting the airport, to ensure that the necessary access capacity can be provided throughout the life of the airport, up to the level of ultimate development, in accordance with the demands of the airport master plan.

REFERENCES

1. Ashford, N., H. P. M. Stanton and C. A. Moore, *Airport Operations*, New York: Wiley-Interscience, 1984.

2. Mullet, L. B., and P. J. Corcoran, "Access to Airports" in *Airports for the Eighties: Proceedings of the Fourth World Airport Conference*, London: Institution of Civil Engineers, 1973.

3. Block, J., "Airports, Towns, Hinterland," in *The Airport, Access by Air and Land*, Paris: Proceedings Institute of Air Transport Conference, 1972.

4. Whitlock, E. M., and D. B. Saunders, *Airport Access/Egress Systems Study*, Wilbur Smith and Associates, DOT-TSC-OST-73-32, September 1973.

5. *Institute of Air Transport Survey*, Paris: Institute of Air Transport, July 1979.

6. Dajani, J. S., and William J. Schneider, "Role of Helicopters in Airport Access," *Transportation Engineering Journal*, New York: American Society of Civil Engineers, November 1978.

7. Homburger, W. S. (Ed.), *Urban Mass Transit Planning*, Berkeley, California: Institute of Transportation and Traffic Engineering, University of California, 1967.

8. *Report on a Study of Rail Links with Heathrow Airport*, London: Ministry of Transport, 1970.

9. Ashford, N. and P. McGinity, "Access to Airports Using High Speed Ground Transport," *High Speed Ground Transportation*, Vol. 9 No. 1., Spring 1975.

10. Ashford, N., *Evidence to the Terminal 5 Heathrow Airport Enquiry*, London: British Airways, BA81, 1982.

11. *Survey of Ground Access*, Los Angeles: U.S. Aviation Industry Group, 1981.

12. Whitlock, E. M. and E. F. Cleary, "Planning Ground Transportation Facilities," *Transportation Research Record No. 732*, Washington, D.C.: Transportation Research Board, 1976.

13. Cherwony, W. and Frank Zabawski, *Airport Terminal Curbfront Planning*, paper presented at Annual Meeting of the Transportation Research Board, Washington, D.C., 1983.

12

REQUIREMENTS OF V/STOL SYSTEMS

12.1 INTRODUCTION

In the late 1960s, a number of developments combined to create increased interest in vertical takeoff and landing (VTOL) and short takeoff and landing (STOL) aircraft. The need for larger and larger airports, the ever-increasing scarcity of available airport sites due to urban growth and sprawl, and the unabated growth in air travel had caused airport operators and aircraft manufacturers to look to V/STOL systems for relief. By diverting short haul air travelers away from major airports, it was envisioned that V/STOL systems could lessen congestion in the air, at airports, and on surface transportation access routes and parking lots.

By the 1970s, the congestion problem had slackened somewhat at most major airports, primarily because of a decrease in air traffic growth and the introduction of wide-bodied jets. Thus the advent of commercial STOL aircraft did not occur as originally anticipated, and VTOL activities are still limited to helicopters performing a variety of specialized functions. Nevertheless, as developing technology produces quieter, more efficient, and larger capacity V/STOL aircraft, an ever-increasing share of the short haul market will be served by these systems, and specialized airport facilities will become necessary.

This chapter considers some of the more important aspects of planning and design of VTOL and STOL airport facilities.

12.2 PLANNING AND DESIGN OF VTOL FACILITIES

VTOL Characteristics and Trends

The VTOL family of aircraft includes all aircraft that have the capability of landing and taking off vertically. It consists of helicopters, the dominant com-

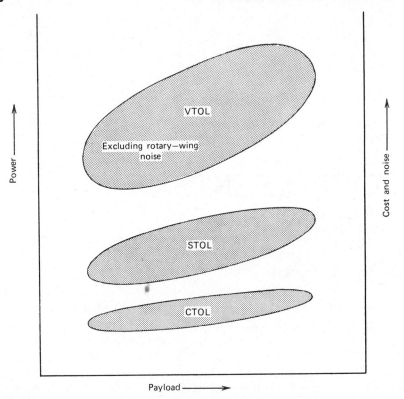

FIGURE 12.1 Basic technical and economic comparisons of various aircraft groups. (*Source:* Reference 2.)

ponent of the current VTOL fleet, plus aircraft in the research and development stages, in which a diversity of concepts (tilt wing, jet lift, etc.) may be called on to achieve vertical lift.

Although Leonardo da Vinci produced a conceptual design for a helicopter as early as about 1500, the first successful helicopters were not produced until 1923—by Pateras Pescara and Étienne Oemichen of France. In 1924, Oemichen's machine traveled 1 km with a payload of 200 kg. The first significant practical application of helicopters for military purposes occurred during the early 1940s, and civilian development followed World War II. Since that time, this versatile aircraft has been used for a wide range of activities including police and traffic patrols, fire fighting, crop seeding and fertilizing, search and rescue operations, and public transportation service.

The helicopter is a rotary wing aircraft that depends principally for its support and movement on the lift generated by one or more power-driven airfoils rotating on vertical axes. Its main value lies in its ability to hover and to fly sideways as well as forward. Because of its maneuverability and its ability to take off and land vertically, it can operate safely from clear areas little larger than the craft itself. Compared to conventional take off and landing (CTOL) and STOL aircraft, helicopters and other VTOL aircraft are costlier, noisier, and require more power for comparable payloads (see Figure 12.1).

Helicopters range in overall length from about 28 to 98 ft and in height from about 7 to 25 ft. The smallest helicopters have a capacity of two people and a maximum payload of about 550 lb. The largest helicopters are capable of transporting 40 or more passengers, plus a crew of three, and have a maximum payload of over 20,000 lb. According to the FAA (1), two- to five-place helicopters make up the majority of the civil helicopter fleet.

Helicopters are relatively slow; normal speeds range from 0 to 100 mph for small models to 0 to 185 mph for larger aircraft. Typical cruising altitude for helicopters is 1000 to 1500 ft, although many can fly at altitudes up to 10,000 ft above sea level. Helicopters are best suited for short haul transportation, typically serving trips up to about 75 mi. However, certain large models such as the Sikorsky S-65C are capable of transporting full passenger loads up to 300 mi.

Table 12.1 gives dimensions of typical small, medium, and large helicopters; Figure 12.2 illustrates popular helicopter configurations.

A number of innovative concepts are likely to be employed in future VTOL designs to provide increased operating speeds and range. For example, a wing

Table 12.1 Dimensions of Typical Helicopters

	Manufacturer and Model		
Data Item	Bell Helicopter Company 206B	Boeing-Vertol 107-II	Sikorsky Aircraft Company S-65
Overall length (ft)	38.8	83.1	88.2
Main rotor diameter (ft)	33.3	50.0	72.3
Overall height (ft)	9.5	16.9	24.9
Static clearance ground to main rotor (ft)	6.2	9.9	10.3
Tail rotor diameter (ft)	5.2	None	16.0
Wheel base (ft)	—	24.8	27.0
Tread (ft)	6.3	12.9	13.0
Static clearance ground to tail rotor (ft)	3.0	16.9	8.8
Wheel spacing (in.)	—	12.5	17.0
Turning radius (ft)	—	51.0	50.8
Number of seats	1 Crew, 4 passengers	3 Crew, 25 passengers	3 Crew, 44 passengers
Maximum payload (lb)	1,685	5,000	15,400
Maximum gross weight (lb)	3,350	22,000	42,00

Sources: Heliport Design Guide, FAA Advisory Circular AC 150/5390, 1B, August 22, 1977, and manufacturers' information.

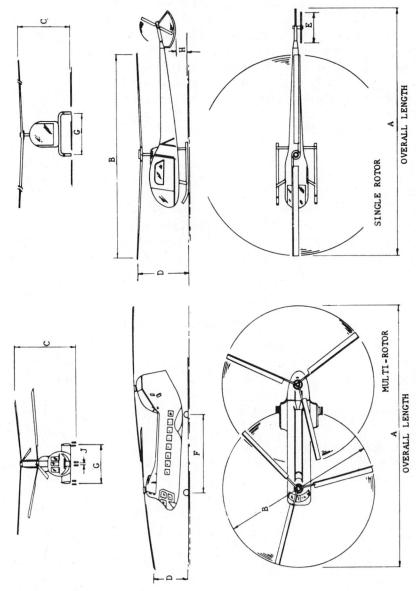

FIGURE 12.2 Typical helicopter configurations. (*Source*: Reference 1.)

could be added to provide lift at cruise speeds, resulting in an unloaded main rotor. This design is known as a *compound helicopter*. The design would offer improvements in both speed and range, but the added wing would increase the empty weight and, because of downwash on the wing, more rotor thrust would be required for VTOL.

A second proposed VTOL design, the *composite aircraft*, would rely for liftoff and descent on a rotor that would be stowed along the top of the fuselage

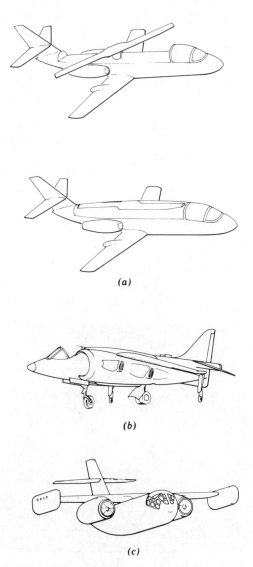

(a)

(b)

(c)

FIGURE 12.3 Innovative VTOL design concepts. (a) Composite aircraft in hover and cruise modes. (b) The Harrier vectored-thrust aircraft. (c) The Ryan XV-5B fan-in-wing aircraft. (*Source:* Reference 2.)

at cruise speeds. Forward thrust for the stowed rotor aircraft could be provided by either propeller or turbofan.

A third innovative concept for VTOL aircraft would omit the rotor completely. Lift would be provided by thrust vectored from the cruise engines. Alternatively, the cruise engines could be supplemented by lift engines in the wings to provide lift (Figure 12.3).

By the early 1980s, research and development of VTOL aircraft systems were progressing on a variety of fronts. Flight research and demonstration testing was being performed by Sikorsky Aircraft Division, United Technologies Corporation on the XH-59 helicopter. That experimental aircraft features two counterrotating rigid rotors mounted one above the other on a common shaft. This system permits the advancing side of both rotor discs to generate lift, offering high speeds without the need for a wing to offload the rotor. With two outboard engines for auxiliary thrust, this helicopter, pictured in Figure 12.4, has been tested at speeds of 240 kt in level flight.

A promising tilt rotor research aircraft, the XV-15, was being developed by Bell Helicopter Division of Textron. The tilt-rotor uses large helicopter rotors for vertical lift in the helicopter mode and for forward thrust in the airplane mode. When the rotors are tilted forward, a wing provides the lift. The tilt-rotor combines the hover efficiency and maneuverability of a helicopter with the cruise efficiency and speed of an airplane. In 1980, the tilt-rotor was tested at a speed of 301 kt in level flight. Figure 12.5 shows the tilt-rotor aircraft in hover and cruise modes.

Both derivatives of the XV-15 and all-new aircraft are being studied by the Bell Helicopter Division. An XV-15 derivative would have a gross weight of 15–18,000 pounds and a passenger capacity of 15 to 18. Capacities of all-new aircraft studied have ranged from 25 to 100 passengers.

FIGURE 12.4 The XH-59 experimental helicopter. (Courtesy United Technologies Sikorsky Aircraft.)

FIGURE 12.5   The XV-15 tilt rotor research aircraft. (a) Hover mode. (b) Cruise mode. (Courtesy Bell Helicopter Division of Textron, Inc.)

During the early 1980s, the McDonnell–Douglas Aircraft Company continued its development of the Harrier vectored thrust aircraft for the U.S. Marine Corps and the Royal Air Force. (See Figure 12.6.)

Although much of the research and development of VTOL systems has been supported by the military, it is expected to impact the future of civilian aviation as well. Nevertheless, by 1982, support from the civil sector remained low for anything other than helicopter developments (3).

FIGURE 12.6   The Harrier vectored thrust aircraft. (Courtesy McDonnell–Douglas Corporation.)

Classification of Heliports

A *heliport* is a prepared area that is used for landing and takeoff of helicopters. It may be either at ground level or elevated on a structure. A minimum facility heliport that does not have auxiliary facilities such as waiting room, hangar, parking, fueling, and maintenance is referred to as a *helistop*. Cleared areas normally used for other purposes can also accommodate occasional helicopter operations. Sites such as these are called "off-heliport landing areas," not heliports.

Heliports are classified by the FAA (1) into the following groups of usage and size:

Public-use
Private-use
Personal-use
Federal
Military

The public designation is an indication of use rather than ownership. A heliport that is used for public transportation is classed as a public-use heliport, regardless of ownership. At private-use heliports, usage is restricted to the owner or to persons authorized by the owner. Special use heliports that do not accommodate public transportation helicopters (e.g., police heliports) are classified as private-use even though publicly owned. Personal-use heliports are owned by individuals, companies, or corporations and are used exclusively by the owner. Federal heliports are those facilities operated by a nonmilitary agency or department of the U.S. government, while military heliports are operated by one of the uniformed services.

The extent of facilities at a public-use heliport may limit operations to helicopters of a specific size or weight. Heliports with complete support facilities, including maintenance and fueling, are capable of supporting helicopters in both the *normal* and *transport* categories.

Normal category helicopters are operated principally in private, business, charter, or commercial flying other than air carrier operations. These helicopters have a maximum gross weight of 6000 lb or less.

Transport category helicopters, which are operated in scheduled or non-scheduled passenger service, are single- or multiengine machines of unlimited maximum gross weight.

Selection of Heliport Sites

The versatility and maneuverability of the helicopter make it possible to operate such aircraft in congested and highly developed areas of a community. However, the potential of the helicopter's unique operating characteristics cannot be fully realized until an adequate system of heliports is provided. One of the most important aspects of planning and design of a system of heliports is the selection of appropriate sites. Site selection studies should be undertaken with the goal of maximizing user convenience, aircraft safety, and community acceptance. The first step should consist of the identification and analysis of available sources of information. Such a desk study should include the following components:

1. A review of available relevant studies (e.g., metropolitan airport system plan, comprehensive land use plan, and areawide transportation plan). Such studies may contain forecasts of land uses, trip origins and destinations, travel time data for surface transport, and other useful information.

2. An analysis of available wind data to determine desirable orientations for heliport approaches.

3. A study of National Geodetic Survey quadrangle sheets, road maps, and aeronautical charts, from which feasible sites are selected for further evaluation.

4. A study of land costs in the areas of interest. An aerial inspection of each site by helicopter can be especially helpful in evaluating possible obstacles to flight, available emergency landing locations along the approaches, wind turbulence, and other features relating to aerial navigation.

Finally, a detailed on-site inspection of each site under study should be made before a final comparison is made of alternative sites.

Heliport facilities do not require a large area and usually are inexpensive to construct because they need not be elaborate installations. Experience has shown that safe and useful heliports can be established by using a small sod or paved plot, fenced to exclude unauthorized personnel, and marked as to use. Roof-top or elevated heliports can be economically advantageous and usually do not involve high additional structural expense, especially if included in the original structural design of the building (4).

At least eight factors should be considered when analyzing potential sites for heliports. These are discussed in turn.

1. Class and layout of the heliport.
2. Convenience for users.
3. Airspace obstructions.
4. Coordination with other aircraft movements.
5. Direction of prevailing winds.
6. Social factors.
7. Turbulence.
8. Visibility.

Class and Layout of the Heliport.   The size or class of the heliport and the size of the largest helicopter to be served will determine the dimensions of the landing and takeoff area as described in the next section. The amount of space needed will be a determinant of the number of potentially suitable sites.

Convenience for Users.   Because helicopters provide a short haul transportation service, landing areas must be as close as possible to the actual origins and destinations of persons using the helicopters. Inordinate delays and inconvenience in accessing the helicopter service will negate the inherent time saving and convenience benefits of the helicopter. Special studies of traffic are recommended to identify areas of highest demand. Comparisons of total travel time with that of other modes will be helpful in making forecasts of helicopter usage.

Airspace Obstructions.   Physical objects such as buildings, poles, towers, and the like may be hazardous to helicopter flights. Thus a study must be made to identify potential hazards. Imaginary obstruction clearance planes have been published by the FAA, and their use is described in this chapter.

Coordination with Other Aircraft Movements.   In the interests of safety, FAA studies must be made to ensure that use of the proposed heliport sites would not interfere with landing and takeoff operations at any nearby airport.

This factor is especially important when the proposed site is at or near an existing airport, since the FAA must approve the use of airspace.

Direction of Prevailing Winds. Landing and takeoff operations by helicopters preferably should be made in the opposite direction of prevailing winds. To the extent that other factors permit, approach-departure surfaces should be oriented to aim landing and takeoff operations into the wind.

Social Factors. Many people consider the noise of helicopters to be objectionable. The need to locate heliports in close proximity to large concentrations of population makes the problem of helicopter noise especially difficult. In selecting a helicopter site, the planner should endeavor to minimize the effects of helicopter noise, especially in the area immediately surrounding the heliport.

Others may find heliports aesthetically unacceptable. The use of landscaping and well-designed service buildings will tend to overcome such objections.

Generally community zoning regulations permit the use of heliports in industrial, commercial, manufacturing, agricultural, and unzoned areas (1). However, it may be necessary to seek revision of the existing zoning regulations to permit the development of needed heliports. Restrictions on the heights of buildings in helicopter approach-departure paths should also be included in the zoning ordinance.

Turbulence. In the case of elevated heliports, nearby buildings or rooftop structures may cause troublesome wind turbulence, possibly necessitating flight tests to determine the nature and extent of the problem. It may be found that a certain potential site is acceptable most of the time, despite adverse turbulence in high winds. In such a case, the FAA suggests that the heliport be approved for use up to a predetermined wind velocity limit.

Visibility. The use of elevated heliports may be restricted because of low clouds, especially on buildings of 100 ft or higher. Fog, smoke, glare, and other restrictions to visibility may rule out the use of some potential heliport sites.

Layout and Design of Heliports

The size and shape of a heliport and the type of service facilities offered depend primarily on three factors:

1. The nature of the available site.
2. The size and performance characteristics of the helicopters to be served.
3. The number, size, and location of buildings and other objects in the vicinity of the heliport.

The principal operational components of the heliport are the touchdown area, the landing and takeoff area, the peripheral area, and the obstruction clearance surfaces, as illustrated in Figure 12.7.

Typically the touchdown area is a square, its sides should be approximately equal to the rotor diameter. A 20 × 20-ft touchdown area will probably be large enough for the smallest helicopters. The touchdown area should be capable of supporting the dynamic wheel loads of the helicopter.

The size of the landing and takeoff area is determined by the overall length of the critical helicopter. Its length and width should be 1.5 times the overall length of the largest helicopter to be accommodated.

The area bordering the landing and takeoff area is called the peripheral area. The minimum width of the peripheral area should be 10 ft or one-fourth the overall length of the helicopter, whichever is larger. Except for certain navigational aids, the peripheral area should be free of obstructions and activities that might interfere with helicopter operations. It is recommended that a safety barrier be erected along the outside edge of the peripheral area and the parking and service apron to exclude unauthorized persons.

In certain circumstances, parking spaces for helicopters may be required at private heliports, and at least two spaces normally are needed at public heliports. A special study of helicopter traffic may be necessary to determine the number of helicopter spaces required. The helicopter parking and service apron is usually located adjacent to the peripheral area. The length and width of each parking space should be equal to the overall length of the largest helicopter, and there should be a minimum clearance of 10 ft between spaces.

At public heliports, the level of helicopter traffic and the volume of passengers, mail, and cargo may justify the construction of one or more buildings to facilitate passenger and cargo movements and the service and storage of the aircraft.

Table 12.2 summarizes design criteria for heliports, including taxiway and shoulder widths, slopes and clearances to buildings, and obstacles, as recommended by the FAA.

These criteria do not apply to offshore helicopter facilities. Recommendations for the design of such facilities are given in Reference 1.

Approach-Departure Paths

The VFR obstruction clearance plane for heliports is part of Figure 12.4. The imaginary approach-departure surfaces shown make it possible to identify objects that may constitute a hazard to helicopter operations. The surfaces shown are applicable to all three classes of heliport.

Note that curved approach-departure paths are permitted. The FAA recommends that the curved path begin at least 300 ft from the landing and takeoff areas. The radius of curvature for the paths will depend on the operating characteristics of the helicopters, but will generally range from approximately 700 to about 1500 ft.

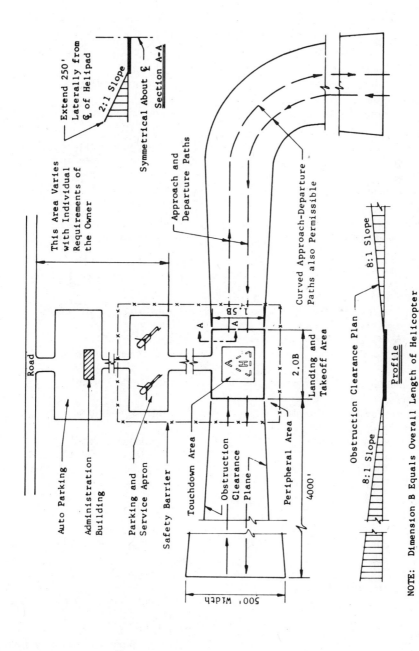

NOTE: Dimension B Equals Overall Length of Helicopter

FIGURE 12.7 Principal components of a heliport area. (Courtesy Federal Aviation Administration.)

369

Table 12.2 FAA Recommended Design Criteria for Heliports

Design Feature	Public-use	Private-use Personal-use
	Heliport Classification	
	Dimension	
Takeoff & Landing Area		
Length, width, diameter	1.5 × helicopter overall length	
Touchdown pad		
Length, width, diameter	1.0 × rotor diameter	
Minimum ground-level		
Length, diameter	2.0 × wheelbase	1.5 × wheelbase
Width	2.0 × tread	1.5 × tread
Minimum elevated		
Length, diameter	1.0 rotor dia.	1.5 × wheelbase
Width	1.0 rotor dia.	1.5 tread
Peripheral area		
Recommended width	¼ helicopter overall length	
Minimum width	10 feet (3 m)	
Taxiway		
Paved width	Variable, 20-foot (6 m) minimum	
Parking position		
Length, width, diameter	1.0 × helicopter overall length	
Pavement grades		
Touchdown pad, taxiways, parking positions	2.0 percent maximum	
Other grades		
Turf shoulders, infield area, etc.	Variable, 1½ to 3 percent	
Clearances, rotor tip to object		
Taxiways, parking positions	10-foot (3 m) minimum	
Helicopter primary surface		
Length, width, diameter	1.5 × helicopter overall length	
Elevation	Elevation highest point takeoff & landing area	
Helicopter approach surface		
Number of surfaces	Two	
Angular separation	90° min., 180° preferred	
Length	4,000 feet (1 220 m)	
Inner width	1.5 × helicopter overall length	
Outer width	500 feet (152 m)	
Slope	8:1	
Helicopter transitional surface		
Length	Full length of approaches and primary surface	
Width	250 feet (76 m) measured from approach & primary surface centerline	
Slope	2:1	

Source: Heliport Design Guide, FAA Advisory Circular AC 150/5390-1B, August 22, 1977.

It is suggested that at least two approach-departure paths be provided, separated by an angle of at least 90°. An angle of separation of at least 135° is recommended for large public heliports. Emergency landing areas, to be used by single-engine helicopters, should be provided along all approach-departure paths.

For precision IFR operations, tentative FAA guidelines call for a 300-ft primary surface, with approach-departure clearance surfaces flaring uniformly to 3400 ft width 10,000 ft from the landing area and having a slope of 15:1. Side transitional surfaces with 4:1 slopes extending laterally from the edge of the primary surface are recommended.

Marking of Heliports

Several marking configurations have been used to identify heliport facilities. The recommended marking for the landing and takeoff area, illustrated in Figure 12.8, consists of a segmented equilateral triangle surrounding a 10 ft high letter "H." This symbol also may be used with a solid segmented border 1.5 ft wide to define the touchdown area.

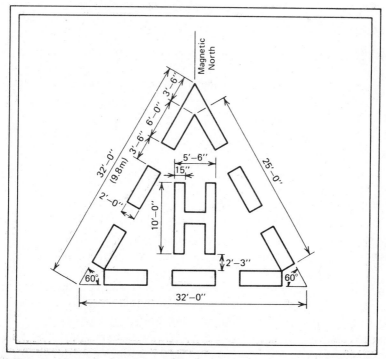

FIGURE 12.8 Recommended heliport marking. Standard marking dimensioned for a pad size of 90 ft or more; for pattern sizes of other than 75 ft, scale dimensions proportionately. (*Source:* Reference 1.)

Standard heliport identifier markings are white, but when placed on a light colored surface they should be outlined in black to make them more conspicuous.

Hospital helistops have traditionally been identified by a red cross on a white background with a red touchdown area border 1 ft wide. In this configuration a white "H" is superimposed on the center of the red cross.

A special symbol may be painted on the roofs of tall buildings to indicate where helicopters can land to evacuate persons in case of fire. The accepted symbol for this purpose is a red numeral at least 5 ft high, centered by a circular marking 2 ft wide. The numeral indicates the allowable gross weight of the helicopter loading in thousands of pounds.

Where the landing and takeoff area at a heliport is unpaved, it may be ringed by boundary markers similar to those used to outline segmented circles. Spacing of these markers may be 25 to 100 ft, depending on the size and configuration of the landing and takeoff area.

The FAA recommends that an 8 ft wind cone be located in a prominent but unobstructive place adjacent to the landing area. The color of the wind cone should contrast with its background, and it should be lighted if night operations are expected.

Taxiway centerline markings and apron parking position markings may also be necessary at busy heliports. These markings are typically yellow.

Lighting of Heliports

The lighting that is necessary at a given heliport depends on the size of the facility and the amount and nature of helicopter traffic that occurs at night. Six types of heliport lighting are described in the following paragraphs:

1. Identification beacon.
2. Obstruction lighting.
3. Perimeter lighting.
4. Landing direction lights.
5. Floodlighting.
6. Taxiway lights.

This listing is not intended to be exhaustive, but it includes the principal types of heliport lighting employed to facilitate helicopter operations during periods of darkness or poor visibility.

An identification beacon is recommended for heliports that are to be used at night, unless the heliport is a part of an airport. The FAA specifies that a heliport beacon have flashing lights coded green-yellow-white, and flashing 30 to 60 times a minute. It should be visible at night at a distance of 3 mi. The beacon should be located within 0.25 mi of a ground level heliport. In the case of elevated heliports, special efforts may be necessary in locating the beacon to avoid problems with glare.

All objects that penetrate the obstruction clearance surfaces described previously constitute a potential hazard to navigation. When it is not feasible to remove such obstructions, they should be marked and lighted in accordance with the publication *Obstruction Marking and Lighting* (5). If nighttime operations are anticipated, standard aviation red warning lights and beacons should be placed on towers, flagpoles, smokestacks, and other objects that penetrate the imaginary surfaces. Specifications on the number, type, and placement of obstruction lights are given in Reference 5.

As Figure 12.9 illustrates, the FAA specifies that five or more yellow lights be equally spaced along each side of the landing and takeoff area. The purpose of perimeter lighting is to positively identify the landing and takeoff area during darkness and times of poor visibility. These lights, which are considered necessary for nighttime helicopter operation, should be of low silhouette and should have a hemispherical light distribution and a power of at least 15 W (1).

Lines of five yellow landing direction lights may be employed, with spacing 2 to 15 ft. Selective illumination of these lines of lights communicate to the pilot the desired direction for landing and takeoffs.

Floodlighting may be used to improve the overall visibility of the heliport landing surface and to illuminate ramps, aprons, and taxiways. Care must be taken to ensure that floodlights do not dazzle or hinder pilots rather than aid

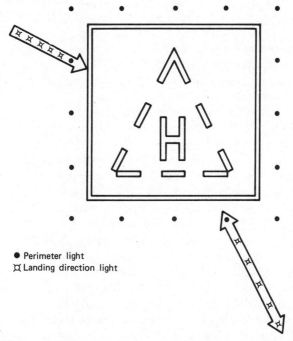

● Perimeter light
◻ Landing direction light

FIGURE 12.9 Heliport lighting configuration. (*Source:* Reference 1.)

them when taxiing or making a landing approach. Taxiway lights consist of omnidirectional blue lights that outline the usable limits of the taxiway route. These lights are usually located 10 ft beyond the edge of the taxiway.

Elevated Heliports

Heliports may suitably be located on rooftops of large buildings and on piers and other waterfront structures. Elevated heliport sites are especially desirable in heavily developed business districts, where open land is scarce and expensive, and buildings would interfere with operations at ground level sites. Elevated sites do not require the acquisition of additional land and may provide better accessibility for the helicopter traffic. On the other hand, suitable elevated sites may be difficult to locate and more costly to prepare than ground level sites, and may be less accessible to the helicopter users.

Landing pads for elevated airports come in two basic types:

1. Roof-level landing pads, which rest directly on the roof.
2. Raised landing pads, which are supported by columns or pedestals and framing that transmit the loads to existing building columns.

In either case, it is recommended that the height of the touchdown area be at least equal to that of the surrounding parapet walls, to provide adequate clearance to helicopters during landings and takeoffs. A safety net or fence at least 5 ft long should be installed around raised landing pads. It is recommended that the net begin below the surface of the touchdown area and not rise above it.

The obstruction clearance requirements described previously are applicable to elevated heliports. The designer should take special care to ensure that elevator shafts, air conditioner towers, and other rooftop structures do not interfere with safe helicopter operations.

The recommended dimensions of rooftop landing and takeoff areas are the same as for ground heliports. When a raised landing pad is used, however, its dimensions should not be less than 1.5 times the rotor diameter to avoid operational problems associated with loss of rotor downwash ground effect.

Many commercial buildings can support small helicopters without major structural modifications. A simple wood or metal pad to spread the concentrated loads over the existing structural members may be all that is required.

The roof landing surface should be designed so that it will not fail under impact loads of helicopters making a hard landing. To allow for the effects of impact, the FAA recommends designing the landing surface to support a concentrated load equal to 75% of the gross weight at each main landing gear (i.e., for dual-wheel configurations, 37.5% at each wheel of the gear). The loads should be applied over the footprint area of the tire or landing skid. For operational areas outside the touchdown area, the maximum static loads may be used in the design of the pad and structural framing.

The surface of the helicopter load-distribution pad or other platform should be solid so that the motor downwash will produce the maximum "ground cushion."

Elevated heliport landing facilities should be constructed of weather-resistant and fire-retardant materials. Arrangements should be made for the safe confinement and disposition of any flammable liquid spillage. The designer should, of course, comply with local building codes and fire regulations.

Heliport Pavement Design

Procedures for the design of heliport pavements differ only slightly from those used to design pavements for light to moderate sized CTOL aircraft. Although a paved surface for the landing and takeoff area is desirable, turf may be used for heliports that serve low volumes of small helicopters. It has been found that if the supporting soil is mechanically stabilized by the addition of granular materials, a turf surface may be suitable for helicopters with gross weights up to 10,000 lb.

The decision to pave the operational areas normally depends on the gross weight of the largest helicopter served, the number of helicopter operations, the local climatic conditions, and the size of wheel loads of the ground service equipment. The thickness of heliport pavements is determined primarily by the characteristics of the supporting soil and the gross aircraft weight. The procedures for the design of airport pavements described in Chapter 10 are generally applicable to the design of heliport pavements.

The downwash from helicopter rotors manifests itself in the form of undesirable erosive velocities. The magnitude of the downwash velocities and the extent of turbulence in the landing area are largely functions of the gross weight of the helicopter. Where large helicopters are to be served, areas in the immediate vicinity of the touchdown area and other areas where helicopters hover must be properly stabilized to control erosion of the surface. At public heliports, the FAA recommends that the entire landing and takeoff area be stabilized. If hover taxiing is to occur, it is suggested that a width equal to approximately twice the rotor diameter be stabilized along the proposed taxiway.

12.3 PLANNING AND DESIGN OF STOL FACILITIES

In recent years there has been a great deal of interest in short takeoff and landing (STOL) systems as a means of alleviating problems encountered at conventional airports. Fundamentally, the problems are those of overcrowding, from too many aircraft and too many people attempting to use an airport at the same time. Increasing congestion and delays have been experienced on the runways and aprons, in the terminals, and on the highway networks leading to the airport. One approach to reducing these delays is to provide STOL facilities to accommodate short haul demand. Such facilities may be added at congested CTOL airports or at separate, more convenient locations closer to the central city. The development of STOL ports should also be considered in outlying areas, especially where the terrain is too rugged to accommodate large conventional airports.

STOL Characteristics and Trends

Some STOL aircraft exist in concept only. Others have been extensively researched and flight tested. Yet by 1983, few of these aircraft had been placed in commercial service.

One approach to STOL service is to employ existing low-wing-loading turbopropeller aircraft. A prominent example of this type of aircraft is the de Havilland DHC-6 "Twin Otter," a twin-engine turboprop aircraft having a capacity of 20 passengers and a cruising speed of 200 mph.

The de Havilland Aircraft Company has also manufactured a larger STOL aircraft, the DCH-7 or "DASH-7" (6). This four-engine turboprop aircraft has a capacity of 50 passengers and a cruising speed of 266 mph. According to the manufacturer, very low noise levels are assured for the DCH-7 because of its large, slow turning propellers and moderate power requirements. In 1984, de Havilland will introduce the DASH-8, a wide-bodied, twin-engine turboprop aircraft with a capacity of 36 passengers and a cruising speed of 310 mph.

One of the shortcomings of existing STOL turboprop aircraft is a low ride quality, especially in gusty winds; this results from low wing loadings (~ 80 lb/ft^2). To improve ride quality, consideration has been given to the use of deflected slipstream turboprop aircraft such as the McDonnell-Douglas 188 transport. "High-lift short-field capacity is attained on this aircraft from large, full-span, triple-slotted trailing edge flaps which are completely immersed in and turn the slipstream from the propellers in a downward direction" (7).

Physical characteristics of selected STOL aircraft are listed in Table 12.3, as provided by the manufacturers.

Aircraft engineers have also studied the feasibility of developing a swept-wing fanjet STOL aircraft, to achieve higher cruising speed, larger capacity (typically 90 to 150 passengers), increased range, and a smoother ride. Such aircraft would attain higher wing loadings (and slower landing and takeoff speeds) by means of action of gas exhaust from the engines on a wing flap. Riebe explains:

> Basically, aircraft with powered-lift systems obtain short field length operation through low-speed flight resulting from generation of high lift on the wing through distribution of a sheet of high-momentum gas from the jet engines along the wing trailing edge and deflected downward by means of a trailing-edge flap. This concept, known as the jet flap, produces supercirculation about the wing, resulting in augmented lift that is added to the vertical component of the thrust vector of the high-momentum gas and the basic conventional wing lift (7).

Table 12.3 Physical Characteristics of Selected STOL Aircraft

Data Item	Aircraft Manufacturer and Model		
	DeHavilland Aircraft of Canada DHC-6 (turboprop)	DeHavilland Aircraft of Canada DHC-7 (turboprop)	McDonnell–Douglas DA-188F (turboprop)
Overall length (ft)	51.8	80.6	80.67
Wingspan (ft)	65.0	93.0	78.48
Overall height (ft)	18.6	26.2	33.16
Type of gear	Single wheel	Dual wheel	Dual wheel
Wheelbase (ft)	14.8	27.5	23.67
Tread (ft)	12.5	23.5	20.0
Wheel spacing (ft)	—	Main wheels: 16.5 in. centers, nose wheels: 14.5 in. centers	1.5
Maximum gross weight (lb)	12,500	44,000	58,422
Maximum static gear load (lb)	Main gear: 5,700 per gear, nose gear: 1,700 per gear	Main gear: 20,559 per gear, nose gear: 5,390	24,600 (main gear/side), 9222 (nose gear)
Maximum impact gear load (lb)	Main gear: 16,000, nose gear: 8,590	Main gear: 38,675 per gear, nose gear: 12,000	58,422 (side, main gear)
Horizontal braking load (lb)	Main gear: 6,650 per gear	Main gear: 9,125 per gear	14,600
Tire footprint area (in.^{2})	Main wheels: 120 in.^{2}/tire, nose wheels: 54 in.^{2}/tire	Main wheel: 30 × 10.00/12.96 in.^{2}/tire, nose wheel: 6.50-10, 20 in.^{2}/tire	109
Turning radius (ft)	41	64	50.75
Number of engines	2	4	4
Powerplant (type and hp)	Pratt & Whitney, PT6A-27, 620 shp	PT6A-50, 1035 shp	General Electric CT58-16, 1600 shp
Number of seats	2 crew, 20 passengers	4 crew, 48 passengers	4 crew, 72 passesngers
Fuel capacity (lb)	3,049	10,000	15,820
Maximum cargo capacity (lb)	5,561	12,000 (all cargo)	NA
Clearance ground to engine (ft)	4.5	10.75	11.25
Clearance ground to wing tip (ft)	9.4	13.25	16.92

Two basic variations of this concept, illustrated in Figure 12.10, have been proposed:

1. *Externally Blown Flap.*   The engine exhaust gas is maintained outside the wing.
2. *Internally Blown Flap.*   The exhaust gas is directed "through a ducting network in the wing to a narrow slot at the wing trailing edge, then downward through a flap system" (7).

A Douglas Aircraft Company report (2) expressed preference for the externally blown flap configuration because of its conventional design and low development risk. On the other hand, a Lockheed Aircraft Corporation report (8) recommended the development of a hybrid OTW/IBF (engines mounted over the wing with an internally blown flap) aircraft for runway lengths of 3000 ft or less. The Lockheed report concluded that the OTW/IBF configuration would give lower fuel consumption, better ride quality, greater speeds, and more potential for further improvement. The report further concluded that from the standpoint of direct operating costs and fuel consumption, the deflected slipstream (turboprop) aircraft would be advantageous.

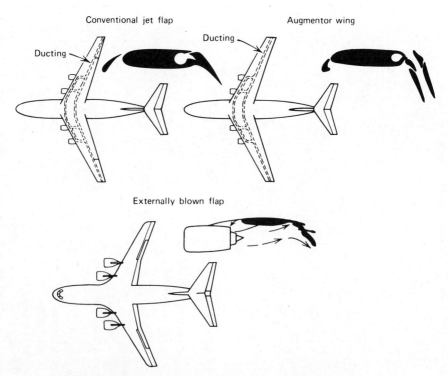

FIGURE 12.10   STOL high lift systems. (*Source:* Reference 7.)

Because aircraft noise is a primary factor in siting a STOL port, aircraft designers have attempted to develop quieter STOL aircraft. Notable progress in noise amelioration has been made by NASA and Boeing with the development of the Quiet Short-Haul Research Aircraft. Flight research and testing of that aircraft was being performed in the early 1980s (3).

STOL Port Location

Almost all the factors that should be considered in selecting a CTOL airport site are applicable in choosing a STOL port location (see Chapter 4). Some of the factors of special concern include the following:

1. *Air Safety Factors.* The air traffic generated by the STOL port must be separated from other air traffic in the area, both existing and proposed. VFR and IFR traffic procedures must be reviewed, and an airspace utilization study by the FAA is required. Each potential site must be evaluated to determine whether man-made or natural obstructions would be present that would adversely affect air safety.

2. *Land and Land Use Factors.* Clearly, a major consideration in the location of a STOL port is the availability and cost of land. Although much less land is required for a STOL port than for a conventional airport (16 to 50 acres vs. 5,000 to 10,000 acres), the desirability of choosing a site in close proximity to the users may make it difficult to identify suitable locations.

3. *Atmospheric Factors.* Atmospheric or climatological conditions that influence the selection to a STOL port site include direction and magnitude of winds (especially turbulence and crosswinds), temperatures, precipitation, and visibility.

4. *Engineering Factors.* The relevant engineering factors relate to the costs of construction and include such considerations as the ruggedness of the terrain (amount of earthwork), the quality of the foundation soil, the availability of construction materials, and problems of surface drainage.

5. *Social and Environmental Factors.* Perhaps the most important consideration is the compatibility of the STOL port with the users of neighboring property, especially with respect to noise.

Land uses that should be avoided are: residential, schools, hospitals, and noise-sensitive commercial land uses. On the other hand, land uses that are considered compatible are transportation ways; that is, railroads, highways, rivers, lakes; industrial, so long as they do not interfere with the airport through smoke or electronic signals, and also commercial and recreational uses to a certain extent (9).

It is important that the evaluation of STOL port sites be closely coordinated with the FAA, state and local governments, and members of the aviation community. In view of the desirability of locating STOL ports near centers of population, the need for participation of citizens groups in the planning process described earlier has special significance.

Layout and Design of STOL Ports

The general principles of airport layout and design given in Chapter 7 are applicable to STOL port design. However, there are major differences in scale between conventional airports and STOL ports. Table 12.4 lists the FAA's recommended design criteria for metropolitan STOL ports that assume bidirectional runway operations and a precision instrument approach. Figures 12.11 and 12.12 present typical ground level STOL port layouts.

A runway length of 1500 to 2000 ft is recommended for STOL operations from a paved surface at sea level and temperatures up to 90°F. The minimum runway length for a given STOL port depends on the FAA's air-worthiness standards, the performance characteristics of the aircraft, and its design mission. Runway lengths for STOL aircraft may be determined from performance curves similar to those in Figures 7.1 and 7.2, taking into consideration the STOL port elevation and temperature, and the aircraft weight.

Both STOL and R/STOL* aircraft have a direct operating cost (DOC) penalty that is a function of the available field length. The shorter the allowable landing and takeoff distance, the higher the DOC penalty. In terms of increase of DOC for a vehicle designed for a 6000 ft runway, the Lockheed study (8) indicated the use of the following penalties:

Field Length (ft)	DOC Penalty (%)
2000	24
3000	17
4000	3

These higher operating costs are, of course, offset by reductions due to lack of congestion and real estate and airport development costs.

In a study of quiet turbofan STOL aircraft for short haul transportation, a Douglas Aircraft Company report (10) concluded:

> The first generation STOL/short haul aircraft should be designed to no less than a 3000 foot field length and to a payload of 150 passengers or more. The economic penalties for designing to 1500 to 2000 foot field lengths are large and the definitive requirement for this type of STOL performance is not well substantiated.

STOL runways should be oriented parallel to the direction of prevailing winds. The designer should try to maximize wind coverage with an objective of at least 95% usability.

* Reduced/short takeoff and landing.

Table 12.4 STOL Port Design Criteria

Design Item	Recommended Criteria	Comment
Protection surfaces		
Primary surface length	Runway length plus 100 ft on each end	
Primary surface width	300 ft	Based on the use of microwave instrument approach equipment
Approach–departure surface length	10,000 ft	
Approach–departure surface slope	15:1	
Approach–departure surface width at:		Approach–departure surface is 765 ft wide at 1500 ft from beginning
Beginning	300 ft	
10,000 ft	3,400 ft	
Transitional surface slope	4:1	
Transitional surface maximum height	100 ft	
Clear zone		
Length	750 ft	
Inner width	300 ft	Begins at end of primary surface
Outer width	532 ft	
Pavement strength	150,000 lb gross weight on dual tandem gear	Based on second-generation aircraft

Source: Planning and Design Criteria for Metropolitan STOL Ports, FAA Advisory Circular AC 150/5300-8, including Change 1, April 3, 1975.

ANNUAL PASSENGERS: 2 - 5 MILLION

AREA: 37 ACRES

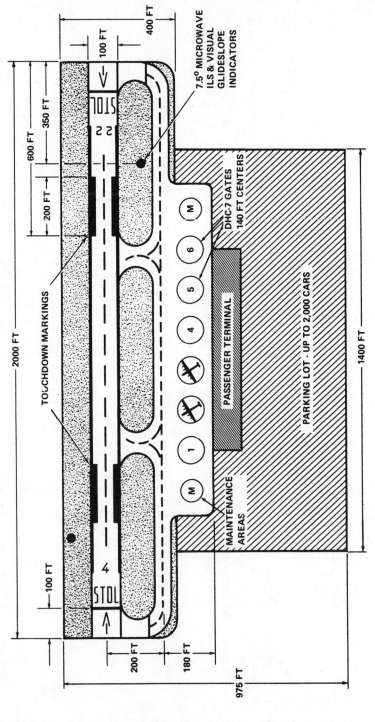

FIGURE 12.11 Typical high density ground level STOL port. (*Source:* Reference 11.)

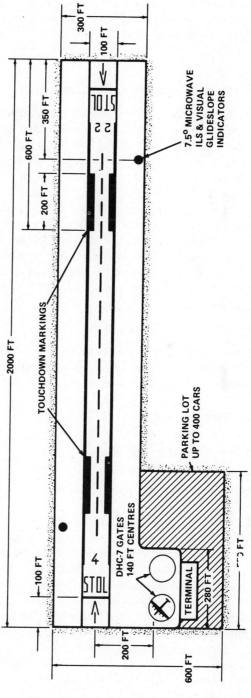

1/2 - 1 MILLION PASSENGERS ANNUALLY   17.5 ACRES   1 - 2 GATES

FIGURE 12.12 Typical low density ground level STOL port. (*Source:* Reference 11.)

The longitudinal slope of a STOL runway should not exceed 1% (9). For determination of pavement slopes, vertical curve lengths, and sight distances, the FAA recommends that the specifications for a general utility airport be employed.

Obstruction Clearance Requirements

Compared to criteria for a conventional airport, the imaginary obstruction clearance surface for a STOL port is characterized by steeper slopes and a much smaller area. As Figure 12.13 illustrates, the approach-departure surface has a 15:1 slope and the transition surface has a 4:1 slope. The length of a typical STOL protection surface is approximately one-fifth that of a CTOL surface (22,000 ft vs. 110,000 ft). The area of the STOL protection surface is only 1.5 mi^2, compared to 93 mi^2 for a CTOL protection surface (11).

The STOL port protection surfaces recommended by the FAA are based on operational tests with the microwave ILS (9). For VFR operations, a curved approach-departure path may be used. The radius of the curved path will depend on the performance characteristics of the aircraft. For planning purposes, a 1500 ft radius is suggested.

Visual Aids for STOL Ports

The recommended pavement markings for STOL ports (Figures 12.11 and 12.12) are similar to those used at conventional airports. The FAA (9) recommends five types of pavement marking:

1. Threshold markings.
2. Runway numbers.
3. Runway centerline marking.
4. Runway edge marking.
5. Touchdown aim point marking.

A transverse stripe 5 ft wide, extending across the end of the runway, is recommended to identify the threshold. Standard 60 ft "STOL" letters should be placed 20 ft from the end of the runway. Beginning 120 ft from each runway end, runway direction numbers should be installed. These are similar to conventional runway numbers but only half the size. A centerline marking 3 ft wide, similar to that used for CTOL runways, is recommended. Runway edge markings, also 3 ft wide, begin at points 120 ft from each runway as illustrated. Touchdown aim point marking consists of solid blocks, 20 ft wide and 200 ft long, placed alongside and including the runway edges, beginning 300 ft from the runway end.

The pavement markings are white, but they may be outlined with black to make them more conspicuous. STOL markings are not used at conventional airports where CTOL and STOL aircraft operate on the same runway.

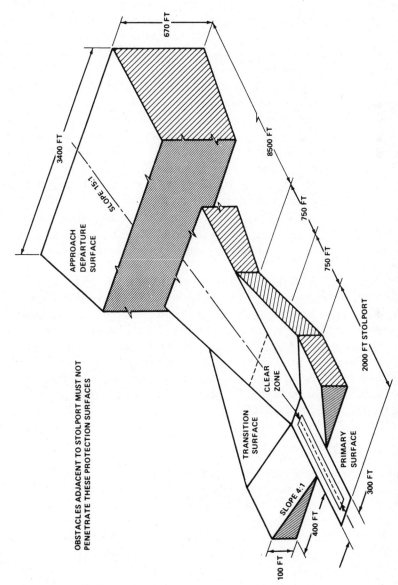

FIGURE 12.13 STOL port obstruction clearance requirements. (*Source:* Reference 11.)

385

The FAA (9) recommends the installation of the following types of runway lighting for STOL runways where instrument or night operations are expected.

1. *End Lighting.* A bar of seven lights installed across the end of the runway, spaced 5 ft apart. For runways with single direction operations, lights with red filters are used. For bidirectional operations, red filters signify the end of the runway, and yellow filters are used to identify the threshold for approaching pilots.

2. *Threshold Lighting.* Two wing bars symmetrically located about the runway centerline, each comprised of four lights. The threshold lights are in line with the end lighting. The innermost light for each bar is placed not more than 10 ft from the runway pavement edge. The lights are green in the direction of approach and red in the opposite direction.

3. *Edge Lighting.* Alternate yellow and white lights, placed not more than 10 ft from each edge of the runway, spaced 100 to 200 ft apart and extending the entire runway length.

4. *Distance-Remaining Lights.* Four lights installed along the runway centerline beginning 50 ft from the threshold. The lights are red in the direction of the rollout and blanked out to approaching pilots.

In addition, the FAA recommends the use of a runway end identifier light system (REILS) and visual approach slope indicators (VASI-2) at STOL ports. The location, glide path angle, and spread between the upwind and downwind units for the VASI-2 system should be especially tailored for STOL port use in accordance with FAA recommendations (9). Furthermore, a lighted wind direction indicator (wind cone) of a color that contrasts with its surroundings should be placed adjacent to the landing area. Standard blue edge taxiway lights are recommended for surface STOL ports, and green centerline taxiway lights are suggested for elevated STOL ports.

Elevated STOL Ports

Because of the scarcity and high cost of suitable ground level STOL port sites near urban areas, consideration should be given to such novel locations for STOL port sites as the tops of buildings, elevated structures over railroad yards, and floating sites along a waterfront. To make the designer aware of special operational problems that may be associated with the use of elevated sites, some of these problems are briefly described here, along with recommended remedial schemes.

An elevated STOL port site should be approximately 1700 to 2000 ft long and at least 300 ft wide. Where a parallel taxiway is needed, the structure should be at least 400 ft wide.

The runway threshold on elevated STOL ports should be located at least 100 ft inboard from the edge of the building to ensure that there are no hazardous undershoots. Special aircraft emergency arresting systems or barriers are required to prevent out-of-control aircraft from rolling off the structure. A number of containment concepts have been considered, but the most promising system seems to consist of cables stretched across the runway and connected to a damping device (7). To prevent passenger injury or discomfort, such a system should have a runout of at least 300 ft (9). Arresting gear of this type has been successfully utilized on aircraft carriers for a number of years. It could be actuated by the pilot by lowering an arresting hook. Automatic systems of this type have also been proposed to protect aircraft that swerve laterally off the runway.

Special design features may be required to help an aircraft decelerate and stop in periods of heavy rain, sleet, or snow. A relatively expensive but promising approach to preventing the accumulation of heavy rain or snow involves piping a heated solution of antifreeze and water 2 in. beneath a concrete runway surface. Grooving the runway surface is a tested means of significantly decreasing the required stopping distance under wet runway conditions.

Because of troublesome problems associated with wind turbulence and crosswinds, the FAA recommends an in-depth analysis of proposed elevated STOL ports to determine the wind effects under various conditions (9). Wind tunnel studies conducted by NASA indicate that the use of curved side overhangs on the edges of the STOL port can significantly reduce the turbulence in the runway area (7). In view of the need to operate with crosswinds up to 30 knots, NASA has also conducted wind tunnel investigations on means of reducing crosswinds along the runway surface. Preliminary results suggest that it is possible to reduce crosswinds at the runway centerline by means of porous fences or screens mounted along the side of the landing surface. Increasing the number of screens tends to reduce velocities at the centerline.

Finally, the designer must be especially aware of problems relating to the structural design of the elevated STOL port. In addition to the maximum static gear loadings, the designer must consider the dynamic loadings that come from the impact of a hard landing, the horizontal forces caused by the braking of an aircraft, and the forces that could be transmitted to the structure by the emergency arresting system stopping an aircraft. In addition, live loads due to snow, service equipment, and personnel must be taken into account.

REFERENCES

1. *Heliport Design Guide*, FAA Advisory Circular AC 150/5390-1B, including Change 1, May 18, 1979.

2. *A Brief Review of V/STOL Aircraft*, Douglas Aircraft Company, Report MDC-J0690/01, March 16, 1970.

3. Perkins, Russell G., "Aerospace Highlights 1981," *Astronautics and Aeronautics*, December, 1981.

4. *Heliport Manual*, 1st ed., Montreal: International Civil Aviation Organization Document 9261-AN/903, 1979.

5. *Obstruction Marking and Lighting*, FAA Advisory Circular AC 70/7460-1F, September 27, 1978.

6. *Dash 7* Aircraft Characteristics for Airport Planning, the de Havilland Aircraft of Canada, Ltd., April 1980.

7. Riebe, John M., "STOL Aircraft Flight and Landing Area Considerations," *American Society of Civil Engineers Transportation Engineering Journal*, Vol. TE2, May 1973.

8. Sweet, H. S., J. H. Renshae, and M. K. Bowden, *Evaluation of Advanced Lift Concepts and Potential Fuel Conservation for Short-Haul Aircraft*, Washington, D.C.: prepared by Lockheed Aircraft Corporation for NASA, September 1974.

9. *Planning and Design Criteria for Metropolitan STOL Ports*, FAA Advisory Circular AC 150/5300-8, including CHG 1, April 3, 1975.

10. *Study of Quiet Turbofan STOL Aircraft for Short Haul Transportation*, Final Report, Vol. II, *Aircraft*, Douglas Aircraft Company, June 1973.

11. *STOL Transportation System Planning*, 2nd ed., de Havilland Aircraft of Canada, Ltd., May 1971.

13

ENVIRONMENTAL IMPACT OF AIRPORTS

13.1 INTRODUCTION

Not many years ago there was little concern about harmful environmental effects that attended the construction of airports and other public facilities. The principal thrust of government aviation actions was to foster the development of the aircraft industry. Complaints regarding environmental issues were rare and were viewed by government officials as irritants that threatened to impede the progress of air commerce.

A dramatic turnabout in public and official concern about the environmental impact of airports developed in the late 1960s. The increased emphasis on the environmental effects of airports was partly a result of heightened public awareness of environmental problems in general. Perhaps more important, it was attributable to the alarming worsening of airport environmental problems that accompanied the sharp increases in aviation activity and the introduction of large jet aircraft.

This chapter calls attention to important federal environmental laws and describes how this legislation has changed the airport planning process. It covers briefly the most important areas of environmental concern and indicates how these effects may be evaluated and ameliorated. Much of the material has been abstracted from a report (1) prepared for the U.S. Department of Transportation by CLM/Systems, Inc., to which the reader is referred for a more comprehensive treatment of the subject.

13.2 ENVIRONMENTAL LEGISLATION

Several important laws require airport sponsors and planning agencies to give appropriate consideration to environmental amenities and values when planning for airports. The most significant provisions relating to environmental planning are contained in the Department of Transportation Act, the National Environmental Policy Act of 1969, the Airport and Airway Development Act of 1970, the Uniform Relocation Assistance and Real Property Acquisition Policies Act of 1970, the Clean Air Act and its amendments.

The Department of Transportation Act, passed October 16, 1966, declared it a matter of national policy to make special efforts to preserve the natural beauty of the countryside. Section 4(f) of that act stated that the Secretary of Transportation may not approve any program or project that requires any land from a public park, recreation area, wildlife and waterfowl refuge, or historic site unless there is no feasible and prudent alternative to the use of such land. Furthermore, transportation programs that require land from such areas must employ all possible measures to minimize environmental harm.

The National Environmental Policy Act of 1969 declared another national policy, namely, that the federal government would use all practicable means and measures "to create and maintain conditions under which man and nature can exist in productive harmony." It established a three-member Council on Environmental Quality in the Executive Office of the President to develop guidelines for agencies affected by the law. Section 102 of the act, quoted in part below, established the requirement for environmental impact statements.

Section 102. The Congress authorizes and directs that, to the fullest extent possible: (1) the policies, regulations, and public laws of the United States shall be interpreted and administered in accordance with the policies set forth in this Act, and (2) all agencies of the Federal Government shall

1. (*a*) Utilize a systematic, interdisciplinary approach which will insure the integrated use of the natural and social sciences and the environmental design arts in planning and in decision making which may have an impact on man's environment.

2. (*b*) Identify and develop methods and procedures, in consultation with the Council on Environmental Quality established by title II of this Act, which will insure that presently unquantified environmental amenities and values may be given appropriate consideration in decision making along with economic and technical considerations.

3. (*c*) Include in every recommendation or report on proposals for legislation and other major federal actions significantly affecting the quality of the human environment, a detailed statement by the responsible official on:

(a) The environmental impact of the proposed action.

(b) Any adverse environmental effects which cannot be avoided should the proposal be implemented.

(c) Alternatives to the proposed action.

(d) The relationship between local short-term uses of man's environment and the maintenance and enhancement of long-term productivity.

(e) Any irreversible and irretrievable commitments of resources which would be involved in the proposed action should it be implemented.

The Airport and Airway Development Act of 1970 authorized the Secretary of Transportation to make grants for airport development and set conditions for the approval of federally sponsored airport projects. Several of these conditions related specifically to the environmental effects of airport development. The act required that appropriate consideration be given to the economic, social, and environmental effects of the location of an airport on nearby communities, and that the proposed development be consistent with the community's planning goals and objectives. It required that citizens of neighboring communities be afforded the opportunity for public hearings. The law directed the Secretary of Transportation to consult with the Secretaries of the Interior and Health and Human Services in the evaluation of possible adverse environmental effects of airport projects. It further required compliance with appropriate air and water quality standards. Under the law, no federally assisted development projects that would have adverse environmental effects may be authorized unless the Secretary of Transportation certifies that no feasible and prudent alternative exists and that all possible steps have been taken to minimize the adverse effects predicted.

The Uniform Relocation Assistance and Real Property Acquisition Policies Act of 1970 provides for equitable and uniform treatment of persons displaced from their homes, businesses, or farms by federally assisted programs. If land is acquired for federally assisted airport development, the airport sponsor must reimburse persons displaced from their homes, businesses, or farms for the costs of moving and for expenses in searching for replacement property. Persons displaced from their homes may be paid an additional amount up to $15,000 for the purchase of comparable housing. Tenants may receive up to $4,000 for rental payments or for a down payment on a house. Under the law, replacement housing may be constructed by a public agency if suitable housing is not available to those displaced by the development program. The act calls on public agencies receiving federal assistance to provide advisory services to assist displaced persons in relocating to new houses, businesses, and farms.

The Clean Air Act, as amended in 1977, provided for the establishment of ambient air quality standards and required that the Governors of the various states submit implementation plans designed to meet those standards. The law provides for sanctions against those states that fail to make reasonable efforts toward compliance with the air quality standards. In such standards, the law states that the Secretary of Transportation shall not approve any projects or award any grants under Title 23, United States Code, other than for safety, mass transit, or transportation improvement projects related to air quality improvement or maintenance.

Thus, federal laws and directives have brought about fundamental changes in the airport planning process. Environmental factors must now be considered with the same degree of thoroughness as safety, efficiency, and construction costs. Whenever possible, airport planning should be accomplished by a multidisciplinary team of engineers, architects, economists, planners, and environmental specialists. A wide range of alternatives should be developed and compared, including the "do not build" option. Airport planners must seek out and consider the views of government agencies, members of the aviation community, and the public at large. Every effort must be made to minimize the hardships to persons displaced from homes, businesses, and farms by airport development, and payments for moving expenses and replacement housing are mandated.

A new dimension has been added to the airport planner's job. Airport development that focuses only on the requirements of the user without emphasis on the protection, and even enhancement, of the environment, will no longer be tolerated. This added dimension should not be viewed as a deterrent to technical progress, but as an opportunity to develop new and innovative ideas that enhance technical progress by linking it to the preservation of natural aesthetic land functions (2).

13.3 ENVIRONMENTAL IMPACT STATEMENTS

As a means of implementing the various environmental laws, directives (3–6) issued by the Department of Transportation provide guidance for the preparation of environmental impact statements. Applicants for federal aid must submit a proposed draft environmental impact statement for all airport developments that would significantly affect the quality of the environment.

Where doubt exists about the need to prepare an environmental impact statement, a document called an "environmental assessment" is prepared concisely describing the environmental impacts of the proposed work and its alternatives. This assessment serves as a basis for deciding the nature of further environmental analysis and documentation. If it is determined that a proposed project would not have a significant effect on the environment, a statement to that effect is prepared. This document, which is called a finding of no significant impact (FONSI), must be made available to the public on request, but normally does not have to be coordinated outside the originating office.

Certain actions are so patently innocuous that they are categorically excluded from the requirement of an environmental assessment or an environmental impact statement. Such actions include administrative procurements, personnel actions, and project amendments that do not significantly alter the environmental impact of the action.

In the early stages of an environmental analysis, local agencies and other affected groups and persons should be invited to participate in a process known as "scoping." In this process, the significant issues to be analyzed in depth are identified, and those that are insignificant are eliminated from further study. The process also provides an opportunity for assigning the preparation of the environmental impact statement among the lead and cooperating agencies, and for the scheduling of these assignments.

In the development of airport master plans and other complex proposals, the Department of Transportation encourages the preparation of tiered environmental impact statements. The first tier of such statements focuses on broad issues such as airport location, area-wide air quality, and land use implications of the development. The second tier is site specific and describes detailed project impacts and measures to mitigate harmful impacts.

The elements of a comprehensive environmental impact statement have been well defined by federal laws and directives. These elements are briefly described in the following subsections.

Description and Purpose of the Project

The statement should contain a quantitative description of the proposed development, including the amount of land to be acquired and cleared and the extent of construction. The purpose of the project should be set forth, showing anticipated aviation and community needs, based on aviation demand and population forecasts. If the work is to be completed in stages, the proposed scheduling of various phases of the development should be indicated. The location of nearby communities and airports should be identified, as well as public parks, historic areas, and wildlife sanctuaries. Such areas of environmental interest should be shown on a map in relation to the proposed airport development. The relationship of the development to short and long range land use plans for surrounding areas should be indicated.

Probable Impact of the Development on the Environment

The environmental impact statement should include a discussion of the likely temporary and permanent impacts on the biosphere. Temporary impacts consist primarily of those related to the construction process, such as siltation and erosion, flooding, and air pollution that results from clearing and burning operations. By following FAA guidelines (7), the harmful effects of construction-related problems can be minimized.

The environmental impact statement should document the probable permanent impact on the human environment, including social as well as environmental concerns. Any potential division or disruption of communities should be described, and the locations of neighboring churches, schools, hospitals, and other places of public assembly should be graphically portrayed. Changes in ground traffic and flight patterns should be described, and the effects of such changes on ambient noise levels should be stated. For significant airport projects, the results of a noise study should be included as an attachment to the environmental impact statement.

The statement should describe the probable permanent impact of the development on fish and wildlife sanctuaries, scenic and recreation areas, and historical or archaeological sites. The potential for the alteration or destruction of wildlife breeding, nesting, or feeding grounds, and possible effects of water pollution on marine life should be described. Locations of open spaces, parks, golf courses, and other public and private recreational areas should be indicated.

Probable Adverse Environmental Effects That Cannot Be Avoided

Except for relatively minor improvements, airport development projects normally produce unavoidable adverse environmental effects. For example, acquisition of additional airport land may cause persons to be displaced and business and farming activities to be relocated. Increased air traffic causes more air pollution and increases in ambient noise levels. Improvements to lighting systems resulting in more nighttime operations may cause greater annoyance to nearby residents.

The environmental impact statement should recognize unavoidable adverse environmental effects and, to the extent possible, describe them in quantitative terms. The statement should provide the numbers of houses, businesses, and farms affected by the development and the type, suitability, and location of relocation housing. It should identify any community interests that conflict with the proposed development and indicate why these interests have not been satisfied. Adverse noise impacts should be described by means of noise contours showing the levels of noise exposure, the land use activities affected, and the extent of such effects.

Alternatives to the Proposed Action

The environmental impact statement should identify and describe alternative actions that have been investigated to meet community interests and to lessen the adverse effect on the natural environment and recreational lands and historic sites. Four different groups of alternatives may be considered (1):

1. Basic alternatives.
2. Site location alternatives.
3. Developmental alternatives.
4. Nonphysical alternatives.

Examples of these classes of alternatives appear in Table 13.1.

Reasons for rejecting the various alternative actions should be stated, and the estimated cost of each alternative should be given. If no feasible and prudent alternative to the proposed course of action exists, the steps that have been taken to minimize adverse environmental effects must be described.

Relationship Between Local Short Term Uses of the Environment and Maintenance and Enhancement of Long Term Productivity

The environmental impact statement should compare the short-term environmental problems with the long term environmental benefits that are claimed for the airport development. The short term problems are generally those associated with the construction process. A variety of long term benefits may

Table 13.1 Examples of Alternative Environmental Actions

1. Basic Alternatives
> Should the airport be built?
> Should part of transport service be provided by another mode?

2. Site Location Alternatives
> Where should new airport be located?

3. Developmental Alternatives
> Which runway alignment should be chosen?
> Should existing runway be extended rather than building a new one?
> What is the best runway configuration?

4. Nonphysical Alternatives
> Should flight schedules be rearranged so that there are fewer night operations?
> Should landing fees be raised to discourage aviation traffic?

be identified, including those related to increased safety and efficiency of aircraft operations, economic advantages associated with increased air commerce, and environmental gains. Table 13.2 gives examples of short term problems and long term benefits that might be included in an environmental impact statement.

Irreversible or Irretrievable Commitments of Resources

The environmental impact statement should list any irreversible or irretrievable commitments of resources that would be made if the airport project were undertaken. Examples of such commitments are as follows:

Table 13.2 Examples of Short Term Problems and Long Term Benefits Due to Airport Development

1. Removal of trees in runway approaches.	1. Turfing and landscaping.
2. Erosion and siltation during construction.	2. Recharging groundwater supplies.
3. Dust, mud, and related annoyances.	3. Supplying need for air transport.
4. Ground traffic congestion due to detours, road closures.	4. Inducement of economic development.
5. Construction-related noise problems.	5. Increase of safety and efficiency of airport.
	6. Diminution of noise by shifting aircraft flight patterns to less densely populated areas.

1. Destruction of wildlife habitats.
2. Creation of groundwater or other hydrologic imbalances.
3. Removal of areas of scenic beauty (e.g., streams, primeval forestland).
4. Use of construction materials for the airport project.
5. Loss of natural resources (e.g., minerals, special crops), which will become inaccessible because of the airport development.

13.4 PUBLIC HEARINGS

As mentioned earlier, the Airport and Airway Development Act directs that airport sponsors afford the opportunity for public hearings on the environmental effects of certain airport development projects. Specifically, citizens must be given such opportunity in the case of federally assisted projects that involve the location of an airport, the location of a runway, or a runway extension. The requirement for a public hearing may be satisfied by publishing a notice of opportunity in a newspaper of general circulation and holding a hearing if one is requested (6). The sponsor must certify that an opportunity for a public hearing was given and must document the various steps taken in the hearing process. If a hearing is held, the sponsor must include a summary of the issues raised and the sponsor's reaction and conclusions on those issues.

13.5 COORDINATION WITH OTHER AGENCIES

During past years, a major stumbling block to the orderly development of airports in urban areas was the multiplicity of political jurisdictions affected. Often a dozen or more local governments with conflicting goals and little direction became involved in the planning of a single airport. The need for coordination was obvious.

Planners of federally assisted airport projects must now coordinate the airport planning activity through an areawide or state clearinghouse (8). In metropolitan areas, the clearinghouse is an areawide agency (e.g., a regional planning commission) that has been recognized by the Office of Management and Budget as an appropriate agency to evaluate, review, and coordinate federally assisted programs and projects. In nonmetropolitan areas, the clearinghouse is a comprehensive planning agency designated by the governor or by state law to review and coordinate such activities. Airport sponsors must notify the clearinghouse of any plans to apply for federal assistance. The clearinghouse is responsible for evaluating the significance of proposed projects to state, area, or local plans and programs. Furthermore, the clearinghouse has the responsibility of assuring that appropriate government agencies are given the opportunity to review and comment on the environmental significance of proposed federally assisted projects.

Many and varied agencies and organizations normally participate in the planning of an airport. With specific reference to environmental matters, airport planners should receive input from the following government agencies, where applicable:

1. Federal Aviation Administration.
2. State aeronautics commission.
3. City planning commissions.
4. State Department of Transportation or Highway Department.
5. Rapid transit authority.
6. Air and water pollution district.
7. Local environmental agencies.

In addition, the planners should consult with members of the aviation community and the public at large. In the former category, air carriers, pilots' associations, flying clubs, and travel industry groups are particularly noteworthy. Input from the general public may be received from civic organizations and environmental groups, and from individual participants in public hearings.

13.6 AIRPORT NOISE

One common environmental impact of airport development is also probably the most troublesome to control: airport noise. We will examine the nature and scope of the noise problem, describe some of the noise measurement and rating techniques, and discuss some remedial programs to reduce noise levels and lessen its harmful effects.

Before 1960, there was little concern about aircraft noise. Earlier airport engineering textbooks and design manuals mentioned airport noise only peripherally, if at all. Solutions to aircraft noise problems were limited almost exclusively to preventing encroachment of urban development in the vicinity of airports.

Since the introduction of commercial jet aircraft in 1959, there have been dramatic changes in the nature and magnitude of the airport noise problem. The sharpening focus on airport noise as a serious environmental problem has resulted from a combination of factors, including the following:

1. Increases in air traffic, especially flights utilizing larger and more powerful jet aircraft.
2. Increased urbanization of airport neighborhoods.
3. Increased public awareness of environmental problems generally and airport noise problems particularly.

The seriousness of the noise problem was manifested in 1969 by the promulgation in Federal Aviation Regulations, Part 36, of FAA noise standards for the certification of turbojet aircraft of new design. The regulations were amended in 1973, extending the same standards to all *new* aircraft of older design. In late 1976, the FAA announced that older, noisier, four-engine jet airplanes must be modified to meet the Part 36 noise levels or be retired from service within eight years (9). The aircraft noise problem is, of course, worldwide in scope, and ICAO similarly has adopted noise certification standards for jet aircraft (10).

The Environmental Protection Agency (EPA) estimated that the total area in the United States subjected to excessive aircraft noise (as evidenced by numerous complaints) grew about sevenfold between 1960 and 1970. By 1976, it was estimated that aircraft noise was a significant annoyance for 6 to 7 million Americans (9).

Noise detracts from the amenities of a pleasant living environment and may cause land values to decrease. It can be a source of great annoyance, interrupting sleep, interfering with conversation, and depriving people from full enjoyment of many recreational activities. Many experts now recognize noise as a serious threat to public health. People repeatedly exposed to high noise levels may exhibit increased irritability, severe nervous tension, loss of ability to concentrate, and impaired aptitude to perform even simple tasks (11).

Noise Measurement Techniques

Noise is defined as excessive or unwanted sound. It is unwanted because it annoys people, interferes with conversation, disturbs sleep, and in the extreme, is a danger to public health. Sound, whether noisy or noiseless, is produced by vibrations in a medium (e.g., air, water, steel). When an object vibrates, it produces rapid small-scale variations in the normal atmospheric pressure. This disturbance is propagated from the source in a repetitive spherical pattern at a speed (in air) of approximately 1100 ft/sec (340 m/sec). It may be reflected, partially absorbed, or attenuated before reaching an eardrum to produce a sensation of sound.

Noise is characterized by its sound level, its frequency spectrum, and its variation over time. "Sound level" refers to a physical measure that corresponds to the hearer's subjective conception of loudness. It is a function of the magnitude of the pressure fluctuations about the ambient barometric air pressure. One can speak of the strength of these fluctuations in terms of several variables, the most common being *sound intensity* and *sound pressure*.

Sound intensity (also called sound power density) is the average rate of sound energy transmitted through a unit area perpendicular to the direction of sound propagation, typically measured in picowatts* per square meter (pW/

* 1 picowatt = 10^{-12} watt.

m^2). The human ear can detect sound intensities as weak as one picowatt and tolerate intensities as high as 10^{13} pW. Because of the difficulties of dealing with such a large range of numbers, a logarithmic measure called the decibel (dB) is used to describe sound level. The sound intensity, expressed in decibels, is

$$\text{sound intensity} = 10 \log_{10}\left(\frac{I}{I_0}\right) \tag{13.1}$$

where

I = sound intensity (pW/m^2)
I_0 = 1 pW/m^2, a standard reference intensity representing approximately the weakest audible sound

Since no instrument is available for directly measuring the power level of a source, sound pressure, which is usually proportional to the square root of sound power, is used as a measure of the magnitude of a sound disturbance (12). The sound pressure, in decibels, is

$$\text{sound pressure} = 10 \log_{10}\left(\frac{P}{P_0}\right)^2 \tag{13.2}$$

$$= 20 \log_{10}\left(\frac{P}{P_0}\right)$$

where

P = the root mean square sound pressure, typically expressed in newtons per square meter (N/m^2)
P_0 = 20 μN/m^2 or 0.0002 dyne/cm^2, a standard reference pressure corresponding to the weakest audible sound

Sound level is measured by a sound level meter, which consists essentially of a microphone that converts the pattern of sound pressure fluctuations into a similar pattern of electrical voltage, one or more amplifiers, and a voltage meter, which is normally calibrated to read in decibels. For practical purposes, the decibel scale ranges from zero, the threshold of hearing, to about 140 dB, the onset of pain. For every increase of about 10 dB, there is a doubling of the sound's apparent loudness.

The apparent loudness of a sound also depends on the *frequency* of the sound. Frequency is the rate of occurrence of the sound pressure fluctuations, commonly expressed in cycles per second or hertz (Hz). The frequency determines the pitch of the sound; the higher the frequency, the higher the pitch. The lowest note on a piano has a frequency of about 27 Hz, and the highest note has a frequency of 4186 Hz. The normal human ear can hear sounds with frequencies from about 20 to 20,000 Hz, but it is more sensitive to sounds in the middle to high frequency range. Since most people consider high frequency noises more annoying than low frequency noises at the same sound level, a frequency analysis may be required to properly evaluate noise sources. Schultz explains:

> Most noises are made up of a mixture of components having different frequencies: the sound of a diesel tractor/trailer at high speed on the freeway combines the high-pitched singing of the tires and the low-pitched roar of the engine and exhaust, both of which the ear readily distinguishes. A landing jet aircraft has a clearly distinguishable whine from the compressor, mixed with the "random" noise of the engine exhaust (sounds like a big waterfall). A flute, on the other hand, if played softly, makes an almost pure tone containing only a single prominent frequency. Depending on how the components of a noise are distributed in frequency, our ears make a subjective judgment of "quality." Consequently, it is important to have an objective measure of the frequency distribution. (11)

A frequency analysis is performed by means of a sound meter that can be tuned to different parts of the frequency range. The meter eliminates or "filters out" all of the sound components except those in a relatively narrow band of frequencies. Thus, it is possible to selectively measure the sound level for different bands and to describe the frequency distribution of noise as a set of partial sound levels in contiguous frequency bands covering the entire audible range. These measurements can be displayed on a graph such as Figure 13.1 showing an octave-band (or third-octave band) analysis of the noise (11).

> [The terms octave and third-octave] describe the bandwidth of the filter according to the ratio of the upper and lower frequencies that bound the band: in an octave band, the upper bounding frequency is always exactly double the lower bounding frequency; in a ⅓-octave band, the upper frequency is always $1.26 (= \sqrt[3]{2})$ times the lower frequency. Each octave band is made up of (or contains) three equal, contiguous ⅓-octave bands (11).

The annoyance a person experiences because of noise depends to a considerable extent on its variation over time. The temporal effect is manifest in the duration of a single noise event, as well as its frequency and time of occurrence. Clearly, the longer a noise lasts, the greater the interruption of human activity and the more pronounced the annoyance. Laboratory tests have indicated that for durations ranging from a few seconds to 60 sec, a noise decreases in acceptability roughly at a rate of 3 dB per doubling of duration (13). Thus, two sounds of equal frequency distribution will be judged equally acceptable if one has an amplitude of 3 dB less than the other and a duration of twice the other.

The number of aircraft operations per day and their time of occurrence can strongly influence the degree of annoyance experienced by those residing near airports. In research performed in the vicinity of Heathrow Airport, a comparison was made of Londoners' noise exposure and the results of social surveys taken

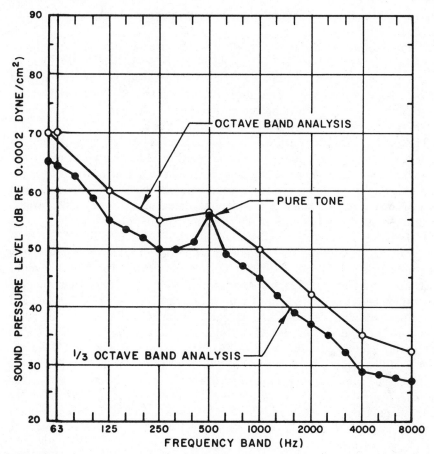

FIGURE 13.1 Typical points on the A-level and EPNL noise scales. (Courtesy U.S. Department of Transportation.)

around the airport. The study identified the number of aircraft exposures as one of the most important factors influencing the degree of public annoyance by aircraft noise. It was found that the number of events alone had a higher contribution to the total variance in response than did the noise level itself (13). This suggests that the very existence of a noise event may be more significant than the magnitude of the event.

For obvious reasons, aircraft noise is more annoying during evening and nighttime hours than during the day. Nighttime aircraft operations cause more interference with social conversation, detract more from recreational activities, and are more likely to interrupt sleep than operations during daylight hours.

Noise Rating Techniques

A great many scales have been used to express noise levels. Although there is no generally accepted noise scale, only a few of the available scales have gained wide acceptance. Several of the more commonly employed noise scales are described below.

One of the simplest and most straightforward noise measurement techniques consists of measuring the *overall sound pressure level*, which is related to total sound energy over the audible frequency range. However, the unweighted overall sound pressure level is not strongly correlated with a hearer's subjective response to the noise. As indicated earlier, the human ear tends to be more sensitive to sounds with relatively high frequencies.

The *A-weighted sound level* was devised to more closely represent a person's subjective response to sounds. In the A-weighted filter network, the lower frequencies are deemphasized in a manner similar to human hearing. Like the overall sound level, the A-weighted sound level is measured in decibels [dB (A)]. The A-weighted scale is a widely accepted measure of surface transportation noises but is less commonly used to measure aircraft noise.

In 1959, K. D. Kryter developed a scale called the *perceived noise level* (PNL) that correlates with the annoying properties of jet aircraft noise. It is measured in decibels and evaluated in units of PNdB. The PNdB level is measured for a single event, such as an aircraft flyover. Its evaluation requires the instantaneous measurement of sound pressure levels in the various octave (or ⅓ octave) bands for each half-second increment of time during the noise event. It is based on a series of calculations that weight the octave (or ⅓ octave) band levels of the noise according to the degree of annoyance it causes.

A modification to the perceived noise level accounts for the duration of the event and the subjective response to pure tones in the noise spectrum. Termed the *effective perceived noise level* (EPNL) and measured in EPNdB, it has been adopted by the FAA and the ICAO as the standard measurement for aircraft noise. Typical points on the A-level and EPNdB scales appear in Figure 13.2. Note that

$$\text{EPNdB} \approx \text{dB(A)} + 12 \qquad (13.3)$$

The procedures for calculating perceived noise levels are complex. For planning purposes, the ICAO (10) recommends that the approximate methods described below be used to determine EPNL values.

To determine the EPNL, a series of instantaneous sound pressure levels is measured in each of the octave bands for each half-second increment of time during the aircraft flyover. Figure 13.2 plots a typical instantaneous measurement for the various octave bands. The following steps are taken to compute the EPNL for a noise event.

Step 1. Let SPL(i, k) indicate the sound pressure level for the ith frequency band measured at time increment k. Convert each SPL(i, k) in the spectrum to perceived noisiness $n(i, k)$ in noys,* by using Table 13.3.

---

* The noy is a subjective unit of noisiness. A sound of 2 noy is twice as noisy as a sound of 1 noy; a sound of 3 noy is 3 times as noisy, and so on.

TYPICAL NOISE LEVELS

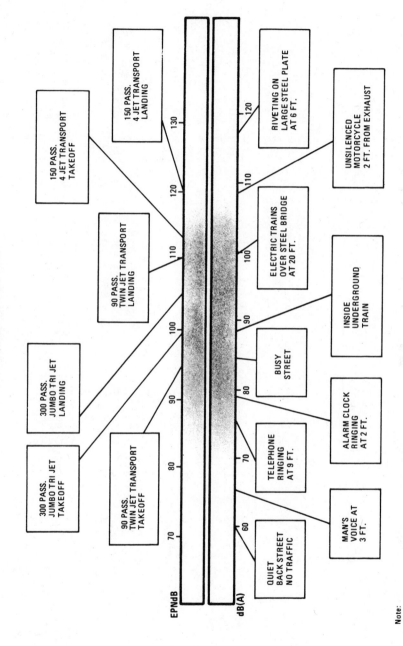

FIGURE 13.2 Typical instantaneous measurement of noise spectrum. (*Source:* Reference 11.)

Note:

Approximate relation between EPNdB scale and dB(A) scale is shown in this comparison of various noise sources.

Table 13.3 Noys as a Function of Sound Pressure Level

Sound Pressure Level (dB)	1/3 Octave Band Center Frequencies (Hz)							
	63	125	250	500	1000	2000	4000	8000
50	—	—	1.56	2.00	2.00	3.46	4.26	3.02
55	—	1.38	2.25	2.83	2.83	4.89	6.01	4.26
60	1.00	2.08	3.26	4.00	4.00	6.90	8.49	6.01
65	1.60	3.12	4.71	5.66	5.66	9.74	12.0	8.49
70	2.55	4.69	6.81	8.00	8.00	13.8	16.9	12.0
75	4.06	7.05	9.85	11.3	11.3	19.4	23.9	16.9
80	6.48	10.6	13.9	16.0	16.0	27.4	33.7	23.9
85	10.3	14.9	19.7	22.6	22.6	38.7	47.6	33.7
90	14.9	21.1	27.9	32.0	32.0	54.7	67.2	47.6
95	21.1	29.9	39.4	45.3	45.3	77.2	94.9	67.2
100	29.9	42.2	55.7	64.0	64.0	109.	134.	94.9
105	42.2	59.7	78.8	90.5	90.5	154.	189.	134.
110	59.7	84.4	111.	128.	128.	217.	267.	189.
115	84.4	119.	158.	181.	181.	307.	377.	267.
120	119.	169.	223.	256.	256.	433.	533.	377.
125	169.	239.	315.	362.	362.	611.	752.	533.
130	239.	338.	446.	512.	512.	863.	1062.	752.
135	338.	478.	630.	724.	724.	1219.	1499.	1062.

Source: *Environmental Protection, Annex 16 to the Convention on International Civil Aviation, Vol. I, Aircraft Noise,* 1st ed., International Civil Aviation Organization, Montreal, 1981.

Step 2. Compute the total perceived noisiness $N(k)$ for time increment k by combining the perceived noisiness values $n(i, k)$ by means of the following formula:

$$N(k) = 0.7n(k) + 0.3 \sum_{i=1}^{8} n(i, k), \qquad \text{noys} \qquad (13.4)$$

where $n(k) =$ the largest of the $n(i, k)$ values

Step 3. Convert the total perceived noisiness $N(k)$ into the perceived noise level PNL(k) by employing the following formula:

$$\text{PNL}(k) = 40.0 + 33.3 \log N(k), \qquad \text{PNdB} \qquad (13.5)$$

Step 4. In case of landing turbofan aircraft operations, correct the PNL(k) value obtained in step 3 for subjective response to the presence of pure tones by adding 2 PNdB. No correction of PNL values is required for other aircraft operations.

Step 5. Following steps 1 to 4, determine the tone-corrected PNLs, designated PNLT, for each of the k half-second increments of time during the noise event. Figure 13.3 shows a typical pattern for a 20 sec aircraft flyover.

Step 6. Compute a duration correction factor, D, by the formula

$$D = 10 \log \frac{[t(2) - t(1)]}{20} \qquad (13.6)$$

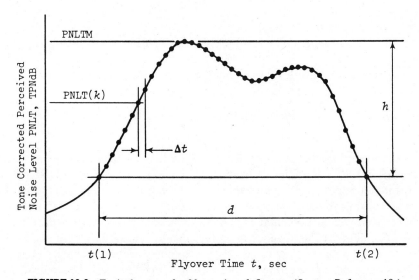

FIGURE 13.3 Typical pattern for 20 sec aircraft flyover. (*Source:* Reference 10.)

where $t(2) - t(1)$ is the approximate time interval during which a recording of PNLT is within 10 dB of its maximum value.

Step 7. Compute the EPNL by adding the duration correction factor D to the maximum value of the tone-corrected perceived noise level PNLTM:

$$EPNL = PNLTM + D, \quad PNdB \quad (13.7)$$

The resulting value of EPNL represents the effective perceived noise level for a single noise event such as a flyover. One is normally interested in evaluating the total noise exposure level (TNEL) produced by a succession of n aircraft. This can be determined by employing the following equation:

$$TNEL = 10 \log \sum_{i=1}^{n} \text{antilog} \frac{EPNL(n)}{10} + 10 \quad (13.8)$$

The ICAO (10) has recommended that the total noise exposure level be adopted internationally for land use planning purposes and that the measure be referred to as the International Noise Exposure Unit.

In a report (14) presented to the British Parliament in 1963, a rating technique called the *noise and number index* (NNI) was introduced to account for the average peak noise level as well as the number of aircraft heard in a given period of time:

$$NNI = \bar{L} + 15 \log_{10} N - 80 \quad (13.9)$$

where

N = number of aircraft heard
$\bar{L}$ = the average peak noise level (PNdB or EPNdB)

The average peak noise level is computed by the following equation:

$$\bar{L} = 10 \log_{10} \frac{1}{N} \sum_{i}^{N} 10^{L/10} \quad (13.10)$$

where L = peak noise level (PNdB or EPNdB) for a single noise event
The constant 80 was included in the NNI equation so that zero NNI would correspond to zero public annoyance due to aircraft noise, as determined by a social survey around Heathrow Airport (11). Figure 13.4 plots relationships between NNI and the percentage of people annoyed by exposures to the aircraft noise. The degree of annoyance in an area can be assessed by multiplying the percentage of people likely to be annoyed by the population density (15).

The composite noise rating (CNR) was developed in the 1950s to deal with problems of noise around military air bases. It has also been used by planners

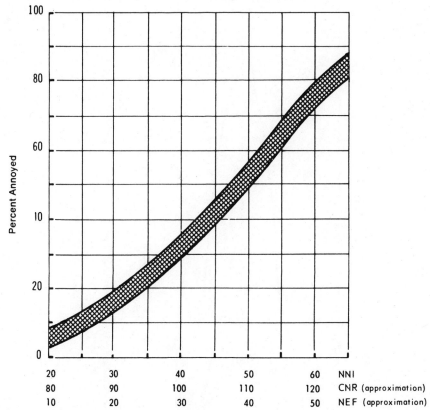

FIGURE 13.4 Percentage of annoyed persons in relation to noise. (*Source:* Ariel Alexandre, "The Social Impact of Aircraft Noise," *Traffic Quarterly*, Vol. 28, No. 3, Eno Foundation for Transportation, July 1974.)

as a land use planning technique and by the Federal Housing Administration to evaluate the suitability of residential housing tracts in the vicinity of airports.

The CNR procedure estimates the size of an area exposed to aircraft noise in the vicinity of airports and relates this exposure to the anticipated response of surrounding residential communities. It is based on four factors:

1. Aircraft noise levels (PNdB or EPNdB).
2. Number of landings, takeoffs, and engine runups.
3. Time of day.
4. Extent of runway utilization.

It is not necessary to measure the noise levels used in the calculation of CNRs with a sound level meter or other such device. The publication of a set of generalized noise contour maps (16) has made it possible to estimate the noise

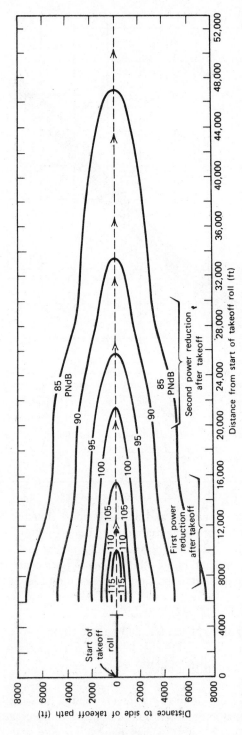

FIGURE 13.5 Standardized CNR curves: perceived noise level contours for takeoffs of four-engine piston aircraft (use contours as drawn) and four-engine turboprop aircraft (reduce all contour values by 5 PNdB). (*Source:* Reference 16.)

produced during takeoff, landing, and runup operations by any of several classes of aircraft. Figure 13.5 presents an example of a noise contour map.

The first step in the CNR procedure is to collect the following information on the aircraft operations at the airport in question: the average number of takeoffs, landings, flight paths, and the percentage utilization of each runway. The average number of movements is determined separately for daytime (0700 to 2200) and nighttime (2200 to 0700).

On the basis of this operational information, the appropriate sets of noise contours is selected and the perceived noise levels (PNdB or EPNdB) indicated for the area in question are read directly from the charts. Corrections are added algebraically to the readings from the noise contour maps to account for other factors such as number of operations, runway utilization, and time of day. (These corrections are summarized in Table 13.4.) The resultant number is called the composite noise rating.

At this point in the analysis, there will be several CNR values, one for each operation being considered. A single CNR value must be chosen to represent noise conditions for the area under study for all flight conditions, according to the following procedure:

Table 13.4 Operational Corrections to Apply to Perceived Noise Levels for Takeoffs and Landings

Number of Takeoffs or Landings per Period		Correction
Day (0700–2200)	Night (2200–0700)	
Less than 3[a]	Less than 2	−10
3–9	2–5	−5
10–30	6–15	0
31–100	16–50	+5
More than 100	More than 50	+10
Runway Utilization (%)		
31–100		0
10–30		−5
3–9		−10
Less than 3		−15
Time of Day[b]		
0700–2200		0
2200–0700		+10

Source: Bolt, Beranek & Newman, Inc., Land Use Planning Relating to Aircraft Noise, Technical Report, Cambridge, Mass., October 1964, p. 10.

[a] If the average number of operations for aircraft type is less than one per time period, that aircraft type should not be considered in the analysis.

[b] In general, the ratio of daytime-to-nighttime operations is such that daytime operations determine the CNR at airports. Only when the nighttime activity is disproportionately high will the nighttime correction affect the CNR.

Only those CNRs that are within 3 units of the maximum CNR need be considered. If there are three or more CNRs fulfilling this requirement, add 5 units to the highest one to determine the CNR that applies for all flight operations; if there are less than three, the highest CNR applies (16).

The final step involves estimating the community response, based on case histories of military and civil airports that experienced aircraft noise problems. Table 13.5 summarizes the types of response that may be expected for various ranges of CNR values. Generally, CNR values of 100 or higher are considered to be incompatible with residential land use.

The FAA has developed a refinement of the CNR methodology called *noise exposure forecasts* (NEFs). According to the NEF methodology, the total noise exposure consists of noise produced by different classes of aircraft flying at different times and along different flight paths. The noise exposure forecast for aircraft class *i*, utilizing flight path *j*, can be expressed as follows (11):

$$\text{NEF}_{ij} = \text{EPNL}_{ij} + 10 \log\left(\frac{N_{dij}}{K_d} + \frac{N_{nij}}{K_n}\right) - C \qquad (13.11)$$

where

N_{dij} = the number of daytime operations for aircraft class *i* and flight path *j*
N_{nij} = the number of nighttime operations for aircraft class *i* and flight path *j*
K_d = 20
K_n = 1.2
C = 75

The values assigned to the constants K_d and K_n mean that one nighttime flight contributes a great deal more to the NEF value than a daytime flight. The value of the constant C was chosen to prevent confusion of the NEF values with CNR values.

The total NEF at a given location is the sum of all the individual NEF_{ij} values and may be computed by the following equation:

$$\text{NEF} = 10 \log \sum_{i} \sum_{j} \text{antilog} \frac{\text{NEF}_{ij}}{10} \qquad (13.12)$$

The NEF procedure utilizes effective perceived noise decibels as its basic measure and, like the CNR methodology, requires detailed information on numbers and types of aircraft, runway utilization, flight paths, operating procedures, and time of day.

In the late 1970s, the FAA adopted the day/night average sound level (L$_{DN}$) procedure (17) as the preferred method of measuring noise resulting from aircraft operations. The L$_{DN}$ is a measure of the noise environment at a specified

Table 13.5   Estimated Response of Residential Communities from
Various Threshold CNR and NEF Values

Description of Expected Response	CNR Takeoff and Landings	Ground Runups	NEF Takeoff and Landings
Essentially no complaints would be expected. The noise may, however, interfere occasionally with certain activities of the residents.	<100	<80	<30
Individuals may complain, perhaps vigorously. Concerted group action is possible.	100–115	80–95	30–40
Individual reactions would likely include repeated, vigorous complaints. Concerted group action might be expected.	>115	>95	>40

Source: Bolt, Beranek, and Newman, *Land Use Planning Relating to Aircraft Noise*, Cambridge, Mass., October 1964, p. 12.

location over a 24-hour period. In terms of sound energy, it is equivalent to the level of a continuous A-weighted sound level with nighttime noises increased by 10 dB to account for the undesirable effects of night noise disturbances. The L_{DN} may be directly measured by a sophisticated integrating noise measurement meter or it may be calculated in several ways.

With the L_{DN} method, the contribution of an aircraft operation is described in terms of the sound exposure level (SEL). The SEL is the A-weighted sound level integrated over the entire noise event and normalized to a reference duration of 1 second. In other words, the SEL gives the level of a continuous 1-second sound that contains the same amount of energy as the noise event (see Figure 13.6).

Empirical graphs, typified by Figure 13.7, have been published (17) giving SEL values in dB for different classes of aircraft, mode of operation, and locations with respect to the flight path. The "partial" L_{DN} value for those conditions can then be calculated by equation 13.13, which accounts for the number and time of day of such operations. For aircraft class i, and operation mode j,

$$L_{DN}(i,j) = \text{SEL}(i,j) + 10\log(N_D + 10\,N_N) - 49.4 \quad (13.13)$$

where

N_D = number of daytime operations for given conditions
N_N = number of nighttime operations for given conditions

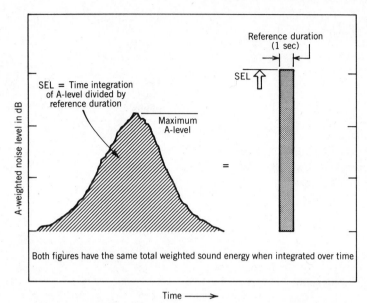

FIGURE 13.6   Illustration of the SEL concept. (*Source:* Reference 17.)

Daytime is taken as the period from 7:00 A.M. to 10:00 P.M., and nighttime is the remainder of the day.

After the "partial" L_{DN} values have been calculated for each significant noise intrusion, they may be summed on an energy basis by Equation 13.14 to obtain the total L_{DN} due to all aircraft operations.

$$L_{DN} = 10 \log \sum_i \sum_j 10^{\frac{L_{DN(i,j)}}{10}} \tag{13.14}$$

Noise Abatement

There are a number of techniques and procedures that can be employed to lessen the undesirable effects of noise in the vicinity of airports. These countermeasures can be grouped into four classes, relating to:

1. Aircraft design or modification.
2. Aircraft operation and use.
3. Airport planning and design.
4. Land use in the airport vicinity.

As a part of the certification process, the FAA places limitations on noise from all new subsonic turbojet aircraft. The noise certification process involves making noise measurements at specified locations along the approach and takeoff paths and to the side of the runway. Maximum noise levels in EPNdB are specified for landings and takeoffs as a function of the aircraft gross weight. Manufacturers have made significant advances in recent years in the design of quieter aircraft, primarily through design of quieter engines and improved aerodynamic design, which permits steeper and quicker ascents and descents.

A number of controls on aircraft operations can be imposed to minimize noise exposure. Perhaps the most dramatic operational control has been the FAA's decision to prohibit civilian aircraft from flying at supersonic speeds over the United States. Where multiple runways are available, aircraft may be assigned to takeoff or approach paths over sparsely populated areas, weather, wind, and other such circumstances permitting. Similarly, turns may be specified

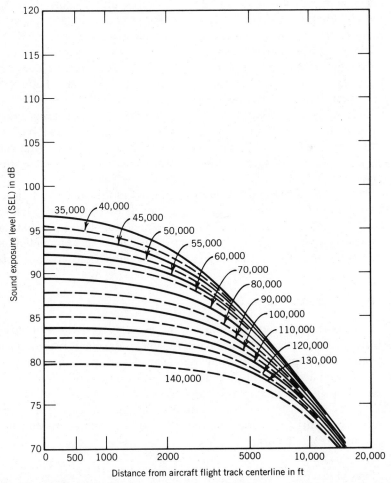

FIGURE 13.7 Example of empirical graph for estimating sound exposure level. (Four-engine HBPR Turbofan Transport (747); landing—3° glide slope; flight track distance range—35,000–150,000 ft from runway landing threshold.)

for takeoff movements, and steeper approach glide paths may be employed. Aircraft speeds may be varied during the takeoff to achieve higher elevations and more rapid movements over noise-sensitive areas. In some cases pilots may be required to cut back on power after achieving a specified elevation, to lessen noise exposure to heavily populated areas. These and other operational controls can be particularly beneficial during evening hours when people are more sensitive to aircraft noise.

Airport planners and designers should consider possible undesirable noise exposures when choosing runway orientation and placement. Once a runway is built, displaced thresholds may be employed to reduce perceived noise levels under the approach and at the end of a runway. Extensive landscaping can also help to shield airport surroundings from aircraft ground operations.

Perhaps the most fruitful countermeasure against aircraft noise is land use planning and control: that is, taking advantage of available land use control techniques to ensure that the land surrounding the airport is used in a manner compatible with the airport environment. With the possible exception of certain outdoor recreational activities, almost all types of land use are compatible with airports, provided the NEF values do not exceed 30. Land that has NEF values between 30 and 40 may be used for commercial and industrial purposes and for offices and public buildings. If the buildings have special insulation, the land may also be suitable for hotels, motels, and apartments. Where the NEF values exceed 40, there are few compatible land uses. Such land can be suitably used for hotels, motels, offices, and public buildings if acoustic insulation is installed.

By means of objective noise studies conducted in the vicinity of airports, it is possible to define areas exposed to noise levels of a specified magnitude. The results of such studies may be displayed in the form of noise contour maps such as that shown as Figure 13.5. Such maps must be used judiciously, recognizing the complexity and variability of the public's reaction to noise.

The Public's Reaction to Noise

The most important factors to influence the public's annoyance with noise relate to the characteristics of the noise itself, namely, its sound level, frequency, and variation over time. It should be emphasized, however, that many other factors are correlated with public annoyance with aircraft noise, and there are wide variations in tolerance to noise among people and communities.

Studies of community reaction to aircraft noise have shown that a variety of factors may contribute to the total impact of aircraft operations on a neighboring community, including:

1.   Fear of aircraft crashing the community.
2.   Perceived importance of the airport to the local economy.
3.   Income, occupational status, and other social factors.

Furthermore, the number of complaints about airport noise may not accurately reflect the extent or intensity of annoyance experienced in a community. Factors such as the degree of community organization and the availability of institutional mechanisms for voicing complaints may bear strongly on the number of persons who complain. It is not surprising, therefore, that forecasting the impact of aircraft noise on nearby neighborhoods is an inexact process that must be applied with considerable attention to its subjective aspects.

13.7 IMPACTS ON LAND USE

Because of its size and nature, an airport can have profound effects on land use in the vicinity. These impacts may be economic, developmental, or visual. Airport planners and designers should endeavor to employ available land use controls and design techniques to minimize undesirable land use impacts in the airport environs and within its boundaries. The following subsections briefly describe airport land use impacts. Chapter 4 covers specific land use planning procedures and controls.

Economic and Developmental Impacts

A large airport may encompass 20,000 or more acres of land and may overlap several political jurisdictions. In large urban areas, tens of thousands of persons may be employed in air transportation activities. The annual payroll for airport employees may total hundreds of millions of dollars, and indirect effects of purchase of local goods and services by airlines and air transport service industries may equal or exceed that amount. Additional benefits to the local economy derive from the purchase of goods and services by business from tourists or convention participants made possible by the airport. Other impacts that may be equally important but more difficult to quantify include increasing the attractiveness of the area to desirable industries, facilitating commercial transactions, and improving access to recreational, social, and cultural opportunities.

Visual Problems and Controls

Unless carefully planned and designed, airports can have a negative visual effect on the community. Outside the airport boundary, uncontrolled motels, car rental establishments, and other airport-related commercial developments can create a garish and ugly visual impression on airport visitors, employees, and nearby residents. Such problems are the responsibility and concern of local governments, which can improve the appearance of the airport neighborhood in a number of ways (e.g., by use of zoning regulations and building codes, by well-planned location and design of airport access facilities, and by careful design and construction of public buildings in the airport area).

Within the airport proper, positive planning and design controls must be employed by the airport operator to provide a functional and visually pleasing environment.

> The visual environment should provide clear orientation for the different segments of population that use or work at the airport, enabling them to find their destinations with relative ease. Ease of orientation on the airport should be considered at the design phase by adopting a functional and readily identifiable terminal area layout; by using the control tower or other tall buildings as landmarks by which persons may orient themselves; by permitting views of destinations from the roadway; by designing a clear sign system; and by differentiating directions of travel on the roadways.
>
> The environment should provide a clear visual image so that persons at the airport can better understand the sections of the airport that they use. . . . The layout of the entire airport may be more easily grasped by designing a clear and simple layout of the entire airport; by reinforcing the layout by use of simplified maps; by visually differentiating between areas on the airport; and by making clear connections between different parts of the airport (1).

The airport operator can also control the location, height, and appearance of private buildings on the airport, and can enhance the airport appearance further by judicious planning and design of parking lots, access roads, fencing, and landscaping.

13.8 AIR AND WATER POLLUTION

Air and water pollution may constitute the most serious environmental impacts caused by an airport development. These problems are also probably the most complex, and their evaluation and control may require the assistance of highly trained environmental specialists. Although a detailed treatment of air and water pollution is well beyond the scope of this book, we describe briefly various types and sources of air and water pollutants and ways of controlling and lessening their impact.

Air Pollution

Air pollutants may be grouped into five major classes:

1. Particulate matter.
2. Carbon monoxide.
3. Photochemical oxidants.
4. Nitrogen oxides.
5. Sulfur dioxide.

Particulate matter is any solid or liquid material less than 500 microns (μ) in size and dispersed in the air. An average annual particulate matter concentration of 75 μg/m^3 may have an adverse impact on human health, as might a maximum 24 hr level of 260 μg/m^3, which occurred only once a year (1).

Carbon monoxide is a colorless, odorless, highly poisonous gas that results from the incomplete combustion of carbonaceous fuels. Gaseous organic compounds of carbon and hydrogen (hydrocarbons) and oxides of nitrogen are also emitted during combustion. Prevailing concentrations of hydrocarbons do not appear to be detrimental to human health, but certain of these substances may react with nitrogen oxides to produce harmful pollutants.

Ozone and other oxidizing agents are formed when hydrocarbons and nitrogen oxides are exposed to sunlight. These photochemical oxidants can cause irritation to the respiratory and alimentary systems, as well as damage to vegetation, metals, and other materials. There is also some evidence that long-term exposure of humans to nitrogen dioxide even in low concentrations contributes to chronic respiratory diseases.

Sulfur dioxide, which is present in the exhaust gases of aircraft, is a colorless, extremely irritating substance that is especially harmful to the respiratory system. Detailed information on these pollutants can be found in publications of the EPA.

The air pollution at an airport may stem from a variety of sources. Some of the major sources are as follows:

1. Aircraft engine exhaust.
2. Aircraft fuel venting.
3. Aircraft fueling systems.
4. Motor vehicles of passengers, employees, and airport visitors.
5. Ground service equipment.
6. Airport heating plant.
7. Construction operations.

The pollutants contained in aircraft engine exhaust gases consist principally of carbon monoxide, carbon dioxide, hydrocarbons, nitrogen oxides, soot, and other particulate matter. The exhaust gases also contain highly irritating organic acids and carbon and sulfur compounds. The amount of compounds emitted into the atmosphere is a function of the type of aircraft and engine, the phase or mode of operations, and how long the engine is operated in each phase. It is useful to consider the pollutants emitted in the following phases of operation:

1. Taxi or idle.
2. Takeoff.
3. Climbout (from liftoff to 3000 ft altitude).

4. Approach (from 3000 ft altitude to touchdown).

5. Landing.

For most jet aircraft, the pollutant rate of emission of carbon monoxide and hydrocarbons is greatest during the taxi or idle phase, and the rate of emission of nitrogen oxides is greatest during takeoff.

Vaporization of fuel from spillages that occur during fueling and from fuel storage tanks can produce a significant amount of airport air pollution. Virtually all the vapor emissions from these sources are hydrocarbons.

As much as 25% of the pollutants emitted by all sources within the airport boundary may come from motor vehicles of passengers, employees, and airport visitors (1). Additional pollution is caused by the operation of gasoline-powered ground service equipment. The amount of pollution from these sources is directly related to the amount of gasoline burned. Estimates of fuel burned by motor vehicles of passengers, employees, and visitors can be made from traffic counts and estimates of average distances traveled within the airport boundary. Studies made at large airports indicate that ground service vehicles consume approximately 7 gal of gasoline per vehicle per day.

At large airports the airport heating plant can be a significant source of air pollution. The quantity of pollutants emitted, of course, depends on the type of power plant and the type and amount of fuel used.

Construction operations at an airport may also contribute to the air pollution problem. Clearing and excavation activities, burning of refuse, demolition of old buildings, and other such operations may add dust, smoke, exhaust emissions, and other pollutants to the atmosphere.

The EPA has the overall responsibility for the establishment of national ambient air quality standards. Such standards have been established and published in the *Federal Register* (18). Enforcement of these standards is the responsibility of state air pollution control agencies supported by the EPA.

Three approaches have been used to measure the air pollution impact at an airport: (1) direct measurement, (2) estimation of emission density, and (3) atmospheric dispersion modeling.

Direct atmospheric measurement of the concentrations of various classes of pollutants is a complex undertaking calling for highly specialized and expensive equipment. Methods for measuring various pollutants have been published by the EPA (18), and assistance for making direct atmospheric pollution measurements may be obtained from state air pollution control agencies.

Estimates of the number of pounds of various classes of pollutants can be based on previous research. For example, using data of the type given in Table 13.6, it would be possible to estimate the number of pounds of carbon monoxide, hydrocarbons, and nitrogen oxide for each phase of an operation of a long range jet. To estimate total quantities of pollutants, the quantities of pollutants for one long range jet would be multiplied by the total number of operations per day by each aircraft. Calculations of this type could be made for other classes of aircraft. From similar computations, the quantities of pollutants

Table 13.6 Example of Available Data for Estimation of Quantities
of Pollutants from Long Range Jets

	Engine Emission Rate (lb/hr)			Average Time in Each Phase (min)
Phase	Carbon Monoxide	Hydrocarbons	Nitrogen Oxide	
Taxi/idle	103	84	1	Variable[a]
Takeoff	10	12	148	1.0
Climbout	10	13	94	2.2
Approach	29	12	20	4.0
Landing	10	13	94	0.4

Source: *Airports and Their Environment*, CLM/Systems, Inc., prepared for the U.S. Department of Transportation, September 1972.

[a] Taxi/idle times should be based on actual operating practices at the airport under study.

from fuel spillages, motor vehicles, the airport heating plant, and so on, could be estimated.

Atmospheric dispersion modeling is a highly complex computer simulation procedure that predicts pollutant concentrations at various locations in the airport vicinity. Detailed information is required on emission sources, topography, air temperature, wind speed and direction, and other meteorological variables. From the computer output, it is possible to develop contour maps showing lines of equal pollutant concentration. Such results readily identify areas that may have high concentrations of various pollutants and makes it possible to evaluate realistically the available countermeasures.

Remedial programs to reduce airport air pollution can be grouped in three categories:

1. Modifications to aircraft engines.
2. Modifications to ground operations.
3. Modifications relating to the planning, design, and construction of the airport.

A great deal can be done to reduce aircraft engine pollution rates by better design, but such modifications are costly and can be implemented only over a long period of time. There are also a number of operational changes that can be inaugurated to reduce air pollution; however, some of the changes can be undertaken only with considerable additional cost or hazard. Apparently, the most desirable operational changes would be to:

Require engines to be shut down at gates.

Use fewer engines, operating at higher rpm when taxiing, to reduce carbon monoxide and hydrocarbon emissions.

Eliminate the problem of fuel venting by providing a means of draining residual unburned fuel at the gate.

Airport planners and engineers may have the greatest success in reducing the impact of air pollution through better airport planning, design, and construction. For example, new airports should be provided with buffer zones between the airport, where pollution concentrations are highest, and the community. To the extent feasible, parking lots, heating plants, and other sources of pollution should be separated and located downwind from locations accessible to the general public. Pollution from vehicular traffic can be lessened by designing access roads to avoid bottlenecks and unnecessary stops. Amounts of water or chemicals used during clearing, grading, and demolition operations to control dust should be minimized, as well as burning activities. These and other measures would decrease the impact of air pollution.

Water Pollution

Water pollution may result directly from the construction and operation of an airport or indirectly from land development induced by the presence of the airport. Removal of natural cover and other airport construction practices can result in unsightly soil erosion and sedimentation. An increase in the sediment load not only can lead to clogged drainage structures and flooding, but is also detrimental to biological activity because it filters out light and covers the bottom of lakes and streams. In addition, the construction process may generate various waste materials (e.g., fuels, lubricants, construction debris, and sanitary wastes from construction personnel).

The water pollution that results from the operation of an airport may be grouped into five classes:

1. Sanitary wastes.
2. Storm water pollution.
3. Wastes related to fueling, operation, and cleaning of aircraft.
4. Wastes related to major aircraft overhaul and maintenance.
5. Industrial wastes.

Sanitary wastes are the wastes generated by the people who use the airport. These wastes are produced by such activities as food preparation, washing, and toilet use. It is estimated that 20 gal of water per passenger per day is used at a typical airport and that 90% of this water returns to the collection system (1). This water must be treated to remove inorganic solids and dissolved impurities and to destroy disease-causing organisms.

Storm water runoff may be polluted by chemicals used for insect control and snow and ice removal, by fuel and oil spills on the runways, taxiways, and aprons, and by fire-fighting foam used for aircraft emergencies.

Wastes associated with the fueling, operation, and cleaning of aircraft may also be carried to nearby lakes and streams through the storm drainage system. Fuel spills and leaks, oil and grease deposits, and harsh cleaning detergents can be serious sources of water pollution unless such wastes are collected and treated.

Even more serious water pollution may be caused by major aircraft overhaul activities. These pollutants consist primarily of the highly toxic chemicals used to remove paint and clean and rechrome engine parts. Similar pollutants may be generated by light industries that are located on or near the airport and use the airport sewage disposal system.

Development induced by the presence of an airport facility also contributes water pollutants and may have a serious impact on the water pollution problem unless suitable countermeasures are undertaken. Coordinated and cooperative regional planning may be required to ensure that the capacity of the streams to absorb waste is not exceeded, nor their usefulness to downstream communities jeopardized.

Strict regulations have been imposed in the United States to prevent the pollution of lakes and streams. Airport sponsors must consult with the EPA and the appropriate state water pollution agency or agencies about the treatment and discharge of wastes, and the discharge of waste materials into navigable waters must be licensed by the Corps of Engineers. Information on water quality standards may be obtained from these agencies. It is generally necessary to collect, separate, and treat all waterborne wastes, regardless of geographic location. The specific procedures for the treatment of wastes are not within the scope of this book; however, some of the more important measures that may be employed to *prevent* water pollution are listed below.

1. Where feasible, use shallow gradients for backslopes and channels to avoid erosion.

2. Protect slopes from erosion by using appropriate ground cover during and after construction.

3. Establish procedures to keep fuel spills from getting into the storm drainage system.

4. Prohibit dumping of waste oil and grease into the storm drainage system.

5. Avoid flushing of fire-fighting foam down storm sewers.

6. Use low phosphate detergents for aircraft washing.

7. Limit the amount and type of chemicals used for insect and vegetation control.

13.9 HYDROLOGIC AND ECOLOGICAL IMPACTS

Now we consider impacts on the life cycles of plants and animals and changes that can occur to the natural circulation and distribution of water as a result of airport construction. Although these effects may be no less objectionable than those previously described, they may be more insidious.

Hydrologic Impacts

Three of the most common hydrologic problems associated with airport construction are flooding, disruption of water movements by filling and dredging operations, and salinity intrusion.

An airport development typically involves the construction of vast expanses of runways, taxiways, buildings, aprons, and other impermeable surfaces. This decreases the infiltration of rainwater into the ground and increases the quantity of runoff and the likelihood of flooding.

There is an additional but less apparent reason for flooding to be caused by an airport development. Impervious surfaces tend to increase the speed at which water runs off or to decrease its time of concentration at the various drainage structures. This means that the impacts of storms of shorter duration and higher average rainfall intensity are likely to be manifest at each drainage structure during the design period. This flooding tendency may be felt throughout the drainage basin, and the effect may extend far beyond the airport boundaries.

Airports are frequently constructed along coastal lands where original subsurface materials are weak and unstable. In these circumstances it may be necessary to relocate channels and drain and fill swampy areas. Such changes to the water environment may cause significant local climatic changes, alter the patterns of water movement, and endanger fish and wildlife. Proposed earthwork changes of this nature should be undertaken only after the hydrologic impact has been carefully evaluated and considered. Interference with water movements may be minimized by constructing airport facilities on open substructures.

When airports are located in coastal areas, the decreased infiltration of rainwater is likely to cause a lowering of the groundwater table. The lowered groundwater table may allow seawater to intrude into aquifers, which serve as a source of fresh water for nearby residents. Hydrologic studies should be made to measure the impact of decreased infiltration, and in extreme cases it may be necessary to recharge the groundwater artificially to prevent salinity intrusion.

Ecological Impacts

"Ecology" is defined as the science of the relationships between living plants and animals and their environments. Impacts of airports on man have been described already. In contrast to those effects, certain ecological impacts on plants and animals are subtle and may be manifest 10, 20, or more years after an airport is developed. Ecological impacts may result from airport construction practices, from activities related to the daily operation of the airport, or from development induced by the presence of the airport.

Unless carefully controlled, clearing, grubbing, and stripping operations may cause sedimentation and siltation to occur in natural waterways. This may destroy the food sources of small fish, and in extreme cases may smother certain species of marine life. Ecological harm may also result from filling, dredging, draining, and other topographic modifications, and from the construction of roads, fences, pipelines, and natural waterways. Such construction activities may destroy wildlife habitat and food sources, as well as create barriers and corridors that impede or enhance the distribution of organisms.

Use of pesticides and herbicides at an airport may contaminate food supplies of aquatic animals. Excessive withdrawal of groundwater may deplete water supplies for wildlife or contaminate those supplies by salinity intrusion. Aircraft and automobile engine emissions may damage certain plant species and suppress growth and yield of crops. Water pollution may deplete the supply of oxygen in natural waterways so heavily that aquatic life cannot survive.

Construction activities associated with development due to the airport can cause the same types of ecological damage described earlier.

Induced developments may also cause a lowering of the water table and flooding, as well as complicating efforts to control water pollution.

Earlier sections described countermeasures that can help control various types of environmental impact of airports on man. Those countermeasures can be employed with similar success to lessen an airport's impact on plants and animals.

REFERENCES

1. *Airports and Their Environment*, CLM/Systems, prepared for the U.S. Department of Transportation, September 1972.

2. *Planning the Metropolitan Airport System*, FAA Advisory Circular AC 150/5070-5, May 1970.

3. *Airport Aid Program*, FAR, Part 152, including Change 11, October 1, 1980.

4. *Procedures for Considering Environmental Impacts*, U.S. Department of Transportation Order 5610.1C, September 18, 1979.

5. *Requirement for Public Hearings in the Airport Development Aid Program*, FAA Advisory Circular AC150/5100-7A, February 25, 1972.

6. *Request for Aid; Displaced Persons; Public Hearings; Environmental Considerations; Opposition to the Project*, FAA Advisory Circular AC 150/5100-8, January 19, 1971.

7. *Airport Construction Controls to Prevent Air and Water Pollution*, FAA Advisory Circular AC 150/5370-7, April 26, 1971.

8. *Evaluation, Review, and Coordination of Federal and Federally Assisted Programs and Projects*, Office of Management and Budget, Circular No. A-95, January 13, 1976.

9. *Aviation Noise Abatement Policy*, U.S. Department of Transportation, November 18, 1976.

10. *Environmental Protection*, Annex 16 to the Convention on International Civil Aviation, Volume I, Aircraft Noise, 1st ed., Montreal: ICAO, 1981.

11. Schultz, T. J. (Bolt Beranek and Newman, Inc.), *Noise Assessment Guidelines: Technical Background*, prepared for U.S. Department of Housing and Urban Development, Government Printing Office, 1972.

12. Peterson, Arnold P. G., and Jr., Ervin E., Gross, *Handbook of Noise Measurement*, 7th ed., Concord, Mass.: General Radio Company, 1972.

13. Galloway, William J., "Predicting Community Response to Noise from Laboratory Data," in *Transportation Noises: A Symposium on Acceptability Criteria*, Ann Arbor, Mich.: Ann Arbor Science Publishers, 1970.

14. *Noise*, Final Report, prepared by the Committee on the Problem of Noise and presented to Parliament in July 1963, London: Her Majesty's Stationery Office, Cmnd. 2056.

15. Richards, E. J., "Noise and The Design of Airports," in *World Airports, The Way Ahead*, London: Proceedings of Conference held at Queen Elizabeth Hall, September 1969.

16. Bolt, Beranek, and Newman, Inc., *Land Use Planning Relating to Aircraft Noise*, Cambridge, Mass.: Technical Report, October 1964.

17. *Calculation of Day-Night Levels (L_{DN}) Resulting from Civil Aircraft Operations*, U.S. Environmental Protection Agency, EPA 550/9-77-450, National Technical Information Service PB 266 165, January, 1977.

18. *National Primary and Secondary Ambient Air Quality Standards*, Environmental Protection Agency, *Federal Register, Vol. 44, No. 28*, February 8, 1979.

BIBLIOGRAPHY

Hauer, E., "Noise and Airport Planning," in *Readings in Airport Planning*, Toronto: University of Toronto, Centre for Urban and Community Studies and Department of Civil Engineering, 1972.

INDEX